DANGEROUS INTERSECTIONS

Feminist Perspectives on Population, Environment, and Development

*A Project of the Committee
on Women, Population,
and the Environment*

*Edited by Jael Silliman
and Ynestra King*

South End Press
Cambridge, MA

D0188750

Library of Congress Cataloging-in-Publication Data
Dangerous intersections : feminist perspectives on population, environment, and development / edited by Jael Silliman and Ynestra King.
p. cm.
"A project of the Committee on Women, Population, and the Environment."
Includes bibliographical references and index.
ISBN 0-89608-598-8. — ISBN 0-89608-597-X (pbk.)
1. Women in development. 2. Economic development—Social aspects. 3. Economic development—Environmental aspects. 4. Environmental degradation. 5. Birth control. 6. Population policy.
I. Silliman, Jael Miriam. II. King, Ynestra.
HQ1240.D37 1999
305.42—dc21   98-30801
                                                              CIP

South End Press, 7 Brookline Street, #1, Cambridge, MA 02139-4146
04 03 02 01 00 99   1 2 3 4 5 6

To Shikha, Maya, and Micah

UCD WOMEN'S CENTER

TABLE OF CONTENTS

ACKNOWLEDGMENTS

This collection reflects the intellectual excitement and shared political commitment that has made working with CWPE such a meaningful experience. We have learned much from each other. Through our collective work, represented in these essays and our collaborations, we have been able to create an agenda for further research and action. This collection would not have been possible without the ongoing political analysis and support of all the CWPE members who laid the foundation for this effort. We are grateful to the Women's Studies Program at the University of Iowa and the Population and Development Program at Hampshire College for their support.

We also want to acknowledge Betsy Hartmann for her ongoing advice, comments, and wise suggestions, as well as Laretta Henderson for her assistance in preparing the essays for publication. Our editors at South End Press, Sonia Shah and Lynn Lu, believed in the importance of our analysis from the start, and made the process of publishing this book less daunting. Their critical comments and suggestions made the collection much stronger. Funding from the MacArthur Foundation and the Noyes Foundation enabled CWPE members to come together to develop the alternative analysis reflected in this book, and we are very grateful for their support.

INTRODUCTION

Jael Silliman

From the Collective Imagination to the Public Policy Arena

The contentious issue of population growth and "overpopulation" looms large in our collective imagination. Since Malthus, and more insistently in the last four decades, we have been barraged with strident claims that proclaim "overpopulation" is at the root of all our problems. Overpopulation is the starting and ending point of discussions on a plethora of global problems. Explaining away the most pressing concerns of the world as a "population problem" is appealing. It is simple and elides other structural and historical causes that may explain the situation. The image of the ticking clock, the incendiary "population bomb" that will set off a massive, earth-destroying explosion, is etched into our collective psyche.

Population increases are associated with faceless and undifferentiated poor women of color in intricately coded and unspoken ways. This fear seeps into public discourses and discussions, bleeding into the public policy arena, indelibly coloring and distorting understanding of the world. Media reporters and public policy "experts," in discussing crises ranging from civil war in Rwanda to deforestation in the Amazon, proclaim them a result of overpopulation. These facile explanations pay little attention to the specifics of each situation: complicated histories of colonialism, corporate extraction, government policies and subsidies, economic inequalities, and growing fundamentalism worldwide that are, in fact, more pertinent than overpopulation. They put the blame on others—those "dark and irrational people" in those equally "dark and primordial places"—who are unaware and ignorant of the "fuses" they are sparking. "They" are the problem. "We" are absolved of all responsibility. In lieu of complicated explanations, cookie-cutter analyses and solutions are advanced and gain political and financial support.

For these reasons, the issue of population growth keeps surfacing. It raises its head menacingly in numerous disguises across public policy arenas.

The common wisdom goes this way: we cannot make headway on any other problems until we take care of population growth.

The Committee on Women, Population, and the Environment (CWPE) investigates the reasons why a variety of environmental, social, and security issues are defined or presented as population problems. We expose the people, the philosophies, the funding, and the politics behind such analyses. In short, CWPE rejects the simplistic projection of population growth as the major source of environmental degradation. We do so in order to redirect attention to the roots of the problem, while working with progressive movements to find socially just solutions. At the same time, we strongly support women's right to safe birth control and abortion as part of comprehensive health care. We take on the double challenge of combating population control forces and the anti-abortion movement, both of which seek to restrict women's reproductive freedom. CWPE is both intellectual and activist in its orientation and mission. This book of essays by various CWPE members who are academics and activists is part of this ongoing political work.

CWPE: Origins, Politics, and Context

Throughout the 1990s, "free market" policies have been ascendant, though fissures are now appearing in the inflexible "free" market approach, and the first challenges are being mounted against it as markets collapse in Asia. However, the power of corporations and a belief in privatization are still strong. The State, as a provider of services and a guarantor of basic needs, is still being undermined by international monetary policies, though as capitalism threatens to crash, some state and capital control mechanisms are coming back into fashion. Structural Adjustment Programs (SAPs) and the new trade regimes of GATT (General Agreement on Tariffs and Trade) and NAFTA (North American Free Trade Agreement) have weakened state authority and regulatory powers in the name of "free trade." States are increasingly beholden to multinational corporate interests rather than to their citizens. The tidal wave of the market has eroded the progress made by environmental and social movements. Across the globe, wages for the majority of workers have declined. There has been an expansion in temporary work and piece-work. Environmental regulations have been relaxed and unions undermined. The thrust toward privatization, in a decade where SAPs have already decimated social safety nets, has been especially debilitating for the poor. In the face of increasing global inequalities and insecurities, fundamentalist movements have gained ground all around the world. They explain the insecurity people are faced with as a product of the decline of "traditional values." Drawing on these traditional values, they divert discontent created by economic policies and reassert a "natural" or "God-given" order in which women are subordinate.[1]

This disturbing political climate, together with preparatory events leading up to the United Nations Conference on Environment and Development in Rio in 1992, brought CWPE together in 1991. In preparations for the Rio Conference, environmental destruction was being linked to population growth. Population control advocates and some leading environmental organizations used the conference as an opportunity to fuel and galvanize a strong neo-Malthusian population control movement. They wanted greater support for population control programs. A propaganda machine went into high gear, proclaiming that "population growth is the principal cause of the environmental crisis." This "public education" effort was well funded by a few key private foundations in the United States, and had considerable political support.

Riding on the momentum created by Rio in preparations for the United Nations International Conference on Population and Development (ICPD) in Cairo in 1994, these population control advocates tried to gain "grassroots" support for an aggressive population control agenda that was staged in "high-tech" citizen's meetings across the United States. The U.S. Agency for International Development (USAID) identified population growth as a key "strategic threat" that "consumes all other economic gains, drives environmental damage, exacerbates poverty, and impedes democratic governance."[2]

CWPE, a loose but politically astute network of feminist scholars and activists, was especially concerned about these developments. We feared the possibility of incipient alliances being forged between environmental organizations, population control advocates, and uncritical feminist organizations (especially in the United States, where a clear distinction between reproductive rights and population control had not been made), based on their mutual support for reducing fertility. We feared that in the "rush" to save the planet, the work of women's health and human rights advocates would be trampled by the expansion and greening of this population agenda.

We saw the tired debates over the relationships between population and environmental deterioration repackaged for the 1990s. These glossy and updated versions made obligatory references to "women's empowerment." The rhetoric of "empowerment," however, was used without any real analysis of the structural reasons for women's impoverishment and lack of access to resources, and was not linked to a concrete policy agenda to improve women's lives or the quality of the environment.

CWPE members, watching this dangerous tide swell, seized the moment to work with the environmental community. We held a number of meetings with members from these national and international organizations to express our concerns about the ways in which the issues were being addressed, and to share our expertise regarding the dangers of a simplistic analysis. Furthermore, as part of this effort to build allies in the environmental community for a feminist agenda, we pulled together a broad range of international women's rights and environmental justice advocates to hammer out a "New Approach" to the problem in May 1992. (See Appendix A: "Women, Population, and the Environment: Call for a New Approach.") In a statement and call for action we challenged the argument that population growth is the major cause of environmental deterioration. We defined the root causes to be social and economic structures, rather than population demographics and women's fertility. We argued that demographically driven population-control programs treat women as objects of control and violate the basic feminist tenets of reproductive choice and bodily integrity for women. In this widely circulated document, endorsed by more than 300 individuals and organizations around the world, we not only launched a well-defined political position but put into place a network of people who shared our approach.

In addition to our targeted intervention in the mainstream environmental movement, CWPE identified the need to serve as a voice within the transnational women's movement, which in the early 1990s was becoming an increasingly powerful actor in the international policy arena. CWPE members were keenly aware of the dangers of the women's movement being "mainstreamed" as it sought to negotiate with governments and international agencies to have women's voices heard on international policy formulations. We noted the "professionalization" of the women's movement as it became an "institutional player" in global politics. We saw how this drained its energies and resources and created further separations between a leadership elite and the grassroots. Given these developments, we were determined to keep space open within the transnational women's movement for an alternative dialogue that was not tied to strategic public-policy objectives or conference politics. In addition to serving as a cross-current within the transnational women's movement, we worked with women-of-color organizations to highlight the problems of the "South within the North." We made the connections between the processes of economic, social, and political marginalization affecting poor women in both the North and the South.

CWPE is not afraid to chart its own course and work outside the mainstream. For example, CWPE was not part of what has been called the "women's consensus position" that placed women's health and rights at the center of population policies at the ICPD in 1994, although we did participate in selected deliberations supporting the most important reforms. Indeed, CWPE critiqued and challenged the prevailing and much-touted "consensus," because of its failure to address structural causes of poverty and disenfranchisement. Since such conferences are set within a framework of liberalization, privatization, and market supremacy, we argued that injecting a feminist and environmental impulse is a contradictory move, because this paradigm runs counter to feminist and environmental values and principles. Moreover, we were troubled by the way in which this "consensus" was orchestrated and financed by a small group of actors. We were concerned with how population control organizations were adopting and adapting the language of women's rights without fundamentally changing their programs and policies. CWPE, together with allies in the South, believed that structural adjustment, "free trade," militarism, consumerism, and corporate pollution were not adequately addressed in Cairo. Through our networks, publications, and conferences, we built allies among Southern and women-of-color organizations, progressive development activists, social justice environmentalists, and anti-racist organizers. It is in these alliances, beyond the confines of orchestrated consensus, that we see the real political space from which positive visions of social, economic, and environmental justice emerge.

While the series of U.N. conferences galvanized CWPE to articulate its position, construction of an alternative analysis is an ongoing effort. We critically read the way in which issues get reworked in contemporary political contexts. In the current U.S. climate, where anti-immigration propaganda and policies are on the rise, we tie our analysis of "the greening of hate" to anti-immigration initiatives that use the population issue as a wedge to penetrate the environmental movement. We participated in the California-based Immigration and Environment Campaign, coordinated by the Political Ecology Group (PEG) to address those environmentalists and anti–immigration rights coalitions that blame immigrants for environmental decline. With PEG and the Hampshire College Population and Development Program, we organized the first National Strategy Session on Immigration and the Environment in March 1996 in California. This meeting brought together key representatives of environmental justice, immigrant rights, feminist, and civil rights movements. We continue to work in partnership to expose the racial and class politics behind the anti-immigration movement. Organizing and public education have been part of the effort led by PEG that prevented the Sierra Club from taking a formal anti-immigrant stand. (See Appendix B: "Immigration and Environment Campaign.")

CWPE members speak out against the targeting of women's fertility in "welfare reform," and for addressing the underlying causes of welfare dependency, such as poverty and joblessness. For example, we challenged child exclusion policies (family caps), which deny extra benefits to women who give birth to children while on welfare; contraceptive-incentive schemes, which interfere with a woman's family planning decisions; time limits, which cut off all welfare benefits to mothers and children after two years; and teen residency requirements, which require minors to live with their parents. We draw the connections between increasing criminalization of people of color and the poor, prisons, and population control. We have ongoing campaigns against hazardous contraceptives such as Quinacrine chemical sterilization, Depo-Provera, Norplant, and immunological contraceptives in the United States and abroad. At the same time, we support the redirection of contraceptive research toward safer, women-controlled alternatives, making us squarely pro-choice and anti–population control.

CWPE continues to challenge dominant representations of population, environment, and development through its biannual newsletter, *Political Environments,* workshops and conferences, and numerous publications by individual members. We make a special effort to draw links between domestic and international policies and to speak across the activist/scholar divide. A crucial feature of our work, which we carry over into this book, is that we have identified and cultivated a political common ground, although we have widely ranging ethnic and national identities. While building common ground, we have maintained and respected differences. This book demonstrates the possibility of common ground where diversity thrives.

This anthology is geared to activists, students, policymakers, and scholars who want to develop an understanding of how population, environment, and development issues are being raised in the current political moment, when a neoliberal agenda and privatization reign supreme. Here, we come together to present a series of works and a coherent political analysis that reflect our five-year collaboration in CWPE. Together, we anticipate and map the development of conservative and neoliberal philosophies and policies, which disempower women and are environmentally hazardous. We integrate population, environment, and development issues through an explicitly feminist analysis, so that they can be understood in relationship to one another and from the standpoint of women's rights, with particular attention to issues of race and class. Through all the essays we reject the "population paradigm." We suggest alternative ways to understand the "ecological crisis" as a crisis of systems of technology, production, ownership, and culture within human society, rather than an inherent opposition between human beings and nature.

The Ubiquitous Population Issue: Its Public Policy Dimensions

In the opening essay Betsy Hartmann examines the way in which "national security" is being redefined in the United States. She traces how, in a "rapidly growing policy enterprise," the relationships between population pressures, resource scarcities, and intrastate conflict in the South are highlighted and presented as threats to national security. Hartmann unmasks the political, economic, and cultural reasons why this analysis is quickly being picked up in foreign policy and environmental circles, as well as by the military complex. She argues that this reformulation of the "Third World" as not only overpopulated but environmentally degraded as well feeds into existing racist and cultural stereotypes. It also allows one to oppose immigration on seemingly progressive or altruistic grounds. While Hartmann focuses her article on how environmentalism is being redefined in national (in)security paradigms, the appropriation and subversion of the language and values of environmental movements are part of a broader process stretching beyond the United States. Through subversion and co-optation, a new "meta-managerial perspective" and policy elite are emerging under the environmental banner. To rationalize and control fertility, labor, and natural resources is part of the new "environmentalism."

Reformulating the Population Equations and Moving Beyond

Asoka Bandarage examines international migration, industrial capitalism, and colonialism as keys to understanding population dynamics. In this way she moves from technocratic magic-bullet solutions to population, immigration, and environmental decline, to a systemic understanding of the interrelationships between these issues. She challenges post-Cairo formulations that privilege improvements in the position of women as a key to reducing fertility. While underlining the importance of empowering women, she argues that this must be accompanied by structural reforms that reduce social and economic disparities. Bandarage insists that persistent and increasing inequality within countries and between countries is the most pressing issue of our time.

Patricia Hynes, in deft and bold strokes, reformulates the I=PAT equation devised by Paul Ehrlich and John Holdren in 1974. This simple but ideologically driven equation has dominated thinking and policy formulations on the relationship between population, consumption, technology, and the environment for almost three decades. Hynes examines the politics that drives its formulation. In sound feminist tradition she refuses to disengage it from structural issues of poverty, male dominance, militarism, and consumerism. In a playful but compelling attempt to insert these factors into the equation, she exposes IPAT's limitations and creates another approach to address this complex set of interactions. "Taking population out of the equation," she brings elements of social and environmental justice into the heart of the analysis.

Andy Smith explains why liberal Protestant organizations have historically supported population control. She argues that even Euro-American Christian feminists do not challenge the population paradigm. She suggests that their failure to incorporate the work done by women of color and Third World women results in a blindspot in their analyses. She finds this especially disturbing because it is these very communities whose populations such organizations advocate reducing. She shows how liberal Protestants have been caught in the politics of the abortion movement. Smith calls for a Christian ethic that takes seriously the lives of Third World women and women of color and rejects the population paradigm. She also comments on the ways in which feminist language and demands for social justice are being co-opted by right-wing populationists and the anti-immigrant movement.

In a case study of Tanzania, Meredeth Turshen examines and analyzes the debates regarding the ecological crisis that have been dealt with more abstractly in the previous essays. Whereas the World Bank describes the poor as both "victims and agents" of environmental damage, and population growth as a major cause of environmental deterioration and agricultural stagnation in Tanzania, Turshen refutes these assertions. She examines unequal gender relationships, the competition for scarce resources among groups of Tanzanians, and the differences between the Tanzanian government and multilateral institutions to understand environmental decline. She concludes that it is SAPs and the privatization of public services that increase poverty and are at the root of the environmental crisis in Tanzania. Such case studies that take into account the particular set of forces at work at each country or regional level are essential for a real understanding of the relationhips between population and environmental deterioration, and for appropriate policy responses.

Development and Civil Society:
Censorship and Accountability

Meredeth Tax is concerned with the way in which "culture" has been divorced from development. Together with politically committed women writers from around the world, she has initiated Women's WORLD (Women's World Organization for Rights, Literature and Development), a global feminist organization for the right to free expression. In a bid to take back and redefine "culture" as "the totality of the ways in which [a] community conducts its life," the members of Women's WORLD assert that culture and cultural development must be a central component of development. By this they mean that people need the time, space, and access to the means of cultural expression to define their own social values. They argue that this kind of authentic expression is increasingly difficult for people to engage in as cultural domination and a global monoculture threaten cultural diversity. Those who challenge the global monoculture are silenced. The members of Women's WORLD argue that women writers symbolize the free speech of all women, and that free speech is essential for democratization.

In my essay I trace the expansion of women's organizations in the increasingly dynamic and politically and economically powerful nongovernmental organization (NGO) sector. I argue that while some NGOs do play important roles in social and political development and can be sites for democratic change, many NGOs enable the privatization and liberalization of nationalized economies. I map how a neoliberal economic and political agenda steered by the major lending institutions and donor agencies increasingly promotes NGOs in efforts to meet social needs. In the process of substituting NGOs for the state in social provisioning, NGOs are often used and restructured in accordance with this new economic agenda. I examine the changing character and roles of NGOs. As women's NGOs are drawn into these imperatives, the tensions between professional and bureaucratized NGOs and grassroots movements are magnified. The paper calls for NGOs to critically examine their current alignment with the State, international development agencies, and social movements.

Justine Smith, from a Native American perspective, shows how activists often address social justice issues in an isolationist manner. While there is a great deal of lip service regarding working inclusively and collaboratively, in reality movements like the women's, environmental, and economic-justice movements work in isolation. Smith shows how Native American communities and activists do not usually fall into this trap. Committed to a sovereignty framework, they are better able to see and make connections between issues. Smith uses the struggle over mining interests in northern Wisconsin to make the point. She then argues that a sovereignty paradigm is useful in broader struggles for environmental and social justice. She concludes by explaining how defending and protecting native rights and sovereignty is the first step toward preservation of the global community.

Environmental Ravagers: Militarism and Consumerism

Joni Seager names militaries as the major environmental abusers—they are privileged environmental vandals. In an insightful and colorful feminist analysis, she focuses on the ways in which patriarchy, power, militarism, and environmental destruction intersect and reinforce each other. She shows how militarized environmental destruction reflects gendered processes and dynamics. She argues that gender is both evident and instrumental in the militarized environmental arena. She brilliantly documents how global devastation caused by militaries is a product of the militarized "cult of masculinity." This hypermasculinity is structurally central to modern militaries. Seager concludes that a failure to come to terms with the military and its gendered structures will severely undermine our ability to change the current global environmental condition.

While there is increasing consensus that consumption must be dealt with as a key environmental variable in the North, Patricia Hynes critiques the limited ways in which consumption is defined and addressed. She argues that consumption—much like demographically driven "population" thinking—has been reduced to a mere empirical per capita phenomenon. In this way, reducing or changing consumption patterns and behaviors becomes an individual responsibility rather than a social and political one. Furthermore, Hynes explains how, using this reductionist approach, consumption gets detached from the structural and ideological forces that make some rich while impoverishing the vast majority. She brings feminist tools to deconstruct recent North American critiques and movements addressing consumption and consumerism.

Reproductive Rights: Barriers and New Frontiers

Marsha Tyson Darling and April Taylor are both concerned with issues related to the social construction of sexuality of African American women. Darling places African American women at the center of the discourse on redistributive justice, with the right to speak for themselves, so that they are not continually represented by others. In a detailed historical account she traces how the State, because of these representations by others, expropriates self-determination of Black females. She shows how the civil rights of Black females have been abandoned and Black women's poverty intensified through this process. In particular she demonstrates how the State has defined the social good as increasingly inimical to the rights of privacy in mother-hood, medical confidentiality for at-risk women, and civil rights protections from coercion relating to informed consent and choice. She raises troubling concerns regarding the genetic revolution and the impacts it may have on the health and well-being of African American women.

April Taylor overlays the set of concerns raised by Darling with a look at new corporate attempts to tap African American women. She discusses the "hypermedicalization" of Black women's bodies for corporate profit. She gives specific examples of pharmaceutical and biotech companies pushing products on African American women even though the health potential of these products is often dubious. She critiques the way in which an increasing array of very questionable contraceptives, like Norplant and Depo-Provera, and genetically based drugs, is marketed to Black women. She warns Black women not to be duped by high-tech, intrusive contraceptive methods that promise "choice," "responsibility," and "freedom." She situates these corpo-rate forays within a history of medical mistreatment and experimentation on Black women, whose fertility is still feared.

Marlene Gerber Fried builds on the analysis presented by Darling and Taylor to expose the links between coercive population control in the devel-oping world and coercive policies in the United States. She advises caution as women navigate between feminist critiques of population policy and the anti-abortion movement's opposition to abortion and all forms of contraception. Her strategy for confronting the double challenge is to continue strong advo-cacy for safe and accessible abortion. She points out how, despite 25 years of legal abortion, abortion rights are an ongoing struggle in the United States. From within the abortion rights movement she speaks to us of the agony of so many women in the United States—young women, women in prison, women who have been raped, undocumented women, women without resources—who lack access to the safest surgical procedure in the United States today. She insists that if we are to move ahead, abortion rights must be placed in the context of a larger human-rights and social-justice agenda.

Conclusion

We hope these essays stir the "collective political imagination" and steer us in a liberatory direction that encourages intellectual and activist work across sectoral concerns and social movements. In all these essays we call on our readers to step out of prevailing paradigms; to consider population, environment, and development concerns; and to imagine alternative approaches. By posing old questions in fundamentally different ways and by posing new sets of concerns and questions, we encourage readers to engage in different intellectual dialogues and political conversations. By refusing to respond to or be contained within a neoliberal framework, we create the possibilities for transformative agendas to take root.

Together we can put in place an expansive vision of population, environment, and development—a vision firmly rooted in human rights and social and environmental justice. We invite readers to be part of this imagining, this creative and political endeavour.

APPENDIX A

Women, Population, and the Environment: Call for a New Approach

We, the undersigned, are troubled by recent statements and analyses that single out population size and growth as a primary cause of global environmental degradation. We believe the major causes of global environmental degradation are:

• Economic systems that exploit and misuse nature and people in the drive for short-term and short-sighted gains and profits.

• War-making and arms production, which divest resources from human needs, poison the natural environment, and perpetuate the militarization of culture, encouraging violence against women.

• The disproportionate consumption patterns of the affluent the world over. Currently, the industrialized nations, with 22 percent of the world's population, consume 70 percent of the world's resources. Within the United States, deepening economic inequalities mean that the poor are consuming less, and the rich more.

• The displacement of small farmers and indigenous peoples by agribusiness, timber, mining, and energy corporations, often with encouragement and assistance from international financial institutions, and with the complicity of national governments.

• The rapid urbanization and poverty resulting from migration from rural areas and from inadequate planning and resource allocation in towns and cities.

• Technologies designed to exploit but not to restore natural resources.

Environmental degradation derives thus from complex, interrelated causes. Demographic variables can have an impact on the environment, but reducing population growth will not solve the above problems. In many countries, population growth rates have declined, yet environmental conditions continue to deteriorate.

Moreover, blaming global environmental degradation on population growth helps to lay the groundwork for the re-emergence and intensification of top-down, demographically driven population policies and programs that are deeply disrespectful of women, particularly women of color and their children.

In Southern countries, as well as in the United States and other Northern countries, family planning programs have often been the main vehicles for dissemination of modern contraceptive technologies. However, because so many of their activities have been oriented toward population control rather than women's reproductive health needs, they have too often involved sterilization abuse; denied women full information on contraceptive risks and side effects; neglected proper medical screening, follow-up care, and informed consent; and ignored the need for safe abortion and barrier and male methods of contraception. Population programs have frequently fostered a climate where coercion is permissible and racism acceptable.

Demographic data from around the globe affirm that improvements in women's social, economic, and health status and in general living standards are often keys to declines in population growth rates. We call on the world to recognize women's basic right to control their own bodies and to have access to the power, resources, and reproductive health services to ensure that they can do so.

National governments, international agencies, and other social institutions must take seriously their obligation to provide the essential prerequisites for women's development and freedom. These include:

• Resources such as fair and equitable wages, land rights, appropriate technology, education, and access to credit.

• An end to structural adjustment programs imposed by the IMF, the World Bank, and repressive governments, which sacrifice human dignity and basic needs for food, health, and education to debt repayment and "free-market," male-dominated models of unsustainable development.

• Full participation in the decisions that affect our own lives, our families, our communities, and our environment, and incorporation of women's knowledge systems and expertise to enrich these decisions.

• Affordable, culturally appropriate, and comprehensive health care and health education for women of all ages and their families.

• Access to safe, voluntary contraception and abortion as part of broader reproductive health services which also provide pre- and post-natal care, infertility services, and prevention and treatment of sexually transmitted diseases, including HIV and AIDS.

• Family support services that include childcare, parental leave, and elder care.

• Reproductive health services and social programs that sensitize men to their parental responsibilities and to the need to stop gender inequalities and violence against women and children.

• Speedy ratification and enforcement of the U.N. Convention on the Elimination of All Forms of Discrimination Against Women as well as other U.N. conventions on human rights.

People who want to see improvements in the relationship between the human population and natural environment should work for the full range of women's rights, global demilitarization, redistribution of resources and wealth between and within nations, reduction of consumption rates of polluting products and processes and of nonrenewable resources, reduction of chemical dependency in agriculture, and environmentally responsible technology. They should support local, national, and international initiatives for democracy, social justice, and human rights.

APPENDIX B

Immigration and Environment Campaign

Position Statement by the Political Ecology Group (PEG) (Reprinted with permission)

We, the undersigned organizations and individuals, believe that immigrants and environmentalists need to unite and work together if we are to progress toward an ecologically sustainable and socially just world.

In the current political climate that blames immigration and environmental regulations for the nation's problems, we commit ourselves to defending the health, environment, and human rights of all of our communities.

We challenge the fear, hate, and divisiveness in today's debate with the following positions that guide our approach to sensible and humane action on immigration and the environment.

• *Current economic troubles are not caused by environmentalists or immigrants but by corporate and governmental practices that neglect public well-being in favor of short-term private gain.* Public policies have bolstered business profits while the majority of U.S. residents face declining incomes and job security. Downsizing, deindustrialization, and the shifting of production overseas by transnational corporations are consequences of the new global economy, where corporations have more freedom than ever to move capital and resources to places with cheaper labor and regulatory costs. At the same time, people are criminalized for moving to find work in areas where natural and economic resources are flowing. Today's economic, social, and environmental woes are only made worse as opportunistic politicians attack immigrants, workers, and the environment.

• *Scapegoating the politically disenfranchised is morally unjustifiable, divides people, and hides the real causes of our problems.* Throughout U.S. history, sentiment has turned against immigrants during economic lows. In response to fears of competition with Chinese workers in the 1870s, Congress passed the Chinese Exclusion Act in 1882, which banned Chinese from entering this country for the next 61 years. In the midst of the Great Depression, more than 500,000 persons of Mexican origin were deported from the U.S., including tens of thousands of American citizens. In the Proposition 187 era, migrants to the U.S. and those who appear "foreign," especially Latinos and Asians, are becoming targets of racist and violent hate crimes. Similarly, anti-immigrant hate groups are on the rise again in Germany, France, and Italy. This mean-spiritedness is spurred on by conservative rhetoric that has blamed not only immigrants and environmentalists, but also the poor, the elderly, and people of color.

• *While we believe that global demographic issues should be addressed in a serious manner, immigration is not a chief cause of environmental degradation in the U.S.* Some extremist population control groups have been wooing environmentalists to support anti-immigrant policies, at a time when environmentalists and immigrants need to be working together. They claim that immigration needs to be further restricted because population growth is a major factor in U.S. environmental degradation. We reject this argument and its results. Blaming population growth is a convenient way to ignore the varying impacts of different groups of people and institutions. The impact of an immigrant family living in a one-bedroom apartment and taking mass transit pales in comparison to that of a wealthy family living in a single-family home with a swimming pool and two cars. That the U.S., with only 5 percent of the world's population, consumes 32 percent of the world's petroleum and plastics, and produces 22 percent of the world's carbon dioxide and chlorofluorocarbon (CFC) emissions is not a reason to close our borders but to change our superconsuming economy. For example, reducing energy use will not be achieved by curbing migration, but by adopting policies promoting energy efficiency, mass transit, and renewable energy technologies.

• *Over-emphasizing the role of population growth in environmental problems ignores who has control of production and consumption decisions.* Many of the causes of environmental decline in this country have little to do with population growth or individual consumer choices. The military—the nation's largest single polluter—and corporations produce much more toxic waste than households do. Corporate advertising drives overconsumption and creates demand for new products that are often more environmentally destructive than old products. Sprawling suburbs, planned and built by developers, gobble up prime agricultural land and wildlife habitat. The public has little control over these decisions. Attempts to make companies clean up after themselves or make new developments more compact and efficient are often undermined by industry lobbying against regulations. Corporate actions have also limited individual decisions for more sustainable lifestyles, such as choosing to take mass transit instead of driving. For example, in the 1930s and 1940s General Motors, Firestone, and Standard Oil (now Chevron) bought out and dismantled the electric trolley system in Los Angeles and 75 other cities in order to create demand for their products.

• *Immigrants are essential allies and leaders of the movement for environmental protection and restoration.* Immigrant communities suffer disproportionately from environmental degradation and poisoning, whether from exposure to pesticides in fields, toxic dumps in neighborhoods, or solvents in factories. But immigrants have begun to fight back and are among the leaders of the environmental justice movement. Efforts like those of the mostly Latino residents of Kettleman City, who recently won their six-year battle against ChemWaste's planned hazardous waste incinerator, are forcing corporations to prevent pollution, rather than dumping it onto those least able to resist. Environmentalists also have much to learn from immigrant cultures and practices. Newcomers to this country often come from places where they had more sustainable lifestyles and a closer connection to the land. The Laotian family that grows its own vegetables without pesticides in a small backyard plot is as much a model of environmentalism as the European-American family that recycles its newspapers.

• *As the environmental justice movement has shown, environmental concerns are integrally linked to human rights, health, livelihood, and social justice issues.* A violation of an immigrant's rights threatens the rights of all and raises the level of conflict and hate in our social environment. No society that tolerates such disrespect of other human beings is capable of building a healthy co-existence with the natural world. A society where rich dominate over poor and white over black cannot muster the cooperation and good will necessary to solve such problems as global warming or preservation of biodiversity. Environmentalists and immigrants must begin to work together to build a sustainable society based on mutual respect and the celebration of diversity.

We commit ourselves to the following strategies:

• Building alliances between the immigrant rights and environmental movements for an environmentally sustainable economy that meets the needs of all people.

• Defending the human and civil rights of immigrants.

• Resisting the rollback of environmental regulations.

• Refuting the myths that blame immigrants for environmental and economic problems, and highlighting immigrants' positive contributions.

• Supporting policies that radically reduce U.S. consumption of the world's resources and promoting the development and use of environmentally sound technologies.

• Insisting that government, corporations, and developers be accountable to community demands for environmental protection and human health.

• Supporting universal and equal access to education, health care, and livable wages—humanitarian goals that are also the most effective means to achieve a sustainable population.

To contact the Political Ecology Group (PEG), write to: PEG, 965 Mission Street, Suite 700, San Francisco, CA 94103

Notes

1. In a parallel development, a number of influential books published in the United States, such as *The Bell Curve: Intelligence and Class Structure in American Life,* by Richard J. Hernstein and Charles Murray (New York: Free Press, 1996), provide biological explanations and justifications for deep-rooted social and economic distress.

2. USAID Strategy papers, LPA Revision, 5 October 1993, 7.

POPULATION, ENVIRONMENT, AND SECURITY

A New Trinity

Betsy Hartmann

The end of the Cold War has forced a redefinition of national security in the United States. While "rogue states" like Iraq have replaced the Soviet Union as the enemy,[1] globalization has ushered in an era of more amorphous threats. Environmental problems rank high among them. "Environment and security" are linked together in a rapidly growing policy enterprise that involves the U.S. Departments of State and Defense, the CIA, academic research institutes, private foundations, and nongovernmental organizations.

There are a number of reasons why "environment and security" is an idea whose time has come. Clearly, serious global environmental problems such as ozone depletion, global warming, and pollution of the seas require new forms of international cooperation. Whether these should be the purview of national security agencies is another question, given their tradition of competition, secrecy, and nationalism.[2]

The environment and security field often focuses less on these legitimate concerns, however, than on a supposed causal relationship among population pressures, resource scarcities, and intrastate conflict in the South. According to the main architect of this theory, Canadian political scientist Thomas Homer-Dixon, environmentally induced internal conflict in turn causes states to fragment or become more authoritarian, seriously disrupting international security.[3]

The scarcity-conflict model is fast becoming conventional wisdom in foreign policy, population, and environment circles, popularized and sensationalized by writers such as Robert Kaplan and Paul Kennedy.[4] Top State

Department officials have blamed political strife in Haiti, Rwanda, and Chiapas, Mexico, in large part on population and environmental stresses.[5] Opportunism no doubt plays a role in making the model a fashionable trend. For the State Department it is a convenient form of ideological spin control that masks the tragic human consequences of U.S. support for military regimes and Duvalier-style dictatorships during the Cold War. For the military it provides new rationales and missions to legitimize its multibillion-dollar budget. Expensive satellite surveillance systems appear more acceptable to the U.S. Congress and public if they are also used for the "softer" task of environmental monitoring. This also means more business for the large aerospace corporations suffering from the loss of Cold War defense contracts. Increasingly, the military-industrial complex is becoming a "military–environmental security complex."[6]

The international relations field also needs new raisons d'être, and environment and security research is well funded. The population lobby has seized on it too, for several reasons. As birth rates continue to fall around the globe more rapidly than anticipated, it is hard to sustain the alarmism that fuels popular support for population control. Building an image of an overpopulated, environmentally degraded, and violent Third World is politically expedient, especially as it feeds on popular fears that refugees from this chaos will storm our borders.

An appeal to national security interests is also a strategy to counter the right-wing assault on international family-planning assistance. For example, a recent Rockefeller Foundation report, *High Stakes: The United States, Global Population and Our Common Future* (whose cover contrasts sad, dark-skinned children with happy, white ones) draws heavily on the scarcity-conflict model in order to move a recalcitrant Congress:

> Resource scarcities, often exacerbated by population growth, undermine the quality of life, confidence in government, and threaten to destabilize many parts of the globe.... Once a resource becomes scarce, a society's "haves" often seize control of it, leaving an even smaller share for the "have-nots." Since population growth rates are highest among the have-nots, this means that an even larger number of people are competing for a smaller share of resources—and violent conflict is often the result.[7]

In a kind of strange déjà vu, the threat of resource scarcities and political instability also featured in Rockefeller's first rationales for population control in the 1950s.[8]

Opportunism and political pragmatism are not the only explanations for the rapid acceptance of the scarcity-conflict model, however. The concept of scarcity has deep resonance in the U.S. cultural and political psyche. Andrew Ross draws the link between the manufacturing of social scarcity essential to capitalist, competitive, individualist regimes and the notion of natural scarcity.[9] The grossly unequal division of wealth in a society of resource abundance and waste demands an ethic of social scarcity to explain poverty. In the 1970s, the wasteful consumer class in the United States spearheaded concerns about a global ecology crisis; worried about the earth's "natural limits," they brought a new paradigm of natural scarcity into being. The result, according to Ross, is that

> for more than two decades now, public consciousness has sustained complex assumptions about both kinds of scarcity. In that same period of time, however, neo-liberalism's austerity regime has ushered in what can only be described as a pro-scarcity climate, distinguished, economically, by deep concessions and cutbacks, and politically, by the rollback of "excessive" rights. As a result, the new concerns about natural scarcity have been paralleled, every step of the way, by a brutal imposition of social scarcity.... The two forms of scarcity have been confused, either deliberately, in order to reinforce austerity measures against the poor, or else inadvertently, through a lack of information about how natural resources are produced and distributed.[10]

Ross concludes that systematic inequalities underlie both shortages of economic resources and environmental degradation. Unlike New Right economists, he does not minimize the severity of environmental problems, but points to the need for redistribution of wealth and power in order to prevent the "lonely hour when biological scarcity is the 'last instance' of determination in planetary life."[11]

Neo-Malthusianism—the belief that rapid population growth is a major cause of poverty, environmental degradation, and political instability—dovetails nicely with the ideology of social and natural scarcity and has proved very compatible with neoliberalism's emphasis on the free market and dismantling of the social welfare functions of the state. It is not surprising that it occupies such an important place in the environment and security framework.

Parables of Scarcity

In 1989 Jessica Matthews's article "Redefining Security" helped set the stage for the linking of environment and security. "Population growth lies at the core of most environmental trends," she wrote, and then she went on to recommend support for international family planning as one of the four most important steps in a new security agenda.[12]

Since that time, references to population pressures as a major strain—if not *the* major strain—on the environment have become seemingly obligatory in the literature. They are usually unsubstantiated, presented as a self-evident truth. The 1996 U.S. National Security Strategy announces in the preface that "large-scale environmental degradation, exacerbated by rapid population growth, threatens to undermine political stability in many countries and regions."[13] "Exacerbated by population growth" (and nothing else) is, in fact, a constant refrain.

Just what is the evidence for these assumptions? Thomas Homer-Dixon's *Project on Environment, Population and Security,* jointly sponsored by the University of Toronto, the American Association for the Advancement of Science, and the Canadian Center for Global Security, has produced a series of case studies (e.g., Rwanda, South Africa, Pakistan, and Chiapas) to investigate the relationship among population growth, renewable resource scarcities, migration, and violent conflict. While the text of the case studies tends to be somewhat more nuanced, the models based on them are simple diagrams of questionable causality.

Figure 1. How Environmental Stress Contributes to Conflict

Environmental Scarcity	**Intermediate Social Effect**	**Result**
Environmental Depletion and Degradation	Poverty	
Population Growth	Inter-Group Tensions	Instability
Limited Access to Resources	Population Movements	Conflict
	Institutional Stress and Breakdowns	

Source: Homer-Dixon, Thomas F. "The Project on Environment, Population and Security: Key Findings of Research." Wilson Center, *Environmental Change and Security Project Report,* Spring 1996, 45-46.

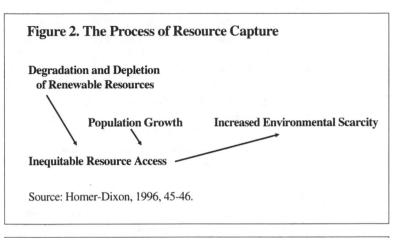

Figure 2. The Process of Resource Capture

Degradation and Depletion
of Renewable Resources

Population Growth   Increased Environmental Scarcity

Inequitable Resource Access

Source: Homer-Dixon, 1996, 45-46.

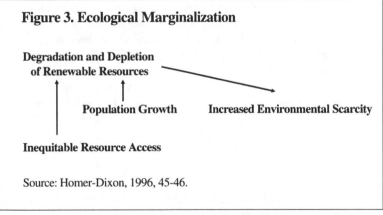

Figure 3. Ecological Marginalization

Degradation and Depletion
of Renewable Resources

Population Growth   Increased Environmental Scarcity

Inequitable Resource Access

Source: Homer-Dixon, 1996, 45-46.

In Figure 1, Homer-Dixon illustrates the main lines of causality between environmental scarcity and conflict. In Figure 2 he depicts the process of "resource capture," and in Figure 3 that of "ecological marginalization."

There are a number of problems with these models. First is the weak definitional foundation upon which they are built. Homer-Dixon defines environmental scarcity as including three factors: the degradation and depletion of renewable resources, the increased consumption of those resources, and/or their uneven distribution. The increased consumption of resources is mainly linked to population growth, hence its prominence.

This concept of environmental scarcity thus conflates distinct processes—the generation of renewable resource scarcities, environmental degradation, population growth, and the social distribution of resources—into a single, overarching term that is "tantamount to analytical obfuscation."[14] Environmental degradation is confused with renewable resource scarcity (indeed, they are often presented as virtual synonyms) although there is no necessary link between the two. Land shortages, for example, can be an incentive to boost productivity through better agricultural techniques and land improvements.[15] By adding the social distribution of resources to the definition of environmental scarcity, Homer-Dixon creates a *de facto* link to conflict, since political conflict often revolves around issues of resource control. This is the main tool by which he is able to force very disparate conflictual situations into his universalizing model, but the result is a model so inclusive as to be banal.[16] Marc Levy makes a similar critique, arguing that it is difficult to imagine that conflicts in developing countries would not include renewable resource issues: "Developing country elites fight over renewable resources for the same reason that Willy Sutton robbed banks—that's where the money is."[17] He also notes that environmental factors interact with such a variety of social processes to generate violence that "there are no interesting mechanisms that are purely and discretely environmental."[18]

The automatic equation of population growth with increased resource consumption is another problem. Not only does it not necessarily follow that if there are more people, they will consume more—per capita consumption could fall for a number of reasons—but the increased resource consumption may have little to do with demographic factors and instead have to do with increased demand in external markets for a particular product, e.g., teak for Scandinavian furniture or shrimp for Western palates.

By their very nature, Homer-Dixon's models homogenize diverse regions with distinct histories and cultures. Clearly, the specific colonial and post-colonial histories of countries such as Rwanda and Haiti, for example, have much to do with the present generation of "scarcity" in those places. Also missing from the picture is serious discussion of economic inequalities. Although Homer-Dixon acknowledges their importance, the place they occupy in his models skews causality, in effect naturalizing the processes of maldistribution. Combined with population growth, he argues, resource scarcity encourages powerful groups within a society to shift distribution in their favor—this is the "resource capture" presented in Figure 2. Similarly, agricultural shortfalls due to population growth and land degradation are seen to induce large development schemes, the benefits of which are then captured by the rich.[19]

The origins of inequalities and the role of powerful forces—agribusiness, mining, timber, and other corporate interests—in environmental degradation receive little attention. The argument that environmental stress weakens state structures, or that it makes them more authoritarian, puts the cart before the horse, since state structures themselves profoundly affect how resources are distributed and managed. The choice of a large development scheme over more sustainable small-scale projects, for example, may have little or nothing to do with agricultural shortfalls and instead reflect the links between foreign donors and domestic elites who stand to gain from lucrative procurement and construction contracts.

Homer-Dixon's view of the state is oddly idealized. Environmental scarcities, he argues, "threaten the delicate give-and-take relationship between state and society." If the state cannot cope with the resulting agricultural shortfalls, economic stress, and migration, then "grassroots organizations" may step in to respond. Focusing only on the needs of their respective constituencies, these organizations supposedly cause society to fragment into groups that do not interact or trust each other. This enhances "the opportunities for powerful groups to seize control of local institutions or the state and use them for their own gain." Homer-Dixon also claims that "environmental scarcity can strengthen group identities based on ethnic, class, or religious differences."[20]

It takes quite a stretch of the imagination to believe that the states he has studied, which include Mexico, Pakistan, and Rwanda after all, had a nice give-and-take relationship with their people before scarcity set in. In fact, one could argue that the real scarcity in those places was and still is the absence of democratic control over the structures that govern access to both economic and natural resources. Characterizing "grassroots organizations" as forces for social fragmentation also neglects the role many such groups have played in building a democratic civil society to challenge corrupt and authoritarian states.

The neglect of external actors constitutes a further lacuna. Intrastate violence is seldom a self-contained phenomenon—where, for example, do the arms trade, geopolitical maneuvering, and international financial institutions figure in Homer-Dixon's models? The models are essentially closed systems in which internal stresses may generate movement outward, mainly through mass migration, but the outside is rarely seen to be pressing in.

Homer-Dixon, for example, depicts ecological marginalization (Figure 3) as a process by which unequal resource access and population growth force the migration of the poorest groups to ecologically vulnerable areas such as steep hillsides and tropical rain forests. The pressure of their numbers and their lack of knowledge and capital then cause environmental scarcity and poverty.[21] But should population growth and unequal resource access really be ascribed equal weight as the "push factors" causing people to migrate to such areas? An extensive study of deforestation by the United Nations Research Institute for Social Development notes that while many observers blame deforestation on forest clearing by poor migrants, they ignore the larger forces attracting or pushing these migrants into forest areas, such as the expansion of large-scale commercial farming, ranching, logging, and mining. "To blame poor migrants for destroying the forest is like blaming poor conscripts for the ravages of war."[22] The study found an absence of any close correspondence between deforestation rates and rates of either total or agricultural population growth.

In most cases the ecological damage caused by poor peasants pales in comparison with that caused by commercial extraction of resources, often for export. The greatest deforestation took place under colonial rule, and today most tropical wood and beef production is destined for foreign markets. Due to good prices and favorable tariff treatment, most beef in Latin America is exported to the United States, much of it for use in fast-food chains or for pet food. The average Central American eats less beef than the average U.S. housecat.[23] Between 1950 and 1980, consumption of tropical hardwoods in the industrialized nations was more than twice that of all the tropical producer nations combined—despite their growing populations.[24] The failure to link the consumption patterns of developed countries and Southern elites to "local" land uses is, in fact, a key shortcoming of Homer-Dixon's approach. The scope of inquiry is surprisingly insular in a period of rapid global economic integration.

The narrow conceptualization of population is also surprising given that the population field itself is opening up to more gender-sensitive analysis and programming. Homer-Dixon and the environment and security literature in general focus mainly on aggregate population size and density, paying little attention to other key dynamics such as age distribution, differential mortality rates, and sex ratios. Neglecting history once again, the literature displays little understanding of the processes of demographic transition to lower birth and death rates.

Nor, except for a few obligatory references to the need for women's literacy programs, does it seriously address gender inequalities, despite a significant body of research in this area. Subsumed into the analytic frame of "population pressure," women implicitly become the breeders of both environmental destruction and violence. Important questions are not asked, much less answered. What are women's property rights, labor obligations, and roles in the management of environmental resources? How have structural adjustment policies affected their health, workloads, and status relative to male family members? Where are investments being made: in basic food production, where rural women most often work, or in export agriculture? If men are forced to migrate to earn cash or to join militaries, how do women cope with the labor requirements needed to sustain food production and maintain infrastructure?

Instead of linking violence to women's fertility, one can ask how violence affects women's capacity to support the family and community institutions on which protection of the local environment depends. Even more than conventional interstate war, current conflicts in Africa brutally target women and children in order to destroy communities, and at the same time depend on them to sustain military forces with both food and fresh recruits.[25] Women are often discriminated against in post-conflict transitions as well. In Rwanda, for example, there are concerns that widows may lose access to land because of women's limited property rights, undermining the process of agricultural rehabilitation.[26]

Violence is also a direct cause of environmental destruction. The German Institute for Peace Policy estimates that one-fifth of all global environmental degradation is due to military and related activities.[27] Feminist geographer Joni Seager argues that whether they are at peace or war, militaries are the biggest threat to the global environment.[28] "In modern warfare," she writes, "the environment has become a militarized target, and 'ecocide' provides another arena for the play of militarized manhood."[29] Even after the cessation of conflict, land mines and the lingering effects of scorched-earth policies and chemical warfare obstruct environmental restoration. Military bases are also a major source of toxic contamination. According to Seager, the U.S. Pentagon produces more toxic waste than the five largest American chemical companies combined.

Militaries are built on a cult of manhood that emphasizes domination— they "feed on and fuel the masculinist 'prerogative' of men conquering nature."[30] They also directly contribute to the creation of both "social" and "natural" scarcities since they take economic resources away from human development and environmental improvements. In developing countries as a whole, for example, military expenditures soared from 91 percent of combined health and education expenditures in 1977 to 169 percent in 1990.[31]

This is not to say that population growth plays no role at all in environmental degradation, but to ascribe to it the leading role is to miss the larger, more complex picture. Doing so fails to address adequately the question of why birth rates have remained high in some places. High infant mortality rates, children as a vital source of labor and support for the elderly in peasant societies, son preference, lack of education and opportunity, and discrimination against women are all factors that can contribute to high birth rates. In El Salvador, for example, the same unequal economic and social relations that have slowed demographic transition—marginalization of the peasantry, gender discrimination, political power monopolized by a small elite—also underlie unsustainable patterns of resource use.[32] These unequal relations need to be addressed, not population growth per se. Indeed, the historical record shows that broad-based improvements in people's living conditions, such as investments in health, education, and job creation, spur fertility decline.[33] Recent research also challenges the neo-Malthusian assumption that population pressure always negatively affects the environment. In parts of Africa, increasing population densities combined with sound agricultural practices have led to environmental improvements.[34] Similarly, the focus on peasant populations as the destroyers of the environment neglects the important role of traditional agriculture in preserving biodiversity.[35]

Moreover, the extent of environmental degradation in Africa is often overstated. Through examination of historical data, the comparison of aerial photographs from different time periods, and oral research in local communities, anthropologists James Fairhead and Melissa Leach, for example, have shown how areas of forest and savannah vegetation have remained remarkably stable in the northern margins of Guinée's forest zones, in contrast to the conventional view, carried over from the colonial period, that farmers are encroaching on the forest and using it unsustainably.[36] The extent of "desertification" on the continent has also been exaggerated due to faulty science and the need for development agencies and other important actors to create a "disaster narrative" for Africa in order to legitimize their interventions.[37]

Even though he focuses on population, Homer-Dixon is not a strict Malthusian doomsdayer in the tradition of triage theorist Garrett Hardin or Stanford biologist Paul Ehrlich. Homer-Dixon believes that social and technical ingenuity can help overcome the problem of resource scarcities. Institutions that "provide the right incentives for technological entrepreneurs" and "family planning and literacy campaigns" that ease population-induced scarcity are among his solutions.[38] Missing from this technocratic framework is the notion of political *transformation*: democratizing control over economic and natural resources and the direction of technological development. Indeed, progressive movements for social change would probably be put into the category of scarcity-induced conflict.

Despite its popularity among liberals, Homer-Dixon's is a conservative worldview where the maldistribution of both power and resources is essentially naturalized and determined by the god of scarcity. When this god of scarcity meets the devil of racism, the result is the greening of hate.

Back to Deepest, Darkest Africa

In 1994 journalist Robert Kaplan popularized Homer-Dixon's views in an *Atlantic Monthly* piece on "The Coming Anarchy," which proclaimed the environment as the most important national security issue of the 21st century.[39] Much of the article dwells on West Africa, which Kaplan presents as a hopeless scene of overpopulation, squalor, environmental degradation, and violence, where young men are postmodern barbarians, and children with swollen bellies swarm like ants. Kaplan's article did for Africa what *The Bell Curve* did for the United States: it reintroduced racism as a legitimate form of public discourse. But whereas *The Bell Curve* was at least attacked by some elements of the liberal press, "The Coming Anarchy" captured the imagination of the liberal establishment, even that of President Clinton himself. "I was so gripped by many things that were in that article," Clinton said in a speech on population, "and by the more academic treatment of the same subject by Professor Homer-Dixon.... You have to say, if you look at the numbers, you must reduce the rate of population growth."[40]

Homer-Dixon, of course, should not be held responsible for all of Kaplan's racist (and misogynist) stereotyping, and he is now careful to distance himself from the journalist's work. Yet the fact remains that the scarcity-conflict model can easily serve as a vehicle for this kind of thinking. Nowhere is this clearer than in the case of Africa.

Kaplan expands on the themes of "The Coming Anarchy" in his book *The Ends of the Earth,* which takes environmental determinism to a new and absurd level. For example, he links violence in Liberia to its dense forests. In the dark rain forest where trees and creepers block the view, "men tend to depend less on reason and more on suspicion," he writes. The Liberian forest, "a green prison with iron rain clouds," is thus responsible for the animism and spirit worship that weakened the civilizing influences of Islam and Christianity. Liberia, "a forest culture" further undermined by overpopulation, is naturally more prone to violence.[41]

Seen through Kaplan's eyes, African women are mainly bare-breasted and pregnant, and their fertility is out of control, with dire consequences. In an interview on *The News Hour with Jim Lehrer,* he went so far as to suggest that if women in Rwanda had lower fertility, the genocide would not have happened:

> Rwanda is a place where women have been giving birth on the average of eight times over their adult lifetime. This has been going on for decades. If those women had been giving birth two or three times instead of eight, imagine how much different Rwandan society would have been. And given that politics is merely a macro expression of social relations, the politics would have evolved differently.[42]

His images of Africa are reminiscent of old colonial accounts of the enlightened white man encountering the primitive savage. In fact, he is enamored of the British colonial writer Richard Burton, who, he notes approvingly, perceived that slaves preferred the "paradise" of the American South and the "lands of happiness" in the West Indies to their native home.[43]

Despite the lack of substantive evidence, Kaplan maintains that Africa's climate and poverty are the breeding ground for AIDS and other deadly diseases, which, along with crime, threaten even our wealthiest suburbs. And that is why self-interest dictates that we care about the continent. He is short on solutions, however. He is not keen on democracy, preferring the "honest" authoritarianism of Singapore's dictator Lee Kuan Yew.[44] Hence, he argues, the West should shift emphasis away from promoting democracy in the Third World and toward "family-planning, environmental renewal, road-building and other stabilizing projects."[45] He ignores the emergence of many positive national and transnational political forces such as the peace, environmental, and women's movements.

Like Kaplan, Jeffrey Goldberg of the *New York Times* also shoulders a modern-day variant of the white man's burden. In a feature article titled "Our Africa Problem," he writes:

> There is a whole new set of what might be called biological national-security issues: environmental destruction, explosive population growth, the rapid spread of disease and the emergence of entirely new diseases. It is widely understood that these things hurt Africa. What is not understood is that they can also hurt America.[46]

Goldberg warns of yet-unknown killer microbes emanating from Central Africa's dense rain forests. "Chaos, though, is the best incubator of disease," he claims, and disease is an incubator of chaos. Africa is caught in a vicious cycle of misery where war and corruption mean no health care and family planning, which leads to "too many sick people" who in turn "create despera-tion and poverty," leading back to corruption and war.[47] This simple closed system leaves out everything from IMF- and World Bank–imposed structural adjustment programs that have seriously eroded African public health systems to declining terms of trade for African products on the international market.

Goldberg offers solutions, however. Watching the sterilization of a poor, naked Kenyan woman, he notes that U.S. aid for family planning can help stem the biological crisis of overpopulation. Add to that the magic bullet of the free market. The export of beef and roses, he believes, will save Uganda. The United States should pursue a policy of heightened engagement in Africa not only to subdue the microbes, reduce population growth, and stem the tide of refugees, but quite simply "to make money."[48]

But making money is not always conducive to protecting the environ-ment. For example, commercial livestock and flower production may well have a negative impact on Uganda's ecology. Methyl bromide, a highly toxic pesticide that is also a major ozone depletor, is now used on neighboring Kenya's flower crops.[49] The limits of Goldberg's environmental under-standing are revealed by his statement that Mobutu, Zaire's recently deposed dictator, was "an effective environmentalist," even if an inadvertent one, because he let the country's infrastructure deteriorate and left its immense forests in near-pristine condition.[50] Underdevelopment thus becomes syn-onymous with environmentalism, as if the human beings inhabiting Zaire do not matter.

A psychoanalyst could have a field day with Kaplan's and Goldberg's images of Africa—the dark, impenetrable rain forest as the subconscious; fears of women's uncontrolled fertility as a manifestation of sexual repres-sion; Africa as the unknown, the other, the enemy; the United States as the su-perpower superego. Whatever the reason, these images have infected the U.S. political psyche, helping to shape public opinion if not public policy. That overpopulation was a major cause of the genocide in Rwanda has become conventional wisdom in mainstream environmental and foreign policy circles. In a much-heralded speech on the environment, former Secretary of State Warren Christopher warned that "we must not forget the hard lessons of Rwanda, where depleted resources and swollen populations exacerbated the political and economic pressures that exploded into one of this decade's great-est tragedies."[51] Similarly, former Undersecretary of State for Global Affairs Timothy Wirth remarked that in Rwanda "there were simply too many people competing for too few resources."[52]

Scholars more familiar with Rwanda's history, and that of neighboring states, offer a much more complex understanding of the tragic events there. While not denying the existence of demographic and environmental pressures, Peter Uvin, who worked as a development consultant in the region, analyzes the role of economic and political inequalities, institutionalized ethnic prejudice, and foreign assistance in generating the conflict. Ironically, the international aid community considered Rwanda a model developing country because of its "political stability" and supposed concern for the rural population. Its main problems, according to World Bank reports, stemmed from the vicious cycle of poverty, rapid population growth, and pressure on the environment. The donors cast a blind eye toward the government's authoritarianism and systematic impunity. Even in the 1990s, when violent repression and genocidal preparations were becoming state policy, foreign aid more than doubled. Uvin writes:

> Rwanda's genocide was the extreme outcome of the failure of a development model that was based on ethnic, regional and social exclusion; that increased deprivation, humiliation and vulnerability of the poor; that allowed state-instigated racism and discrimination to continue unabated; that was top-down and authoritarian; and that left the masses uninformed, uneducated, and unable to resist orders and slogans. It was also the failure of development cooperation based on ethnic amnesia, technocracy and political blindness.[53]

In his study of the population-resources dilemma in Rwanda and Burundi, economist Leonce Ndikumana explains why agriculture has stagnated in the region, noting the lack of substantive improvements in farming technologies. At the same time the demand for children has remained high. Yet despite pressure on the land, he argues that the political crises in both countries are mainly the result of institutional failure caused by a long history of ethnic divisions between the Hutu and Tutsi: "These countries have promoted nepotistic and dictatorial political systems that reward ethnic identity rather than merit while miserably failing to protect the rights and interests of the individual and minority groups.... Population growth is only a scapegoat for people willing to put the blame of failed development policies on rural populations."[54] The failure of the international community to acknowledge the genocide and take swift action can also be seen as profound institutional failure on the global level.

Even Homer-Dixon's case study of Rwanda acknowledges that environmental and population pressures had at most "a limited, aggravating role" in the Rwandan conflict.[55] The case of Rwanda clearly points to the importance of in-depth case-study research to counter simplistic explanations of conflict. In his analysis of population-environment models in Africa, Robert Ford urges scholars and policy makers "to take the longer road" and confront the complex and constantly changing political, economic, cultural, historical, and environmental dynamics of a specific locale. Neo-Malthusianism, he concludes, "is not a sound basis for environmental security."[56]

Faulty Diagnoses, Faulty Prescriptions

It is too early to judge whether the scarcity-conflict model will have a direct impact on foreign policy or continue to play a more indirect role of (mis)shaping public opinion by masking the deeper political and economic forces generating poverty, environmental degradation, violence, and migration in the South. Much will depend on the extent to which it is challenged by alternative voices. Failing an effective challenge, one can foresee a number of serious consequences. These include:

Distortion of population policy

By overemphasizing the role of population growth in environmental degradation and violence, the model legitimizes population control as a top priority. Already in India and Bangladesh, population control absorbs from one-quarter to one-third of the annual health budget, and in a number of African countries undergoing structural adjustment, public health systems have been decimated while funding of population programs has increased.[57] In Nigeria, for example, contraceptives may be available, but maternity care is no longer affordable, even though pregnancy and childbirth complications are on the rise, largely as a result of poor nutrition and bad housing conditions.[58] The quality of family-planning services is also undermined when there is no basic health infrastructure to ensure the safe, effective, and ethical use of contraception.

Viewing population pressure as a security threat creates a false climate of fear and urgency, eroding the progress made by the women's health movement in moving the population establishment away from a narrow focus on fertility reduction to a more comprehensive women's reproductive health and rights perspective. The plan of action of the 1994 U.N. International Conference on Population and Development in Cairo endorses a broad reproductive health strategy, in which women have access not only to contraceptives but to sexuality education, pregnancy care, and treatment of sexually transmitted diseases. The plan also highlights the need for male responsibility in birth control, and for programs to raise the status of women.

This perspective is likely to be lost if family planning is viewed as the magic bullet to pacify Third World trouble spots and save the environment. Dennis Pirages, a key academic exponent of the scarcity-conflict model, believes that dealing with population growth is the place to begin a "paradigm shift" in foreign and defense policies. He laments the Cairo conference's "emphasis on rights at the expense of responsibilities" and instead advocates tough and resolute action on family planning.[59]

This kind of security mind-set could relegitimize the use of targets, incentives, and coercion in family-planning programs, with grave repercussions for women's health and human rights. It could reinforce the persistent bias in the choice of contraceptive technology toward long-acting, provider-dependent methods such as Norplant over safer barrier methods, which also protect against sexually transmitted diseases such as HIV/AIDS.[60]

Homer-Dixon's project shows no sensitivity toward these issues, as it neglects to look at the ethical implications of its focus on population pressures and the actual population programs that exist in the case-study countries. In one article he briefly mentions coercive policies in China leading to lower fertility rates, but he does not criticize them. Rather, his concern is that "experts are not sure this accomplishment can be sustained for long."[61] It hardly bodes well for women's rights when forced abortions and sterilizations are considered an "accomplishment."

Gender bias and blindness

This approach to population is part of a larger gender bias and blindness in the environment and security field. It is in fact far behind the development field in this respect, perhaps because it takes so little notice of literature and ideas outside of its disciplinary boundaries. Poor people, when they are differentiated at all, are mainly categorized by ethnicity and religion.

While the neglect of gender issues could easily lead to policies that reinforce male hegemony and treat women as objects rather than subjects, it also prevents recognition of the leading role women have played in reconciliation efforts, such as the peace movements in the Middle East and Somalia and the anti-communalism struggle in India. Women have been at the forefront of attempts at ecological restoration too, such as the Green Belt Movement in Kenya and the Chipko movement in India. Rather than targeting their fertility, it would make more sense to learn from women's organizing efforts and engage them in the processes of conflict resolution.

Dehumanizing and depoliticizing refugees

By naturalizing poverty and political violence in the South, the scarcity-conflict model dehumanizes refugees of color, turning them into faceless invaders fleeing the chaos and environmental degradation they brought upon themselves.[62] This view feeds racism and helps legitimize current U.S. immigration "reforms" that, among other restrictive measures, severely curtail the rights of asylum-seekers.

Using the scarcity-conflict model, political refugees from countries like El Salvador could potentially be recast as less worthy "environmental refugees." Already, senior U.S. intelligence officials are rewriting the history of the war in El Salvador as having been caused by environmental impoverishment and overpopulation, failing to acknowledge U.S. support for the Salvadoran military's death squads and scorched-earth policies.[63]

Militarizing sustainability

A particularly pressing issue is what impact the scarcity-conflict model will have on U.S. defense policies. Currently, the Environment and Security Office of the U.S. Department of Defense has a budget of about $5 billion, almost equivalent to that of the civilian Environmental Protection Agency.[64] While much of this money is directed toward activities such as cleaning up bases and protecting military personnel and facilities from biological hazards, another top priority is "helping neutralize environmental conditions which could lead to instability."[65] The State Department's Bureau of Intelligence and Research focuses more explicitly on "the linkages between increasing ethnic tensions ... and resource scarcity," and since 1991 the annual U.S. National Security Strategy document has included environmental issues.[66]

Using military satellites for environmental surveillance seems to be the most important practical application of the new national security focus on the environment. In the MEDEA project, a select group of environmental scientists is working with the CIA to identify key sites for surveillance. The data collected will be kept in secret archives and then released to "unspecified 'future generations' of scientists."[67] Given the intelligence community's long history of deeply institutionalized secrecy, duplicity, and paranoid distrust of outsiders, Deibert is skeptical that environmental researchers, especially those from other countries, will have confidence that the information, when it is finally released, has not been altered or manipulated for "national security reasons."[68]

The existence of alternative satellite-monitoring systems, controlled by civilians, can act to some extent as a hedge against intelligence misinformation. But Deibert points to the worrying trend of merging both civilian and military environmental reconnaissance systems under one umbrella, so that the military effectively becomes the "clearinghouse" for environmental data. He cites as an example the Brazilian government's purchase of a $1.4-billion Amazon Surveillance System from the United States, which will be used to monitor borders, airspace, and the environment.

Also problematic is the kind of technocratic, quantitative analysis of environment and conflict emerging from both official and academic security circles, which substitutes for rigorous qualitative and historical research. The CIA's "State Failure Task Force" is testing the effect of 75 possible independent variables, including demographic, environmental, social, and economic ones, on various political crises from 1955 to 1994. But in a world of complex causality, how can such variables be considered "independent"?[69] (In keeping with neoliberal trends, "openness to international trade" was found to be one of the most important predictors of state stability.)

Gareth Porter of the Environmental and Energy Study Institute has argued for the creation of a quantitative "national security impact index" that would reveal the importance of major global environmental threats.[70] Researchers in Norway are using quantitative analysis to test whether environmental scarcity and population density are major contributors to civil conflict.[71] Such studies are no doubt the wave of the future and could serve as the empirical basis for the formation of defense policies. As such, they require detailed critical scrutiny.

The U.S. military is already directly involved in promoting "sustainable development" in Africa, assisting almost 20 countries in environmental activities such as fisheries management, game park preservation, and water resource management.[72] The Defense Intelligence Agency has also identified ecological deterioration in Lake Victoria "as a cause of potential instability in East Africa."[73] While these are real environmental concerns, why is the U.S. military addressing them and not civilian agencies in partnership with local people themselves? Isn't it a fundamental contradiction in terms to have the military engaged in "sustainable development" when it is has been the cause of so much environmental devastation and is hardly known for its democratic, participatory, and gender-sensitive approach?

International relations scholar Daniel Deudney argues convincingly that turning the environment into an object of national security risks undermining the positive forms of global environmental thinking and cooperation that have been emerging in recent years. He writes:

The movement to preserve the habitability of the planet for future generations must directly challenge the tribal power of nationalism and the chronic militarization of public discourse. Ecological degradation is not a threat to national security; rather, environmentalism is a threat to national security attitudes and institutions. When environmentalists dress their arguments in the blood-soaked garments of the war system, they betray their core values and create confusion about the real tasks at hand.[74]

It is also important to remember that national security agencies need an enemy, and who is the enemy when violence and instability are blamed on population pressures and resource scarcities? Implicitly, if not explicitly, the enemy becomes poor people, especially poor women, and the social movements that represent them. It may be an ironic outcome of the scarcity-conflict model that environmental groups are themselves targeted as security threats when they challenge the control and degradation of natural resources by local elites, governments, and transnational corporations.

Anti-environmentalist repression is already occurring in many countries. Witness the violent suppression of the Ogoni people in Nigeria who are trying to protect their lands from destruction by Shell Oil. Sooner or later, when their lands are rendered uninhabitable, they too will probably be written off as resource-scarce.

It is time to challenge the population, environment, and security trinity before it exercises a firmer hold on public policy and consciousness. While a watchdog role is necessary, it is not sufficient. The integration of progressive social science research with the experiences and activism of environmental, women's, peace, and refugee rights movements can create a new and deeper understanding of the forces generating poverty, environmental destruction, and violence. Solutions will come not from the barrel of a gun, a spy satellite, or coercively imposed contraceptive technologies, but from the wisdom and actions of those who have been working long and hard to overcome the scarcity of justice.

Notes

I would like to thank Jael Silliman and Meredeth Turshen for their comments on a previous draft. I would also like to refer readers to the Woodrow Wilson Environmental Change and Security Project Reports, which provide a useful compilation of information.

1. Michael T. Klare, *Rogue States and Nuclear Outlaws: America's Search for a New Foreign Policy* (New York: Hill and Wang, 1995).

2. Daniel Deudney, "Environment and Security: Muddled Thinking," *Bulletin of the Atomic Scientists,* April 1991, 22–28.

3. Thomas F. Homer-Dixon, "Environmental Scarcities and Violent Conflict," *International Security,* Vol. 19, No. 1 (1994), 5–40.

4. Robert D. Kaplan, "The Coming Anarchy," *Atlantic Monthly,* February 1994, 44–76; and Matthew Connelly and Paul Kennedy, "Must It Be the Rest Against the West?" *Atlantic Monthly,* December 1994, 61–84.

5. Timothy Wirth, "Sustainable Development Vital to New U.S. Foreign Policy," speech presented to National Press Club, Washington, DC, July 12, 1994; and Warren Christopher, "American Diplomacy and the Global Environmental Challenges of the 21st Century," speech delivered at Stanford University, Palo Alto, CA, April 9, 1996 (reprinted in Wilson Center, *Environmental Change and Security Project Report,* spring 1996, 81–85).

6. Ronald J. Deibert, "From Deep Black to Green? Demystifying the Military Monitoring of the Environment," in Wilson Center, *Environmental Change and Security Project Report,* spring 1996, 29.

7. Rockefeller Foundation, *High Stakes: The United States, Global Population and Our Common Future* (New York: Rockefeller Foundation, 1997), 9, 21.

8. Betsy Hartmann, *Reproductive Rights and Wrongs: The Global Politics of Population Control* (Boston: South End Press, 1995).

9. Andrew Ross, "The Lonely Hour of Scarcity," *Capitalism, Nature and Socialism,* Vol. 7, No. 3 (1996), 3–26.

10. Ibid., 6.

11. Ibid., 26.

12. Jessica T. Matthews, "Redefining Security," *Foreign Affairs,* Vol. 68, No. 2 (1989), 163, 177.

13. White House, *1996 U.S. National Security Strategy of Engagement and Enlargement.* Excerpted in Wilson Center, *Environmental Change and Security Project Report,* spring 1996, 72.

14. James Fairhead, "Conflicts over Natural Resources: Complex Emergencies, Environment and a Critique of 'Greenwar' in Africa," paper presented to the UNU/WIDER and QEH Meeting of the Project on the Political Economy of Humanitarian Emergencies. Queen Elizabeth House, Oxford, England (July 3–5, 1997), 18.

15. Ibid., 15.

16. Ibid., 18.

17. Marc A. Levy, "Is the Environment a National Security Issue?" *International Security,* Vol. 20, No. 2 (1995), 57.

18. Ibid., 58.

19. Homer-Dixon, "Environmental Scarcities," op. cit., 13.

20. Thomas F. Homer-Dixon, "The Project on Environment, Population and Security: Key Findings of Research," in Wilson Center, *Environmental Change and Se-*

curity Project Report, spring 1996, 48.

21. Ibid., 47.

22. Solon Barraclough and Krishna Ghimire, "The Social Dynamics of Deforestation in Developing Countries: Principal Issues and Research Priorities," Discussion Paper No. 16 (Geneva, Switzerland: United Nations Research Institute for Social Development, 1990), 130.

23. Daniel Faber, "Imperialism, Revolution and the Ecological Crisis of Central America," *Latin American Perspectives,* Vol. 19, No. 1 (1992).

24. Nicholas Guppy, "Tropical Deforestation: A Global View," *Foreign Affairs,* Vol. 62, No. 4 (1984).

25. Meredeth Turshen and Clotilde Twagiramariya, *What Women Do in War Time: Women and Conflict in Africa* (London: Zed Books, 1998).

26. Bridget Byrne, Rachel Marcus, and Tanya Powers-Stevens, *Gender, Conflict and Development,* Vol. 2. *BRIDGE Report,* no. 35 (Brighton, UK: Institute for Development Studies, University of Sussex, 1995).

27. H. Patricia Hynes, *Taking Population Out of the Equation: Reformulating I=PAT* (Amherst, MA: Institute on Women and Technology, 1993).

28. Joni Seager, *Earth Follies: Coming to Feminist Terms with the Global Environmental Crisis* (New York: Routledge, 1993).

29. Ibid., 19.

30. Ibid., 15.

31. United Nations Development Program, *Human Development Report 1993* (New York: Oxford University Press, 1993).

32. Faber, "Imperialism, Revolution and the Ecological Crisis of Central America," op. cit.

33. Hartmann, *Reproductive Rights and Wrongs,* op. cit.

34. Mary Tiffen, Michael Mortimore, and Frances Gichuki, *More People, Less Erosion: Environmental Recovery in Kenya* (London: Overseas Development Institute and J.W. Wiley, 1994).

35. M.A. Altieri and L.C. Merrick, "In Situ Conservation of Crop Genetic Resources through Maintenance of Traditional Farming Systems," *Economic Botany,* Vol. 41, No. 1 (1987), 86–96.

36. James Fairhead and Melissa Leach, "Rethinking the Forest-Savanna Mosaic: Colonial Science and Its Relics in West Africa," in Melissa Leach and Robin Mearns, eds., *The Lie of the Land: Challenging Received Wisdom on the African Environment* (Oxford and Portsmouth, NH: International African Institute with James Currey and Heinemann, 1996).

37. Jeremy Swift, "Desertification: Narratives, Winners and Losers," in *The Lie of the Land,* op. cit.

38. Homer-Dixon, "Environmental Scarcities and Violent Conflict," op. cit., 16–17.

39. Kaplan, "The Coming Anarchy," op. cit.

40. U.S. Department of State, remarks by the president to the National Academy of Sciences (Washington, DC: White House, Office of the Press Secretary, June 29, 1994).

41. Robert D. Kaplan, *The Ends of the Earth: A Journey at the Dawn of the 21st Century* (New York: Random House, 1996), 28–29.

42. Robert D. Kaplan, interview on *The News Hour with Jim Lehrer,* U.S. Public Broadcasting System, April 5, 1996.

43. Kaplan, *The Ends of the Earth,* op. cit., 80–81.

44. Ibid., 377.

45. Robert D. Kaplan, "For the Third World, Western Democracy Is a Nightmare." *International Herald Tribune,* December 30–31, 1995, 4.

46. Jeffrey Goldberg, "Our Africa Problem." *New York Times Magazine,* March 2, 1997, 35.

47. Ibid., 35.

48. Ibid., 80.

49. Political Ecology Group and Transnational Resource and Action Center, *The Bromide Barons: Methyl Bromide, Corporate Power and Environmental Justice* (San Francisco: Political Ecology Group, 1997).

50. Goldberg, "Our Africa Problem," op. cit., 38.

51. Warren Christopher, "American Diplomacy" speech, op. cit., 83.

52. Timothy Wirth, "Population Pressure and the Crisis in the Great Lakes Region of Africa," remarks at the Center for National Policy, December 18, 1996. Excerpted in Wilson Center, *Environmental Change and Security Project Report,* spring 1997, 118.

53. Peter Uvin, *Development, Aid and Conflict: Reflections from the Case of Rwanda,* Research for Action 24 (Helsinki, Finland: United Nations University World Institute for Development Economics Research, 1996), 34.

54. Leonce Ndikumana, "Institutional Constraints and the Population-Resources Dilemma in Burundi and Rwanda" (working paper, University of Massachusetts Economics Department, Amherst, MA, 1997), 21, 30.

55. Valerie Percival and Thomas Homer-Dixon, *Environmental Scarcity and Violent Conflict: The Case of Rwanda* (Washington, DC: Program on Science and International Security, American Association for the Advancement of Science, 1995), 2.

56. Robert E. Ford, "The Population-Environment Nexus and Vulnerability Assessment in Africa," *GeoJournal,* Vol. 35, No. 2 (1995), 215.

57. Hartmann, *Reproductive Rights and Wrongs,* op. cit.

58. Adetoun Ilumoka, "Reproductive Health and Rights: Principles, Policies and Commitments in Context" (paper presented at the Seventh International Association for Women in Development Forum, Washington, DC, September 5–8, 1996).

59. Dennis Pirages, "Demographic Change and Ecological Security," in Wilson Center, *Environmental Change and Security Project Report,* spring 1997, 43.

60. Hartmann, *Reproductive Rights and Wrongs*, op. cit.

61. Homer-Dixon, "Environmental Scarcities," op. cit., 37–38.

62. See, for example, Connelly and Kennedy, "Must It Be the Rest Against the West?" op. cit.

63. Richard Smith, "The Intelligence Community and the Environment: Capabilities and Future Missions" (presentation to the Woodrow Wilson Center, June 22, 1995), in Wilson Center, *Environmental Change and Security Project Report*, spring 1996, 103–8.

64. William Nitze, "A Potential Role for the Environmental Protection Agency and Other Agencies" (presentation to the Woodrow Wilson Center, November 21, 1995), in Wilson Center, *Environmental Change and Security Project Report*, spring 1996.

65. Sherri W. Goodman and Admiral William Center, "Military Capabilities and Possible Missions Related to Environmental Security" (presentation to Woodrow Wilson Center, May 18, 1995), in Wilson Center, *Environmental Change and Security Project Report*, spring 1996, 98.

66. *Environmental Change and Security Project Report* (Washington, DC: Woodrow Wilson Center, 1997), 209.

67. Deibert,"From Deep Black to Green?" op. cit., 28–32.

68. Ibid., 31.

69. *Environmental Change and Security Project Report* (Washington, DC: Woodrow Wilson Center, 1997), 212.

70. Gareth Porter, "Advancing Environment and Security Goals Through 'Integrated Security Resource Planning,'" in Wilson Center, *Environmental Change and Security Project Report*, spring 1996, 35–38.

71. *Environmental Change and Security Project Report* (Washington, DC: Woodrow Wilson Center, 1997), 200.

72. Kent Butts, "National Security, the Environment and DOD," in Wilson Center, *Environmental Change and Security Project Report*, spring 1996, 26.

73. J. Brian Atwood,"Towards a New Definition of National Security" (remarks to the Conference on New Directions in U.S. Foreign Policy, University of Maryland, College Park, November 2, 1995). Excerpted in Wilson Center, *Environmental Change and Security Project Report*, spring 1996, 85–88.

74. Daniel Deudney, "Environment and Security: Muddled Thinking," *Bulletin of the Atomic Scientists*, April 1991, 28.

POPULATION AND DEVELOPMENT

Toward a Social Justice Agenda

Asoka Bandarage

Rapid population growth in the world today is not simply attributable to igno-
rance, irrationality, and apathy of the poor, or to their lack of access to contraceptives. The fundamental reasons for population growth in the South and
population decline in the North (apart from immigration) lie in the evolution
of industrial capitalism and Western imperialism. Contemporary international
migration also has its origins in these historical developments.

During the early stages of European imperialism, the European population "exploded across the face of the earth" while natives, especially tribal
peoples, experienced massive depopulation.[1] Of the millions of slaves taken
out of Africa, only a small proportion reached North America, many having
died en route on slave ships. Approximately 50 million of the world's tribal
people were wiped out due to conquest and the spread of new diseases by
European colonizers and their descendants between 1780 and 1930.[2]

Tribal depopulation has continued apace due to war, poverty, and disease,
which have accompanied Western demographic, politico-economic, and cultural expansion over the past 500 years. For many Native American and other
indigenous peoples, the primary issue continues to be survival, not population
control. Understandably, then, when sterilization and experimental contraceptives are pushed on native women, they see this as a form of genocide.

Unequal Population Dynamics

Appropriation of wealth from the colonies laid the basis for the industrial
revolution and improvements in general standards of living in the imperialist

24

countries. In the West, the demographic transition from large to small families was achieved first among the middle classes, who absorbed the greater measure of benefits from imperialism and the industrial revolution. Among the working classes, who bore most of the detrimental effects of these forces, the demographic transition was not achieved until well into the second half of the 19th century and even later. The shift from labor-intensive agriculture to less labor-intensive industrial production, improved wages, legislation against child labor, reduction of child mortality, mandatory schooling for children, and wage employment of women were among the factors contributing to a gradual reduction of births among the working classes.[3]

The demographic transition achieved in the West, however, could not be repeated in the colonies, due to the wholly different trajectory of socio-economic evolution set in motion there. As Barry Commoner has pointed out, the demographic transition in the imperialist countries involved a kind of "demographic parasitism," in that the second "population balancing phase of the demographic transition in the [economically and militarily] advanced country ... [was] fed by the suppression of that same phase in the colony."[4] In other words, the exploitative relationship between the metropolitan and colonial countries resulted in differential demographic dynamics in the two regions.

Production and Reproduction under Colonialism

The extractive operations introduced into the colonies, such as plantation agriculture and mining, required large supplies of labor. Starting from the early years of merchant capitalism, European overseas investors and colonizers were hampered by labor shortages—that is, a crisis of "underpopulation" rather than "overpopulation." When native people refused to abandon subsistence production and traditional lifestyles to work for Europeans, the Europeans resorted to the African slave trade and indentured labor from Asia and Europe.

Colonial state policies were strongly pro-natalist—for example, equating the value of African slave women with "breeding power." At least some "birth strikes" are known to have occurred among colonized women in the Americas and the African continent who refused to produce children for the hated white masters and their harsh enterprises.[5] In the long run, however, the interests of colonial capitalism prevailed over the interests of subjugated peoples. The imposition of monocultural export agriculture and private property rights robbed colonized people of their lands and natural resources. Taxation policies and the integration of markets in colonized territories into European economies forced many indigenous people to neglect or abandon types of production that formerly had served their needs well and become wage laborers, sometimes migrating to distant lands seeking employment. For increasing numbers of people without other sources of survival in the expanding global market economy, their labor became their only marketable commodity, their survival mechanism.[6]

Colonial capitalism, and the exploitation and poverty it created, made large families a rational choice for most people. Within the United States, too, poor tenant farmers and sharecroppers, black and white, found large families a necessity in order to ensure the many hands it took to survive.

The roads, communications, engineering, agricultural technology, and medical services introduced by European colonizers and extractors of natural resources to increase both the number and productivity of laborers in their enterprises initiated the first phase of the demographic transition in the colonies. Imported technologies of public health, in particular, led to a dramatic reduction of mortality rates. However, the persistence of pro-natalist norms, high infant mortality, and conditions of economic insecurity prevented birth rates from declining significantly. The result was a disruption in precolonial demographic equilibrium between birth rates and death rates followed by rapid population growth, particularly in the post-independence period due to the exponential growth rate.

The demographic explosion in the Third World, then, is a product of contradictions within the twin forces of modern technology and capitalism. These forces brought down death rates through modern technology, but they could not bring down birth rates because they increased social inequality and undermined economic security and self-sufficiency for the masses.

Almost everywhere, parents in lower economic classes tend to have more children than do middle-class parents. There are two primary reasons for this. First, in poor communities the marginal cost of raising an additional child is very little—certainly when compared with the exorbitant costs of raising a child at middle-class consumption levels in the North. Second, for poor people without other resources, children are often economic assets, not liabilities.

Unlike middle-class children, who remain dependent on their parents until adulthood, poor children in the Third World start to work at an early age. In rural communities, children engage in a variety of unpaid, as well as underpaid, work, including agricultural fieldwork, export craft production, domestic work, rearing young siblings, and so on. In urban slums, many families depend entirely on the labor of children working as street vendors, beggars, thieves, and prostitutes. Such children are trapped in a catch-22: they must engage in such activities for lack of survival alternatives in the first place, and then their very labor keeps them from the schooling that might enable them to move beyond such poverty. This contributes to the intergenerational propagation of class status and the perpetuation of the cycle of poverty and high fertility.[7]

Colonialism and Subordination of Women

The relationship between poverty and fertility cannot be understood fully without looking at the economic and social subordination of women. Under colonial capitalism, men were favored for wage labor over women; women's labor became increasingly marginalized as unpaid, invisible domestic labor. Private property rights, education, and new technology were given largely to men, although women continued to be central economic producers in most regions. Where women were absorbed into wage labor as field hands, maids, and so on, they were restricted to lower-paid, lower-status "women's work." Even when women became the primary breadwinners of families (for example, because of male unemployment or migration), they continued to be defined in colonial practice largely as dependent housewives and mothers. Christian proselytization and the Victorian morality of the 19th and early 20th centuries helped reinforce the sexual and social subordination of women.

Economic marginalization and deepening poverty have not allowed women to challenge patriarchal social relations. In the absence of improvements in women's economic and social status, children continue to be their primary source of social esteem as well as economic security and power.[8] Childless women—in particular, women without sons—are ostracized and often abandoned by husbands in patriarchal cultures. The pressure to bear sons, coupled with high infant mortality rates, makes it rational for poor women to have many children. Under such conditions, many poor women see demands for fertility control, including economic incentives to accept sterilization, not as a choice but as a threat to their very social identity and well-being.

These observations have some validity for poor women in the North as well. For example, lack of access to abortion and contraception are not why teenage girls bear children in the United States. The causes of high teenage pregnancy in poor neighborhoods are largely rooted in economic and social structures that undermine self-esteem, hope, and upward mobility. As many analysts have shown, where poverty is the "dominant factor" in the lives of black teenage men and women, many choose to bear children as a way of expressing their adult status in a harsh and racist world that denies their sense of being.[9] Early childbearing and the burdens of child-rearing, whether among whites or people of color, hinder young parents from furthering their education and improving their lives. As in the Third World, these factors often lead to the intergenerational transmission of poverty and a continuation of the mutually reinforcing cycle of poverty and high fertility.

Population control advocates are not entirely wrong when they point out that many poor women do not have access to reliable contraceptives and that they would like to use them in some cases, regardless of the disapproval of their boyfriends or husbands. However, historical evidence from the West as well as other regions has shown repeatedly that, for family planning and contraceptives to be accepted and used, social conditions compatible with low fertility must exist. Voluntary family planning has succeeded only in societies where economic security—including access to material resources, health, and education—has been improved for the general population and for women in particular.

Social Justice and Fertility

The dominant capitalist development model assumes that social improvements can come about only as a result of rapid economic growth. However, even in Europe and the newly industrialized countries, such as South Korea and Taiwan, economic growth alone was not sufficient to improve general living standards. State intervention in the provision of universal education and health care, and in some cases land reform, were vital for improving living standards and lowering birth rates.

Frances Moore Lappe and Rachel Schurman have observed that by the 1980–85 period, among the more than 70 poor countries in the world, only six—China, Sri Lanka, Colombia, Chile, Burma, and Cuba—and the south Indian state of Kerala had managed to cut their total fertility rates by a third and to reduce population growth rates to less than 2 percent annually. Yet, unlike European countries and newly industrialized East Asian "success" economies that had experienced the demographic transition to low birthrates, these seven areas did *not* have very high levels of economic growth, per capita incomes, industrialization, or urbanization. Nor did they have strong family planning programs in common.

What China, Sri Lanka, Colombia, Chile, Burma, Cuba, and Kerala did have in common were guarantees of basic necessities, especially access to sufficient food. Four of the seven areas (China, Sri Lanka, Cuba, and Kerala) provided more extensive food guarantees than any other Third World countries.[10] These examples suggest that what is most essential for poverty alleviation and declining birth rates is not overall economic growth, but rather equitable income distribution, the reduction of economic inequality, and improvements in women's lives.

In Sri Lanka, benefits provided by the social welfare state such as universal education, health care, and food subsidies helped to improve the quality of life and to lower mortality and birth rates, despite low per capita incomes and low economic growth rates (prior to economic liberalization in 1977). The high rate of women's literacy, 84 percent, and the delayed age of marriage, nearly 24.7 years for women on average in 1981, are indeed unusual in an economically poor country, as is women's low fertility rate of only 2.5 children for the 1990–95 period.[11]

The demographic transition in Kerala is even more instructive, because it stands in sharp contrast to the rest of India, which has not achieved the same. Despite large-scale programs of population stabilization conducted by the Indian government over several decades, using conventional Western approaches to family planning, the annual population growth rate in India has averaged 2.1 percent during the past 40 or so years. While Kerala's population density is three times the Indian average and for many decades Kerala was considered among the most "backward" and "overpopulated" of Indian states, within an astonishingly short time span, both Kerala's mortality and fertility rates declined. Thus, Kerala's annual population growth rate went from 2.26 percent in 1971 to 1.74 in 1981.[12]

The demographic transition of Kerala was not the achievement of stringent population control. Rather, it was the result of structural reforms that reduced social and economic disparities. Transfer of resources to the poorest groups occurred through such mechanisms as abolition of tenancy through land reform, enforcement of child-labor and minimum-wage laws, widespread health facilities, pension funds, universal education, public work programs, expansion of agricultural labor unions, and a minimum food and grain distribution system. All have contributed to Kerala's successful demographic transition. These reforms led to overall improvements in the quality-of-life index—reduced infant mortality, longer life expectancy, higher literacy. When mortality levels fell, and when the value of children as an economic asset declined across the social spectrum, even some of the poorest landless laborers became amenable to family planning.[13]

The fertility decline in Kerala must also be seen in relation to the relatively high status of women, a fact visible in the relatively longer life expectancy of girls and women over boys and men (the human biological norm). Among Indian states, Kerala's sex ratio of 97 males per 100 females is exceptionally favorable to women. Although Kerala's matrilineal traditions have weakened in recent years, they have nevertheless been important in giving Keralan women a relatively high social status. Recent social reforms in Kerala have been particularly beneficial to women. They have increased women's educational levels, labor force participation, and age at marriage, which is the highest of any state in India. Fully 22 percent of Keralan women never marry, apparently because attractive alternatives to marriage are available to educated women.[14]

Kerala's success is not simply the result of top-down action from a benevolent leftist state. Without grassroots mobilization and continued pressure by peasant and labor groups, the Communist Party of India (CPI), despite being elected to power, would have been unlikely to initiate and successfully carry out land-reform, minimum-wage, child-labor, and similar progressive legislation. Even when the CPI was out of power, it was able to influence the continuation of social welfare policies due to its popularity with the poor. In Sri Lanka, too, the welfare state was the product of very high levels of popular participation in electoral politics.

The welfare state may not be a panacea for all social problems or women's concerns. Certainly, the Keralan and Sri Lankan models have not been perfect. The lessons of these cases, however, is that if reduction of population growth rates is a priority, then social structural changes are essential. Social equity concerns must take priority over aggregate growth concerns, and human needs must come before the "needs" of externally imposed family planning programs and other institutional structures.

Although the rhetoric of "basic needs," "human development," "women's rights," "sustainability," and so on have been incorporated in documents of the dominant world institutions, these same institutions have been vigorously blocking efforts toward social justice and democracy. The World Bank, for instance, has consistently opposed income redistribution even when some of its own studies have shown that increased income correlates with lower fertility.[15] Studies from Bangladesh and other areas show that one of the central questions guiding the population-control enterprise is, "Can family planning programs ... succeed without extensive socioeconomic development?"[16] Population control is increasingly promoted as a substitute for income and wealth redistribution in the face of worsening global inequality.

Widening Global Inequality

Over the past three decades, disparities in wealth and income between North and South have been increasing, as well as disparities based on class, race, and gender. In 1960, the richest 20 percent of the world's population had incomes 30 times greater than the poorest 20 percent. By 1990, the richest 20 percent were getting 60 times more. And this is based on the distribution between rich and poor countries. When the maldistribution of income within countries is taken into account, the richest 20 percent of the world's people in 1990 got at least 150 times more than the poorest 20 percent.[17]

Within countries too, income disparities and equity ratios between the richest and poorest groups have been widening. The experience of Chile during its recent so-called economic miracle (referring to high economic growth rates) is an example. The income share of the richest fifth was 7.6 percent in 1969. By 1988, that ratio had changed to 54.6 percent for the highest group and 4.4 percent for the poorest group. The result has been an increase in the percentage of Chileans living under the poverty line, from 28.5 percent in 1969 to 36 percent in 1979, and 42 percent in 1989. Caloric intake among the poorest 20 percent decreased more than 23 percent between 1969 and 1989.[18]

Inequalities have been widening in the North as well. In 1988 in the United States, the lowest income quintile had 7 percent of the national income, while the highest quintile held 44.4 percent. In 1991, 32.7 percent of blacks, 28.7 percent of Hispanics, 13.8 percent of Asians and Pacific Islanders, and 11.3 percent of whites fell below the poverty line (the poverty threshold in 1991 for a family of four was $13,924).[19]

Examination of wealth holdings (property and capital assets) in the United States reveal even greater disparities. In 1988, the poorest 25 percent of the U.S. population held 0.3 percent of the wealth, while the richest 8.8 percent of the people controlled nearly 50 percent of total wealth. Within the latter group, just 2.8 percent controlled 27.2 percent of total national wealth.[20] Income and wealth differentials are rapidly increasing also in Europe, especially in the former Soviet bloc countries.

Gender disparities in income and wealth are continuing. According to United Nations estimates in 1980, women comprised 52 percent of the world's population but owned 1 percent of the world's property, performed two-thirds of the world's work hours, and received one-tenth of the world's wages. The amount of land available to women food producers in the Third World is declining. Although more and more women are employed, they receive 30 to 40 percent less pay than men worldwide, even when they do the same work as men. Female-headed households tend to be disproportionately poorer than male-headed households across the world.[21] In 1987, nearly half of all female-headed households (67.2 percent of black and 70.3 percent of Hispanic female-headed households) in the United States fell below the poverty line.[22]

Persistent and often increasing inequality in income and resource distribution is the main issue of our time. Social inequality underlies the worsening problems of poverty, environmental destruction, repression of human rights, and resistance to democratic change, as well as population growth. "Overpopulation" is not the root cause of the global political and economic crisis. To understand the source of the crisis, we have to move farther away from Malthusian analysis and the focus on population and toward an analysis of the unequal integration of regions, social classes, races, and men and women into the expanding global capitalist economy.

Deepening Poverty

In the post–World War II neocolonial period, the chains of economic dependency binding the Third World—the South—to the industrialized North were tightened. Worsening terms of trade and continued distortion of Third World economies toward export-led growth further undermined the subsistence and living standards of the poor. In this period, transnational corporate dominance greatly expanded. For example, three to six transnational corporations based in the North now control 75 percent of the South's exports in the 21 main categories of commodity trade.[23] In many countries, corporate control of the production and distribution of food is a significant cause of hunger.

In the 1970s, the Third World as a group demanded a New International Economic Order with better terms of trade and more equitable distribution of wealth and income between the ex-colonies and the industrialized nations of the North. It was also in this context that the Third World delegates at the 1974 United Nations Population Conference in Bucharest called for development assistance over population control, arguing that "development itself is the best contraceptive." Instead of heeding these demands, the North continued to strangle the economies of the South, thereby exacerbating poverty and destitution. GATT (the General Agreement on Tariffs and Trade) and NAFTA (the North America Free Trade Agreement) represent two instruments for widening and deepening control of global resources and markets by transnational corporations, most of them based in the North. Not only will GATT and NAFTA constrict and depress wages, GATT will also allow transnational corporations to extend their control into the service sector, as well as to impose patent rights on plants and gene materials through new developments in biotechnology. As Vandana Shiva and other critics have pointed out, the survival rights of indigenous forest dwellers and farmers will be undermined by these forces.[24]

The Debt Crisis

Widening gaps in terms of trade between the North and the South and aggressive lending policies of commercial banks, among other factors, gave rise to the Third World debt crisis. At the beginning of 1989, "developing nations" owed foreign creditors $1.3 trillion—that is, just over half their combined gross national products and two-thirds more than their export earnings. The annual debt service bill on this approximated $200 billion, and total debt principal and interest have continued to grow.[25] Since 1983, the South has been a net exporter of financial resources to the North, and no longer a net recipient. In other words, Third World people have to pay for their own oppression.

The response of the North to the problems of Third World debt is "Structural Adjustment": a set of "free market" economic policies imposed by the International Monetary Fund and the World Bank as a condition for receiving "assistance" in the form of further loans (i.e., future debt). Structural Adjustment Policies (SAPs) seek to improve the foreign investment climate of loan recipients by eliminating barriers to capital expansion and international trade. Adjustment loans come with stringent conditions—for example, trade "liberalization" and export promotion, devaluation of local currencies (which automatically raises the price of every essential consumer good in local markets, including food), curbs on import substitution, privatization of government services and enterprises, wage and salary freezes, cutbacks in state social welfare expenditures and subsidies, and so forth. Frequently, the World Bank also requires acceptance of strong population-control programs by Third World governments as a condition for receiving adjustment loans.

Corrupt government leaders and officials are known to have pocketed many loans received, and a small elite has prospered from export-led growth and the neoliberal programs. But a growing body of data from around the world shows that the pressures created by debt repayment and SAPs have been disastrous for the poor, particularly for women. Mandated cuts in government spending, freezing of wages, abolition of food subsidies, and cutbacks in expenditures for basic infrastructure, maternal child health, clinics, schools, and other essential public goods have not only reduced services needed especially by the poor but have also increased unemployment and driven down wages, further exacerbating their poverty and vulnerability, particularly for women.[26]

Not only has adjustment ignored the impact on women, but SAPs have been built upon the very exploitation of women. Cutbacks in social services have forced women, as the primary nurturers and caretakers of families, to stretch their own and their families' limited resources to the breaking point.

Further shifts of natural resources into export production have threatened women's subsistence production and their ability to feed their families. When dismissed from their jobs or when their wages are cut due to SAPs, women are forced to seek additional work, often in the informal sector as vendors, domestic workers, or prostitutes.

The recent report of the Commonwealth Expert Group on Women and Structural Adjustment reveals that female nutrition and health have declined in many countries where IMF/World Bank SAPs were put into effect. By inducing declines in female schooling and health as well as by increasing infant mortality, SAPs have in many cases helped maintain the conditions of high fertility. As Ingrid Palmer has written in an International Labor Organization working paper for the World Employment Program:

> What can be stated at once is that all the signs point to a pronatal impact of structural adjustment policies in the short term. On every count—the value of children's assistance, the threat to women's personal income, and the reduction in public expenditure on health-giving facilities—the outcome for fertility is forbidding. More will be expected of the household labor supply with its gender and age allocation.[27]

The vast system of global political and economic inequality created by colonialism and neocolonialism is maintained by militarism, particularly increased arms exports and armed intervention. The five permanent members of the United Nations Security Council account for 85 percent of global arms exports. The United States alone is responsible for 40 percent of the global arms trade.[28]

While arms sales are vital to Northern economies, particularly that of the United States, they exacerbate global income disparities, cut into social welfare expenditures, drive down living standards, and aggravate the problems of poverty as well as environmental destruction and violent conflict. As much as 20 percent of the original debt of the Third World was for military expenditures to help maintain repressive regimes. Some of the highest spending on defense prevails in some of the poorest regions. Indeed, where inequalities are greatest and threats to governments high, military expenditures tend to be high as well. For example, South Asia spends $10 billion a year on the military and sub-Saharan Africa spends $5 billion. When countries increase spending on weapons and armed forces, fewer resources remain for social welfare. As the United Nations Development Program's 1990 *Human Development Report* points out, there are now eight times more soldiers than physicians in the Third World.[29]

The combined effect over the past decade of declining terms of trade for most Third World exports, debt, structural adjustment, increasing military expenditures, and population growth has been a reduction in real social expenditures per person in many "developing" countries (which can hardly be called "developing" at all). Relentless expansion of industrial capitalism and the development model of "free trade, export growth first" are depressing wages, constricting self-reliance, and undermining the very subsistence of the poor majority. There is no guarantee that even a progressive people-first state like Kerala can withstand the penetration of international capital and privatization and be able to hold on to its hard-won social improvements in the years ahead. In Sri Lanka, for example, the welfare state has been gradually dismantled due to the confluence of economic liberalization since 1977, IMF/World Bank policies, and militarism. As a result, income disparities have widened, and hunger and malnutrition among the poorer groups have increased.[30]

According to U.N. estimates, 1.2 billion people in the world live in deep poverty. More than a quarter of the world's population fails to receive sufficient food for a normally active life, and nearly one-fifth goes hungry everyday. Of the world's children under five years of age, 180 million are seriously underfed, and 14 million die each year before their fifth birthday.[31] Impoverishment forces many poor people to deplete their own resource base through overcultivation, deforestation, overfishing, and so on. And many others are forced to enter the growing "skin trade," a trade in human bodies. Parents sell children to anyone who will take them. Prostitution of both women and children flourishes. The most desperate even sell body parts; in India and Egypt, for example, the illegal trade in kidneys is booming. Some countries also report an illegal trade in human fetuses.

Poverty and deterioration of living standards is not peculiar to the South. During the Reagan-Bush administrations in the United States, for example, increased military expenditures; "supply-side economics," with changes in income tax laws to favor the wealthy; and cutbacks in social welfare programs sharpened social inequality and increased poverty. Here, too, the brunt of the burden has been borne by women and children, especially blacks and Hispanics. In 1988, one in seven women in the United States was poor, one in six could not afford health insurance, and one in three female-headed families lived below the poverty level.[32] African American women and their children constituted the largest single group living in poverty. Like "adjustment" policies in the South, neoliberal policies in the United States, too, may have a pronatal impact, in that they have increased poverty, particularly the poverty of women.

Neither the population issue nor the broader politico-economic crisis that it represents can be resolved by increased funding for family planning programs and quick-fix contraceptives. Poverty alleviation and the economic empower-ment of women must be the cornerstones of population policy. To eradicate poverty and to reduce economic inequality, however, we must move away from the capitalist, competitive, "growth first" model of development and toward a new model that places survival of humans and the environment before the needs of corporate profit and technological advancement. We need sustainable and democratic models of development that honor social, ethical, and ecological principles, including the essential oneness and equality of all human beings.

Statement Presented at the NGO Forum on the ICPD, Bureau for Refugee Programs, U.S. Department of State, Washington, D.C., April 29, 1993

Poverty contributes to high fertility, environmental destruction, political unrest, and migration. To eradicate poverty and to achieve sustainable development, the global disparity between the poverty of the majority and resource overconsumption by the minority must be reduced. The agendas of the United States of America for the International Conference on Population and Development must provide specific measures for poverty alleviation.

When people have genuine choices, they will not seek to emigrate overseas. The solution to the influx of economic, environmental, and political refugees to the United States is the provision of economic opportunity for people in their lands of origin. To curb the number of refugees coming here, the U.S.A. must vastly reduce its weapons sales abroad. To avoid intensification of North-South conflicts, the U.S.A. must allow the less industrialized countries to control their genetic resources.

Alleviation of women's poverty is urgent. There is evidence around the world that improvements in women's status through education and economic op-portunity are crucial for voluntary reductions in birth rates. United States funding must be directed towards economic development programs for women rather than top-down family planning programs.

Birth control programs must offer genuine choices to women. Women must be able to choose from a range of contraceptives, including barrier methods. They must have full information on side effects and contraindications of high-technol-ogy methods. Targets and incentives must be abolished in the Third World and must not be extended to the U.S.A. Male methods and male participation in birth control must be increased.

Women of color (Native American, African American, Hispanic American, and Asian American women) must be fully included in the decisionmaking process for the United States agenda for the ICPD. Members of the Committee on Women, Population, and the Environment offer our assistance in: (1) planning the agenda for the ICPD, (2) transforming family planning programs into democratic partici-patory models, and (3) directing U.S. population funding toward social and eco-nomic development projects for women in the United States and abroad.

Notes

1. Georg Borgstrom, *The Food and People Dilemma* (North Scituate, MA: Duxbury Press, 1973), 1–2.

2. John Bodley, "Demographic Impact of the Frontier," in Scott W. Menard and Elizabeth W. Moen, eds., *Perspectives on Population: An Introduction to Concepts and Issues* (New York: Oxford University Press, 1987), 23.

3. Marvin Harris and Eric B. Ross, *Death, Sex and Fertility: Population Regulation in Preindustrial and Development Societies* (New York: Columbia University Press, 1987), 119–21.

4. Barry Commoner, *Making Peace with the Planet* (New York: The New Press, 1992), 160.

5. Maria Mies, *Patriarchy and Accumulation on a World Scale: Women in the International Division of Labour* (London: Zed Books, 1986), 91, 99.

6. Asoka Bandarage, *Colonialism in Sri Lanka: The Political Economy of the Kandyan Highlands, 1833–1886* (Berlin: Mouton, 1983).

7. John G. Patterson and Nanda R. Shrestha, "Population Growth and Development in the Third World: The NeoColonial Context," *Studies in Comparative International Development,* Vol. 23 (Summer 1988), 23.

8. Frances Moore Lappe and Rachel Schurman, *The Missing Piece in the Population Puzzle,* Food First Development Report No. 5 (San Francisco: Institute for Food and Development Policy, 1988), 27.

9. Leon Dash, *When Children Want Children* (New York: Penguin Books, 1989); also Constance Willard Willlares, *Black Teenage Mothers: Pregnancy and Child Rearing from Their Perspective* (Lexington, MA: Lexington Books, 1991), 131.

10. Lappe and Schurman, *The Missing Piece,* op. cit., 55–63.

11. Asoka Bandarage, "Women and Capitalist Development in Sri Lanka, 1977–1987," *Bulletin of Concerned Asian Scholars,* Vol. 20, No. 2 (1988), 77–78; John Caldwell, Indra Gajanayake, Bruce Caldwell, and Pat Caldwell, "Is Marriage Delay a Multiphasic Response to Pressures for Fertility Decline? The Case of Sri Lanka," *The Journal of Marriage and the Family,* Vol. 51, No. 2 (May 1989).

12. John Ratcliffe, "Social Justice and the Demographic Transition in India's Kerala State," *International Journal of Health Services,* Vol. 8, No. 1 (1978); T.N. Krishnan, "Population, Poverty and Employment in India," *Economic and Political Weekly,* November 14, 1992.

13. Joan Mencher, "The Lessons and Non-Lessons of Kerala: Agricultural Labourers and Poverty," *Economic and Political Weekly,* Special Number (October 1980), 1987.

14. Ratcliffe, "Social Justice," op. cit., 139.

15. World Bank, *World Development Report 1984,* 109.

16. Cited in Betsy Hartmann and Hilary Standing, *The Poverty of Population Control: Family Planning and Health Policy in Bangladesh* (London: Bangladesh

International Action Group, 1989), 67.

17. United Nations Development Programme, *Human Development Report 1992* (New York: Oxford University Press, 1992), 1.

18. Cathy Schneider, "Chile: The Underside of the Miracle," *NACLA Report on the Americas,* Vol. XXVI, No. 4, 30.

19. U.S. Department of Commerce, Economics and Statistics Administration, Bureau of Census, *Poverty in the United States, 1991,* No. 181, vii, x.

20. Stephen J. Rose, *Social Stratisfication in the U.S.: The American Profile Poster Revised and Expanded* (New York: The New Press, 1992), 21.

21. United Nations, *The World's Women, 1970–1990: Trends and Statistics, Social Statistics and Indicators,* Series K, No. 8 (New York: United Nations, 1991), 3.

22. U.S. Department of Commerce, Economics and Statistics Administration, Bureau of Census, "Distribution of All Children and of Poor Children by Family Type and Race: 1987," in *Statistical Abstract of the U.S. 1990* (Washington, DC: U.S. Government Printing Office, 1990), 463.

23. Canadian University Student Organization, *Here to Stay: Linking Sustainable Development and Debt, Part I: Understanding the Third World Debt* (Ottawa: Education Department, November 1990), 9.

24. Vandana Shiva, "North Blocks South in Biodiversity," *Third World Resurgence,* No. 28 (1992), 12–22.

25. United Nations Development Programme, *Human Development Report 1990,* 79, and *Human Development Report 1992,* 45 (New York: Oxford University Press, 1990 and 1992, respectively).

26. Commonwealth Expert Group on Women and Structural Adjustment, *Engendering Adjustment for the 1990s* (London: Commonwealth Secretariat, 1989).

27. Ingrid Palmer, *Gender Issues in Structural Adjustment of Sub-Saharan African Agriculture and Some Demographic Reflections* (working paper No. 166, World Employment Programme, ILO, 1980), cited in Jeanne Vickers, *Women and the World Economic Crisis* (London: Zed Books, 1991), 22.

28. Asoka Bandarage, "Global Peace and Security in the Post-Cold War Era: A 'Third World' Perspective," in Michael Klare, ed., *Peace and World Security Studies: A Curriculum Guide* (Boulder, CO: Lynne Rienner Publishers, 1994), 34.

29. Ibid., 31–32.

30. Bandarage, "Women and Capitalist Development in Sri Lanka, 1977-1987," op. cit., 77–78.

31. UNDP, *Human Development Report 1992,* op. cit., 14; and *Human Development Report 1991,* op. cit., 23–24.

32. Marc L. Minnghoff, *The Index of Social Health, 1990: Measuring the Social Well-Being of the Nation* (Tarrytown, NY: Fordham Institute for Innovation in Social Policy, Fordham University, 1990), 5.

TAKING POPULATION OUT OF THE EQUATION
Reformulating I=PAT

H. Patricia Hynes

In the mid-1970s, Paul Ehrlich and John Holdren put forth a simple algebraic equation that largely determined the parameters of the population-environment debate in the North in the ensuing years. Metaphors like "population bomb" and "population explosion" and images of teeming Third World cities fortified their algebraic model. Subsequently adopted by most mainstream environmental and population organizations of industrial countries, the formula became widely known as the I=PAT or IPAT equation.[1] The impact of humans on the environment (I) is a product of the number of people (P), the amount of goods consumed per person (A), and the pollution generated by technology per good consumed (T). Thus:

$$\text{Environmental Impact} = \text{Number of People} \times \frac{\text{Goods}}{\text{Person}} \times \frac{\text{Pollution}}{\text{Good}}$$

or $I = PAT$, where I is units of pollution

The appeal of IPAT lies in its simple, physical insight: All people use resources and create waste, and many have children who use more resources and create more waste. Complex, close-grained social and political factors that identify *who* among the universal P is responsible for *what*, and the *how* and the *why* behind much pollution—such as the military, trade imbalances and debt, and female subordination—are outside the scope of the formula. With IPAT, an atomistic view of humans' impact on the environment has been promulgated as sufficient analysis for public policy on population and environment.

The trademark of IPAT is its arithmetic integrity. The three factors inter-act in multiplicative fashion, so that an increase in any one of them—popula-tion, level of affluence, polluting technology—results in an increase in I. A small decrease in A and T is quickly offset by a small increase in population; conversely, a small decrease in P is countervailed by a small increase in A or T. IPAT works algebraically and thus appears to be internally consistent and correct.

Another drawing point of IPAT is the seeming geopolitical balance in the parameters. Regions with high P generally have low AT, and regions with high AT generally have low P. For example, just under 25 percent of the world's population consumes about 75 percent of the world's resources and energy and 85 percent of all wood products, and the same fraction of the population generates most of the world's waste and global atmospheric pollu-tion. Most of the high consumers and polluters live in the developed coun-tries. The world's population of 5.4 billion people is growing at a rate of 1.7 percent per year and is projected to reach 10 billion by 2050. More than 90 percent of that growth will be in developing countries.[2] These statistics, with their alleged evenhandedness to North and South, are used to corroborate the universality of the formula and frame the parameters of the international public policy debate on environment and development. (How balanced, though, is the environmental impact of developing and developed countries if developing countries are more responsible for the impact of only one factor, P, while developed countries are more responsible for the impact of two fac-tors, A and T?)

Debates from Within

So entrenched is IPAT that critics and advocates alike debate from within it; like a mental boxing ring, it locks in those who take it on. Some critics have argued that A and T are more egregious than P in impact; others, that the im-pact of an increase in population is variable and contextual, depending on such factors as population density and robustness or fragility of the ecosystem. This leads advocates to propose a country-by-country assessment of popula-tion limits based on a given country's ecological carrying capacity, C; ulti-mately I=PAT regenerates as I=PACT. In other cases, critics charge the North with hypocrisy because of its inflated focus on P, near silence on A, and insuf-ficient action on T. International mediators then propose North-South negotia-tions where each gives something—for example, carbon dioxide reductions in the North for demographic reductions in the South. I=PAT persists as I=P[A]T, where A sidesteps negotiation as T and P are traded off against each other.

The environmentalist Barry Commoner, one of the early and fiercest critics of IPAT, has analyzed population, consumption, technology changes, and pollutant increases in the United States between 1950 and 1970, the years of rapid industrial growth for four categories of pollutant: nitrogen oxides, phosphates, synthetic pesticides, and discarded beer bottles. Using regression analysis, he found that "the dominant contribution to the sharply rising pollution levels during that period of time was the technology factor rather than increasing population or affluence."[3] In the post–World War II era, disposable containers replaced reusable ones; manufacture and use of synthetic fertilizers and pesticides increased exponentially; truck freight replaced rail freight; and national transportation policy favored the automobile. In a comparable but modified analysis for developing countries, Commoner demonstrated similar results: The increase in motor vehicle use and electricity generation between 1970 and 1980 was significantly higher than the increase in population. He concludes that "environmental quality is ... largely governed ... by the nature of the technologies of production."[4] While Commoner forcefully propounds the overriding role of industrial technology in pollution, he nevertheless leaves the IPAT paradigm intact for another generation of analysts to compute and compare the impacts of population, consumption, and technology on the environment.

In analyzing the 1992 United Nations Conference on Environment and Development in preparation for the 1994 UN International Conference on Population and Development (ICPD), senior policy analyst Susan Cohen of the Guttmacher Institute packaged the key global threats to environment within the IPAT formula. The thorniest issue of her analysis was, What would make P palatable to feminists?

Feminists are the group that environmentalists and populationists[5] find the most fractious in the population debate, because feminists will not disengage structural issues of poverty, male dominance, militarism, and consumerism from the population-environment debate. Cohen quotes populationists who are willing to talk reproductive rights as well as responsibilities and to link national demographic targets with economic and health ones for women. Environmentalists have a mixed record in public support for abortion and women's rights, she notes, but some are rapidly recognizing that the antidote to population explosion is "empowering women," as a 1993 issue of the National Wildlife Federation journal puts it.[6] Cohen sifts and sorts through the points of consensus that feminists, environmentalists, and populationists could have. The common ground that she maps includes linking population programs with programs for women's literacy and economic development, engaging women in designing family planning programs from the bottom up, combining demographic with social targets, taking a reproductive health approach to family planning, and lobbying for more and better contraceptive research.[7] Throughout the analysis, however, an undertow lurks: Feminists must break their silence about population pressures. In other words, feminists must buy into the P of IPAT, and then work from within that atomistic black box.

The authors of *Beyond the Limits*, sequel to *The Limits to Growth*, employ a system-dynamics computer model to show a range of environmental and human outcomes from ecosystem collapse to sustainability, with varying rates of population growth, consumption of resources, industrial output, and generation of pollution.[8] The simulations forecast the capacity of the earth at various scenarios of P, A, and T to sustain life and to avoid or suffer overshoot (going beyond ecological limits) and environmental collapse. The authors' simulations lead them to conclude that a sustainable world would support about 7.7 billion people at a standard of living comparable to that of a Western European in 1990, provided that technologies to reduce pollution emissions, land erosion, and resource use are adopted by 1995 and that these technologies are continually improved.

A prototypical graph of a simulation reinforces the premise of IPAT, which underlies their analysis: Since people can be counted numerically, population is fundamentally a quantitative phenomenon and therefore can be treated as a physical unit comparable to pollution and industrial output.

When the number crunching is finished, the authors call for a revolution in sustainability and, admirably, recognize that "equity" and "justice,... truthtelling," and "love" are necessary for that revolution. "The sustainability revolution will have to be, above all, a societal transformation that permits the best of human nature rather than the worst to be expressed."[9] It's a pity—and the nemesis of *Beyond the Limits*—that the social ideals of equity and justice are a humanistic afterword to a numerical analysis of humans in the world, rather than beacons of enlightenment that would recast the analysis up-front. The quest for a sustainable world has to originate from a passion for justice, not merely conclude with an appeal to truth and love, Scotch-taped like some ethical appendage onto a quantitative input-output model of humans in the world.

Critics and advocates alike, as these examples demonstrate, are locked into the argot of the IPAT model; their results become the talking points for

Figure 1. Scenario of Stabilized Population and Industry with Technologies to Reduce Emissions, Erosion, and Resource Use Adopted in 1995.

State of the world

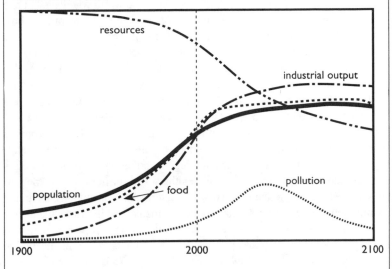

Reprinted from *Beyond the Limits*, © 1992 by Meadows, Meadows, and Randers. With permission from Chelsea Green Publishing Co., Post Mills, VT.

public policy and international negotiations. Wittingly and unwittingly, they buy into the P of IPAT. An alternative feminist approach would reform IPAT so that key structural factors that have been omitted—the elements of social and environmental justice—are brought into the heart of analysis and ultimately reframe public policy on environment and population.

Rethinking IPAT

As the environment and population debate becomes more nuanced, P increasingly refers to the one-fifth of humanity who are absolutely poor and have the highest fertility rates, while A and T are associated with the consumption and technology of the wealthiest and most industrialized fifth of the world's population. A 1991 United Nations study states: "These 'poorest of the poor,' being most in need of the benefits of development, are often responsible for a disproportionate amount of environmental degradation, and feature the highest fertility rates.... These 'bottom billion' people may often pose greater environmental injury than the other 3 billion of their fellow [developing country] citizens put together."[10] In the same vein, the editor of the Worldwatch Environmental Alert Series points to "some 2.2 billion people ... wreaking havoc on the world"—"the one-fifth of the world who have but one goal: surviving the next day," and the other fifth who have set record levels of consumption over the past 40 years and show no signs of abating.[11]

Can the poorest 1.1 billion people compare in environmental impact to that of the technology and consumption of the wealthiest 1.1 billion? Is this one-to-one ratio accurate, and is it just? The P of most concern for fertility control—the "poorest of the poor"—are institutionally powerless yet collectively resilient women who have larger numbers of children for complex reasons that range from immediate survival and necessity to lack of appropriate reproductive health services to coercion by a male partner, patriarchal religion, or the state. The T of concern, the highest-polluting industrial processes that provide consumer goods for the wealthiest fifth of humanity, belong almost entirely to men in the most powerful, interlocking institutions, including multinational oil and gas corporations, governments, and industrial giants like car makers and chemical and weapons manufacturers, whose goal is maximizing economic growth and profit.[12] The A of concern are the 1.1 billion who consume 85 percent of all wood products and 75 percent of all energy and resources; they generate almost 90 percent of ozone-depleting chlorofluorocarbons (CFCs) and two-thirds of carbon dioxide emissions and spend a significant portion of their lives dieting, watching television, and riding in air-conditioned cars.

If the wealthiest 20 percent use at least 16 times more energy and 17 times more wood than the poorest 20 percent, then how can the one-to-one ratio of environmental impact hold? It strains credulity to equate the poorest, least politically powerful human beings on earth with the most potent industrial expressions of corporate capitalism and former state socialism, the T of IPAT. It strains arithmetic to equate the lowest consumers of natural resources on earth with the highest consumers, who haven't a clue whether the 85 percent of the world's wood products they purchase and discard were sustainably harvested or come from the last remaining trees on a denuded mountain slope. The wealthiest one-fifth are the major meat-eaters of the world, yet they could not trace the links between, on the one hand, the hamburger they eat and the dog food they buy and, on the other, the patch of Latin American rain forest razed for beef cattle that supply the North American beef and dog food markets. (Perhaps the number of domestic pets and the number of animals eaten per year per person should be calculated into the P of IPAT.)

If the wealthiest 20 percent of the world harbors 80 percent of nuclear, chemical, and biological weapons,[13] and none of the poorest 20 percent makes, owns, tests, or uses any weapons of comparable ecological destruction, then how can the one-fifth richest and one-fifth poorest be held equal in environmental impact? (IPAT does not account for this difference in rates of military pollution.) If, as Indian environmentalists argue, we apportion the earth's capacity to absorb wastes among the human population equally, then all of the global climate change gases released by the poorest one-fifth of humanity (the " 'survival emissions' of the poor") are more than assimilated by the earth. Global climate change, by this calculation, is threatened by the " 'luxury emissions' of the rich," which exceed the earth's assimilative capacity.[14]

The permutations of IPAT, which conflate the poorest people with the wealthiest, equate thousands of women from Rwanda and Bangladesh in environmental impact to the DuPont Corporation, the U.S. and former USSR military, and thousands of overweight North Americans and Western Europeans. Some of the poorest 1.1 billion people are indigenous people who have been driven from their ancestral lands by governments and multinationals that privatized and exploited the resource base for a market economy. Some of the 1.1 billion poorest are African women who lost access to land when communal rights were replaced by European title-deed systems that restricted land ownership to men. "In Africa, where market organizations of women traders once allowed women political and economic power, and where sister/brother inheritance and kin cooperation patterns allowed women an alternative to dependence on a husband, European patriarchy undermined both."[15] How much imprecision and injustice is built into IPAT when an Indian tribal woman uprooted by state privatization of forests she used for subsistence, or a destitute African woman impoverished by Western "development," is considered comparable in environmental impact to a corporate or government or military person from the wealthiest one-fifth of the world? Within this model, the chasm in equity between the absolute poor and the extravagantly wealthy is invisible and irrelevant.

Differences of power and decision-making between individuals who own nothing and must resort to scavenging local biomass to survive and multinational corporations whose wealth is accrued in part from exploiting the resource base of impoverished countries are set aside in IPAT, a power-blind equation. The responsibility of those few at the pinnacles of government and industry who first colonized and then devised the post-colonial models of development that have altered and restricted inheritance and land ownership for women in Africa—and thus disempowered and impoverished some of the "bottom billion"—is unexamined in IPAT, an agent-less equation. That the majority of the bottom 20 percent of the world's poor are women of color and their children (the P of concern), and the majority of the top 20 percent of the world's affluent are white men (the AT of concern) is not noted in IPAT, a gender- and color-blind equation. Finally, the environmental good created by those who reclaim wastelands, restore woodlands, use natural resources wisely, preserve their local ecosystems from industrial exploitation and commodification, and participate in what Finnish economist Hilkka Pietilä calls a "cultivation economy"[16] is not factored into the IPAT model of human impact on the environment, a niggardly and negative equation.

Humanism and Environmentalism

A first correction to IPAT would split apart the impact made by humans using resources such as land, forests, and water for survival from humans consuming luxury goods and services that generate significant pollution, such as golf courses, speedboats, and private planes.

$$I = (PAT)_S + (PAT)_L$$

where S is survival
L is luxury

A humanistic environmental public policy would work first to enhance $A_{SURVIVAL}$ through investment in primary health care and women's health, including the availability of appropriate birth control, education, and opportunities for women equal to those of men; and through access to credit, land reform, and the reduction of foreign debt. Simultaneously, humanistic public policy would prioritize reducing T_{LUXURY} and $T_{SURVIVAL}$ through investment in appropriate technologies and pollution prevention such as energy efficiency, public transportation, and organic agriculture, as well as streamlining technology transfer. A national and individual commitment to change consumption patterns and to reduce A_{LUXURY}—that is, unnecessary consumption of nonrenewable and endangered resources (e.g., oil and gas, primary metals, and rainforest timber)—is crucial for industrial countries; as yet, there is a vacuum of analysis, information, political will, and public policy on this issue.

This correction to IPAT introduces social justice to environmental protection. We give priority to reducing poverty, redistributing power and wealth, ensuring the equality of women with men, as we simultaneously employ technical fixes such as eliminating ozone-depleting chemicals and making motors and appliances more energy-efficient. Widely celebrated cases, like that of Kerala, India, described below, demonstrate that when a society invests in universal education, primary health care, land reform, and the full participation of women in society—that is, when women have social security and power in their lives—they choose to have fewer children, and that choice is respected. Rather than pursuing a classic trickle-down development model—tax breaks and incentives for private internal and external investment in infrastructure and industry—the progressive government of Kerala applied the majority of its resources and efforts to the redistribution of wealth through land and wage reform as well as the general improvement of all human services. These reforms and the progressive government were the fruit of society-wide popular movements, especially vibrant women's, labor, and environmental movements.[17] Kerala—while poor and densely populated—has universal primary health care, the highest rate of female literacy in India, the lowest infant mortality rate, the longest life expectancy, and a population growth rate that is close to that of Australia.

A humanistic environmental agenda would critically address consumerism, for all industrial countries are living off the land, forests, biota, minerals, and energy base of developing countries and indigenous habitats. Many U.S. environmental organizations have established a population program, yet none has a program exclusively dedicated to overconsumption or consumerism. Not one industrial country or region has, as a matter of environmental public policy, committed to a reduction in consumption of pollution-intensive, resource-degrading luxury goods. We have no national net consumption reduction rate, no concept of consumption replacement rate, no mainstream nonprofit environmental organizations whose mission is zero economic growth or zero consumption growth. Total global advertising—which reflects and stimulates consumerism—"multiplied nearly sevenfold from 1950 to 1990 ... three times faster than world population."[18] Yet the rhetoric of "population bomb" and "population explosion" has gained currency in environmental organizations while concepts like "consumption bomb" and "consumption explosion" barely have a toehold.

In the early 1990s the Natural Resources Defense Council took a step in the direction of addressing consumption by initiating a program on population and consumption. If, however, environmentalists increasingly believe that the key to lower fertility rates is "empowering women," as the journal of the National Wildlife Federation proclaimed, then why haven't environmental organizations renamed their population programs "Empowering Women" or "Women's Rights" or "Reproductive Health"? Why not emulate Conservation International, which has a Gender and Social Policy Program rather than a population program?

Military and Environment

The second correction to IPAT would introduce a factor for military pollution, a mammoth pollution impact caused by a very small but politically powerful population. Thus,

$$I = (PAT)_{SURVIVAL} + (PAT)_{LUXURY} + MAT$$

where	M is	military population, particularly those with authority over budget, arms technology, and defense policy.
	A is	consumption of renewable and nonrenewable resources such as land, oil, metal, and solvents for military hardware, testing, maneuvers, and war.
	T is	pollution generated by research, weapons manufacture, testing, maneuvers, uranium and metals mining, and waste disposal.

Worldwide, the military is the most secretive, shielded, and privileged of polluters; thus, estimates of I for MAT are patchy and understated in many cases. Most of the extant data concern the United States, because increasing pressure on the Department of Defense and Department of Energy (DOE) by citizens, the Environmental Protection Agency, and Congress has forced those agencies to inventory, assess, and disclose the extent of their environmentally hazardous activities. Further, by the mid-1980s, the split in percent of global military spending between the developed and developing world was 80-20; and within the developed world, the United States and the former Soviet Union were the dominant military powers. For this cluster of reasons, the analysis of I=MAT will focus mainly on the United States' military activity.[19]

In the United States, some 20,000 military sites—including weapons production plants; chemical and biological warfare research facilities; training and maneuver bases; plane, ship, and tank manufacture and repair facilities; and abandoned disposal pits—rank as the most polluted hazardous waste sites. The Pentagon generates a ton of toxic waste per minute, more toxic waste than the five largest U.S. chemical companies together, making it the largest polluter in the United States. This figure does not include DOE's nuclear weapons plants and the Pentagon's civilian contractors. The 100-acre basin at Rocky Mountain Arsenal near Denver, Colorado, which was used to store waste from the production of nerve gas and pesticides from World War II through the Vietnam era, has been called "the earth's most toxic square mile" by the Army Corps of Engineers.

The Pentagon is the largest sole consumer of energy in the United States and, very likely, worldwide. Military energy use can jump from 2 to 3 percent to 15 to 20 percent in wartime, estimates that do not include energy demand for weapons manufacture. Altogether the world's military may use as many petroleum products as Japan, the world's second-largest economy. The estimated worldwide military use of aluminum, copper, nickel, and platinum surpasses the entire Third World demand for these metals.

Military nuclear reactors generate 97 percent of all high-level nuclear waste and 78 percent of all low-level nuclear waste in the United States. Some 300,000 citizens—more than half of those who ever worked for the U.S. nuclear weapons complex—are believed to have been harmed by radiation exposure. By 1989, more than 3,000 sites at 100 nuclear weapons manufacturing facilities were found to have contaminated soil and groundwater. As individual states spurn the siting of permanent subsurface storage facilities for nuclear waste within their boundaries, the federal government is heavily lobbying cash-poor Native American tribes to accept interim storage facilities for nuclear waste: 15 of the 18 federal grants for studies to establish a nuclear waste storage facility went to Indian reservations. Two-thirds of all uranium in the United States lies under Indian reservations. "We have nuclear radiation all over our land but no major environmental group in this country has a uranium campaign," remarked Winona LaDuke in the Sierra Roundtable on Race, Justice and the Environment.[20]

Without good data, researchers estimate that the military accounts for 5 to 10 percent of global air pollution, carbon dioxide, ozone depletion, smog, and acid-rain-forming chemicals. The Research Institute for Peace Policy in Starnberg, Germany, estimates that 20 percent of all global environmental degradation is due to military and related activities. One policy analyst at Worldwatch Institute concludes that "the world's armed forces are quite likely the single largest polluter on earth."[21]

What, then, is the military? The military is an institution invented and peopled by a small number of men who perpetuate masculinism by proliferating and parading about phallic weapons and by treating nuclear capability as a signifier of national manhood, and who sustain the morale of soldiers by victimizing women in rape and prostitution camps around military bases in rituals called rest and recreation. A well-glued solidarity between the military, national security advisers, civilian defense contractors, and elites of governments cloaks the degradation of women, the glorification of male pugnacity, and the extraordinary debt of pollution, destruction of land, and use of nonrenewable resources in the paternalistic mantle of national security. How can any of the 1.1 billion poorest and least intensive resource-using people, who are mainly women and children, be compared in environmental impact to the military population, a numerically small, sheltered male elite that is responsible for as much as 20 percent of all global degradation?

The implications of this analysis for public policy on environmental protection are rich with possibility. Reduce MAT, nationally and worldwide, through reductions in military spending, through better global regulation of arms exports and imports, through aggressive retooling of defense industries into civilian projects,[22] through linking the environmental movement with the peace movement, the feminist movement, and indigenous peoples. The military ought to be subject to the same right-to-know laws and the same environmental legislation as industry, and not permitted to police itself with regard to environmental protection. A system of national accounts for military costs to environment—including direct and indirect land, sea, and air use; waste emissions from military and civilian defense contractors; radioactive contamination throughout the life cycle of nuclear weapons production; and environmental losses from war—would enable environmentalists to apportion blame and accountability for environmental impact justly.

In a zero-sum economy, investment in weapons is public investment taken from literacy projects, infant, and maternal care, and condoms, for that matter. "It is immoral," Oscar Arias Sánchez, former president of Costa Rica, told an audience at MIT,

> for the wealthy nations to grow wealthier by selling arms to poor countries for money that they should be spending to feed and house their people, for education and health care and not on weapons designed to kill. Deferring human development programs in poor countries costs us as much misery and death as would a generalized war among all the nations of the world. This delay is due mainly to a distortion of priorities that places military ends over social investment.[23]

And what of the connection between war and unwanted/inflicted pregnancy? Postwar "baby booms" are common subjects of demographic and economic analysis; yet why haven't demographers studied the link between military bases, war, prostitution, rape, and pregnancy when evidence from World War II to Vietnam and Bosnia abounds?

Any environmental organization that has established a program on population policy ought to rethink an indiscriminate targeting of the population at large that fails to examine the excessive environmental impact that a relatively small population in military and defense industries has. A program on military and the environment would address more structurally, more accurately, and more justly the most damaging human impact on the environment.

Zero Population Growth announces that "it's time to break the silence on overpopulation"; but the best-guarded secret, the most pervasive silence engulfs the subject of military overpopulation, that is, the growing global traffic in weapons and the intensifying military usurpation of land and natural resources. With a few exceptions, notably Citizens Clearinghouse for Hazardous Waste, which has helped organize citizens to confront the military over military toxics,[24] environmental organizations have avoided the issue of the military and the environment. Doing so, they have enabled the military—the global toxics leviathan—to remain the most secretive, shielded, privileged, and largest of polluters, while targeting the poorest one-fifth of human beings for "wreaking havoc on the environment" as they try to survive day to day.

Environmental Guardians: The Lacuna in IPAT

> Native communities possess the experience of sustainability, learned from years of observation, careful behavior, and strong community— evidenced in thousands of years of living in the same place, whispering the same prayers, and walking the same paths.
>
> —Winona LaDuke

The most telling shortcoming of IPAT is its singular view of humans as parasites and predators on the natural environment. I, or the impact of humans on the environment, is fundamentally a negative measure of degradation and destruction of natural resources, calculated in units of pollution. This truncated, culture-bound view of humans in their environment originates from an industrial, urban, consumerist society. People in industrial countries meet their needs and seek happiness by purchasing commodities, nearly all of which use nonrenewable materials and energy and generate waste, a minimum of which is reduced, reused, or recycled. At best most people in industrial countries have recreational knowledge of nature and natural resources, and they often unknowingly leave the world much more degraded than they find it. These are the cultural roots of IPAT, an environmentalism that "comes out of the industrial mind, not the indigenous mind," to borrow from Winona LaDuke.

Indigenous peoples, rural peasants, and tribal peoples in developing countries, on the other hand, with their immediate and direct relationship to forests, land, water, and biodiversity, offer many stellar examples of humans knowing firsthand the living resource base from which they subsist, restoring and replenishing their local environment as they use it, and guarding it from maldevelopment projects. The Green Belt Movement, which originated in Kenya and spread to 12 other African countries; the Chipko Movement and wasteland restoration projects in India; agriculture among indigenous farmers of Central America and the American Southwest who preserve biodiversity among food crops—all are accomplished expressions of humans who have direct knowledge of, who love, use wisely, and conserve, the environment that is their "home, habitat, and workplace."[25] This positive human impact on environment—the lacuna of IPAT—is neither imagined nor accounted for in the model conceived within an industrial worldview where "everyone is an atomized individual whose home is wherever their lease or their mortgage is, whose work is wherever there is a job with a paycheck, and whose habitat can be projected into special times and spaces by vacationing in national parks and wilderness areas or just knowing that it exists somewhere."[26]

The impact of humans on the environment—if that impact is to encompass the significant environmental conservation of some humans and also hold out hope that the rest of humankind can learn from them how to live with a net positive impact—must include a factor for environmental conservation.

$$I = C - [(PAT)_{SURVIVAL} + (PAT)_{LUXURY} + MAT]$$

where   C is   environmentally beneficial work of natural resource management, preservation, and restoration; indigenous door-yard gardens, urban forests, gardens and composting, etc.

Within our own backyards in the United States are community-based models of people who leave the world better, richer in "natural and human capital," than they found it. The urban garden and greening movement offers a modest but stellar example from within industrial countries of people engaged in environmental conservation and education while reclaiming urban neighborhoods and the people of those neighborhoods.[27] Many urban conservationists are "people of low income and no income," as Rachel Bagby of Philadelphia Green describes her community. "In 100 years," forecasts Blaine Bonham, the director of Philadelphia Green, "when the suburbs have destroyed themselves with ugly sprawl and banal strips of malls, the viable parts of our cities where neighborhoods are thriving will be places like Strawberry Mansion and Point Breeze," two of Philadelphia Green's low-income neighborhoods with extensive gardens and tree-lined streets. The Greening of Harlem and Philadelphia Green are our native Chipko and Green Belt movements in which *ecociudadanos,* or urban environmentalists, are the key to the greening of U.S. cities.

Greening of Harlem

Central Harlem alone has 662 vacant, garbage-strewn lots—one out of every eight building lots, the equivalent of 112 acres—largely the legacy of disinvestment by absentee landlords, abandonment, and arson. Looking at any one of them, Bernadette Cozart, director of the Greening of Harlem coalition, gets "this land reclamation thing" in her head. She sees vacant lots as sources of jobs and places to grow vegetables and herbs that would go all the way from seed to shelf, restoring nature absent for more than 100 years. "Add the beauty of nature to Harlem and you give kids who have only known New York City as concrete and steel the chance to get to know nature."

The Greening of Harlem coalition members come from key community institutions, such as Harlem Hospital and the Marcus Garvey Park Conservancy, and from local tenant groups, including the Edgecomb Avenue Block Association. There is Dr. Barbara Barlow, chief of pediatric surgery and director of the Childhood Injury Prevention Program at Harlem Hospital, who insists that every playground in Harlem that is renovated with safe playground equipment and surfaces also have a community garden. Lorna Fowler, president of the Edgecomb Avenue Block Association, is an eminent manager—of people, of buildings, of budgets, of the large and small scale from tree-pit gardens on Edgecomb Avenue to Jackie Robinson Park. Ethel Bates has a single-minded passion for the "place" of Marcus Garvey Park, with its first-rate urban architecture and unique granite outcropping. She has reclaimed it from a public space colonized by drug dealers and abandoned by police to a green space where children can play. Bernadette Cozart envisions no less than a flower and vegetable garden, a horticultural resource center, maybe even a greenhouse and bird and butterfly garden in every school in Harlem as the basis for ecological science in Harlem for adults as well as kids. Since 1989, the Greening of Harlem has helped neighborhood people design, build, and tend 17 organic gardens and rejuvenate three key Harlem parks. In 1994 the Goddess Garden and a plant nursery for Harlem were opened.

Philadelphia Green

In a 100-block neighborhood of North Philadelphia called Susquehanna, 11 African American retirees (nine women and two men) run the Philadelphia Community Rehabilitation Corporation. The opaque and institutional-sounding name obscures the local social genius at work restoring abandoned buildings, greening vacant lots, and rescuing human beings of Susquehanna who have no other safety nets. Executive Director and founder Rachel Bagby explains that "we do *lives,* not houses": putting mothers back in school, providing tutoring, infant care, more than 40 units of low-income housing, the equivalent of five acres of trees, and community vegetable and sitting gardens. She points to her teaching aid—a whole, sprouting sweet potato from last year's garden, kept in a cool place all winter and then wrapped in newspaper to start it sprouting. This she will cut and plant, with the help of children in the three-lot Garden of Life. There she will pique the children's interest with the story of the sweet potato's life cycle—one that will finish in a sweet potato pie if they are good gardeners and keep the sweet potato patch watered and weeded. At the children's garden on 20th Street she had kids paint the three-story corner building wall with faces like their own, the faces of child gardeners looking, curious and eager, onto the garden and out to the street. "So they could see themselves…. It will transform them into human beings. I know it can be done."

Eighteen blocks away, Sister Maureen O'Hara explains why she left teaching to work in the Penn State Urban Gardening Program. "It's one thing to garden; it's another to cultivate the earth." Some city folks—like residents of the largely Puerto Rican neighborhood at Second and Dauphin Streets, where she is currently working on a demonstration garden for parents and children—are barely a generation away from cultivating the earth. The memory is fresh and beckoning, but the obstructions are colossal: local cocaine rings on the streets, vandalism, demolition waste, buried garbage and syringes on local lots. Maureen O'Hara recognizes the global pattern of inequality between the industrial countries and developing countries replicated in North Philadelphia, where the urban poor live in the most polluted environment. And she also sees community gardens as a link in the chain of worldwide activism that joins tree planting in Kenya and wasteland restoration in India with organic community gardens and composting in Norris Square, North Philadelphia.

This environmentalism, unlike one that clumps all humans together as ecological parasites and predators and sets up biodiversity preserves without people, is based on the belief that humans can live and learn to live in symbiosis with nature. This environmentalism unites social justice with a profound respect for nature and elevates environmental protection to the plane of environmental justice.

Agency in IPAT

Population is the raging monster.

—E. O. Wilson

No goal is more crucial to healing the global environment than stabilizing human population.

—Al Gore

The I=PAT equation is the key to understanding the role of population growth in the environmental crisis.

—Paul and Anne Ehrlich

"English," writes linguist Julia Penelope, "allows us to suppress reference to the agents who commit specific acts particularly when the speaker/writer wishes to deny or cover up responsibility.... We suppress human agency and sometimes try to imply grander forces at work by doing so, appealing to an unspecified, perhaps illusory, universality or evading the issue of who will be or is responsible for some action."[28] The word "population" is an unspecified universal that evades the issue of who among the P of IPAT is responsible for the high fertility of poor women, their lack of access to safe birth control and abortion, and the higher rate of illiteracy and poorer nutrition among girls relative to boys.

Words like "fertility rates" delete human agency in pregnancy by implying that an abstract factor—fertility—is responsible for environmental degradation, and thus they enable the speaker to avoid discussion of who is responsible for what. Words like "population bomb" and "population explosion" suppress any agent and create the impression that the situation and its consequences are "occurring in a social vacuum ... disconnected from the cultural, social and historical context in which they arise."[29] Beneath the abstract, agentless word "population" is the substrate of sexual politics—the crosscutting domain within culture, social relations, history, economy, science, and sexuality in which women become pregnant. Environmental knowledge, no less than any other knowledge, begins by naming the agents within.

Agency and P

How often do women choose to become pregnant? How free are women to avoid pregnancy? Studies and interviews with women worldwide suggest that more than "125 million couples who want to delay or stop having children have no reliable means of doing so.... Moreover, the number of children that Third World women say they want is declining."[30] Other sources cite an estimated 300 million women without access to safe and affordable family planning and the often-quoted U.N. survey that found women in Africa, Asia, and Latin America wanting an average of one-third fewer children than they have.[31] Critics have pointed out that these statistics are questionable on the grounds that the studies were conducted to serve the interests of contraceptive manufacturers and population-control programs. While the findings and numbers may reflect the bias of the interviewers, the problem that many women do not have access to safe abortion and safe contraception when they want them stands.

Does reproductive choice for women rest fundamentally on technology or on social relationships with men—proximate and remote, intimate and institutional? What are the links between fertility rates and male subordination of girls and women—through rape, unavailability of safe birth control and abortion, refusal to use or allow birth control, feminization of poverty, compulsory heterosexuality, and through penetration as the paradigm of sexuality?

If a country spends twice as much on military armaments as on health and education, who is responsible for high fertility rates in that country if infant and child mortality is high, if contraceptives are not available when people want them, and if girls drop out of school sooner to help with the household work? If the Philippines (and 70 other countries) is suffering a hemorrhage of capital, including human and natural resources, to service their foreign debt, who is responsible for the resulting debt-aggravated environmental degradation—the 41 percent of the Philippine population that lives under the poverty level because 50 percent of their country's budget flows out in reverse foreign aid to Western creditors, or those, within and without, who indemnified that country? Should not the agents of poverty, debt, and militarism, that mix of elite government officials, global economic institutions, and multinationals that engineers the international economic agenda—rather than an agentless and unspecified universal "population"—be named and held accountable for their role in the environmental crisis and the P of IPAT?

Even when reproductive choice is primarily a question of access to birth control technology, the sexual politics of research, family-planning-program priorities, and reproductive responsibility prevail. The trend in contraceptive technologies is in the direction of longer-acting, so-called woman-controlled methods, such as Norplant, that can be monitored and removed only in family planning agencies—in other words, contraceptive technologies that give family planning programs more control over women's fertility and more potential to abuse the rights of poor women. Why are the hormonal and chemically altering birth control technologies that carry risk of cancer, infection, and death developed for use on women, while indigenous methods are ignored and low-tech methods for men are underutilized? Why do so few, including women's health advocates, "question the joined interests of the population establishment and the pharmaceutical industry that determine the contraceptives that are available"?[32]

Only a handful of researchers worldwide (an estimated five to ten) are doing research on male fertility control: Why has research on male birth control that is nonhormonal and reversible, or the male pill, been so trivial and dismal? Dr. Mostafa Fahim, director of the Center for Reproductive Science and Technology at the University of Missouri, was forced to abandon research on a promising ultrasound technique—a simple, painless, nonsurgical, and reversible method of halting sperm formation. Fahim was not granted funding to collaborate with the Chinese on this method, and the university restricted him to testing his method on human subjects with prostate cancer who were to have their testes removed.[33] Even where there are breakthroughs—such as vas deferens–based methods and heat methods to reduce sperm production, which are reversible, efficient, and nontoxic—they have not seen the global marketing and promulgation that more risk-laden female contraceptives have. Nor do men have a history of contraceptive abuse and human rights violations comparable to that of women, particularly that of poor women of color, with Norplant, Depo-Provera, the Pill, and the IUD.

One researcher, who analyzed research on male contraceptives, concluded that it is a defeatist attitude and low prioritization by researchers, funding agencies, and pharmaceutical companies, and not the limits of the technology, that account for the retarded state of male contraceptive technologies.

The tone of most of the studies [on male contraception] seems to weigh heavily on the drawbacks and failures instead of trying to take an approach to overcome the obstacles. There is also a definite unwillingness to tolerate even mild side effects like acne or weight gain (some of the symptoms that are common among women on the pill).[34]

If there were a supermarket of choices for men, would men take responsibility for reproduction? "No woman can entirely rely on her partner to avoid a pregnancy," the (Manchester) *Guardian* editorialized on the 30th anniversary of the birth control pill.[35] "Many high level personnel of family planning thinktanks, like ... the Alan Guttmacher Institute and ... Planned Parenthood Federation of America, reason that men would not be willing to tamper with their bodies let alone alter their body chemistry in the name of controlling fertility" because they aren't the ones bearing the risk of pregnancy.[36] The ripple effect of this fatalistic view results in little investment in male contraceptive research, lackluster engagement of boys and men in family planning, and little protection for women and girls against sexually transmitted diseases. If women bear the risk and do the work of pregnancy, and if women have to undergo abortion for an unwanted pregnancy, then shouldn't their partners in sex and reproduction at least share the responsibility of birth control? Why don't men love women enough to use a condom or undergo a vasectomy and collectively demand more research on male birth control methods?

Women and Men and Power

"Empower women and many of the world's most fundamental social and environmental ills will begin to solve themselves," *International Wildlife* forecasts.[37] Ills do not solve themselves, people solve them. What the authors imply is that women with economic and political power will have more clout in their relationships with men and can insist on or negotiate having fewer children. Further, the authors may be surmising that empowered women will seek an economic and political role in their society and then want to have smaller families. In a similar optimistic spirit, Mostafa Tolba, Director of the United Nations Environmental Program, addressed women in Nairobi in 1985: "If there must be a war, let the weapons be your healing hands, the hands of the world's women in defense of the environment."

If power enables women to heal the earth's ills, why haven't "empowered men" solved fundamental social and environmental ills? Why are the most powerful men in the most powerful governments and institutions also the largest polluters and the most intensive consumers of our environmental resource base? If women and power are the key to environmental protection, what is to be done about countervailing male dominance and male reaction to women's power? If economic and political power in men's hands has given us the base of technology, the expanse of military, and the systematic subordination of women that endanger our planet, then environmental public policy must also address men and their power, and male backlash to women and power.

In response to a male attorney's question on the eve of World War II about how to prevent war, Virginia Woolf replied,

> To fight has always been the man's habit, not the woman's.... Scarcely a human being in the course of history has fallen to a woman's rifle; the vast majority of birds and beasts have been killed by you, not us. Your question is how to prevent war? Obviously there is some glory, some necessity, some satisfaction in fighting which we never felt or enjoyed.[38]

Her answer to how we are to prevent war was: to educate women.

Why are educated women the antidote to "educated men"? For it is educated men who have perfected and expanded military weapons and strategy, so much so that often the majority of technically trained men in highly militarized countries work for the defense industry. Clearly, while women are being educated, men must be re-educated—in peace studies; in environmental studies; in health studies that discuss men's role and responsibility in sex, reproduction, and birth control; and in men's studies that analyze the glorification of violence against women, against each other, against the earth.

Agency and A

> Although women represent half of the world's population and one-third of the official labor force, they receive only one per cent of world income and own less than one per cent of the world's property.
>
> —United Nations, 1980

> A 1982 study of the funding practices of specialized United Nations agencies ... estimated that only 0.5 percent of all United Nations allocations to the agricultural sector went to programs for rural women.
>
> —Jodi Jacobson

Do men and women consume differently? Women earn an average of 30 percent less than men in the United States, and U.N. statistics document the universal feminization of poverty. Women as a class are poorer than men worldwide: They eat less, own less, possess less, are invested in less, earn less, spend less. Income is a surrogate for consumption, and we can only conclude that women consume less, proportional to income, than men. Further, many studies of men and women demonstrate that women and men in developed and developing countries spend their money differently—men more on luxury items for themselves, such as business junkets, golf courses, gambling, alcohol, tobacco, and sex (A_{LUXURY}), and women more on necessities for their families and households, such as food, clothing, and health care ($A_{SURVIVAL}$).

If women and their children are the poorest people of the world, and if women are sharing their lesser income with children on survival items, then certainly many men hold more responsibility for luxury consumption, the A_{LUXURY} of IPAT. Environmental programs on consumption, to be fair and accurate, need to bring a gender-conscious perspective to a critique of over-consumption by asking what is consumed, how much is consumed, who consumes how much and what, and whose needs and wants are being met. When a husband, for example, buys his wife a Cadillac for her 40th birthday, whose image and whose "needs" does it serve? Both his car and his wife reflect him back to himself at twice his size. And she, someone else's mirror, may futilely seek her self-esteem in cosmetics and clothing purchased in endless shopping sprees. His and her paths out of consumerism are marked by these differences and inequities in their economic and sexual power.

Environmentalists in the West have endeavored to wrest some control over industrial production and marketing of new products by launching a "green consumer" movement. "Consumers have the power to change the market" was the upbeat salvo sounding forth from Earth Day 1990 events. Most green consumerism, however, is not equivalent to the economic boycott movement and the movement to create economic alternatives, both of which operate in the marketplace and use the power of not purchasing and purchasing differently to change corporations and the context of production. These consumer movements have historically used a social and political analysis of labor conditions (as did United Farm Workers boycotts), economic exploitation of Third World women (as exemplified by the boycott of Nestlé), racism, and the torture of animals. The economic boycott was integrated into collective action and letter-writing campaigns, framed as actions of conscience. The sum of the parts—thousands of individual green consumers—will not be a whole—an organized, environmentally politicized citizenry—unless environmentalists shift from the shallow notion of green consumer to the substantive notion of green citizen.

In Japan a unique consumer's co-op, the Seikatsu Club Consumers Cooperative (SCCC), combines the vision of a people-centered, communitarian economy with sophisticated business skills and a framework of social and ecological principles. The co-op began in 1965 when a Tokyo housewife found that she could not buy pure, fresh, unadulterated milk. She organized 200 women as a cooperative to buy milk directly from dairy farmers. Today Seikatsu has 500,000 members and distributes 500 different minimally packaged products that are fresh and unadulterated. Great emphasis is placed on knowing the producer in order to humanize the market, and consumers regularly visit the producers, especially farmers. SCCC has set up many paid women-workers' collectives for the work of the cooperative and other service enterprises, such as recycling, health, education, food preparation, and child care. "The aim [of Seikatsu] is the creation of a new culture, which depends upon minimum consumption and a rich life.... It is no accident," writes Jeremy Seabrook, "that the impulse of Seikatsu came from women, particularly wives of corporation men, women who found their reduced function as shoppers in supermarkets, as well as the indirect servicers of their husbands' employers, both inadequate and diminishing."[39]

Agency and T

> The male monopoly on science is no mere relic to be easily tossed aside.
>
> —David Noble

Women have been systematically barred and discouraged from the physical sciences and engineering. Because of sex discrimination, we have had no role in inventing the technologies that have initiated global climate change, the depletion of the ozone layer, acid rain, and nuclear meltdowns. U.S. and Canadian undergraduate engineering schools began to recruit women students in the early 1970s (when many had fewer than 1 percent women students), but they have failed to achieve more than 15 to 20 percent sustained enrollment even with strong intervention programs to attract and retain female students. Studies show that the obstacles range from neglect and early discouragement by parents and teachers, to sexual harassment by boys and male teachers, to the 300-year-old tradition of Western science as a lofty, male, secular priesthood whose standards women would pollute and lower.[40] Further, many girls and women—preferring connected knowing and socially useful activity—are alienated from the reductionistic methods of science and the anti-human and anti-environment impacts of much technology.[41]

In December 1989, the National Academy of Engineering picked the top ten engineering accomplishments of the past 25 years:

> moon landing, application satellites, microprocessors, computer-aided design, CAT scan, advanced composite materials, the jumbo jet, lasers, fiber optics, genetic engineering.

What could have been developed and selected in the fields of energy, transportation, pollution control, agriculture, and health technology, were the social usefulness and ecological impact of technology primary considerations? Perhaps:

> photovoltaics, wind turbines, high-speed trains, biodegradation of solid and hazardous waste, alternatives to CFCs, widespread use of integrated pest management and organic agriculture, an effective male birth control device.

The dramatic differences in these two sets of technologies lie not in their technical and intellectual challenge but rather in their values, purpose, and design relationship. The former showcase human mastery over nature and devices for faster, more extensive manipulation of information. The latter tend to work in partnership with nature, to be extensions of natural resources, to manifest consciousness of social and environmental impact, to link the human and natural world.

These differences resonate with what women and men scientists reported in in-depth interviews that probed why they were attracted to science, how they see technology, and how they solve problems with technologies. A significant number of women said that what excited them about technology was making it transparent and accessible to others, while men more often cited being excited by technical design and function. When asked about technology of the future, women imagined technologies that linked the private and public worlds in collaborative and communication-enhancing ways, while men tended to imagine technologies that gave absolute control, extremely high speed, and unlimited knowledge, extending their power over the universe.[42] The world of science and technology—a "world without women"—has given us the T of IPAT.

Accounting for Agency

> In mixed-sex, action-oriented groups, it is hard to ask questions about the relationships between men and women and our environmental crisis. It is not easy to ask about militarism and masculinity, sovereignty and sex, and it's not considered polite to point out that men have been far more implicated in the history of destruction than women. But

there's too much at stake to stick to the easy questions and polite conversation.

—Joni Seager

The appeal of an equation like IPAT is its simple, sound-bite presentation; the downside is that it shuts out complex, structural causes of environmental destruction. This "fast-food" formula, which has such appeal in the land of junk food franchises, could be salvaged with a small but critical emendation: Take the "population" out of IPAT and replace it with "patriarchy."

$$I = C - PAT$$

where	I is	human impact on environment.
	C is	natural resource management, conservation, and restoration that link humans with nature.
	P is	patriarchy (subordination of women; paradigm of power as economic and military dominance).
	A is	consumption of world's resources shaped by colonial relations, debt-induced poverty, and resistance to redistributive policies—such as land reform, tax reform, and affirmative action in pay scales—and supported by economic models that encourage human satisfaction through consumerism and commodification.
	T is	technology that by scale, inefficiency, use of nonrenewable resources, pollution-generating capacity, destructiveness, and mechanistic control of nature is environmentally injurious.

The new formula does not have the "pat" appeal of the old one. *Patriarchy is not a simple number or a quantitative concept like population, and thus the equation does not work arithmetically.* Rather, A and T are functions of P. That is, there is a relationship between patriarchy and the reduction of nature to natural capital and market commodities, the appeal and growth of militarism, the mechanistic model of nature that underlies industrial technology, the second-class status of women, the "feminization of poverty," women's unwanted pregnancies and unsafe abortions, the lack of male contraception, and the lack of male responsibility for contraception. Being a universal phenomenon, patriarchy does not divide neatly between North and South, so the new I=C-PAT wouldn't work so efficiently for international negotiations—unless negotiations were held between women and men.

You can't do number crunching with the new model: Increase *conservation* by 15 percent; reduce *patriarchy* by 10 percent, *consumption* by 5 percent, and *technology* by 5 percent, for example. There is no sustainable level of patriarchy, no carrying capacity for it. On the other hand, opportunities arise for population organizations to refocus their mission onto the root causes of poverty and unwanted pregnancies. Zero Population Growth could change its name and mission to Zero Patriarchy Growth, or better yet, Zero Patriarchy. And the former Population Crisis Council, now Population Action Council, could become the Patriarchy Crisis Council.

Countries have been analyzed and compared as to the status of women versus that of men, using indices such as education, wages, representation in government, reproductive rights, and maternal and infant health. Within a women's human rights framework—and within this framework only—does an analysis of fertility belong. The first ecological limit to high fertility is a woman's own body, her health and energy; aware of those limits, women have almost universally reported wanting fewer children. The "population problem," if women are believed, is a consequence of their having less than full human rights. And this second-sex plight of women is a consequence of patriarchy.

Feminists and Population: A Cautionary Tale

Thus far, feminists have introduced the language of women's rights, reproductive health, and women's empowerment into the environment and population debate. But the power-blind framework of population as a universal pressure equivalent to overconsumption and industrial technology has stayed intact. If anything, population analysis has focused its gender- and race-blind lens more sharply on the "bottom billion," those mainly African, Asian, and Latin American women and children described as "marginal people on marginal lands," "wreaking havoc on the environment." A women's rights agenda has become a rhetorical means for a populationist end—a reduction in numbers of the poorest people on Earth—without a structural change in the analysis. Wittingly or unwittingly, many women's health advocates are buying into the P of IPAT.

Many collaborative policy statements on population—which endeavor to include input from international development, population, environmental, and women's organizations—have turned out to be incongruous hybrids. They leave demographic targets intact as they call for women's rights, and they avoid challenging economic growth and overconsumption in industrial countries while advocating for sustainable development, especially among the poor, in developing countries. A working paper on U.S. policy recommendations to the U.N. ICPD Secretariat states that "women and girls are the subjects, not the objects, of population policies and have the right to determine whether, when, why, with whom, and how to express their sexuality; they have the fight to determine when and whom to marry, they have the right and responsibility to decide whether, how, and when to have children."[43]

The statement "women and girls are the subjects ... of population policies" is an oxymoron; for, as many have noted, if women and girls had full human rights, fertility rates would be significantly lower. Population policies and programs have historically abused the rights of many women and some men. They are not family planning programs gone wrong only because of poor service at the ground level. Rather, the prevailing agent-less analysis of population policy—as this chapter has argued—is fundamentally flawed.

The same U.S. policy statement, which frequently calls for reducing and stabilizing population as soon as possible and suggests numerical targets, has only a tepid, passing mention of consumption associated with environmental degradation. While the statement contains strong recommendations for gender equality and male sexual and reproductive responsibility, and speaks against coercion and intimidation in family planning programs, an ideological framework of population prevails, and the silence on overconsumption and the role of industrial technology is deafening. Further, calling for demographic targets as the statement does ("age-specific birth rates") sets the stage for coercion and abusive incentives in future family planning and reproductive health programs. Overall, the policy, although improved by women's rights advocates, comes off as reform populationism.

What of policy statements initiated by women's health advocates that have the express purpose of "reshaping the population agenda to better ensure reproductive health and rights"?[44] In September 1992 women's health advocates from around the world met to discuss how to make women's voices heard during preparations for the 1994 International Conference on Population and Development. A statement on population policies was drafted, and more than 100 women's organizations reviewed, modified, and finalized the *Women's Declaration on Population Policies*. It has been subsequently circulated and endorsed widely.

The *Women's Declaration* contains strong statements, ethical principles, and recommendations on women's human rights; on the elimination of sexual, social, and economic inequalities; and on male personal and social responsibility for sexuality and reproduction. However, women's reproductive health and rights are placed within a population policy and programs framework. Population policies and programs, as the declaration puts it, should be "framed and implemented within broader development strategies" that redress the inequities among countries, racial and ethnic groups, and men and women.[45] Nested like a series of Chinese boxes, women's health and reproductive rights—the smallest box—are lodged within population policy and programs that are framed by broader equitable development policy. What happens to women's health and reproductive rights in this trickle-down model if development policy is not woman-centered, if it comes with a package of demographic targets? And why subsume a women's rights agenda within population policy?

The first ethical principle of the declaration states, "Women must be subjects, not objects, of any development policy, and especially of population policies."[46] This statement, adapted and used in the U.S. policy recommendations to the ICPD Secretariat, illustrates a complexity about language. The best-intentioned, politically correct language ("women must be subjects, not objects"), removed from the crucible of sexual politics, is rhetoric, not reality. Like oil and water, population policy and "women as subjects" are immiscible even if they can be linguistically linked within a policy statement.

Addressing the same point, the Women's Global Network for Reproductive Rights comments:

> The *Women's Declaration* is based on the acceptance of population policies which is at best confusing and at worst dangerous. It adds to a growing general consensus among established organizations and increasingly among women's groups, that population policies are unavoidable to solve major problems like poverty and environmental degradation, whereby the underlying causes are once more neglected.[47]

Why can't the framework of women's human rights be a big enough, bold enough, and sufficient structure from which to lobby the world for women's reproductive health and rights?[48]

Implications for Public Policy

To make women's human rights an end in itself and to place environmental justice at the core of "environment-population-development" programs, I recommend the following strategies.

For Women's Health and Environmental Organizations

1. *Replace the population framework with a feminist framework.* Make women's health, reproductive self-determination, and equality independent ends in themselves and not means to population goals, or idealistic slogans for environmental programs that target population reduction. Environmental organizations can change the titles and missions of population programs into ones that support "gender and social change," "reproductive rights and responsibilities," and "women's empowerment." This will demonstrate that women's equality is a goal in itself and not merely a means to population reduction.

Do not advocate for women's equality and self-determination within a framework that is defined by population analysis; otherwise women's health networks and organizations risk trading off inclusion for co-optation.[49] "Continue," as the Women's Global Network for Reproductive Rights recommends, "to position this struggle for women's reproductive rights within the larger feminist struggle and movement."[50]

Campaign against family planning and population policies that advocate demographic, fertility, or birth-rate targets. Demographically driven programs have consistently resulted in persuading and forcing poor people, especially women of color, to have fewer children whether or not their conditions of poverty have changed.[51]

Develop international networks and coalitions to monitor and act against population and family planning abuse, including sterilization abuse; lack of information on contraceptive risks and side effects; insufficient medical screening and follow-up care; and lack of barrier protection, male contraceptive technology, and safe abortion services. .

Support the ratification and enforcement of the U.N. Convention on the Elimination of All Forms of Discrimination Against Women and the Convention on the Elimination of All Forms of Sexual Exploitation proposed by the Coalition Against Trafficking in Women in conjunction with UNESCO.

2. *Introduce agency.* Replace the universal, agent-less concepts of population and demographic targets with more fine-grained, causal, and agent-identifying concepts, such as the military, international debt and poverty, and patriarchy. Distinguish among symptoms, consequences, proximate causes, and ultimate causes of our global environmental crises, and establish environmental programs that target the ultimate causes.

3. *Educate women and men.* Support the education of women and girls and also the education of men and boys in such areas as peace studies, the ethics of hunting for sport (the key organizational priority of mainstream U.S. environ-

mental organizations is fish and wildlife management for sport/recreation), violence against women, and responsibility for sexuality and reproduction.

4. *Redirect contraceptive technology and research.* Call for research on appropriate male contraceptive technology together with sex education programs for men and women. Unite the goals of birth control with barrier protection against sexually transmitted diseases in advocating for contraceptive availability. Take public stands supporting women's right to abortion. Borrow from the criteria of appropriate technology (democratic, low technology, low cost, participatory, reversible, nontoxic, local and de-linked from multinational interests, integrative) for the evaluation of contraceptive technology.

For Environmental Organizations

1. *Teach ecological literacy.* Distinguish between environmental science and ecological literacy, and then apply that difference in thinking to the "population" issue. "Real ecological literacy is radicalizing in that it forces us to reckon with the roots of our ailments, not just with their symptoms."[52] It involves a sense of wonder and kinship with life, the capacity to make connections between seemingly distinct events, and knowledge "that changes the way people live, not just how they talk."[53] The Green Belt Movement of Kenya has taught ecological literacy to women and children who participate in it, including the connection between people's use of land, the finite limits of the land's resources, and the carrying capacity of that land.

2. *Examine consumption.* Hold society-wide forums for discussing and educating on issues such as:

• Human satisfaction and consumerism.

• The role of advertising and media in creating consumer demand.

• The masculine values of self-interest, detachment, and individualism implicit in *Homo economicus* of neoclassical economics.

• The connections between consumption, jobs, gross national product, and the imperative of economic growth.

• The obstacles to making overconsumption a substantive environmental and political issue.

• The differences between green consumerism of the 1990s and older economic cooperative and consumer movements organized to protect health, to improve labor conditions, to make products affordable, and to humanize the market.

• The distinctions between the cultivation economy and the extractive economy, between economic growth and economic development.

- The difference between survival consumption and luxury consumption.
- The gap between women's and men's poverty and wealth across cultures, between their earning, access to resources, spending, and reasons for spending.

Environmental organizations could begin by applying the unremitting arithmetic of population growth to consumer advertising and consumption growth rates in order to hold consumption rates and patterns fully accountable for their role in environmental degradation.[54]

3. *Support grassroots and urban environmentalism.* Search out, learn from, and support—but do not colonize—the ecological contributions and knowledge of women, when developing global biodiversity strategies and green cities projects. Field researchers in the United States and developing countries have documented that community-based and grassroots environmental preservation is done primarily by women, and financed by low budgets, subsistence labor, and sweat equity. Yet the value of this work is generally not counted in the economy, or recorded in environmental history or on resource management maps, or documented by environmental media. Further, it is often the more valuable, though invisible, local ecological work: The cultivation and preservation of the widest range of biodiversity in the Brazilian Amazon, in rural Kenya and India, and in many communities throughout the world is done by women at the local and household level, where the surrounding land is "at once home, habitat, and workplace."[55]

Notes

This essay was first published by the Institute on Women and Technology as the pamphlet *Taking Population Out of the Equation* (North Amherst, MA, 1993).

1. The IPAT formula was first published in Paul Ehrlich and John Holdren, "The Impact of Population Growth," *Science*, Vol. 171 (1974), 1212–17. In 1977 the two coauthored *Ecoscience* with Anne Ehrlich, in which they propounded the same formulaic approach to population. See also Paul Ehrlich and Anne Ehrlich, *The Population Explosion* (New York: Simon and Schuster, 1990).

2. United Nations Population Fund, *Population, Resources and the Environment: The Critical Challenges* (New York: United Nations Publishing, 1991).

3. Barry Commoner, "Rapid Population Growth and Environmental Stress," *International Journal of Health Services*, Vol. 21, No. 2 (1991), 201.

4. Ibid., 225.

5. By "populationists," I refer to those people and organizations that contend that sheer numbers of people are the major threat to environmental stability. They advocate control of human population as the most significant act of environmental protection.

6. Susan O. Stranahan, "Empowering women," *International Wildlife*, Vol. 23, No. 3 (May/June 1993), 12–19.

7. Susan Cohen, "The Road from Rio to Cairo: Toward a Common Agenda," *International Family Planning Perspectives*, Vol. 19, No. 2 (June 1993), 61–66.

8. Donella H. Meadows, Dennis L. Meadows, and Jorgen Randers, *Beyond the Limits* (White River Junction, VT: Chelsea Green, 1992).

9. Ibid., 233.

10. United Nations Population Fund, *Population, Resources and the Environment*, op. cit., 15, 18–19.

11. Linda Starke, series editor introduction in Alan Durning, *How Much Is Enough?* (New York: W.W. Norton, 1992), 11–12.

12. "The decision-making echelons of major corporations are almost entirely male," writes Joni Seager. In 1987, three of the U.S. Fortune 1,000 companies had a woman as chief executive; two of the three were replacing deceased husbands. "White males still hold 95 percent of the top [U.S.] management jobs.... The situation is remarkably similar around the world: women hold only 2 percent of senior executive posts in most West European countries, and ... 0.9 percent in Japan." Seager argues that analyses of profit motive and the imperatives of capitalism are insufficient to explain the international environmental degradation for which corporations and corporate bureaucracies are responsible. The culture of the international economic order is masculinist. "Attributes for success in the corporate world—a privileging of emotional neutrality, of rationality, of personal distancing, loyalty to impersonal authority, team playing, scientific rationality, and militarized paradigms—reflect characteristics that define 'manliness' in our culture." Joni Seager, *Earth Follies: Coming to Terms with the Global Environmental Crisis* (New York: Routledge, 1993), 82.

13. Michael Renner, "Assessing the Military's War on the Environment," in Worldwatch Insitute, *The State of the World* (New York: W.W. Norton, 1991).

14. Anil Agarwal and Sunita Narain, "A Case of Environmental Colonialism," *Earth Island Journal*, spring 1991, 39. The entire report may be ordered from Center for Science and the Environment, 807 Vishal Bhawan, 95 Nehru Place, New Delhi, 110 019, India.

15. Irene Dankelman and Joan Davidson, *Women and Environment in the Third World* (London: Earthscan, 1988), 16.

16. Pietilä distinguishes between the cultivation economy and the extractive economy. The former is based primarily on living resources ("agriculture, forestry, animal husbandry, fishing, and all indigenous livelihoods"), the latter on non-renewable natural resources, minerals, and fossils, which are dead materials extracted from the earth. She characterizes the cultivation economy as renewable and partially monetized, with important inputs of sun, air, and water; limited mechanization; good longevity; poor competitiveness; and limited increase of efficiency and productivity. The extractive economy is fully monetized and mechanized, with good competitiveness

but poor longevity and ongoing increase of efficiency and productivity. Hilkka Pietilä, *The Environment and Sustainable Development. Kvinner, miljo og utvikling.* Proceedings from the Conference on Women, Environment, and Development, sponsored by NAVF and the University of Oslo (Oslo, Norway: November 1990).

17. There is extensive literature on Kerala analyzing the many positive effects of a human welfare-oriented government and a politically engaged society. See Richard W. Franke and Barbara H. Chasin, *Kerala: Radical Reform as Development in an Indian State* (San Francisco: The Institute for Food and Development Policy, 1989) and Mafia Helena Moreira Alves et al., "Four Comments on Kerala," *Monthly Review,* January 1991, 24–39.

18. Lester Brown, Hal Kane, and Ed Ayres, eds. *Vital Signs 1993* (New York: W.W. Norton, 1993).

19. Much of the data for this section rely on Michael Rennet, "Assessing the Military's War on the Environment," in Lester Brown et al., *State of the World 1991* (New York: W.W. Norton, 1991). Also see Seth Shulman, *The Threat at Home: Confronting the Toxic Legacy of the U.S. Military* (Boston: Beacon, 1992).

20. "A Place at the Table: A Sierra Roundtable on Race, Justice and Environment, *Sierra,* May/June 1993, 51–59.

21. Renner, "Assessing the Military's War on the Environment," op. cit., 132.

22. In what it titles a "job-oriented defense," the *New York Times* reports that the Pentagon spending plan for the next five years has as much to do with protecting U.S. defense industry and jobs as national security. The article cites orders for a new nuclear submarine and aircraft carrier that are not necessary for "national security" but will sustain a particular industry until new orders are needed (Schmitt, 1993). This entitlement program for the weapons industry reinforces the moral vacuum in which weapons manufactured and sold on the international market are treated as economic goods like food, cotton, or rubber.

23. Oscar Arias Sánchez, "Dialogue on Peace and Permanent Security," *Special Issues,* January 1993, SPURS Program, Massachusetts Institute on Technology, Cambridge, MA, 5.

24. "Dealing with Military Toxics" (Citizens Clearinghouse for Hazardous Waste, Falls Church, VA, 1987).

25. Diane Rocheleau, "Women as Farmers in Rural Landscape," in Lea M. Borkenhagen and Janet N. Abramowitz, eds., *Proceedings of the International Conference on Women and Biodiversity* (Washington, DC: World Resources Institute, 1992), 49.

26. Ibid.

27. All quotations in the following section are from conversations with individuals that took place while I was doing research on community gardens in U.S. inner cities. See H. Patricia Hynes, *A Patch of Eden* (White River Junction, VT: Chelsea Green, 1996).

28. Julia Penelope, *Speaking Freely: Unlearning the Lies of the Fathers'*

Tongues (New York: Teachers College Press, 1990), 144.

29. Ibid., 158.

30. Betsy Carpenter, "Defusing the Bomb," *U.S. News & World Report,* February 8, 1993, 54.

31. Stranahan, "Empowering Women," op. cit.

32. *Women's Global Network for Reproductive Rights Newsletter,* Amsterdam, 1993, 5.

33. E.A. Lissner, "Frontiers in Nonhormonal Male Contraceptive Research," unpublished paper, 1991.

34. Carol Gomez, "Issues in the Development of Male Contraception," unpublished paper, 1993, 9.

35. "The Pill's Birthday," *The Guardian,* June 13, 1990, A22.

36. Gomez, "Issues in the Development of Male Contraception," op. cit., 9.

37. Editorial, *International Wildlife,* May/June 1993, 3.

38. Virginia Woolf, *Three Guineas* (New York: Harcourt, Brace, 1938), 8–9.

39. Jeremy Seabrook, *Pioneers of Change* (Philadelphia: New Society, 1993), 195.

40. *The AAUW Report: Executive Summary. How Schools Shortchange Girls* (Washington, DC: American Association of University Women Educational Foundation, 1992); and David Noble, "A World without Women," *Technology Review,* May/June 1992, 52–60.

41. Bank Street College of Education, "Women and Technology: A New Basis for Understanding," *News from the Center for Children and Technology and the Center for Technology in Education,* Vol. 1, No. 2 (1991), 1–5.

42. Ibid.

43. Timothy E. Wirth, "U.S. Policy Recommendations to International Conference on Population and Development Secretariat" (draft), United States Department of State, Washington, DC, August 3, 1993, 4.

44. *Women's Declaration on Population Policies,* 1993, 1. A copy of the declaration may be ordered from the International Women's Health Coalition, 24 East 21st Street, 5th Floor, New York, NY 10010.

45. Ibid., 3.

46. Ibid., 4.

47. *Women's Global Network for Reproductive Rights Newsletter* (Amsterdam, The Netherlands: 1993), 4.

48. The Committee on Women, Population and the Environment has circulated a statement that identifies the structural roots of environmental crises in economic systems, pollution-intensive technology, overconsumption, and militarism, and that locates women's freedom and development, including reproductive health and fights, within a context of democracy, social justice, and human rights. The committee is an alliance of women activists, community organizers, health practitioners, and scholars of diverse races, cultures, and countries of origin. A copy of the statement may be obtained from Population and Development Program, Social Sciences, Hampshire Col-

lege, Amherst, MA 01002.

49. See Janice Raymond, *Women as Wombs: Reproductive Technologies and the Battle over Women's Freedom* (San Francisco: HarperSanFrancisco, and Melbourne: Spinifex Press, 1993), 19–21. Raymond addresses the disturbing trend in alliances between various women's health organizations and population-control groups that often results in the justification of drugs, such as Norplant, that are risky and dehumanizing for women. In the United States, these alliances between women's health groups and population groups have also expanded to include pharmaceutical companies and medical and family-planning groups, all of which have joined forces to stage a legislative and media blitz to promote RU 486/PG, the new chemical abortifacient. See Janice G. Raymond, Renate Klein, and Lynette J. Dumble, *RU 486: Misconceptions, Myths and Morals* (Amherst, MA: Institute on Women and Technology, and Melbourne: Spinifex Press, 1991), especially the introduction and conclusion.

50. *Women's Global Network for Reproductive Rights Newsletter*, op. cit., 5.

51. For an excellent historical analysis of the shift from noncoercive family planning to population control in India, see Sumati Nair, "Population Policies and the Ideology of Population Control in India," *Issues in Reproductive and Genetic Engineering*, Vol. 5, No. 3 (1992), 237–52. The author documents the central role of aid donors, including the United States, the World Bank, and the International Monetary Fund, in pressuring India into fertility targets and coercive population programs. Also see Betsy Hartmann, *Reproductive Rights and Wrongs,* revised edition (Boston: South End Press, 1995) for a thorough critique of the narrow birth-rate reduction goals of international family-planning programs. She demonstrates how these programs have abused women's reproductive rights and continue to ignore barrier methods while promoting long-lasting hormonal methods for women.

52. David W. Orr, *Ecological Literacy* (Albany, NY: State University of New York Press, 1992), 88.

53. Ibid., 91.

54. Some thoughtful initiatives on consumption, consumerism, and the role of the economy in environmental degradation are emerging from diverse pockets of U.S. society, including groups in the Northwest committed to voluntary simplicity and the Frontiers Thinking in Economics Project, directed by Dr. Neva Goodwin at Tufts University in Medford, Massachusetts.

55. See Agarwal, Rocheleau, and Hecht in Lea M. Borkenhagen and Janet N. Abramovitz, eds, *Proceedings of the International Conference on Women and Biodiversity* (Washington, DC: World Resources Institute, 1992).

CHRISTIAN RESPONSES TO THE POPULATION PARADIGM

Andy Smith

Although many religious communities have been tackling population issues, I focus here on Christian communities because of their increased attention to these issues as a result of the Vatican's response to the U.N. International Conference on Population and Development (ICPD) held in Cairo in 1994. Liberal Protestant organizations have historically been supportive of population control. Dianne Moore, a Christian feminist ethicist, notes that a relationship (albeit a complex one) exists between the eugenics movement of the 1930s and the first church statements supporting birth control.[1] In 1969 Reinhold Niebuhr of Union Theological Seminary, Henry Fosdick of Riverside Church, and Henry Knox Sherrill of the World Council of Churches signed a full-page ad in the *New York Times* calling for mass population control efforts in Latin America.[2] Today, most mainline denominations have issued statements supporting population control, and the writings of European and Euro-American liberal Christians concerned with environmental issues also tend to accept the population paradigm.[3]

Euro-American Christian feminists such as Sallie McFague, Rosemary Radford Ruether, Catherine Keller, and Christine Gudorf devote much of their writings on population to analyzing the relationships between overconsumption, socioeconomic injustice, and population growth. Even so, they do not sufficiently challenge the population paradigm. Consequently, although these authors are certainly concerned about racial and economic justice, many of their statements on overpopulation have unintended negative consequences for women of color and Third World women. One reason these writers do not challenge the population paradigm may be that they do not base their analyses on work done by Third World women or women of color. In recent writings by each of these authors on this issue, they do not reference a single work by a person of color. It is ironic that, given their feminist commitments, they do not take as the starting point for their discussions the communities whose populations they advocate reducing. They do, however, approvingly quote individuals who have supported notoriously racist population programs, such as Paul Ehrlich of Carrying Capacity Network (CCN), Margaret Caticy-Carlson of the Population Council, and Werner Fournos of the Population Institute.[4] This gives the impression (mistaken, one hopes) that Ruether, Keller, and Gudorf consider these people to have greater expertise on the situations facing Third World women and women of color than do the women themselves. Keller, in particular, puzzlingly states that there is a "conspiracy of silence" on population, despite much work done on population by women of color and Third World women.[5] It is also interesting that Keller, and not a woman of color, was apparently asked to write the contribution on population control in *Ecotheology*.[6]

One reason for the omissions may be that these authors inadequately grapple with the racial aspect of the "overpopulation" issue. Ruether, for instance, states, "The challenge that humans face ... is whether they will be able to visualize and organize their own reproduction, production, and consumption in such a way as to stabilize their relationship to the rest of the ecosphere and so avert massive social and planetary ecocide."[7] She seems to assume that all humans contribute equally to ecological disaster, that all are equally affected by population policies, and that all have the same access to power to organize their production and consumption.

This is not to say that all these authors completely ignore the differing positions between Western women and Third World women. McFague, for instance, does say in her discussion on environmental degradation that "we are not all equally responsible, nor does deterioration affect us equally."[8] But then she says that ecology is a "people" issue in relationship to nonhuman creatures.[9] The problem, then, is "human overpopulation." However, because most industrialized countries have replacement-level fertility, with some even experiencing declining populations, clearly it is not these citizens who are considered to be "overpopulating" the earth and who are the targets of most population programs.[10] Keller and Gudorf further say that all women should make the commitment to have no more than one child.[11] Keller makes an exception for women from communities that have been targeted for genocide, implying that population policies are not in themselves genocidal in intent. (In fact, many population policies violate the U.N. Convention on Genocide.)[12] It would logically follow from Keller's analysis that only Europeans and Euro-Americans should reduce their populations. In addition, this one-child recommendation implies that a Third World woman and a white woman are equally affected by having only one child. But a white, middle-class woman stands to gain economically by having only one child, whereas a Third World woman stands to face tremendous economic hardship as a result of such a policy. Gudorf does acknowledge this point, but it does not seem to affect her policy recommendation in any way.[13]

Keller also erases the particularity of women of color by saying that "the rising global population rate is a catastrophic trend variously underplayed both by right-wing anti-abortionists and feminists combating the misogyny implied by monofocal emphasis on population (often encouraging female infanticide and forced sterilization)."[14] She describes these population practices as "misogynist" but not racist as well, as though they significantly affect all women and not primarily women of color and Third World women. In addition, she implies that feminists are concerned only with "abuses" in population programs instead of with the fact that the programs are designed as a smoke screen for larger structures of socioeconomic injustice (from which European and Euro-American middle-class women gain many privileges). Also, given that it is women of color and Third World women who primarily suffer the brunt of environmental destruction, it might be helpful for Keller to consider what these women have identified as the real "catastrophic trends"—namely, colonization, Western overconsumption, and racism.

Each of these authors discusses the environmental destruction caused by Western consumption patterns. Each also analyzes how population growth is affected by colonialism. Keller, for instance, states: "Justice-centered Christians speaking on behalf of the world of the poor make the irrefutable point that ... it is the exploitation of the resources of the Third World for the sake of the First World and its client elites—not overpopulation—which deprives those others of the resources they need. Is not the focus on population control thus dangerously akin to the genocidal policies which seek to rid the world of the troubling, potentially revolutionary masses of the poor?"[15] Keller then proceeds to ignore this issue in the rest of her essay. If population is a symptom rather than a cause of other global trends, as these authors state, why do they value the population paradigm so highly? Ruether and Keller, in fact, describe overpopulation as one of the "four horsemen of doom," the others being economics, war, and environment.[16] Essentially they argue that the patterns of reproduction for Third World women and women of color that have developed as a result of colonization are as bad as colonization itself. Ultimately, Christian feminists' claim—that population growth is as much a problem as are colonization and Western consumption patterns—is not really an improvement on the argument that overpopulation is wholly to blame for the world's problems. This claim still mitigates the responsibility of those in power.

Gudorf seems to let the rich off the hook when she prioritizes population stabilization over social justice by arguing that "getting the rich to agree to any standard significantly below what they now receive seems ... doubtful."[17] The implication seems to be that we should focus on imperialistic population control policies because they will be easier to implement than economic justice. Further, she states that "combating hunger and ... malnutrition must come primarily through population stabilization."[18] This seems to suggest that ending hunger through economic justice is not Gudorf's primary concern. Ruether does not say that population and overconsumption are equally to blame; rather, "the major cause of destruction of species comes *simply* from the expanding human population" (emphasis mine).[19] Furthermore, she says, it is overpopulation that leads to "war, famine, and disease," not the other way around.[20] Ruether then calls for "the promotion of birth control" instead of the provision of women's unmet needs for contraceptives. She seems to be oblivious to the devastating health effects that such "promotions" have had for women of color and Third World women.[21] Her vision of "a good society," outlined at the end of *Gaia and God,* entails population control, but it does not include redistribution of resources from the North to the South, or anything that would significantly affect the privileges the North enjoys at the expense of the South.[22]

In addition, these writers uncritically espouse rather questionable ideas about population growth. Keller, Ruether, and McFague regard Malthusian orthodoxy as indisputably true.[23] As mentioned previously, Ruether describes population in the Third World as rising independently from patterns of colonization. She also uncritically employs Paul Ehrlich's formula: Environmental Impact = Population x Affluence x Technology (I = PAT). (See H. Patricia Hynes, "Taking Population out of the Equation," in this volume.) Many feminists have argued that this formula is problematic because it assumes that all populations are the same, ignoring different peoples' different impacts on the environment. It also views "all humans as takers from, rather than enhancers of, the natural environment. This truncated, culture-bound view of humans in their environment originates from an industrial, urban, consumerist society."[24] Affluence is conceived only as per capita consumption. This view neglects the fact that the Third World sustains not only its own consumption but also the consumption of industrialized countries.[25] All technology is assumed to be equally harmful. In addition, the environmental impact of the military is lacking in this equation. As Betsy Hartmann states, "I = PAT obscures power relations at the global level; the precise dynamics of environmental degradation at the local, regional, and national levels are also hidden behind a Malthusian veil."[26] Also disturbing is Gudorf's approval of incentive and disincentive programs (such as paying women to use contraceptives) so long as they are as "voluntary" as possible.[27] Given the oppressive conditions most Third World women live in, it is unclear how incentives can be considered even remotely voluntary. If one is living hand to mouth, is the offer of financial resources in exchange for controlling one's reproductive capabilities any kind of a choice? The use of incentives in population programs has been devastating for Third World women and women of color.[28] Even the United Nation's ICPD *draft* proposal condemned the use of incentives and disincentives.[29]

Finally, these writers speak quite eloquently about the responsibilities of the Western world for addressing environmental degradation by targeting consumption patterns. But ultimately they say that the West should accomplish this so that Third World people will reduce their populations. McFague states, "Unless and until we drastically modify our life-style, we are not in a position to preach population control to others."[30] This is true, but it also suggests that if one is morally scrupulous in one's own "lifestyle," then one can excuse coercive control over others, and that the reason one should modify one's lifestyle is to be able to preach population control. This attitude motivates too many population program planners. Many policy makers attempt to determine the minimum amount of social and/or health reforms necessary to reduce population. For example, the International Center for Diarrheal Disease Research in Matlab, Bangladesh, determined that only a minimum amount of health care was necessary to induce women to accept contraceptives. Consequently, additional health care was withheld from them.[31] As Hartmann states, "Once social reforms, women's projects, and family planning programs are organized for the explicit goal of reducing population growth, they are subverted and ultimately fail.... These basic rights are worthy of pursuit in and of themselves; they have far more relevance to the general improvement of human welfare than reducing population growth alone ever will."[32]

Liberal Christians, particularly Christian feminists, focus their energies on countering claims made by the Vatican and other "pro-life" forces. Although this is important, it often fosters a false dichotomy between being pro-population control and anti-choice. Consequently, the experiences of Third World women and women of color become lost in these discussions. As Thais Corral, a Brazilian feminist, said about the proceedings in Cairo, population proponents insist that Third World women must join them in combating the fundamentalists and the Vatican.[33] Thus, as is typical of populationists, columnist Anna Quindlen argues:

> It has become increasingly evident that Americans should not permit the Vatican to go unchallenged in its opposition to birth control and population control. We can do this best by giving our own vocal support of U.S. funding of family planning as an important measure that can deal with unintended pregnancies, burgeoning population, and poverty.[34]

But the Vatican is a closer ally than Quindlen knows. Although the Vatican rejected abortion and all forms of birth control other than natural planning at Cairo, it did not necessarily reject the premises of overpopulation. Said Vatican Secretary of State Cardinal Angelo Dodana: "Everyone is aware of the problems that can come from a disproportionate growth of the world's population. The Church is aware of the complexity of the problem, but the urgency of the situation must not lead into error in proposing ways [of] intervening."[35] In fact, it is because of population control that some Catholics are willing to oppose the Vatican's policy on birth control.[36]

Similarly, many "pro-life" Christians, including evangelicals, wholeheartedly support population control policies.[37] For instance, in her book *Six Billion and More,* Susan Bratton states that abortion is unethical. However, she sees no problem with population incentives. She also thinks coercive techniques are an option if all else fails to stabilize the population. In addition, she favors the use of long-acting hormonal contraceptives (such as Norplant and Depo-Provera), which she considers "safer," for some reason, than barrier methods. She does not address the AIDS crisis or the devastating impact of emphasizing non-barrier methods of birth control. Such is Bratton's "pro-life" position on population stabilization.[38]

Many conservative Christians who do not support population control are not motivated from a larger concern for social justice. Cindy Rollins argues against population policies for eugenic reasons; more Christian babies are needed to offset the growing numbers of non-Christians.[39] Similarly, in his exposé of Human Life International (HLI, founded by Father Paul Marx in 1981), Tom Burghardt claims that the Vatican supports HLI for racist reasons. HLI's purported goal is to stop the Jewish doctors who control the abortion industry and the Muslim conspirators who support their own large families by performing abortions on Christian women. HLI wants to "reeducate Western Europe to help fulfill Pope John Paul II's dream of a re-Christianized, united Europe from the Atlantic to the Urals."[40]

Other conservative Christians argue against population control because they think the world needs nothing but a free-market economy to thrive. They believe the earth has an endless capacity to sustain billions in Western-style comfort. Furthermore, Christians can trust God not to allow the earth to seriously deteriorate (as if it has not already done so).[41] Clearly, these "pro-life" positions are not pro–women's lives, particularly the lives of Third World women and women of color.

If the Christian pro-life position is not pro–women's lives, and particularly not the lives of women of color and Third World women, what of the Christian pro-choice movement? I argue that unless the Christian and secular pro-choice movements come to terms with the racial aspect of the population paradigm and its concomitant *lack of choice* for women of color and Third World women, Native women, like many other women of color and Third World women—although they are overwhelmingly pro-choice—will remain skeptical about the mainstream pro-choice movement. Although in many ways the "pro-choice" populationist movements and the "pro-life" movements seem very different, as Hartmann states, they "share one thing in common: they are both anti-woman," and, in particular, they are anti–woman of color.[42]

A Christian ethic that takes seriously the lives of women of color and Third World women must reject this false polarity and be truly pro-life *and* pro-choice for *all women.* To do so, such an ethic must reject the population paradigm completely. Some women choose to work within this paradigm in the hope that they can reform the system. Others are concerned about population but, like the Christian feminists previously described, are working toward social and economic justice as well. However, continuing to work within this paradigm is problematic, given the manner in which reactionary forces attempt (usually successfully) to co-opt the demands for social justice within the population movement, particularly within Christian churches.

Gudorf states in an article for *Second Opinion* that "There is a very real danger that religion ... will decide that (1) there is a population crisis that threatens the whole society; (2) the birthrate must be lowered; and (3) controlling women's bodies is necessary to lower the birthrate."[43] Ironically, this article was funded by Pew Charitable Trusts, which is campaigning to get religious organizations to adopt these very attitudes. Pew, the largest environmental grant maker in the United States, spent more than $13 million to increase public support for population control for the Cairo conference. Population control, one of Pew's top priorities, is organized through the Global Stewardship Initiative. The initiative's targeted constituencies are environmental organizations, internal-affairs and foreign-policy initiatives, and religious organizations.[44] In conjunction with the Park Ridge Center, Pew organized a forum on religious perspectives on population, consumption, and the environment in Chicago in February 1994. Then, in May 1994, it hosted a consultation that brought together thinkers from major world religions to deliberate on population issues and to issue a statement contradicting the Vatican's anti-choice position.[45] Pew has also targeted evangelicals by funding a report and institutes on population control for *Christianity Today*.[46] Pew provides large amounts of denominational support for work on this issue, including all the funding for the National Council of Churches' (NCC) ecojustice program.[47] The NCC general secretary sits on Pew's Global Stewardship advisory committee.

As part of its program to target religious communities, Pew organized focus groups with different constituencies, including religious constituencies. It identified as "problem" constituencies those who "accept overpopulation as a problem in terms of unequal distribution of resources and mismanagement of resources—not numbers of people."[48] According to its report, mainstream Protestants tend to fall into this category. Consequently, the best way to "convert" Protestants, as it were, was thought to be through an "environmental message."[49] The report then attempted to ascertain how messages could be crafted to reach different communities. It concluded that the most effective messages would have an emotional appeal, would emphasize how individuals would personally suffer from overpopulation, and would appeal to the specific concerns of different constituencies.[50] Pew planned to target the "elites" of the religious communities—i.e., those it thought would understand the problem of overpopulation.[51] It seems to have met with success; in 1993, a Pew survey of 30 U.S. denominations found that 43 percent had an official statement on population.

Through this work, Pew has, in Hartmann's words, managed to "manufacture consensus" about the Cairo conference among Protestant denominations. Church leaders in both evangelical and liberal denominations came out in support of the Cairo conference, lauding its steps forward on women's reproductive health issues. However, as Carol Benson Holst argues, the issue of reproductive rights at the Cairo conference was just a smoke screen concealing the fact that issues of economic injustice between Northern and Southern nations were barely addressed. Also, while claiming not to be number-centered, the conference "Programme of Action" calls for nations to stabilize the population at 9.8 billion by the year 2000. Although the program denounces incentives and coercive measures, it contains no safeguards against them. The program also covenanted the signer nations to increase funds to population programs from $5 billion to $17 billion per year. Jane Hull Harvey, the United Methodist Church's assistant general secretary of the General Board of Church and Society, argues that this increase is a blessing and speculates that perhaps "we will even be able to redirect some of the enormous amounts of military aid the United States pours into Egypt, and translate those dollars into work on sustainable development, consumption and family planning for men and women."[52] Of course, nothing in the Cairo "Programme of Action" addresses redirecting funding from the military; in fact, as Hartmann points out, money for population programs usually comes from money that might otherwise go for reproductive or general health care.[53] Finally, Harvey also does not mention that two-thirds of the money is supposed to come from *developing* nations.[54]

Holst points out that, contrary to impressions manufactured by the media, many people were very critical of the Cairo program. For instance, Holst's former organization, Ministry for Justice in Population Concerns (MJPC), issued a statement that was not allowed to be read at the Cairo plenary even though the ICPD had requested a statement from the organization. The statement charged that the "Programme of Action" was "nothing but an insult to women, men, and children of the South who will receive an ever-growing dose of population assistance, while their issues of life and death will await the Social Development Summit of 1995."[55] At the Pew-Park Ridge conference, Holst also called for the "dominant culture to relinquish control of the economic infrastructure." Consequently, Pew (which had funded the MJPC, knowing it was concerned primarily with the relationship between social justice and population growth) defunded the MJPC because it "was too accommodating to people of color."[56] Holst says that, although Pew at first seemed concerned about justice issues, it became clear that Pew was interested only insofar as the MJPC furthered Pew's own population agenda. Other church-based organizations, Holst says, have privately questioned Pew's slant on population but cannot do so publicly without jeopardizing their funding. As Stephen Greene reports, Pew, through its financial resources, has the clout to change the agendas of environmental organizations to suit its own interests.[57] Consequently, even Gudorf's Pew-funded article—which calls for the transfer of resources from the North to the South, denounces dangerous contraceptives, and cites many social justice concerns—participates in the Pew-engineered consensus by stating that "the Cairo Programme of Action is correct."[58]

Populationists are also becoming adept at appropriating feminist language of increasing women's status to increase contraceptive use. According to Zero Population Growth, for example, "In cultures where a woman's value often depends upon her fertility, she is subject to violence and abandonment if she does not produce the expected number of children.... Oftentimes, without her husband's approval, she cannot use contraceptives without fearing for her safety."[59] Setting aside for the moment that violence against women does not happen in just "those" cultures, what populationists generally refuse to acknowledge is the role of imperialism in perpetuating sexism in Third World communities and communities of color. For instance, as writer and historian Paula Gunn Allen notes, violence against women was almost unheard of in most indigenous nations prior to colonization.[60] Similarly, colonial policies of overturning communal land systems to vest private ownership of land with the male "head of the household" in Africa and other parts of the world only exacerbated sexism in these societies.[61] Gita Sen further notes that Western domination can breed conservatism, particularly regarding women's status, as colonized societies attempt to resist assimilation and cultural erosion. Women, who are seen as the bearers of culture, are often blamed for cultural breakdown: "Historically, in unsettled economic and political times, attacks on women go hand in hand with reactionary tendencies and impulses."[62] Ending neocolonial practices against Third World nations would significantly improve the status of women in those countries. However, populationists are generally concerned neither with ending colonialism nor with raising women's status. At the nongovernmental organization (NGO) forum of the Fourth U.N. Conference on Women in Beijing, for example, a woman from Bangladesh complained that population planners were simply adopting "feminist" rhetoric without changing their coercive policies: "*Now* they [population planners] say after Cairo that we just have to start calling our programs 'women's health' rather than 'population planning,' but we don't need to change anything."[63]

Another example of how demands for social justice are being co-opted by the right wing is the anti-immigration movement's appropriation of the demand for curtailed Western consumption patterns. Anti-immigration groups note that the United States consumes far more resources than does the Third World, but they conclude from this fact that the answer is to restrict immigration into the United States. They reason that immigrants who come to this country imitate the consumption patterns of the well-to-do. Thus, while claiming to be concerned about overconsumption, the right wing employs anti-consumption rhetoric to protect the "desired way of life"—that is, the unsustainable consumption patterns—of the elite in the United States.[64] Challenging consumption patterns without questioning the population paradigm leaves us vulnerable to this kind of co-optation.

These trends suggest that as long as we retain the population paradigm where the term *population* operates as a code word to signify people of color and Third World people, these people will be seen as "the problem population." This is particularly problematic at present as people of color have reached new heights in organizing around environmental justice. Government and business interests recognize the potential power of the environmental justice movement and have taken measures to divide the potential collaboration between civil rights and environmental organizations. For example, an internal memo of the Environmental Protection Agency (EPA), leaked to the press by Rep. Henry Waxman (D-Calif.), announced its plan to drive a wedge between civil rights and environmental justice organizations.[65] The EPA was planning a public relations campaign, directed toward environmental organizations, that would hype the EPA's commitment to racial diversity so that environmental organizations would be less likely to join in coalition with civil rights organizations to target the EPA's historic racist policies. It is interesting that the hype over population growth seems to coincide with the growing strength of the environmental justice movement. Now millions of dollars are being used to support programs that will divide people of color and the mainstream environmental movement. Furthermore, anti-immigrant population control groups like CCN are targeting African Americans to disrupt organizing among people of color.[66] The Federation for American Immigration Reform, for instance, attempted to appeal to the African American community by holding a conference in which it blamed immigrants for the Rodney King riots.

Because it is the structures of global injustice that are decimating the earth and its inhabitants, we must target these structures rather than population growth. A focus on population only distracts us from the needed task of dismantling the "new world order." As Mary Mellor states, "The future of the planet [is] in the hands of a capitalist market economy united with other powerful forces—feudalism, patriarchy, colonialism, imperialism, militarism and racism—to form a monstrous global structure of economic, cultural and political power."[67] Reducing population without taking the fate of the earth out of these hands will not help us or the earth. And as long as communities of color continue to be subject to racist population policies, the banner of reproductive rights as defined by Europeans and Euro-Americans will not meaningfully address the needs of these communities.

Notes

1. Dianne Moore, "Gender Essentialism and the Debate over Reproductive Control in Liberal Protestantism" (Ph.D. diss., Union Theological Seminary, 1995).

2. Reprinted in Dale Hathaway-Sunseed, "A Critical Look at the Population Crisis in Latin America" (unpublished paper, University of California at Santa Cruz, 1979). The efforts these men supported led to the sterilization of 30 percent of women in Puerto Rico and 44 percent of women in Brazil, despite the fact that sterilization was illegal in Brazil; see Betsy Hartmann, *Reproductive Rights and Wrongs* (Boston: South End Press, 1994 [1986]), 248, 250.

3. For a discussion of population statements issued by the Lutheran, United Methodist, Southern Baptist, and United Presbyterian Churches, see Arthur Dyck, "Religious Views," in *Population and Ethics,* ed. Robert Veatch (New York: Halsted Press, 1977), 277–323. See also Jfirgen Moltmann, "The Ecological Crisis: Peace with Nature," *Scottish Journal of Religious Studies* (Spring 1988), 5–18; John Swomley, "Too Many People, Too Few Resources," *Christian Social Action* 5 (November 1992), 10–12; Nancy Wright and Donald Kill, *Ecological Healing: A Christian Vision* (Maryknoll, NY: Orbis, 1993), 7–9, 119–21; Roger Shinn, *Forced Options* (San Francisco: Harper & Row, 1982), 85–105; James Nash, *Loving Nature* (Nashville: Abingdon, 1991), 44–50; and John Carmody, *Ecology and Religion* (New York: Paulist Press, 1983), 140–42.

4. See Rosemary Radfor Ruether, *Gaia and God: An Ecofeminist Theology of Earth Healing* (San Francisco: HarperSanFrancisco, 1992), 23; Catherine Keller, "Chosen Persons and the Green Ecumancy: A Possible Christian Response to the Population Apocalypse," in Margot Kassman, "Covenant, Praise and Justicae in Creation," in *Ecotheology,* ed. David Hallman (Maryknoll, NY: Orbis, 1994), 301; and Christine Gudorf, *Body, Sex and Pleasure* (Cleveland: Pilgrim Press, 1994), 43.

5. Keller, "Chosen Persons," op. cit., 301.

6. Ibid., 300. A similar experience happened at a conference on ecofeminism (sponsored by the Feminists for Animal Rights) that I attended in Washington, DC, in April 1994. For a panel on overpopulation, a man from the right-wing Population-Environment Balance *was* asked to speak, but *no* women of color were asked to speak. The organizers claimed that they "couldn't find any women of color."

7. Ruether, *Gaia and God,* op. cit., 47.

8. Sailie McFague, *The Body of God* (Minneapolis: Fortress, 1993), 4.

9. Ibid., 5.

10. Hartmann, *Reproductive Rights and Wrongs,* op. cit., 6.

11. Keller, "Chosen Persons," op. cit., 307; and Gudorf, *Body, Sex and Pleasure,* op. cit., 48.

12. See United Nations, *Convention of the Prevention and Punishment of the Crime of Genocide,* II(d), which condemns imposing any measure intended to prevent births within a targeted group.

13. Gudorf, *Body, Sex and Pleasure,* op. cit., 48.

14. Catherine Keller, "Talk About the Weather," in *Ecofeminism and the Sacred,* ed. Carol J. Adams (New York: Continuum, 1993), 31.

15. Keller, "Chosen Persons," op. cit., 301.

16. Ruether, *Gaia and God,* op. cit., 111; and Keller, "Chosen Persons," op. cit., 307.

17. Gudorf, *Body, Sex and Pleasure,* op. cit., 42.

18. Ibid., 59.

19. Ruether, *Gaia and God,* op. cit., 101.

20. Ibid., 263.

21. Ibid., 264. Even the United Nations' *Report of the International Conference on Population and Development* (Cairo, September 5–13, 1994) calls for meeting unmet needs for contraceptives rather than promoting their use to women who do not want them.

22. Ruether, *Gaia and God,* op. cit., 258–68.

23. Keller, "Chosen Persons," 302; Ruether, *Gaia and God,* op. cit., 263; and McFague, *The Body of God,* op. cit., 56.

24. H. Patricia Hynes, quoted in Hartmann, *Reproductive Rights and Wrongs,* op. cit., 24.

25. Maria Mies and Vandana Shiva, *Ecofeminism* (London: Zed Books, 1993), 283.

26. Hartmann, *Reproductive Rights and Wrongs,* op. cit., 26.

27. Gudorf, *Body, Sex and Pleasure,* op. cit., 50.

28. See Hartmann, *Reproductive Rights and Wrongs,* op. cit., 66–72.

29. United Nations International Conference on Population and Development, *Draft Programme of Action,* 7.20.

30. McFague, *The Body of God,* op. cit., 4–5. See also Keller, "Chosen Persons," op. cit., 309.

31. Hartmann, *Reproductive Rights and Wrongs,* op. cit., 235–40.

32. Ibid., 40.

33. Thais Corral, speech delivered at Hampshire College's Fight for Abortion Rights, April 1, 1995.

34. Quoted in Swomley, "Too Many People, Too Few Resources," op. cit., 12.

35. Ibid., 11. For other papal statements on the urgency of population stabilization, see Dyck, "Religious Views," op. cit., 316.

36. The Pontifical Academy of Sciences, for example, recommended that couples have only two children to help curb "the world population crisis." See "Vatican Contradiction on Population Control," *Christian Century,* September 7–14, 1994, 809.

37. Loren Wilkinson, "Are Ten Billion People a Blessing?" *Christianity Today,* January 11, 1993, 19; Wendy Steinberg, "The Population Problem," *Christianity Today,* December 12, 1994, 6; Nigel M. de S. Cameron, "Cairo's Wake-Up Call," *Christianity Today,* October 24, 1994, 20–21; Andrew Steer, "Why Christians Should Support Population Programs," *Christianity Today,* October 3, 1994, 51; Loren Wilkinson, ed., *Earthkeeping in the '90s* (Grand Rapids, MI: Eerdmans, 1992), 51–86; and Ronald J. Fasano, "A Biblical Perspective on Ecology," *Christianity To-*

day, June 20, 1994, 7–8.

38. Susan Bratton, *Six Billion and More* (Louisville, KY: Westminster, 1992), 178, 181, 193, 198. However, Bratton does not think Christians should advocate withholding funds from population programs that supply abortions, given the dire need to stabilize the population. She particularly supports the international Planned Parenthood Federation, which has a history of distributing hormonal contraceptives without providing follow-up care or properly educating users about contraindications and side effects. See Hartmann, *Reproductive Rights and Wrongs,* op. cit., 194, 294, regarding Depo-Provera and the Pill.

39. Cindy Rollins, "Don't Limit the Size of the Family," *Alliance Life,* November 23, 1988, 21.

40. Tom Burghardt, "Neo-Nazis Salute the Anti-Abortion Zealots," *Covert Action* 52 (Spring 1995), 30.

41. See Michael Coffman, *Saviors of the Earth?* (Chicago: Northfield Publishing, 1994). See also Tim Stafford, "Are People the Problem?" *Christianity Today,* October 3, 1994, 45–60. Stafford suggests that there are two positions on the population issue: Ehrlich's radical Malthusianism and oppressive population policies and Julian Simon's cornucopianism, which holds that the Earth is in better environmental shape than ever before. E. Calvin Beisner states, "From the Christian perspective of faith in a God of providence, we can be confident that human population will never present an insuperable problem." Quoted in John W. Klotz, review of *Prospects for Growth: A Biblical View of Population, Resources and the Future,* by E. Calvin Beisner, *Concordia Journal* 18 (April 1992), 218.

42. Hartmann, *Reproductive Rights and Wrongs,* op. cit., xvii.

43. Christine Gudorf, "Population, Ecology, and Women," *Second Opinion* 20 (January 1995), 63.

44. Pew Global Stewardship Initiative, *White Paper* (July 1993), 12.

45. Amy L. Girst and Larry L. Greenfield, "Population and Development: Conflict and Consensus at Cairo," *Second Opinion* 20 (April 1995), 51–61. "Varied Religious Stands on Population," *Christian Century,* July 27–August 3, 1994, 714–15. "Morals and Human Numbers," *Christian Century,* April 20, 1994, 409–10.

46. Stafford, "Are People the Problem?" op. cit., 45–60.

47. Carol Benson Holst, conversation with author, March 13, 1995. All subsequent citations of Holst will refer to this conversation.

48. Pew Charitable Trusts, *Report of Findings from Focus Groups on Population, Consumption and the Environment,* July 1993, 64.

49. Ibid., 67.

50. Ibid., 73; and GSA Focus Group Report Memorandum, October 22, 1993, 7.

51. Pew Charitable Trusts, *Report of Findings,* op. cit., 73; *Global Stewardship,* Vol. 1 (March 1994), 1.

52. Jane Hull Harvey, "Cairo—A Kairos Moment in History," *Christian Social Action* 7 (November 1994), 15.

53. Hartmann, *Reproductive Rights and Wrongs*, op. cit., 139.

54. Holst, conversation.

55. Ramona Morgan Brown and Carol Benson Holst, "ICPD's Suppressed Voices May Be Our Future Hope," *Ministry for Justice in Population Concerns* (October–December 1994), 1. For another critical view of Cairo, see Charon Asetoyer, "Whom to Target for the North's Profits," *Wicozanni Wowapi* (Fall 1994), 2–3. Asetoyer writes: "Early into the conference, it became obvious that the issues facing Third World countries such as development, structural adjustments, and capacity building were not high on the list of issues that the superpowers wanted to address. It was clear that the issues facing world population were going to be addressed from the top down with little regard for how this may affect developing countries."

56. Ministry for Justice in Population Concerns, *Notice of Phase-Out,* January 1, 1995. Pew's March 1994 newsletter also dismissed as "rumor mongering" the concerns of women of color about the racist implications of population control. *Global Stewardship,* Vol. 1 (March 1994), 3.

57. Stephen Greene, "Who's Driving the Environmental Movement?" *Chronicle of Philanthropy,* Vol. 6 (January 25, 1994), 6–10.

58. Gudorf, "Population, Ecology, and Women," op. cit., 64.

59. Zero Population Growth, "Bearing the Burden," fact sheet, Washington, DC, Spring 1992, 2.

60. Allen writes, "The assault on the system of woman power requires the replacing of a peaceful, nonpunitive, nonauthoritarian social system wherein women wield power by making social life easy and gentle with one based on child terrorization, male dominance, and submission of women to male authority." From Paula Gunn Allen, *The Sacred Hoop* (Boston: Beacon Press, 1986), 40.

61. Isis, *Women in Development* (Geneva: Isis, 1983), 79.

62. Gita Sen, *Crises and Alternative Visions* (New York: Monthly Review Press, 1987), 75.

63. Audience participant at the NGO Forum, Fourth UN Conference on Women, Beijing, China, August 30–September 8, 1995.

64. Carrying Capacity Network, *Clearinghouse Bulletin* (June 1991), 4, 6; and (October 1991), 2, 7, 8.

65. House Subcommittee on Health and the Environment, "Staff Report," 24 February 1992.

66. Carrying Capacity Network, fund-raising appeal, December 1994. In this appeal, CCN asks for lists of organizations representing minorities, particularly African Americans, so that it can send them copies of its *Immigration Briefing Book.*

67. Cathi Tactaquin, "Environmentalists and the Anti-Immigrant Agenda," *Race, Poverty and the Environment,* Vol. 4 (Spring 1993), 6.

68. Mary Mellor, "Building a New Vision: Feminist, Green Socialism," in Richard Hofrichter, ed., *Toxic Struggles* (Philadelphia: New Society, 1993), 39.

THE ECOLOGICAL CRISIS IN TANZANIA

Meredeth Turshen

This essay analyzes the debates about the current ecological crisis in Tanzania to explore the impact of development, environmental, and population policies on a single country. It focuses on economic and political changes, examining these changes from a gender perspective. It also maps new and recurring disease epidemics in relation to changing gender relations, ecological change, and the political economy. The key factors commonly identified in the environmental crisis are the rate of population growth, patterns of population mobility, urbanization, and women's roles in production and reproduction. The central questions often asked are: Did the Tanzanian people bring about the ecological crisis we observe today, or were national and international policies responsible? Is there a causal relationship between the ecological crisis and economic and social dislocation—or, in other words, is the ecological crisis related to the declining economy and migration? What are the respective roles of the Tanzanian people, the government of Tanzania, foreign powers, and the international financial institutions in economic and social dislocation?[1] Public health analysts wonder also whether the ecological crisis is related to epidemics of AIDS, tuberculosis, and malaria.

At the heart of this essay is the controversy about the role of peasants, especially women farmers, in the current decline of living standards in Tanzania. Policy makers like those at the World Bank see willful or unwitting ecological destruction occuring at the hands of peasants. These analysts believe that farmers and herders are ignorant victims of their own self-perpetuating poverty, unavoidably destroying the environment (for example, by cutting too many trees for firewood and overgrazing pastureland). Critics of the World Bank say that this narrow focus on low-tech agricultural practices ignores class and gender power struggles in Tanzania. We believe that the proper framework for analysis is the context of unequal power relations between men and women, of competition for resources among groups of Tanzanians, of conflicts between Tanzanians and their government, and of disagreements between the Tanzanian government and international aid and banking institutions.

Farming Practices and Ecological Deterioration

That the environment is deteriorating in parts of Tanzania is widely accepted.[2] Desertification—the process by which land is turned into desert—is well advanced in parts of central Tanzania and severe in adjacent areas to the north and west (Singida and Shinyanga). At issue is whether the Tanzanian people (especially women) or their government are responsible for the deterioration. Kevin Cleaver and Götz Schreiber, writing for the World Bank in 1993, link rapid population growth and poor agricultural performance to environmental degradation; they understand the linkage as a synergistic interaction that constitutes a causal chain—in schematic terms, overpopulation leads to environmental degradation, which in turn causes poor crops. The factors they cite are *traditional* African production methods, *traditional* land tenure and use, *traditional* responsibilities of women, and *traditional* use of forest resources.[3]

The World Bank describes the poor as both victims and agents of environmental damage. As victims,

> It is often the poorest who suffer most from the consequences of pollution and environmental degradation. Unlike the rich, the poor cannot afford to protect themselves from contaminated water ... in rural areas they are more likely to cook on open fires of wood or dung, inhaling dangerous fumes; their lands are most likely to suffer from soil erosion.[4]

As agents, the Bank continues, the poor cannot avoid degrading their environment because, for example, they cultivate unsuitable areas—steep slopes, semi-arid land, and tropical forests. Again, their "*traditional* uses of land and fuel have depleted soil and forests and contributed to agricultural stagnation."[5]

The World Bank explanation of environmental deterioration blames the victim. Such interpretations were widespread in the colonial period when it was thought that Africans were the architects of their own degradation. Absent from the World Bank studies is any discussion of large-scale commercial agriculture, transnational agribusiness, and big public and private estates. In Tanzania, 70 percent of commercial agriculture is in private hands. Of total acreage cultivated, 3 percent is large-scale farming—state farms, estates, settler farms, and large African farms.[6]

Here is an example of the debate reframed in progressive terms: Handeni is a dry area of northeastern Tanzania suffering from environmental deterioration that was caused by colonial policies. Historians trace current ecological problems to colonial policies that introduced taxation and new commercial labor relations.[7] Colonists required payment of taxes in cash on specific dates (irrespective of shifting weather patterns), and they substituted short-term labor contracts and casual labor for the old-style patronage under which farmers worked for tribal leaders. In times of scarcity the traditional response of Handeni's farmers was to turn for aid to their patrons, through whom they had long-term access to food reserves. Without that patronage and with the new demand for cash, farmers had no alternative but to migrate in search of paid work. In their absence, their cattle were more subject to infections because farmers were not present to control vegetation, wildlife, and disease-bearing insects. The resultant death of livestock led, in turn, to famine and more migration. Under direct German rule, tribal leaders struggled with German authorities over these policies; under indirect British rule, peasants waged political struggles with the chiefs appointed by the British to impose the new policies. In Handeni, a declining, not a rapidly growing, population had specific negative effects on the environment.

Ecological Decline and Population Growth

The World Bank singles out rapid population growth as a major cause of environmental degradation and agricultural stagnation. Their economists censure Africans for failing to adapt to conditions of rapid population growth, and they name high population densities as the cause of decline in agriculture and the environment. The World Bank argues that when population densities are high, farmers cannot leave fields fallow long enough to restore fertility to the land, and they claim that family size is higher where land damage is greatest and fuelwood supplies are depleted.[8]

Discussing these issues, a Tanzanian demographer claims that "high population growth and economic backwardness are dependent variables which contribute significantly to rapid resource depletion and environmental degradation."[9] It should be possible to refute this statement empirically with regional data. For example, Rukwa, a region in the southern highlands, has the highest population growth rate in the country outside the capital of Dar es Salaam, yet it is fertile, productive, and relatively prosperous. In contrast, Kilimanjaro, a mountainous region in the northeast, has a low population growth rate and reports declining agricultural yields. Unfortunately, the production data for Kilimanjaro are not trustworthy because it is one of the regions that smuggles produce across the Kenyan border; as a result, official data severely underestimate production.[10]

The World Bank's thesis is that high population growth has led to economic backwardness, and their evidence is a stagnant agricultural economy in Tanzania. But crop production flourished in the 1970s. The World Bank hid these trends by aggregating all crop yields together, but the reality became clear when skeptics disaggregated the data. Again, official statistics on agricultural performance are unreliable because crops, especially food crops, are marketed in unofficial channels. "For example, in the mid-1980s some 90 percent of maize was said to have been marketed in unofficial channels."[11] It is important to read this unofficial trade as peasant resistance to government crop-buying agencies and as an attempt to take back control of marketing.

If the data on agriculture and environment are ambiguous, the information on forest resources is clear. The most rapid and extensive deforestation in Tanzania took place in the colonial period, when large tracts of tropical forest were cleared for plantations of export crops such as coffee, tea, rubber, sisal, cotton, and tobacco. Public policy, not population growth, drives deforestation. Detailed case studies at the local level in Tanzania refute reductionist generalizations about population growth causing deforestation. For example, in Lushoto District, deforestation did not occur even as the population tripled, because peasants adapted farming practices, consumption patterns, even architecture, to the new situation. Kondoa, cited as the classic picture of desertification, experienced land degradation in the mid-18th century from trading caravans; war caused further environmental damage in the colonial period, and while conservation measures slowed land degradation in the highlands, they accelerated it in the lowlands. Rufiji, which suffered extensive deforestation for complex reasons, has seen its population fall.[12]

The claim that rapid population growth is the cause of environmental degradation and agricultural stagnation can be refuted at another level. The position is predicated on the idea of a fixed "carrying capacity" without specifying the meaning of the concept. The term has historical roots in British colonial tax policies in Africa. Colonial authorities arrived at the carrying capacity of districts by using a formula based on land, labor needs, and peasant surpluses, which allowed them to calculate taxes and production available for export.[13]

There is a voluminous literature on human carrying capacity—26 definitions published since 1975—but no single generally accepted sense of the term and no formula that can be used to calculate convincingly the number of people the earth can support.[14] The dozen or so definitions of nonhuman carrying capacity—derived from basic and applied ecology—are no more useful in determining sustainable ratios of population and resources. Most definitions recognize the need to extend ecological criteria of carrying capacity to include technological enhancement of productivity and cultural standards. Technology and culture set limits on population size well before the physical requirements for sheer subsistence do. People have the capacity to create new systems of material production, and human labor has the potential to transform nature; labor, technology, and productive systems can transcend contemporary economic constraints and the environmental problems that are symptomatic of economic malaise.[15] Above all, a rigid notion of carrying capacity dismisses political struggles around the control of resources.

Claims that rapid population growth is the direct cause of environmental deterioration oversimplify highly complex interactions. They lead too easily to the conclusion that population control is the answer to environmental deterioration, while avoiding most of the hard policy and power issues. Tanzania's population *is* growing rapidly at 3.2 percent per year. The high total fertility rate of 6.8 children has not changed since 1970; contraceptive use is a low 10 percent, and abortion is available only on medical indication. The World Bank rates Tanzania's birth control efforts as weak (the government supports a private family planning association, UMATI). But even the unmet need for family planning should be understood as a consequence of international policies that raise the price of imported pharmaceuticals (including contraceptives) and curtail government support of public health services.[16]

The International Financial Institutions and the Ecological Crisis

Several feminist analysts incriminate development policies, particularly structural adjustment plans pursued at the insistence of the international financial institutions, in environmental degradation; these policies compound the debt problem and cause widespread misery, deprivation, and destitution. In Tanzania, macro-policies of structural adjustment forced the government to shift priorities "from human to economic development, from food to cash crops, from small-scale to large-scale enterprises, and from inward-orientation to an export-led policy in development."[17] The link to environmental degradation is direct: the Tanzanian government and its foreign donors prioritize cash crops for export and divert labor and land away from food crops; structural adjustment directives reduce public investment in extension services, credit, and other inputs necessary for smallholder farming and move resources to the large-scale plantation and the large farm sector. Transnational corporations and big companies, which own and/or manage many plantations, are the major beneficiaries of external support for agricultural rehabilitation.

Intensification of agricultural production by both small and large producers has contributed to growing soil and environmental degradation. Vegetation has been burned or otherwise removed to open new pastures and farm land. Large-scale growers plunder the land with large-scale mechanized farming systems, the same way big timber companies plunder the forests, and mining companies the earth. Once soil fertility (or timber/mineral output) declines, they move on to other locations and countries. Smallholder growers have fewer options and are more dependent on sustainable use of the environment.[18]

Exports of nontraditional goods have also increased with possibly irreversible ecological consequences. Sales of wildlife products (illegal trophies, ivory, crocodile skins, ostrich and other birds), forest products (timber, black woods, mangrove, mahogany, medicinal plants), and marine products (prawns, lobsters, sea slugs) have all increased with liberalization under structural adjustment policies.[19]

This exploitation for purposes external to Tanzania and the environmental ramifications of structural adjustment policies do not end with a description of the physical impact on the land. The displacement of people and the spatial consequences of dislocation are further aspects of the story.

Population Mobility, Disease, and Environmental Deterioration

Although large-scale population movements are scarcely new in Africa, new patterns of migration and new social dislocations have had profound effects on the vulnerability of Africans to disease and on their ability to maintain control over their physical and political environment. The relation between population mobility and the spread of disease is well documented. The late-19th-century introduction of new diseases—rinderpest (a disease of cattle) and sand fleas—is clearly traceable to European treks across Africa; the epidemics of endemic diseases—smallpox and trypanosomiasis (a disease of people and cattle)—are also bound up with the movement of people directly related to colonization. The question here is, what is the relation today between population mobility, the circulation of new and old diseases, and the deterioration of the environment? In answering this question, three groups of people in circulation need to be mentioned because of their particular relation to disease and environmental change—labor migrants, the armed forces, and refugees. Besides seeking work, doing military service, and fleeing from political violence, reasons for population mobility include villagization, which is unique to Tanzania, and rapid urbanization, which is a global phenomenon.[20]

Labor Migration

Industry and industrial agriculture recruit some labor directly, but more typically the need for cash income forces peasants to seek jobs in distant labor markets, much as colonial taxation schemes compelled subsistence farmers to seek waged work. Over the past two decades, as farm incomes declined, more young men sought work in non-farm activities, a trend reflected in the continuing decline of female-to-male ratios in urban areas (92 women per 100 men in 1995). As immiseration increased on small holdings, more young women joined this migratory movement, seeking casual employment on sugar cane and tea plantations, on large farms, and in the urban informal sector. Common non-farm activities are brewing and selling beer, petty trade, preparing and selling food, domestic service, bar work in clubs and pubs, and prostitution.[21]

Marjorie Mbilinyi offers this analysis of farm labor trends in Rungwe District, Tanzania:

> The crisis of labour for capital and the crisis of reproduction for peasant farming result from the related movements of labour out of capitalist farming and peasant agriculture. First, male labour withdrew from capitalist farm labour, as men sought higher-paying non-agricultural wage employment or entered non-agricultural petty commodity production and trade during the 1960s and early 1970s. This followed the earlier (though ongoing) withdrawal of male labour from the peasant labour force and the intensification of female labour in peasant farming as women entered non-farming petty commodity production and trade or got wage employment during the 1970s and early 1980s.... One consequence of these movements is the decline of a reservoir of cheap labour to work as casual labour for large-scale farm enterprises or peasant labour in export crop production.[22]

Both women and men withdrew from peasant farming because of its low returns and sheer drudgery. The decisions of young women and men to refuse unpaid work on family farms can be read as resistance to exploitation, as can the choice to produce food or engage in petty commodity production and trade rather than follow state exhortations to grow more export crops.[23] Informal sector activities are not taxed, it should be noted, and for now escape government regulation.

These trends should be read together with data on falling percentages of women and men marrying young, because the statistics on age at first marriage convey a sense of how uprooted and insecure this generation is. At the beginning of the 1970s, 50 percent of women and 6.6 percent of men ages 15 to 19 were married; by the end of the decade, 35.7 percent of women and 3.5 percent of men in this group were married.[24]

Armed Forces

Tanzania has one of the largest standing armies in sub-Saharan Africa. The Tanzanian army saw active service in the 1979 invasion of Uganda and in the 1980s in Mozambique.[25]

In epidemiological terms, the relation between the mobility of armies and the spread of disease is direct. The armed forces act as transmitters of venereal diseases and HIV/AIDS between infected groups and the general population.[26] Whether in regular armies, militias, or groups of bandits, young single men attract commercial sex workers to their barracks, kidnap women from villages to provide sexual services in their camps, or harass women serving in their own ranks. HIV is transmitted by blood transfusions as well as during sexual intercourse. When injured in battle, soldiers often require blood transfusions, and blood supplies, often drawn from army recruits, may be contaminated with HIV or other viruses. When soldiers use the same health services as the general population, they may diffuse contaminated blood. It should be noted that women and children receive the most blood transfusions.

Refugees

While Tanzania is fortunate to have escaped the prolonged civil conflicts that have afflicted so much of the continent since independence, it is a major recipient of refugees from six neighbors: Burundi, Mozambique, Rwanda, Sudan, Uganda, and Congo (formerly Zaire). Between 1964 and 1992, Tanzania accepted 292,000 refugees; after the 1994 upheaval in Rwanda, an additional 591,000 refugees entered the country. To avoid the sort of ecological destruction that typically occurs around refugee camps, Tanzania has pursued a policy of resettlement and strict control of refugee mobility.[27]

Refugees face immediate health crises of cholera, diarrheal diseases, and malnutrition, even starvation. Refugee women face particular sexual, mental, and physical health hazards during their flight because they are especially vulnerable to violence and exploitation. Refugee camps are high-risk situations where women are at the mercy of the army, camp guards, and unrelated male refugees. Any of these men may violate women or force them to exchange sex for food and other necessities. Despite women's vulnerability to sexual abuse, health programs for refugee populations have not systematically targeted sexually transmitted diseases (STDs) and especially HIV infection. In general Tanzania has no formal STD program, and the government does not properly report or record cases, though the ministry of health has proposed clinics and services. At least some of the high risk of this situation can be lowered by making women participants in refugee camp administration from the outset, but this is not the practice in Tanzania.[28]

Urbanization

The immiseration, environmental degradation, and deterioration of health and education services in the countryside have pushed many young men and women toward the city. In one sense, urbanization mitigates the direct impact of rapid population growth on the rural environment, but indirectly, a larger urban population increases demand for resources, such as timber and fuel, extracted from rural areas. Tanzania has seen its urban population grow to 22 percent of total population in 1992 from 5 percent in 1960. According to the urbanist Larry Sawers, urban and regional planning in Tanzania has been largely unsuccessful in preventing or even slowing the growth of Dar es Salaam, which has tripled in size.[29]

Urban areas play a particular role in the circulation of disease in late-20th-century Africa. Diseases related to the urban environment include the common diarrheas, associated with contaminated water and lack of sewerage, and tuberculosis, which is one of several diseases of poverty associated with malnutrition and urban overcrowding to which migrants are especially susceptible. Tanzania has a rising number of cases of tuberculosis, thought to be connected with the AIDS epidemic. The TB case rate was 95 per 100,000 population in 1994.[30]

Cities everywhere are sometimes painted as dens of iniquity that breed sexual promiscuity and sexually transmitted diseases. For many women and men, cities do offer freedom from restrictive rules of rural behavior and may be perceived as sites of decadence where important cultural values are destroyed; but other migrants experience more repressive patterns of social organization in urban than rural areas. So, the urban space is a site of contradictions, and the circumstances of migration determine whether migrants find themselves at high risk of disease in the city. A new and growing phenomenon is the number of unsupervised street children in Dar es Salaam (and elsewhere), many of whom are migrants from rural areas and are subject to particular forms of sexual and other exploitation.[31]

Villagization

Massive population redistribution occurred during villagization, the policy of moving people from scattered rural homesteads into villages. The most damaging evidence indicting the Tanzanian government for this policy, which caused environmental deterioration and agricultural stagnation, comes from recent reappraisals. This program entailed the introduction of modern farming techniques, including a degree of mechanization. It was a homegrown policy forcibly imposed in the 1970s by the state and not by external agents, though some analysts maintain that it resembled certain colonial resettlement policies and that its goals were compatible with those of the World Bank.[32]

There is a growing consensus that this modern development policy (rather than traditional methods of farming and herding, as the World Bank would have it) is responsible for crop losses, declining soil fertility, and increased erosion. Environmental destruction occurred because the authorities forced cultivators to live close to one another instead of close to their farms, causing villagers to overcultivate and overgraze nearby plots in their efforts to avoid the increased traveling time to and from fields. Accelerated deforestation occurred because the new settlements required building materials and fuelwood previously gathered and distributed over a wide area by dispersed groups.[33] Peasant resistance to villagization was widespread.

But villagization does not explain the large-scale features of underdevelopment, and the ecological crisis cannot be understood by looking only within the country.[34]

Environmental Destruction and Disease Epidemics

The link between disease and development is well established. The expansion and intensification of agriculture, in the absence of effective public health services, leads to epidemics of old and new diseases. Malaria spreads with large-scale cultivation of cotton, sugar, and rice and with heavy use of pesticides to which malarial mosquitoes become resistant. Throughout the 1980s, malaria was the major cause of death in Tanzania and responsible for 20 to 30 percent of all morbidity. In the last decade, it has spread in the Tanzanian highlands. Epidemiologists attribute increased transmission to the active colonization of areas like the Usambara Mountains in the northeast, the intensification of agriculture, and the attendant terracing and leveling of land in and around villages, which increases the number of breeding places for mosquitoes. And with the increase of malaria comes the increased use of antimalarials and increased drug resistance.[35]

AIDS is another disease that can be linked to environmental destruction.[36] The medical literature typically portrays AIDS in Africa as a heterosexually transmitted disease, with many references to individual sexual behavior but none to the economy, beyond the economics of prostitution.[37] In the Kagera region of northwestern Tanzania, for example, researchers found a linkage between businessmen, young women, economic seductions, sexual transactions, and AIDS deaths among the Haya people of that area. In the past, social sanctions regulated the lives of the young and effectively protected many girls from sexually transmitted diseases before marriage. Today, young girls are exposed to sexual exploitation that carries the risk of AIDS, particularly in urban areas with their preponderance of young men, and women recognize that alternative urban networks fail to protect them.[38]

One exception to the typical portrayal of AIDS is an article arguing that social and economic forces play a critical role in promoting the spread of HIV, and that International Monetary Fund (IMF) and World Bank structural adjustment policies create conditions favoring the disease's circulation. AIDS is best understood as an environmental disease, embedded in the nexus of economic and social relations of power and exploitation. It is an expression of political violence, labor migrancy, and poverty. In settings of political and structural violence that put people at high risk for HIV/AIDS, individuals have little agency and few choices; personal sexual behavior is not at issue. The underlying determinants of the spread of HIV are policies that undermine development and create structures that force the young out of their homes in search of work, destroying the social and familial networks that protect people from some types of disease experience.[39]

Conclusions

What is the magnitude of the current ecological crisis? Is it as great as the one that occurred 100 years ago? Writing in the mid-1980s, development economist Phil Raikes thought people were exaggerating.[40] Table 1 gives critical

Table 1. Critical Indicators for Tanzania

Population in millions	mid-1977	16.4
	mid-1995	29.6
GNP per capita	1978	$230
	1995	$120
Currency depreciation	1980–90/91	182.2%
World Bank ranking	1980	25[1]
	1997	3
Annual deforestation	1981–90	4,400 sq. km, or 1.3% of total area
Daily calorie supply	1986	2,192
	1992	2,021
Median age at death	1990	5 years[2]
Population per doctor	1960	21,600
	1976	18,490
	1990	24,880
Population per nurse	1960	8,300
	1976	3,300
	1990	5,470
Total health expenditure per capita	1990	$4

Percent of Total Central Government Expenditure

Health	1980	6.0	**Education**	1980	13.3
	1987	5.7		1990	11.4
Housing, Social Security, and Welfare	1980	2.5	**Defense**	1980	9.2
	1987	1.7		1987	15.8

Sources: World Bank, *World Development Report* (Washington, DC: World Bank, various years), and UNDP, *Human Development Report* (New York: Oxford University Press, various years).

[1] The World Bank ranks countries by GNP per capita in ascending order.

[2] Median age at death is the age below which half of all deaths occur in a year. The average figure for developed countries is 75 years.

data summarizing changes over the past 20 years that seem to indicate an unparalleled crisis. If the data are to be believed, Tanzania is now one of the poorest nations of the world, along with Ethiopia and Mozambique.

This decline in living standards has not occurred without popular resistance.[41] Despite a climate of fear created by the public security system, Tanzanians voiced criticisms indirectly, "using the double-talk found in most authoritarian societies."[42] Examples of "everyday resistance" mentioned above, coupled with overt defiance in the form of strikes, riots, theft, looting, and civil disturbance, are evidence of opposition, discontent, and anger.

The political economy of Tanzania changed dramatically over the 1980s as economic reforms designed by the World Bank and the IMF failed to resolve the debt crisis. Agricultural intensification and the accompanying environmental deterioration caused more workers to migrate in search of work, upsetting family life and provoking behavior associated with the spread of disease. In several neighboring countries, economic instability led to political instability, ruining livelihoods, dislocating populations, and sending many refugees into Tanzania. The breakdown of social unity in these nations can be traced to structural adjustment policies; the same process is now occurring in Tanzania, giving rise to an ascriptive identity politics that pits African against Asian and Christian against Muslim in ways not seen since independence.[43]

Reduced access to health, education, and other social services—also consequences of cutbacks and the privatization of public services that are part of structural adjustment programs—considerably increased poverty and the hardships of the poor, deepening the crisis for young people and their families in Tanzania. Surely these changes in the political economy, not tradition, are the root causes of the environmental crisis.

Notes

An earlier version of this article was presented at the 39th annual meeting of the African Studies Association on 23 November 1996 in San Francisco, California.

I am grateful for the research assistance of Bea Vidacs, and I thank Daniel Volman and Dorothy Hodgson for sharing resources with me. Several people generously provided useful critical comments on an earlier draft: Karim Hirji, Frank Popper, and David Wilson.

1. The most prominent international financial institutions include the International Monetary Fund and the World Bank.

2. M.B.K. Darkoh, "Desertification in Tanzania," *Geography,* Vol. 67 (1982), 320–31; M.B.K. Darkoh, "Land Degradation and Soil Conservation in Eastern and Southern Africa: A Research Agenda," *UNEP Desertification Control Bulletin,* Vol.

22 (1993), 60–68.

3. Kevin Cleaver and Götz Schreiber, *The Population, Agriculture and Environment Nexus in Sub-Saharan Africa* (Washington, DC: The World Bank Agriculture and Rural Development Series, No. 9, 1993), 1, emphasis added. Reading this volume, one has the impression of entering a time warp; for a contrasting study of contemporary rural life, see Marjorie Mbilinyi, "Agribusiness and Women Peasants in Tanzania," *Development and Change*, Vol. 19 (1988), 549–83.

4. World Bank, *Development and the Environment: World Development Report 1992* (Oxford: Oxford University Press, 1992), 1–2.

5. Ibid., 27. Emphasis added.

6. Werner Bierman and Jumanne Wagao, "The IMF and Tanzania: A Solution to the Crisis?" in Peter Lawrence, ed., *World Recession and the Food Crisis in Africa* (London: James Currey, 1986), 140–47; F. Kjaerby, "The Development of Agricultural Mechanisation in Tanzania," in J. Boesen et al., eds., *Tanzania: Crisis and Struggle for Survival* (Uppsala: Scandinavian Institute of African Studies, 1986), 173–90.

7. James Giblin, *The Politics of Environmental Control in Northeastern Tanzania, 1840–1940* (Philadelphia: University of Pennsylvania Press, 1992). I apologize for this schematic presentation, which is a disservice to the rich economy of Giblin's thesis.

8. Cleaver and Schreiber, *The Population, Agriculture and Environment Nexus*, op. cit., 7; World Bank, *Development and the Environment*, op. cit., 27.

9. Ndalahwa Faustin Madulu, "Population Growth, Agrarian Peasant Economy and Environmental Degradation in Tanzania," *International Sociology*, Vol. 10 (1995), 35–50.

10. Population data from Michael Barke and Clive Sowden, "Population Change in Tanzania 1978–1988: A Preliminary Analysis," *Scottish Geographical Magazine*, Vol. 108 (1992), 9–16; agricultural data from J.K. Van Donge, "The Continuing Trial of Development Economics: Policies, Prices and Output in Tanzanian Agriculture," *Journal of International Development*, Vol. 6 (1994), 157–84. T.L. Maliyamkono and M.S.D. Bagachwa note that remote interior areas like Rukwa with high transportation costs benefited from the pan-territorial pricing policy; this policy penalized areas with easy access to Dar es Salaam, prompting growers to resort to "selling grains in the second economy food market [including cross-border transactions] where prices were more than twice the official producer prices." T.L. Maliyamkono and M.S.D. Bagachwa, *The Second Economy in Tanzania* (London: James Currey, 1990), 75.

11. The Bank's negative figures arise from the relative weight attributed to sisal and cotton; these crops did decline due to a complex array of factors. Falling world sisal prices, rising labor costs, inadequate labor supplies, rising capital costs, and severe shortages of machinery, spare parts, and inputs due to the foreign exchange crisis account for the dramatic and sustained decline in sisal production. Undue state interven-

tion, lower producer prices at the national level, and village resettlement are not to blame. Marjorie Mbilinyi, "Structural Adjustment and Agribusiness in Tanzania: Struggles over the Labour of Women Peasants and Farm Workers," *Taamuli,* Vol. 1 (1990), 89, 90.

12. Solon L. Barraclough and Krishna B. Ghimire, "Deforestation in Tanzania: Beyond Simplistic Generalization," *The Ecologist,* Vol. 26 (1996), 104–9.

13. Ben Wisner, "The Limitations of 'Carrying Capacity,'" *Political Environments,* Vol. 3 (1996), 1–6.

14. Joel E. Cohen, *How Many People Can the Earth Support?* (New York: W.W. Norton, 1995). See especially Appendix 6, 419–25.

15. Theodore Trefon, "The Challenge of Attaining Sustainable Use of Forest Products by Central African City Dwellers" (paper presented at the Annual Meeting of the African Studies Association, Orlando, FL, November 1995).

16. Sources for this paragraph: The average annual growth for the years 1980–93 is higher than the sub-Saharan average of 2.9 percent. World Bank, *World Development Report 1995* (Washington, DC: The World Bank, 1995), 210–11. The total fertility rate is the average number of children born to each woman in accordance with current fertility patterns; it estimates the total number of children a woman will eventually bear if her child-bearing follows current patterns and she survives her child-bearing years. United Nations, *The World's Women 1995: Trends and Statistics* (New York: UN, 1995), 30; World Bank, *Population Growth and Policies in Sub-Saharan Africa* (Washington, DC: The World Bank, 1986), 61; Joe Lugalla, "The Impact of SAPs on Women and Children's Health in Tanzania," *Review of African Political Economy,* Vol. 63 (1995), 43–53.

17. Tanzania Gender Networking Programme, *Gender Profile of Tanzania* (Dar es Salaam, Tanzania: TGNP, 1993), 46. Sources for the rest of this paragraph: Rosina Wiltshire, *Environment and Development: Grass Roots Women's Perspective* (Pinelands, St. Michael, Barbados: DAWN, 1992); Rosi Braidotti, Ewa Charkiewicz, Sabine Hausler, and Saskia Wieringa, *Women, the Environment and Sustainable Development: Towards a Theoretical Synthesis* (London: Zed Books, 1994); Mbilinyi, "Structural Adjustment and Agribusiness in Tanzania," op. cit.

18. Tanzania Gender Networking Programme, *Gender Profile,* op. cit., 55. Between 1983 and 1993, sisal sales declined 78 percent, coffee declined 90 percent, tobacco declined 95 percent, and cashew nuts declined 78 percent; the only crops showing rising sales were cotton (212 percent) and green tea (127 percent). Ibid., 47. Tanzania has made negative progress in repaying its external debt, which rose from $2.9 billion in 1980 to $7.5 billion in 1993. World Bank, *World Development Report 1995,* 200.

19. C.S.L. Chachage, "Forms of Accumulation, Agriculture and Structural Adjustment in Tanzania," in P. Gibbon, ed., *Social Change and Economic Reform in Africa* (Uppsala: Nordiska Afrikainstitutet, 1993), 215–43.

20. Sources for this paragraph: John Lonsdale, "The European Scramble and

Conquest in African History," in *Cambridge History of Africa*, Vol. 6 (Cambridge: Cambridge University Press, 1985), 688–91; R.M. Prothero, "Disease and Mobility: A Neglected Factor in Epidemiology," *International Journal of Epidemiology*, Vol. 6 (1977), 259–67; Meredeth Turshen, *The Political Ecology of Disease in Tanzania* (New Brunswick, NJ: Rutgers University Press, 1984).

21. Sources for this paragraph: Patricia Daley notes that "refugees, not only provided casual labour on local tobacco farms, but were directly recruited by state-owned plantations. Both Tanzania's sisal industry and the Tea Authority recruited workers within the settlements in the 1980s." Patricia Daley, "The Politics of the Refugee Crisis in Tanzania," in H. Campbell and H. Stein, eds., *The IMF and Tanzania* (Harare: SAPES Trust, 1991), 175–99. See below for a discussion of the refugee situation in Tanzania. United Nations, *The World's Women 1995*, op. cit., 62. Tanzania Gender Networking Programme, *Gender Profile*, op. cit., 66.

22. Mbilinyi, "Structural Adjustment and Agribusiness in Tanzania," op. cit., 574.

23. Marjorie Mbilinyi, "Gender and Structural Adjustment," in *Structural Adjustment and Gender: Empowerment or Disempowerment, Symposium Report* (Dar es Salaam, Tanzania: Tanzania Gender Networking Programme, February 1994).

24. United Nations, *The World's Women 1995*, op. cit., 35. Latest available data.

25. In 1992, the armed forces consumed 3.6 percent of GDP, which is greater than the 3.2 percent spent on health. UNDP, *Human Development Report 1995* (New York: Oxford University Press, 1995), 183. Military spending in Tanzania (in current dollars) declined to $106 million in 1994 from $119 million in 1987; the strength of the armed forces has also declined to 32,000 in 1995 from 46,800 in 1992. In addition, Tanzania supported a Citizens' Militia of 80,000 in 1995. International Institute for Strategic Studies, *The Military Balance, 1995–1996* (London: IISS, 1995), 258.

26. M. Baldo and A.J. Cabral, "Low-Intensity Wars and Social Determination of HIV Transmission: The Search for a New Paradigm to Guide Research and Control of the HIV-AIDS Pandemic," in Z. Stein and A. Zwi, eds., *Action on AIDS in Southern Africa: Maputo Conference on Health in Transition in Southern Africa, April 1990* (New York, Committee on Health in South Africa, 1990). See my speculations on the relation between the army and the spread of AIDS in East Africa. Meredeth Turshen, *The Politics of Public Health* (New Brunswick, NJ: Rutgers University Press, 1989), 219–41.

27. Sources for this paragraph: UNDP, *Human Development Report 1995*, op. cit., 161; Charles David Smith, "The Geopolitics of Rwandan Resettlement: Uganda and Tanzania," *Issues: A Journal of Opinion*, Vol. 23 (1995), 54–57; data as of December 23, 1994. Because the incidence of HIV/AIDS was so high in Rwanda before the genocide (15.2 AIDS cases per 100,000 people in 1993), this population faces and poses special health risks. UNDP, *Human Development Report 1995*, 171; Daley, "The Politics of the Refugee Crisis," op. cit., 180.

28. Sources for this paragraph: H.A. Cossa et al., "Syphilis and HIV Infection

among Displaced Pregnant Women in Mozambique," *International Journal of STD and AIDS*, Vol. 5 (1994), 117–23. This study of displaced pregnant women in Zambezia Province, Mozambique, found the prevalence of past or current syphilis was 12.2 percent (within the range of prevalences found elsewhere in Africa); at least 8.4 percent of the women had been sexually abused during displacement. Women reporting more than five events of sexual abuse were more likely to be HIV-infected. Forbes Martin says that in the early period of an emergency, medical facilities rarely can deal with more than saving lives; women's reproductive and other health needs, including the need for protection from STDs and AIDS, go unattended. S. Forbes Martin, *Refugee Women* (London: Zed Books, 1991). See also Anne V. Akeroyd, "HIV/AIDS in Eastern and Southern Africa," *Review of African Political Economy*, Vol. 60 (1994), 173–84; Daley, "The Politics of the Refugee Crisis," op. cit., 189.

29. UNDP, *Human Development Report 1995*, op. cit., 185; Larry Sawers, "Urban Primacy in Tanzania," *Economic Development and Cultural Change*, Vol. 37 (1989), 841–59.

30. Sources for this paragraph: see Lugalla, "The Impact of SAPs on Women and Children," op. cit., for a dismaying description of unsanitary conditions in Dar es Salaam. AIDS and TB interact because persons with an AIDS-lowered immune system run an increased risk of TB infection or progression from asymptomatic infection to overt disease, and they often have more severe forms of TB than persons who are not HIV-positive. World Bank, *Tanzania: AIDS Assessment and Planning Study* (Washington, DC: The World Bank, 1992), 62–63; UNDP, *Human Development Report 1997* (Oxford: Oxford University Press, 1997), 177.

31. Sources for this paragraph: C.S. Blanc, *Urban Children in Distress: Global Predicaments and Innovative Strategies* (Yverdon, Switzerland: Gordon and Breach, 1994), 25–27; C. Boyce Davies, "Epilogue: Representations of Urban Life in African Women's Literature," in M. Turshen and B. Holcomb, eds., *Women's Lives and Public Policy: The International Experience* (Westport, CT: Greenwood, 1993), 171–81; M. Turshen, H. Bretin, and A. Thébaud-Mony, "Migration, Public Policy and Women's Experience," in M. Turshen and B. Holcomb, eds., *Women's Lives and Public Policy*, op. cit., 83–96. For a review of the literature on AIDS and migration, see R. Lalou and V. Piché "Migration et sida en Afrique de l'Ouest: Un état des connaissances," document de travail (Montréal: Université de Montréal, Département de Démographie, 1994). Lalou and Piché find a high correlation in demographic studies between labor migration and the spread of HIV, but they warn that more empirical research is needed to discover how workers, the majority of whom come from areas of low prevalence, can be carriers of HIV. They point out that several little-studied factors are critical to HIV dissemination: whether the migration is seasonal or long-term, whether families travel together, the frequency of return, and attitudes about extramarital sex in both places of origin and destination. See Lugalla, "The Impact of SAPs on Women and Children," op. cit., for a distressing account of street children in Dar es Salaam.

32. Phil Raikes, "Eating the Carrot and Wielding the Stick: The Agricultural Sector in Tanzania," in J. Boesen et al., eds., *Tanzania: Crisis and Struggle for Survival* (Uppsala: Scandinavian Institute of African Studies, 1986), 105–41.

33. Michael McCall, "Environmental and Agricultural Impacts of Tanzania's Villagization Programme," in J.I. Clark, et al., eds., *Population and Development Projects in Africa* (Cambridge: Cambridge University Press, 1985), 123–40; Barraclough and Ghimire, "Deforestation in Tanzania," op. cit.

34. Joel Samoff, "Theory and Practice in the Analysis of Tanzanian Liberalisation: A Comment," in Campbell and Stein, *The IMF and Tanzania*, op. cit., 226–46.

35. Sources for this paragraph: C.C. Hughes and J.M. Hunter, "Disease and Development in Africa," *Social Science and Medicine*, Vol. 3 (1970), 443–93. Space does not permit a discussion here of the many ways in which the policies of the international financial institutions have undermined public health services in Africa. See J. Lugalla, "The Impact of SAPs on Women and Children," op. cit., and Meredeth Turshen, *Privatizing Health Services in Africa* (New Brunswick, NJ: Rutgers University Press, 1999). World Bank, *Tanzania: AIDS Assessment,* op. cit., 3–4. The malaria case rate was 4,261.7 per 100,000 people in 1992. UNDP, *Human Development Report 1997*, 177. J.A. Nájera, B. H. Liese, and J. Hamner, "Malaria," in D.T. Jamison et al., eds., *Disease Control Priorities in Developing Countries* (Oxford: Oxford University Press, 1993), 281–302.

36. Usher spells out the relation of AIDS to ecological collapse in Thailand:

The increasing centralisation of the state, and the intensification of resource use for industrial development, is causing the gradual erosion not only of natural resources but also of people's customary rights to land, cultural integrity, local knowledge and sense of belonging. For people living in a weakened environment, the "goods and services" that were derived to a significant extent from nature must now, increasingly, be replaced by the market. But purchasing food or drugs or cultural commodities (through television, for example) demands the exchange of items that have the equivalent outside market value, forcing people either to extract more and more from the ecosystem, or to leave the village altogether. In the extreme case, when nature is so degraded that it can no longer provide, one of the only remaining local resources in the community that has value on the market is the bodies of the young. In those places where adolescent women—and, to a less extent, men—leave home to sell their labour in the sex industry, AIDS, which appears to have infected a huge proportion of the country's half-million prostitutes, has become a physical manifestation of political dispossession.

From "After the Forest: AIDS as Ecological Collapse in Thailand," *Development Dialogue*, Vol. 1–2 (1992), 13–49.

37. H. Standing, "AIDS: Conceptual and Methodological Issues in Researching Sexual Behaviour in Sub-Saharan Africa," *Social Science & Medicine*, Vol. 34 (1992), 475–83. The medical literature fails to indict development strategies such as tourism, sponsored by national governments and encouraged by international agencies as a solution to underdevelopment, which promote prostitution. There is considerable research on the links between tourism, prostitution, and the spread of AIDS in Southeast Asia, but almost nothing comparable in Africa. Mechtild Maurer, *Tourisme, Prostitution, SIDA* (Paris: L'Harmattan, 1992).

38. B. Weiss, "Buying Her Grave: Money, Movement and AIDS in North-West Tanzania," *Africa*, Vol. 63 (1993), 19–35; E.M. Ankrah, "AIDS and the Social Side of Health," *Social Science and Medicine*, Vol. 32 (1991), 967–80; M.T. Bassett and M. Mhloyi, "Women and AIDS in Zimbabwe: The Making of an Epidemic," *International Journal of Health Services*, Vol. 21 (1991), 143–56. None of these women advocates a return to traditional institutions of patriarchal domination.

39. Sources for this paragraph: P. Lurie, P. Hintzen, and R.A. Loew, "Socioeconomic Obstacles to HIV Prevention and Treatment in Developing Countries: The Roles of the International Monetary Fund and the World Bank," *AIDS*, Vol. 9 (1995), 539–46; M. Turshen, "The Political Ecology of AIDS in Africa," in M. Singer, ed., *The Political Economy of AIDS* (Amityville, NY: Baywood, 1998); D. Sanders and A. Sambo, "AIDS in Africa: The Implications of Economic Recession and Structural Adjustment," *Health Policy and Planning*, Vol. 6 (1991), 157–65; M. Turshen, "Societal Instability in International Perspective: Relevance to HIV/AIDS Prevention," in *Assessing the Social and Behavioral Science Base for HIV/AIDS Prevention and Intervention. Workshop Summary and Background Papers* (Washington, DC: National Academy Press, 1995), 117–28.

40. Raikes, "Eating the Carrot," op. cit., 139.

41. The law limited challenges until the adoption of a bill of rights in 1984 guaranteeing freedom of assembly, and even then it restricted political association to the ruling party, Chama Cha Mapinduzi. Mounting opposition in the 1990s brought about a multiparty system, independent trade unionism, and a free press. Nakazael Tenga and Chris Maina Peter, "The Right to Organise as Mother of All Rights: The Experience of Women in Tanzania," *Journal of Modern African Studies*, Vol. 34 (1996), 143–62.

42. Mbilinyi, "Gender and Structural Adjustment," op. cit., 53. The symposium report says: "In the current situation, physical and psychological torture are widespread. People are not happy with government decisions but the political environment is dominated by fear and hatred, as well as the denial of basic rights."

43. Paul J. Kaiser, "Structural Adjustment and the Fragile Nation: the Demise of Social Unity in Tanzania," *Journal of Modern African Studies*, Vol. 34 (1996), 227–37.

POWER OF THE WORD

Culture, Censorship, and Voice

Meredith Tax with Marjorie Agosin, Ama Ata Aidoo, Ritu Menon, Ninotchka Rosca, and Mariella Sala

We are politically committed women writers from around the world, involved in a range of cultural struggles. Because of our gender and our politics, some of us have been the targets of religious or state censorship. Some have known imprisonment or survived death threats. Some live in exile. Some have experienced mainly the free-market forms of censorship, such as denial of access to publication, marginalization, ghettoization, and stereotyping. Some have resisted such pressures by setting up alternative means of publishing women.

We have been investigating gender-based censorship[1] since 1986, when a few of us first came together within International PEN. We have now formed a separate organization, Women's WORLD (Women's World Organization for Rights, Literature and Development), in order to initiate global feminist work on the right to free expression, as has already been done by activists in the areas of development, the environment, reproductive health, and violence against women.

Women's WORLD is concerned with two issues: (1) the importance of cultural struggle and the role of women writers in it, and (2) gender-based censorship—the historic, worldwide silencing of women's voices—as a major obstacle to women's achievement of equality, sustainable livelihoods, and peace. Our essay begins with an analysis of the world crisis and goes on to examine the role of women writers in the emancipation of women and the construction of civil society. We then look at the many ways gender-based censorship operates and present some examples.

This essay was originally published as a pamphlet by Women's WORLD. It was written by Meredith Tax, president of Women's WORLD, and discussed at international meetings in September 1994 and March 1995 by a working group consisting of Marjorie Agosin (Chile/United States), Ama Ata Aidoo (Ghana), Ritu Menon (India), Ninotchka Rosca (Philippines), and Mariella Sala (Peru); the September 1994 meeting was also attended by Denisa Comanescu (Romania), and Aïcha Lemsine (Algeria). The draft was then sent to a larger group of writers, who were asked for comments and examples. The administrative and publication costs of the pamphlet and the presentation of these ideas at the Nongovernmental Organizations (NGOs) Forum of the Fourth U.N. World Conference on Women were generously supported by the Education and Culture program of the Ford Foundation, without whose help our work would have been difficult indeed.

The following writers worked on this essay: Marjorie Agosin (Chile/United States), Ama Ata Aidoo (Ghana), Ifi Amadiume (Nigeria), Nadezhda Azhgikhina (Russia), Cristina da Fonseca (Chile), Paula Giddings (United States), Merle Hodge (Trinidad), Eva Hung (Hong Kong), Rada Ivekovic (Croatia), Aïcha Lemsine (Algeria), Ritu Menon (India), Ninotchka Rosca (Philippines), Mariella Sala (Peru), Svetlana Slapsak (Serbia), Meredith Tax (United States).

The Global Crisis

In the ten years since the U.N. Women's Conference in Nairobi in 1985 at the end of the Decade of Women, the world has changed so much as to become almost unrecognizable. Among these changes are:

• The accelerating destruction of the environment, which makes Earth's survival an open question.

• A catastrophic subsistence crisis in Africa, Asia, and Latin America, brought about by the failures of the growth model of development and the imposition of structural adjustment policies, aided by the corruption of local ruling elites. Uneven development, conflicts over resources, and the threat of starvation have fanned ethnic rivalries, aggravated domestic tensions, and led to an unprecedented increase in the international traffic in women and children. Although Africa is the worst hit, even parts of Eastern Europe are now feeling a subsistence crisis, due to dislocations caused by war and their rush into market capitalism.

• Vast movements of population from the countryside to the city and the global South[2] to the North in search of employment or in flight from war and famine. While these migrations have accelerated the disintegration of traditional forms of the family and fed ethnic and racial conflicts, they have also laid a potential foundation for new, culturally diverse societies.

• The end to the Cold War period's uneasy equilibrium between socialist and capitalist "camps," and the triumph of the discourse of the North in its most extreme form—the dog-eat-dog worldview of 19th-century free-market capitalism. In North America and the formerly communist countries of Eastern Europe, social and trade union protections and welfare state benefits of all kinds are being rolled back to encourage capital accumulation, which will supposedly create jobs. The consequences are devastating for children, the aged, and the women who must care for both in economies that offer them few options but unemployment, prostitution, and crime.

• The release of previously stockpiled Cold War weapons and nuclear technology into the world, facilitating an epidemic of wars and civil conflicts in the former Soviet Union, the former Yugoslavia, Africa, West Asia, South Asia, and Latin America, leaving hundreds of thousands dead and creating vast refugee populations alienated from their land and self-sufficient production. A parallel development, especially in Latin America, has been the formation of paramilitary groups and narco-mafias that conduct private wars and land grabs against indigenous peoples, "dissidents," "subversives," and even street children. In response, some civil societies are becoming increasingly militarized, with large parts of the population buying arms as an answer to criminality, particularly where the state is perceived as inept or itself criminal.

• The growing dominance of transnational corporations as a global force not accountable to any state or international body, ruling partly by economic domination and partly through a global monoculture that marginalizes or wipes out local and individual forms of cultural expression and autonomy.

• The rise of religious fundamentalism, regional nationalisms, and communalism as political movements targeting women and ethnic minorities. The increasing internationalization and collusion of these movements raises the possibility of a worldwide reactionary movement similar to fascism in the 1920s and 1930s.

The past ten years have also seen positive developments, like the democratic revolution in South Africa, the dismantling of military dictatorships in Latin America, the fall of the Berlin Wall, and the growth of civil societies in Eastern Europe. Struggles for social and economic justice, minority rights, national liberation, and the rights of indigenous peoples have begun to be linked by three international movements:

• A world movement for human rights, including the rights of women, with visible impact on U.N. conferences in Vienna, Cairo, and Copenhagen. Despite an early history of use as an instrument of Northern state policy, the international human rights movement has in recent years shown its potential to humanize justice by coupling demands for economic and social rights with personal and cultural ones.

• A world movement for ecology that links the future of humanity with that of other species and of the planet itself, in which feminists opposed to the growth model of economic development have begun to articulate an alternative that links sustainable livelihoods, bio- and cultural diversity, and gender rights.

• The international women's movement, of which we are a part. Like any broad movement, this has contradictions over policy, priorities, and vision, yet it alone has the potential to create the conditions that will allow women to have a voice in determining their own fate and the fate of the world.

Competing Visions of the Future

As the century ends, three visions of the future are before us. The first is that of the New Economic Order, led by transnational corporations, the World Bank, and the International Monetary Fund—the embodiment of a new international ruling class that is superseding national and local forms of governance. Accountable to no one but their stockholders, the transnationals move industries, crops, and populations around like pieces in a board game. Their New World Order offers us a future in which the profit motive will replace all intellectual and spiritual goals as the prime reason for human existence; in which the only standard of human value will be cash; in which regional and cultural distinctions will slowly vanish, to be replaced by the one great distinction between rich and poor; and in which people will be valued only in terms of their market price. In the New Economic Order, all local, particular, and diverse cultures will be superseded by a global monoculture that exalts sex, violence, and purchasing power, and portrays women mainly as commodities.

A growing network of conservative clerics and politicians superficially opposes the "internationalism" of the New World Order in the name of tradition and national sovereignty, making war on women and ethnic or religious minorities, while invoking a dream of benign communities ruled by them.

They dislike the New World Order's encouragement of secular modernity and its assumption of universal human rights, and fear the anarchic, creative, and populist aspects of mass culture, with its glorification of individual desires and its tendency to stir up women and children against patriarchal control. Their cultural strength must not be underestimated, for they represent a serious threat to women and minorities wherever they are strong. But they do not have the economic strength to oppose the New World Order effectively, and are prepared to collude with it if the price is right, as long as they can maintain local control. They offer us a future in which the world will be divided up between Export Processing Zones and traditional enclaves ruled by the transnationals.

Our main hope is the developing alliance between the global women's movement and other progressive social movements. All our movements face the same oppressive forces: a New World Order that props up modern dictatorships and a reactionary traditionalism that represents the worst form of patriarchal control. We have a common vision of a future in which extremes of wealth and poverty will vanish; in which human rights, sustainable livelihoods, universal literacy, and cultural diversity will become the norm; and in which decisions will be made and social conflicts resolved by negotiation, rather than by force or domination.

A problem remains. While progressive social movements should be natural allies of movements for the emancipation of women, this has not always been the case. Again and again, women have fought beside men in movements for social change, only to see them set up new ruling elites that leave gender and family hierarchies intact, continue to practice the power politics of dominance and submission, and resolve social and personal conflicts through violence or repression. This must change if any of us are to succeed in our goal of social transformation.

Many male revolutionary theorists have seen the struggle for women's emancipation as a "sectoral" one, like the struggles of national minorities or indigenous peoples, and concluded that it is subordinate. Any theory that creates a hierarchy even among liberation struggles, rather than emphasizing their complex, dialectical interactions, will have difficulty transcending power politics. In the words of the African American poet Audre Lorde, "the master's tools will never dismantle the master's house."

In fact, female emancipation is not a subordinate struggle but a majority struggle. Today, women, particularly women of the South, make up the vast majority of the poor and politically disenfranchised people of the world, the true "prisoners of starvation" and "wretched of the earth." Thus, any movement for real transformation must make the demands of women central. And because so many of the chains that bind women are located in the realm of tradition rather than pure politics or economics, a thorough transformation must involve struggles over culture.

What Is Culture, and Why Does It Matter?

Feminist theory has yet to come to grips with culture and religion, while traditionalists have tainted the word "culture" by defending "cultural practices" harmful to women. So we must pause to define our terms.

In the words of Ama Ata Aidoo, "The culture of a community really is the totality of the ways in which that community conducts its lives: its births, growths, study, work, entertainment, and death."[3] Or, as Marjorie Agosin puts it, "Culture is who we are and who we are becoming."[4] It is the food we put on the table; the way we cook it; the utensils with which we eat it; the relations between the people who sit at the table and the people who cook and serve; what is done with the leftovers; what is discussed during the meal; what music, dancing, poetry, or theater accompany it; and the social and spiritual values of those present—for, when we say culture, we include the visions, dreams, and aspirations of humanity.

How is it possible to talk of social and economic development without talking about culture? To treat literacy and art in a purely instrumental way, as most development programs do, is to reinforce values that are part of the problem, not the solution. Do we want only materialist development? Have we no interest in spiritual and political development? How can we address the question of literacy if we ignore the question of what there is to read? Do we want women to learn to read and write merely so they can follow the instructions in packages of birth control pills? Or do we want them to be able to read their own lives, write their own destinies, and claim their share? As Mariella Sala says:

> Without attention to culture, sustainable development is not possible, because profound changes must necessarily be culture-related. We must understand that women's silence is as serious a problem as poverty itself, and is both the cause of poverty and its effect. It is a vicious circle that must be broken. Women writers all over the world are mute; they are without a voice because so many social institutions are deaf to their plight and totally unaware of the importance of creative expression in mobilizing people's energies for change. The impact of creative literature and its ability to point out crucial aspects of

social problems and to envision better ways of living cannot be denied, yet few see that sustainable development, political equality, and peace must be based on full human development, and that art and culture are therefore strategic questions.[5]

Carolina Maria de Jesus, a barely educated woman from a Brazilian *favela*, collected wastepaper from garbage heaps to feed her children, but, fiercely intelligent, wrote in her diary every day:

> I have a mania to observe everything, tell everything, and note down the facts.... We are poor and we live on the banks of the river. The river banks are places for garbage and the marginal people. People of the favelas are considered marginal. No more do you see buzzards flying the river banks near the trash. The unemployed have taken the buzzards' place.[6]

This diary not only gave her a reason to live; it gave the rest of the world a way to understand the world of the *favelas* and inspired a generation of other testimonies by Latin American women. Like Carolina Maria de Jesus, women in the early U.S. labor movement often spoke of their longing for the beauties of art and nature, so that life should not be made up merely of ceaseless toil. In 1912, women textile strikers in Lawrence, Massachusetts, coined the slogan, "We want bread and roses too!" That slogan is still appropriate. But the categories of most development programs do not have room for people like the Lawrence strikers or Carolina Maria de Jesus or their successors, like Dolores Huerta, Wangari Maathai, and Rigoberta Menchú. Because they isolate economic questions, such development programs fail to deal with the complex web of social relations that enmesh women.

A web doesn't move if you pull at only one strand; all you can do that way is break it. The historic cultures and family ties of much of the world are already under attack, if not altogether destroyed. We must find ways to preserve what remains while at the same time refusing to accept those parts of tradition that treat women and children as less than human. Imposing colonialist definitions of progress while ignoring the cultural lives of indigenous peoples has already had devastating consequences. As Ama Ata Aidoo puts it, describing the condition of Africa:

> What happens to a society whose own arts have been killed off, dangerously marginalized or ridiculed out of existence through colonial intervention? What happens to such a society especially if, at the end of formal colonization, it does not seem capable of mobilizing resources, encouraging its cultural workers, or does not have any peace,

necessary to recreate newer forms of cultural manifestations?...
Clearly such a society would be heading towards confusion, inertia,
decay and death.... In Africa ... both governmental and non-governmental agencies ... have adopted the most pragmatic, the most insen-
sitive and the most humiliating policies of development. This attitude
either says: "the people don't know anything, so let's ignore them
completely," or "let's sink a few wells and sell them family planning."

Within this view of development in Africa, nobody—but absolutely
nobody—is asking about what is happening to the human body and
the human mind at the end of a hard-working day. And Africans have
been working hard for a long time. We have a continent filled with
more than 500 million of the most tired people in all history. We have
been exhausted for more than 500 years. Today's Africans cannot afford even the mere notion of vacation, holiday, or entertainment. People have lost touch with earlier forms of rest and have not acquired
any new ones. How do we get even our memories to function at all
when we are not rested or relaxed? What is going to happen to us?

It is an enormous question. When we zero in on women, we shall confront a plight so grim it will break your heart.[7]

Because most programs for women's economic development, education,
and political equality either bow to patriarchal culture or try to impose the culture of the developers, they have fundamental conceptual flaws:

• Their economic programs are reductionist, as if everything else would
fall into place if only economic relations were changed. This is a variant of the old
belief that if you can just get women jobs outside the home, they will automatically become equal, a belief that generations of experience have disproved.

• Their education programs see women as an economic resource—in the
World Bank's phrase, "women are the best investment"—rather than as full
human beings. They thus promote narrow vocational training that stops at
functional literacy and low-level technical skills. Women need a broad humanistic and scientific education for the same reasons men do—so they can
understand and appreciate life, give intellectual and political leadership, and
make the greatest social contribution of which they are capable.

• Their programs for equality are flawed by legal fetishism, a belief that
if you can just pass the right laws, women will become equal. Approaches
that focus on law while ignoring culture will not change things sufficiently for
the majority of women; we can all think of countries where women are equal
in law but not in fact. Our problems would not be solved even if every country elected or appointed women to 50 percent of its positions of power, for, in

many countries, these women would be the wives, lovers, sisters, or daughters of important men, or members of a small group of ruling families. Besides, women politicians do not necessarily serve the interests of most women. And even if progressive women held half the offices in a few countries, that wouldn't change the relations between countries.

These approaches are flawed because they fail to address the cultural factors that impede women's progress. Programs for cultural, political, and economic development must work with, not against, each other. It is naive to think that women will be helped by poverty eradication programs dependent on World Bank loans when these loans insist on changes in the national economy that further impoverish the poor, who are largely women. It is absurd to fight patriarchal culture with one hand and fund it with the other, as do international agencies and NGOs that funnel their money for family planning and female education through religious institutions. The aim may be to reach religious women, but the result is to subsidize the growth of a traditionalist bureaucracy that seems committed to the subordination of women. Campaigns for reproductive rights in the United States, Poland, and Nicaragua; the fight against amniocentesis in South Asia or female excision in West Asia and Africa—these are not merely struggles for better health care, but battles against traditional patriarchal culture, and they must be fought in those terms.

Cultural work that asks questions about the position of women is a central element in our strategy for female emancipation, but this work must develop as a dialectic with the cultures that already exist. Culture has a life and rhythm of its own that cannot be laid out on an economic grid or simply "used" for propagandistic purposes. All too often, the cultural modules of development or health projects merely take the cultural values of the developers, dress them in local costume, and put them on stage. This is not what we mean. In the words of Ninotchka Rosca, "When we say cultural development is central, we mean that people need the time and space and access to means of cultural expression to be able to articulate their own social values." This process is as necessary to overall development as roads and wells and health care.

Cultural Domination and Censorship

Until the age of mass electronic communications, most cultural forms were local or national. Cultural indoctrination was carried out mainly through educational institutions. Today, a soap opera produced in New York can be seen within weeks in an Indian or Latin American village.

The media have made possible a new form of cultural domination, the

global monoculture, which has become a threat to cultural diversity and speci-
ficity the world over. Its products are pitched to the broadest level of taste,
emphasizing sex and violence in order to reach as wide a market as possible
with commercials for cigarettes, soft drinks, or beer. Throughout the world,
the mass media are increasingly dominated by commercial cultural products
from the North, especially the United States.

A parallel development has taken place in the publishing industries of
Europe and North America, where production is increasingly concentrated in
the hands of a few transnational conglomerates. Ten years ago, the U.S. publishing industry, for instance, included many medium- and small-sized companies expressing the individual tastes of their editors. While the reading
audience was somewhat smaller and "best-sellers" sold fewer copies than
they do now, there was room for considerable diversity of taste, interest, and
audience. Now the field has been leveled; small- and medium-sized companies have been driven out of business or gobbled up by conglomerates, so that
the major U.S. publishers are now actually a film company, an oil company, a
newspaper company, etc.

These conglomerates make few concessions to individual editorial taste;
their interest is the bottom line, and they see writing as just another product,
like soft drinks or sneakers. "Big" authors are brand names; the publishers'
goal is to have writers who are different enough from each other to create a
brand preference, but similar enough so that all can reach the broadest possible market. "Little" authors are of little interest, no matter what they say, unless they too can be commodified. Publishers may encourage such writers to
direct their attention to some suitably commercial subject; in Chile, they tell
writers, "Your stories are very well-written and beautiful, and maybe we will
publish them someday but, for the moment, could you write a special story for
us about this or that other subject?"[8] Similarly, Northern publishers stress the
importance of turning out a book every two years, on schedule, preferably all
similar in length, style, and subject matter, in order to create a predictable
product line.

It will soon be possible, if it is not already, to go into the bookstores in
the commercial section of any city in the world and find only the same ten international "big best-sellers," written in the North. Local literature and individual, idiosyncratic voices that emphasize language and expression will have
been driven to the margins. This has already happened in the United States, as
the poet Adrienne Rich describes:

Here is a chain bookstore, stacked novels lettered in high-relief luminescence, computer manuals, intimacy manuals, parenting manuals, investment-management manuals, grief-management manuals, college-entrance manuals, manuals on living with cancer, on channeling, on how to save the earth.... I'm on a search for poetry in the mall. This is not sociology, but the pursuit of an intuition about mass marketing, the so-called free market, and how suppression can take many forms—from outright banning and burning of books, to questions of who owns the presses, to patterns of distribution and availability.[9]

The growing world domination of the North American commercial monoculture Rich describes is an extremely unhealthy development, the equivalent in culture to the hegemony of commercially bred seeds and the practice of monoculture in farming. Both drive out diversity. Both impoverish the soil they feed on. Both produce sterile seeds without a living relationship to their environment.

Conservative politicians and religious demagogues react to the commercial monoculture by calling for censorship. Frightened by the violence and the exploitative use of sex in the media, some in the women's movement echo their cry. As writers, we know this is not the solution, for there is no government that we trust enough to give it control over our access to art and information. We know the first people any government censors are its critics, and that anti-pornography laws have in the past often been used against women who did sex education or expressed an antipatriarchal view of sexuality. With censorship, pornography merely gets driven to the back streets and becomes a profitable illegal business, while people who offer new, critical ideas or agitate for human rights are jailed, driven out of the country, or killed.

Our dislike of censorship does not, however, mean we think all forms of cultural expression are equally benign or that the free market will encourage the best to prevail. We are repelled by the cult of violence in Northern commercial culture and the way its mass media sexualize and racialize every aspect of life, down to the exploitation of racial stereotypes and eroticized images of children in advertising campaigns. But we believe this degradation should be fought by methods that strengthen the women's movement rather than the state. Such methods include satire, public protest, criticism, consumer boycotts, and the creation of independent cultural productions by writers, artists, and filmmakers whose values are not shaped by the market.

Our problems lie not in creating such works but in finding ways to get them into the hands of those who need them. When we try to do so, we run into the censorship that, in one way or another, confronts all genuine social critics and that, when added to the disabilities piled on women simply because of gender, poses a considerable obstacle to the right of free expression.

What Do We Mean by Gender-Based Censorship?

Our definition of censorship is broader than that used by most human rights organizations, which see censorship as the silencing of writers by "jailers, assassins, or official censors."[10] We define censorship as any means by which ideas and works of art that express views not in accord with the dominant ideology are prevented from reaching their intended audience. Such works may be seized or banned; they may be ignored, defamed, diminished, or purposely misinterpreted in order to silence their authors and maintain the existing order.

Every society has some degree of censorship, which it carries out by its normal means of social organization and control. In a military dictatorship, censorship is exercised by the military; in a communist country, by the "dictatorship of the proletariat"; in a market-driven society, by market forces, though the state may be necessary if these do not suffice.

Women who write on issues of state politics are silenced by the same means used to silence men in opposition, though, in practice, even these forms of censorship are affected by gender. But gender-based censorship, as we see it, is much broader and more pervasive than this official, organized suppression. It is embedded in a range of social mechanisms that mute women's voices, deny validity to their experience, and exclude them from the political discourse. Its purpose is to obscure the real conditions of women's lives and the inequity of patriarchal gender relations, and prevent women writers from breaking the silence, by targeting women who don't know their place in order to intimidate the rest.

While some of those who silence women are government officials or religious fanatics, others are parents who decide it doesn't pay to invest in a girl's education, teachers who discourage girls from having ambitions beyond motherhood, publishers who don't think it worth their while to publish books by women, and critics who are unable to take work by women seriously. Censorship often takes place within the family, where manuscripts may be destroyed, suppressed, or altered by husbands, parents, or siblings because of what they reveal about "family secrets." Fathers or husbands may also suppress or appropriate the work of their daughters or wives because they do not wish them to have an independent identity, and feel the work of women in their family properly belongs to them.

In political groups, gender-based censorship is likely to descend on any woman who blows the whistle on sexual harassment and discrimination. In addition, right-wing movements attack women members merely for violating their traditional role by becoming writers or even working outside the home. Left-wing movements, on the other hand, go after those who place too much emphasis on women's issues or say the oppression of women is not caused by economics alone. Movements of oppressed peoples will chastise those who expose sexist practices that should be talked about only "among ourselves." And feminist movements yell foul at women who question their version of the truth or criticize other women too sharply. Such pressures from one's family or closest associates often lead to the most pervasive form of censorship, self-censorship, that holding-back-inside when one cannot face the consequences of speaking the truth—consequences that can range from loss of love to causing pain to being thrown in jail, pushed into exile, or killed.

Gender-based censorship can also be seen in the economic and political priorities that mandate widespread female illiteracy, and in educational systems designed to subordinate and invalidate women's experience. The terrible illiteracy in which so many of our sisters are kept is not just the consequence of poverty, overwork, and discrimination within the family; it is a social mechanism designed to ensure female quiescence and to deny women a public voice. Attacks on female education are a manifestation of the same desire to keep women silent and subordinate that is apparent in death threats against women writers.

Censorship by death threat is becoming common, particularly in societies at war or gripped by religious fundamentalism, nationalism, and communalism. Rada Ivekovic makes the point in relation to the countries of the former Yugoslavia: "Censorship is the effect of any death threat that is meant more or less seriously. It can come from the militias, armed groups, 'other' ethnic groups. It can be more or less legal and official in areas on the brink of war or near the war zone."[11]

In Algeria, gender-based censorship has taken the form of an explicit war on women, as Islamist militants have targeted women, particularly educated, "modern" ones and women journalists, for rape and murder. While the militants make war on women out of policy, government death squads disguised as militants do so to discredit the Islamists, or simply because they can. Young girls are killed merely for going to school, and more than 200 women writers and journalists have been murdered since 1983. According to Aïcha Lemsine:

> Algerian women writers live under the twin threats of religious fundamentalism and a quasi-fascist military regime. For us, women's issues

are issues of survival, our financial resources are nil, and our psychological balance is weakened by fear and anxiety.... The intimidations of the regime and the threats of the Islamists have one purpose: to reduce us to silence. Fear is supposed to drive us away from critical thinking and writing, or stress and exile render us unable to produce any literary creation, or the need for cash makes us more receptive to the pressures of the government.... For all these reasons, Arab and Moslem women need not only to have their lives saved, but also opportunities to create and write. Our voices must be strengthened; we need a network that will give us space for free expression, publication, and international media exposure.[12]

If female education in Algeria is prevented by murder, in other places it is deterred by sexual harassment, rape, or changing economic priorities that devalue girls. The level of literacy among girls is rapidly decreasing in the new market economies of Eastern Europe. Kenya has been the scene of mass unpunished rapes at girls' boarding schools. In the United States, the system's abandonment of youth has taken the form of withdrawing funds for education, particularly in the inner cities, where most students are minorities. Combined with the influence of the media in sexualizing youth, this abandonment has resulted in an epidemic level of sexual harassment in schools, while many girls see so little hope of further education or a career that they become pregnant before they are 14.

Pressures on female education and discrimination within the educational system add up to censorship, for women without education can seldom find a voice. This is its explicit purpose in Russia, according to Nadezhda Azhgikhina:

If ten and fifteen years ago, schoolteachers wanted all their pupils to enter prestigious high schools and universities, now they speak about the importance of higher education only for boys; they insist on "natural destiny" for girls. The pioneer of this viewpoint was without any doubt Michael Gorbachev in his famous book, *Perestroika,* where he proclaimed the importance of "natural destiny" for Soviet women, "so tired from emancipation."…. The result has been the growth of real discrimination…. In Russia only men can apply to the most prestigious institutes, like the Foreign Affairs Institute (to become a diplomat) or the International Journalism department in Moscow State University. Men have more places in any university department—this is the official position of deans and chairs.[13]

Discrimination in higher education can also be found in North America, where whole fields of study, such as surgery and the "hard sciences," are often closed to women. Those who trespass on these precincts are considered fair game for anything from constant sexual innuendo to murder, like the women engineering students killed by a disgruntled male sniper at McGill University in Canada. Academic women who take the alternate route and concentrate on Women's Studies may not be killed, but their concerns may be marginalized, their work discounted, and their academic credentials questioned. In India, says Ritu Menon, "Those who write from a gender perspective are often charged with 'bias' or with practicing 'unsound scholarship,' while those who are politically engaged are told to become more scholarly and not waste so much time on activism."[14]

Those women who persevere enough to become writers face other obstacles. Even in countries where women have made significant strides toward equality, the pinnacles of culture and politics remain almost exclusively male and are heavily guarded. In 1986, for instance, a world Congress of International PEN, billed as a gathering of the world's greatest minds, was held in New York. Out of 117 panelists, only 16 were women. When women writers called a protest meeting, Norman Mailer, then President of PEN American Center, told the press there were so few women speakers because this was a Congress of intellectuals, and very few women were intellectuals.[15] He was also heard to say that a leading woman writer "dressed like a housewife," that he was not going to let her "pussywhip" one of his male guests, and that these women were just making a fuss because they were "too old to catch men anymore." While a number of male writers supported the protesters, others criticized them for making a fuss and being ill-mannered.

If this was the situation in the United States after 20 years of feminist education and organizing, it is unlikely to be better in countries where the feminist movement is new and weak and the dominance of patriarchal culture has gone virtually unchallenged. Some languages do not even use the same word for male and female writer, making women writers seem even more of an anomaly. Says Nadezhda Azhgikhina:

> In the Russian language the word "woman writer" has a female gender, and using this word is problematical for many because men begin to smile and speak about "some stupid woman things." As a result, most serious poets and prose writers prefer to use the word for "man writer" to defend the quality of their creative activity. Women's creative activity is regarded by men as something inherently non-serious, non-talented, second-rate.... Most important literary critics ... speak about very strong, popular books written by contemporary women as exceptions to the rule.[16]

The situation is even more complicated for women who dare to write about the body or sex, thus becoming "bad girls." In most countries of the North, "badness" is commercially viable and women novelists are encouraged to write bedroom scenes if they wish to sell. In others, writing about sex targets women for condemnation. "In Russia, for instance, fiction that touches on women's sexuality, birth, health and other 'non-aesthetic' things is criticized as being written in a 'dirty style' or 'in bad taste.' A typical statement on women's prose appeared in the national literary weekly, the *Lituraturnya Gazeta*, which said 'women have no soul because their soul is too near to their body.' "[17]

Patriarchal attitudes affect women's chances of getting published, regardless of the quality of their work. Women in some countries are denied publication altogether on the grounds that women should not be writers, or that they write in a manner inappropriate to women, or that they are writing on subjects women know nothing about—for censorship assigns or disallows certain subjects and styles as "appropriate" for women, then attacks women who cross the line. Lifestyle too can become an issue. In Nepal, one established writer had problems after her divorce; publishers said, "We can't publish her; she's not even living with her husband." In Russia, during the Soviet period, publishing houses preferred male authors and published women mainly on March 8, International Women's Day; they still do.[18] Publishers have the same preference in Africa, according to many writers. Tsitsi Dangarembga, author of an acclaimed first novel, *Nervous Conditions,* which was published abroad, wrote about how impossible it was for her to get published at home:

> Part of my problem getting published in my own country was certainly commercial. Fiction, no matter by whom, hasn't a wide market in Zimbabwe; textbooks do…. Into the bargain I was beginning to suspect that the "unsafe issues" I chose to investigate would simply not facilitate publication of my works. As a case in point, one of the rejected plays, "Baines Avenue Way," presented as its protagonist and narrator a woman who earns her living by selling her body to men. Opposite her was a second young woman, this one married, who had suffered a history of abuse at the hands of both her husband and her in-laws. This respectable married lady commits suicide outside the first woman's house, where her husband is entertaining himself. I had the distinct impression that the sympathetic young male editor found these women too nasty to be allowed to exist…. The entire situation was a double bind. It was imperative that someone write about these

issues. Yet once the literature was written no one would publish it.[19]

Politically engaged writers and feminists who write honestly about the conditions of their sex, and whose criticisms hit home, have the most trouble. Often they are unable to remain in their own countries, and some meet the most severe forms of censorship: imprisonment, violence, death threats, exile, or murder. But even when there is no overt government or religious censorship, they cannot reach their audience without a struggle because of obstacles within the publishing industry. Publishing industries in most of the South are small and embattled, while in the North many publishers are interested only in books they think will make money. Most publishers in any country tend to shy away from voices that are too sharply critical, particularly in conservative periods. "We don't want books that are purely negative," they will say when faced with critiques of sexism, racism, or colonialism, or, "Not this sixties stuff again!" Or, "So few black people buy books that we can't afford to publish political books about the black experience."

Ama Ata Aidoo recalls the prominent German publisher's representative who told writers at the Zimbabwe Book Fair in 1992 that Europeans were tired of hearing about colonialism; they wanted to hear about something fresh, something new. Today, publishers in the United States tell women "We've heard enough victim stories," or "The time for anger is past," while those in Chile say, "We must not dwell on the sufferings of the past; this is a time of reconciliation."

If it were not for the existence of feminist-controlled alternative presses, many creative works and works of social criticism by women writers would not be published at all. The novelist Flora Nwapa (1931–93), knowing that African women were unable to get published in their own countries and feeling that Northern publishers lacked enthusiasm for their work, attempted to redress the balance by founding her own publishing company, Tana Press, in eastern Nigeria, to publish her work and that of other African women. Efua Sutherland, the Ghanaian dramatist, began a publishing house in order to make well-written, noncolonialist children's literature available to Ghanaians. Similar responses to gender-based censorship have led to the formation of feminist presses in Asia, Latin America, and the North.

As Ritu Menon, copublisher of Kali for Women, the first feminist press in Asia, says:

> The resolve to break the silence has found an echo in cultures and communities across the world, and has given rise to new cultural forms. All over the world, women have spontaneously, consciously,

deliberately—through periodicals, theoretical debates, books, and journals—created another world, and commented on the world they lived in. In cultures where education was denied to women, they demanded it. Where access to print was difficult, they used posters, songs, and low-cost materials. If some women were diffident about writing, others took down what they said and then published it. All the testimonies by women over the last few years have come to us through transcripts, interviews, documents, and dossiers put out by small groups of women, networks like Women Living Under Muslim Law and Women Against Fundamentalism; like Red Feminista Latinoamericana y Caribe contra la Violencia Domestica y Sexual; like Fempress, Naiad, Firebrand, Sister Vision.

Many writers, however, need to publish with mainstream publishers for economic reasons. They may also fear their work will be marginalized or ghettoized if it is published by an alternative press. But large publishers too may ghettoize work by assuming its audience is limited to women, gays, blacks, or whatever group the author comes from, as if parochialism were inevitable. Booksellers do the same—in Chile, according to Cristina da Fonseca and Marjorie Agosin, booksellers refuse even to put books by women in their windows, saying they won't sell—a self-fulfilling prophecy if ever there was one.

[...]

But the age-old methods of silencing women are not working as well as they used to. Despite all the obstacles, an increasing number of women write and publish, stimulated by the growth of women's movements and often nurtured by alternative presses and magazines. Consequently, traditionalists who wish to keep women in their place have had to turn to more active forms of censorship. Self-appointed free-enterprise censorship groups, often religious in origin, are a growth industry in the United States, where, unlike reviewers, they recognize the importance of children's literature. Each year, Christian conservatives mount national campaigns to keep sex education materials and stories that question traditional values out of the schools and public libraries.

Cases of Gender-Based Censorship

In addition to the forms of gender-based censorship described above, women writers experience traditional political censorship—but even then, their treatment is affected by their gender. To take an extreme example, a male and a female writer may both be arrested and tortured, but only the woman is likely to be gang-raped or publicly branded as a prostitute. And, in fact, the types of censorship that afflict women do not come neatly packaged and separated. A woman's personal life is likely to be part of any smear campaign or indictment against her. And politically active women writers make tempting targets because of their presumed vulnerability, not to mention the perverse titillation that persecuting them seems to provide conservative men. Several years of analyzing cases of women writers have led us to the conclusion that women writers who become human rights cases tend to be heterodox in three distinct ways:

• They remove themselves from the authoritarianism and protection of the patriarchal family. They may refuse to marry, be gay, marry too many times, marry someone from the wrong ethnic group or nationality, or simply decide they don't want to live with their parents or husband any more. In some cases, particularly in revolutionary countries, the "patriarchal family" may be the party, government, or national liberation movement.

• They write about the oppression of women in a way that offends. Often they have too impassioned or militant a voice, a voice that men call "strident" or "too angry." They may give specific examples of oppressed women, naming those who have harmed them and calling the government to account. The more specific their examples, the more likely they are to get into trouble.

• They move out of specially marked gender categories of discourse and trespass in areas considered outside of women's realm, meddling in subjects that men consider their own, like scriptural interpretation, law, communalism, corruption, national conflicts, or war and peace. They thus multiply their enemies and increase their vulnerability.

Even in cases that appear on the surface to be purely about state politics, gender considerations are often raised in the form of speculation about the writer's personal life, and persecution is usually conducted partly through "trials by public opinion" in the press. There are many countries in which any outspoken feminist is immediately branded as a lesbian, and thus further stigmatized and endangered.

Censorship campaigns that draw on puritanical sentiments about female sexuality and notions of women's proper place threaten the freedom of all women. Such puritanism was certainly an element in the most visible case of gender-based censorship in recent years, that of Taslima Nasrin, the Bangladeshi writer who was attacked and threatened with death by political fundamentalists for her views on women and religion, and censored and denied her passport for months by a government embarrassed by her revelations about the persecution of its Hindu minority. Targeted by a long press campaign in which government, Islamists, and the liberal opposition all united against her, Nasrin was eventually driven underground and forced into exile by a warrant for her arrest on charges of offending religious sensibilities.[20] Nasrin's case is not unique, but merely the tip of an iceberg. The writers below were all censored because of their ideas about gender relations, their views on state politics, or both:

• Svetlana Alexievitch of Belarus had her most recent book on the Afghani War—called *Zinky Boys* because Russian soldiers were sent home in zinc coffins—prosecuted in the courts by former generals and the KGB, resulting in the exhaustion of her income by court costs and the confiscation of her research materials.

• Judy Blume is one of many writers of children's books in the United States today whose works are being attacked by the religious right, which wants to remove them from school curricula and public libraries. Other authors under attack include Maya Angelou, Annie Garden, Norma Klein, Betty Miles, Katherine Patterson, and Meredith Tax.

• Lindsey Collen, a writer and activist in the trade union, squatters', and women's movements in Mauritius, was threatened with rape and acid attacks following publication of her novel *The Rape of Sita*.

• Rona Fields, an American social psychologist and expert on terrorism, has experienced both state and gender-based censorship. Her 1973 book on Northern Ireland was killed by its English publisher (Penguin) under pressure from the government and British military intelligence; her 1976 book on the Portuguese revolution was suppressed by her American publisher (Praeger) under CIA pressure; and her academic career was derailed by the fact that in 1972 she filed the first academic sexual harassment complaint against Clark University.

• The "Five Croatian Witches" are five women writers—Slavenka Drakulic, Rada Ivekovic, Vesna Kesic, Jelena Lovric, and Dubravka Ugresic—who, because of their fame abroad and their insufficient nationalism, were subjected to an intense campaign of personal and sexual vilification in 1993, after the breakup of the former Yugoslavia, by government-sanctioned newspapers and writers' organizations. Two of these writers have been forced into exile.

• Bessie Head (1937–86) was born in South Africa of a black father and a white mother. After becoming interested in politics, she was driven into exile in Botswana, where, despite her gifts, she was unable to make a living writing because of sexist and colonialist publishing conditions. Her American publisher, for instance, gave her an advance of $60 on her first novel. She died in poverty at the age of 49.

• Aïcha Lemsine found that when she wrote novels criticizing the Algerian socialist government's family code and its treatment of women militants, her books were banned and she was ignored by the print and broadcast media; only after she wrote a general work about the condition of women in other Arab countries, which won an important prize in France, was she allowed to publish and speak in Algeria.

• Fatima Mernissi, a Moroccan sociologist, had her books *Beyond the Veil* and *Islam and Democracy* banned, making them unavailable to the women of her own country in either Arabic or French.

• Irene Petropolous, editor of *Amphi,* the magazine of the Greek Lesbian and Gay Liberation Movement, was fined and sentenced to five months in prison for "publishing material indecent and offensive to public feeling," namely, an editorial notice requesting heterosexual men to stop writing letters requesting sex from the gay women who put notices in the Personals section of the paper.

• Margaret Randall, a poet and essayist born in the United States, gave up her U.S. citizenship because she needed a work permit while residing in Mexico. After many years of living in Latin America, where she edited an important literary magazine, wrote more than 40 books, and supported various liberation movements, Randall returned to the United States, married a U.S. citizen, and applied for permanent residency in 1985. The government attempted to deport her on the grounds of her political beliefs.

• Eliane Potiguara, a writer and organizer of indigenous women in the Amazon rain forest, was subjected to threats of violence and a newspaper campaign branding her a thief and prostitute because of her advocacy of Indian rights. The real issue was that she organized women and wrote political exposés for *Grumin,* the newspaper of her women's organization, about latifundia and timber baron atrocities (including chemical pollution and payment of Indian laborers in rum).

• Nawaal el Saadawi, an Egyptian physician and writer, had her books censored as pornography because they contained medical information, such as that a girl can be born without a hymen or lose it by other than sexual means. In 1981, she was imprisoned because of her political views. Upon her release she founded the Arab Women's Solidarity Association (AWSA), despite opposition by the authorities, who denied its magazine, *Noun,* a license. In 1991, the government dissolved AWSA, and fundamentalist threats to her life forced Saadawi into exile.

In the United States, a conservative political climate and the mass media's tendencies toward seeing only one trend at a time have combined to make gender-based censorship an increasing problem for even well-established writers, if they have a controversial critique of their society or of the position of women. Andrea Dworkin and Shere Hite have moved from being highly commercial writers to being writers published by small or university presses, while Marilyn French, whose first novel was an international bestseller, had her recent pathbreaking book, *The War Against Women*, reviewed in only five places.

The only way to fight gender-based censorship is to persevere in treating taboo subject matter, presenting critical points of view, and getting them published. Chinese women writers deserve special notice for their determination to write about sexuality and personal life, treating subjects like forced abortion, the one-child rule, prison camps, marital rape, and the traffic in women and children. Latin American writers have refused to let the crimes of the past be papered over by a reconciliation without justice, and have persisted in writing not only about the costs of dictatorship, but about patriarchy as well, despite the fact that they are often branded as lesbians for doing so.

Why Censorship Must Be Fought

The subordination of women is basic to all social systems based on dominance; for this reason, conservatives hate and fear the voices of women. That is why so many religions have made rules against women preaching or even speaking in houses of worship. That is why governments keep telling women to keep quiet: "You're in the Constitution," they will say. "You have the vote, so you have no right to complain." But having a voice is as important, perhaps more important, than having a vote. When censors attack women writers, they do so in order to intimidate all women and keep them from using their right to free expression. Gender-based censorship is therefore a problem not only for women writers, but for everyone concerned with democracy.

Women writers are a threat to systems built on gender hierarchy because they open doors for other women. By expressing the painful contradictions between men and women in society, by exposing the discrepancy between what society requires of women and what women need in order to be fulfilled, the woman writer challenges the status quo. Fadwa Tuquan, the Palestinian poet born in 1917 in Nablus, writes in her autobiography:

> Although confined and deprived of a homeland, my father wanted me to write political poetry…. I was expected to create political poetry while the corrupt laws and customs insisted that I remain secluded be-

hind a wall, not able to attend assemblies of men, not hearing the re-
current debates, not participating in public life…. My commitment to
life weakened as I remained secluded from the outside world. My soul
was tormented because of this seclusion. My father's demands may
have initiated my turmoil, but the pain always stayed with me, taking
different forms throughout the journey of my life.[21]

Women writers like Fadwa Tuquan make a breach in the wall of silence.
They say things no one has ever said before and say them in print, where anyone can read and repeat them. This is a vital step in the creation of modern
civil societies, for civil societies are based on discussion, the public use of free
expression. Social differences can be bridged only when they are discussed
openly and all sides are given room to express their own reality. Any democracy worthy of the name must have room for women's voices as well as
men's. But governments that censor women say, "Our country isn't ready for
this writer. She makes the conservatives too angry. Our democracy is still too
weak to tolerate such extreme views." How is their democracy to become
stronger? Censorship does not strengthen the democratic forces in any society.

Women writers symbolize, in their work and life, the free speech of
women. That is why they become targets, and that is why the global women's
movement and all democrats must defend them even when what they say or
the way they live is controversial. Women have a right to be controversial;
you don't have to agree with someone to defend her right to speak. Women
have a right to be celibate or childless, to get divorced, to be lesbians, or to
have many lovers. You don't have to live the way they do to defend their
rights. A democracy is defined by its ability to tolerate differences. The problem here is not the strength of conservatives but the lack of commitment of
liberals when it comes to defending the free speech of women. When their
own rights are threatened, it's a different story.

The progressive response to an imposed monoculture is not censorship,
but the development of democratic, diverse, lively cultures with room for all
our voices. Cultural development—women's development as full human beings, ready to speak out and take their place in running society—is an essential
part of remaking a world in which the dreadful imbalance between rich and
poor, strong and weak, men and women, humans and other species, is becoming a death sentence not only for millions of people, but for the earth itself.

Notes

This article was first published in 1995 by Women's WORLD, New York, NY. It
was published by Kali for Women in New Delhi in 1995. In 1996, it was translated

into Spanish and published in Peru, and translated into Serbo-Croatian and published in the Belgrade journal, *Pro-Femina*. In 1997, it was translated into Urdu and published in Pakistan, and translated into Russian and published in the nonprofit magazine *Vyi I Myi* (You and We) in Moscow. It will soon be published in Arabic by the Egyptian PEN Club in Cairo and in Telugu, a central Indian language, by ASMITA in Hyderabad; its translator is currently seeking a publisher in Japan. The English version of the pamphlet has been posted on two international websites directed at women writers and activists: aviva.com and womenbooks.com. The board of Women's WORLD would be glad to hear comments. For more information, contact: Women's WORLD, 208 W. 30th Street, No. 901, New York, NY 10001.

1. A term coined by Filipina writer Ninotchka Rosca in 1993.

2. This is the term in current international usage for what was formerly called the Third World or the "developing world."

3. Ama Ata Aidoo, keynote speech at "Cultural Dynamics and Development Processes and Africa at the Century's End," UNESCO Conference, Utrecht, June 9, 1994.

4. Letter to author, March 16, 1995.

5. Mariella Sala, speech at "Write Against Silence," Women's WORLD forum, New York, March 15, 1995.

6. Carolina Maria de Jesus, *Child of the Dark*, translated by David St. Clair (New York: New American Library, 1962), 53. The original edition, *Quarto des Despejo*, was published in Brazil in 1960.

7. Aidoo, op. cit.

8. Cristina da Fonseca, letter to author, May 6, 1995.

9. Adrienne Rich, *What Is Found There: Notebooks on Poetry and Politics* (New York: W.W. Norton, 1993), 30–31.

10. Siobhan Dowd, "Women and the Word: The Silencing of the Feminine," in Julie Peters and Andrea Wolper, eds., *Women's Rights, Human Rights: International Feminist Perspectives* (New York: Routledge, 1995), 319–20.

11. Rada Ivekovic, letter to author, June 3, 1995.

12. Aïcha Lemsine, manuscript essay, 1995, in Women's WORLD collection.

13. Nadezhda Azhgikhina, "Culture and Censorship from the Russian Side," June 11, 1995, manuscript in Women's WORLD collection.

14. Ritu Menon, manuscript notes, 1995, in Women's WORLD collection.

15. "Women at PEN Caucus Demand a Greater Role," *New York Times*, January 17, 1986. The protest was organized by Grace Paley and Meredith Tax, who followed it up by organizing a Women's Committee in PEN American Center. In 1989, Tax began to try to form a similar committee in International PEN, which was done in 1991. By 1994, a number of leading women in the International PEN Women Writers' Committee had become convinced that the problem of gender-based censorship was so serious and extensive that it necessitated an independent organization. They organized Women's WORLD, of which Paley is chair and Tax president.

16. Azhgikhina, op. cit.

17. Ibid. This criticism has been made of the young women writers Marina Paley, Svetlana Vasilenko, and Yelena Tarasova, and particularly of the eminent Ludmila Petrushevskaya.

18. Azhgikhina, op. cit.

19. Tsitsi Dangarembga, "This Year, Next Year," *Women's Review of Books,* Wellesley, MA, July 1991.

20. The Women Writers' Committee of International PEN was heavily involved in her defense. The difficulties in this case helped convinced many of us to form Women's WORLD.

21. Fadwa Tuquan, "Difficult Journey—Mountainous Journey" (1984), in Margot Badran and Miriam Cooke, eds., *Opening the Gates: A Century of Arab Feminist Writing* (London: Virago, 1992), 27–29.

EXPANDING CIVIL SOCIETY, SHRINKING POLITICAL SPACES

The Case of Women's Nongovernmental Organizations

Jael Silliman

Collective action from the local to transnational has increased exponentially in the "Third World" over the past two decades. An array of groups, loosely identified as nongovernmental organizations (NGOs), now carry out a broad spectrum of activities, including formulating and implementing social and development programs, promoting social justice and rights, protecting the environment, monitoring governments and selected agencies, and numerous other functions. They encompass neighborhood, professional, service, and advocacy groups. Some are secular, while others are religiously affiliated. They raise funds from a variety of sources, including their membership, donors, governments, national and international organizations, foundations, and the sale of products or services. These nonprofit associations span the political spectrum. By and large, in the popular imagination and in much of the literature, they are idealized as organizations through which people, unmotivated by profit or politics, act from a sense of obligation to achieve a social good. While NGOs do play important roles in social and political development and are sites for democratic change, many NGOs actually enable the privatization and the liberalization of nationalized economies. The growing number of women's NGOs illustrates the challenges that the NGO sector faces.

In many instances, the widespread reliance on NGOs is an indictment of the state's failure in social development. Many NGOs foster democratic practices and supplement the needs of citizens where governments have failed in addressing these tasks. Today, NGOs deliver more official development assistance than the entire United Nations system (excluding the World Bank and the International Monetary Fund).[1] The financial resources, expertise, and access to information technologies concentrated in NGOs sometimes exceed those of smaller governments. NGOs are considered by the development establishment as *the* answer to the difficulties experienced by government-led development and are urged to take over some aspects of development from "autocratic, inefficient and corrupt states.... They are [to] provide countervailing power to government expansionism; [to] strengthen people's ability to hold public servants and politicians accountable for their [in]actions; and [to] foster democratic change by expanding social pluralism."[2]

A neoliberal agenda charted by the major lending institutions (the Bretton Woods Institutions, BWI) and donor agencies has shaped development policies and programs in many countries.[3] This economic paradigm views markets and private initiatives as the most efficient mechanism for achieving economic growth, and for providing most services to most people.[4] NGOs, because they are considered more cost-effective, are favored over governments in efforts to extend welfare services to those unreached by the markets. In many instances, NGOs have become the "preferred channel for service provision," and are a "deliberate substitute for the State."[5] The neoliberal agenda positions NGOs as vital to a thriving civil society for their roles in building democracies.

Women's NGOs are among the fastest-growing groups within the NGO sector. While one may expect that women's NGOs differ from other NGOs, in fact they mirror what is occurring throughout the NGO sector. Many women's NGOs too are being restructured in keeping with the dictates of a neoliberal political and economic agenda. In this essay, I show how women's NGOs are often co-opted through the process of institutionalization, and examine the transformations being wrought in their structures by the interventions of funding agencies. I lay bare and discuss the tensions that are developing between professionalized and bureaucratized NGOs and feminist and grassroots movements. I distinguish between social movements and NGOs and assess the ways in which women's NGOs operate within transnational spaces. Finally, I draw attention to ways in which NGOs compete with other political and religious organizations for power and influence.

Defining the Terms and the Turf:
Some Key NGO Definitions and Characteristics

The NGO sector is not monolithic. It includes a broad spectrum—from unstructured associations with no funds comprised of a handful of volunteers who espouse a social cause, to elaborate organizations with broad membership bases, large budgets, professional staff, and considerable political clout. There are both "David" and "Goliath" NGOs. NGOs may, on occasion, work together, remain apart, or be pitted against one another on ideological grounds, or be divided around issues relating to differential access to power and resources. NGOs straddle the political and social spectrum as well; they may embody the philosophy and practice of a range of ideologies including Marxist, liberal, conservative, traditionalist, religious, socialist, radical, and others, or a combination of these and other ideological strains. While there is now a mandate for NGOs to be active formulators and participants in building "civil society," the appropriate roles for and definitions of NGOs are contested.

The core element of the NGO approach is to induce social change through the organization of people into nonparty structures for collective action.[6] NGOs are established voluntarily and managed independently of government, yet must operate within the laws of the country in which they are located. NGOs have been defined as part of the nonprofit service subsection of the private sector.[7] A primary distinction made between NGOs and the private sector lies in the latter's use of the market to service its clientele, whereas NGOs provide social subsidies.[8] Contrary to the dominant trend in the literature, this distinction highlights the similarities rather than the differences between NGOs and the private sector, which is a refreshing move away from stark categories that often do not hold.

Most NGOs are created and managed by their members and produce or distribute benefits to others. For example, an NGO dedicated to improving women's health might conduct health advocacy and provide health education and services. NGOs often serve as intermediaries that catalyze and broker existing services for clients. For instance, the very same women's health NGO may work as an advocate to ensure that women have access to a government health service. This may include informing women of their rights to health care and letting them know what health services exist, or should exist, in the community. The women's health NGO may create the demand for the service and ensure its utilization through the creation of a pressure and outreach group. NGOs can also serve as a framework through which groups pursuing a common goal can work together. For example, an NGO may serve as an umbrella for members of a community concerned about women's health, such as government agencies, health care providers, women's NGOs, and the private sector, to work together around a common cause.

NGOs can function as lightning rods—raising concerns to shape social policies and public opinion. They incubate new ideas and do legal, scientific, and technical analyses to effect policy changes. They galvanize support and shape, implement, and monitor national and international commitments. They often act as alternative conduits through which external and transnational agencies deliver funds and expertise to local communities, bypassing governments in this process. Many NGOs have become, in effect, guardians of the welfare of hundreds of thousands of poor people, and are watchdogs against government malfeasance and the evasion of accountability. As the potential for NGOs to affect policy has increased and their access to funds has expanded, so the term "NGO" has been stretched to suit a growing number of interest groups. This has led to many debates among scholars and activists regarding what organizational entities can be legitimately defined as NGOs.

This debate played out at the series of recent U.N. conferences. Transnational corporations (TNCs) attended the U.N. conferences, identifying themselves as NGOs. TNCs created business and industry advocacy organizations in the guise of NGOs in order to play a role in various U.N. and other international forums. According to the Women's Environmental and Development Organization (WEDO):

> TNCs depend on trade associations that are granted official non-governmental organization ... status which allows business representatives to observe and participate in official meetings. From this vantage point, they can circulate position papers, meet with delegates, gather information as do other NGOs.... The wealth of TNCs allows them greater political reach, far more than any non-profit organization, small business or women-owned business.[9]

In this way, TNCs have the opportunity to influence international agendas, and their economic clout gives them an unfair advantage. Whether business-interest NGOs should be dealt with in the same manner as public-interest NGOs is a subject of debate; however, there is broad agreement that NGOs are distinct from profit-making corporations. NGOs are not created to make profits but to serve a social purpose in the public interest. Distinctions need to be made between economic actors that seek to fulfill their own interests and social, cultural, and environmental organizations that develop public interest policy.[10]

Many within the women's movement stress the need to make clear distinctions among various types of NGOs. For example, women's health organizations at the March 1995 NGO preparatory meetings leading to the Fourth World Conference on Women adopted a resolution banning the participation of TNCs in their caucus meetings. They wanted to ensure that public interest NGOs were free to meet, reach consensus, and plan without the presence and influence of business interests.[11] They contested the monolithic representation of NGO voices in international forums, arguing that subsuming all NGOs under one category privileges the larger and more conservative groups, and drowns out alternative, less well funded voices. The need for NGOs' accountability to their own immediate constituencies, and to companion actors in movements for social transformation, were serious concerns.[12] Thus, as the potential power of NGOs to affect public policy and debates has increased, there are new contenders that seek to have a voice in international forums of significance.

NGO Expansion and Diversity of Forms

While it is impossible to make generalizations about NGOs for political or analytical purposes, it is necessary to understand the forces that fuel their rapid expansion and increase their political muscle. NGOs have proliferated and evolved significantly in size, funds, scope, character, influence, and transnational dimensions since the 1970s. Except for a few countries where authoritarian regimes severely limit civil society, NGOs have taken firm root. Some analysts have described the Third World as being swept by a "quiet" NGO revolution, and one analyst has gone so far as to suggest that the growth of NGOs in the late 20th century may be as significant as the rise of the nation-state in the late 19th century.[13] Attempts to quantify the number of NGOs estimate them to be in the millions.[14] In response to the phenomenal growth in NGOs, a complex of alliances, networks, and coalitions has been forged to connect various NGOs and strategically push forward the range of issues they represent. Increasingly, some NGOs are being consulted in the development of policy objectives, and NGOs have had success in pushing even the more powerful governments toward changing the tightly closed world of government negotiations.[15] For example, the World Bank consults with NGOs on several of its initiatives. Governments have had NGO members as part of its official delegations in preparation for a series of United Nations conferences that took place in the 1990s, starting with the Summit for Children in 1990 and culminating in the Fourth World Conference on Women in 1995 in Beijing.

NGO roles and functions vary across geography, reflecting situationally and historically specific processes. For example, the predominance of lobbying groups, grassroots voluntary organizations, and nonprofit community-based services in supplementing a weak welfare state characterize the NGO community in the United States.[16] The character of these civic organizations are extremely different from NGOs in Africa that have been shaped "by colonialism, post-colonial politics of development, and the funding priorities and practices of Northern development agencies."[17] Political traditions and historical experience in Latin American countries like Chile and Brazil have emphasized human rights as a central concern, whereas poverty alleviation is a major priority in South Asia.[18] International interest in improving the position and status of women has led to a great deal of outside assistance for women's NGOs in many parts of the Third World.

The politics and activities undertaken by NGOs determine the type of support they receive; the staff or volunteers they attract; and their relationship to social movements, the state, and funding sources. For example, NGOs that challenge accepted power structures and hierarchies at the community level tend to be more controversial than NGOs that seek to provide health care or other forms of development assistance. Moreover, the impact of an NGO trying to change power structures or dominant social values cannot be easily quantified through standard evaluation procedures to fit neatly into a project report for a funding agency or government. Such NGOs find it difficult to gain financial support from local or outside sources. Consequently, they tend to attract more idealistic volunteers and do not rely on professional staff.

Women's NGOs: Current Concerns and Commitments

Neoliberal women's NGOs that adhere to or enhance international or government priorities have found it easier to attract funds than NGOs promoting alternative or radical agendas. For example, as international agencies have deemed that family planning and birth control are central for the development process, they have generously funded NGOs, including women's NGOs, that carry out these functions. International directives and imperatives make more funds available to groups seeking to improve the "condition" of women rather than transforming the position of women. Women's practical needs are prioritized over their strategic needs. As many women's NGOs seek to improve women's condition by providing them with resources, access to health care, credit, skills training, etc., they have expanded rapidly in the last two decades.

Thus, the more formalized women's groups that provide direct services have grown in number and power relative to consciousness-raising, grassroots women's groups formed to challenge patriarchal ideology. In fact, some women's NGOs have been so successful in providing services that this has led, in some instances, to the withdrawal of the government from providing these services. Donor agencies now often prefer to fund NGOs rather than governments to provide some basic services. In other instances, women's NGOs have stepped in to fill the vacuum when governments have withdrawn from providing health care and other services to comply with structural adjustment formulations. For example, in Peru, when the government withdrew food subsidies, women, through their own neighborhood and NGO associations, filled the void even when no support was forthcoming.

In many cases an NGO's priorities may be donor-driven and donor-controlled (such NGOs even have their own term, DONGOs, or donor-organized NGOs), which may distort or divert local priorities and the character of NGO interventions. For example, the emphasis on controlling women's fertility as part of an environmental agenda that has been pushed by many foundations and donor agencies has further consolidated population-control initiatives rather than strengthened valid environmental interventions. The example below illustrates the changes being wrought in NGOs:

> While the impetus for many of those in the NGO movement draws upon these local cultural patterns of social welfare and redistribution, today NGO programs are more likely to operate under market principles.... As these values come to shape both the organizational strategies of the sector and the criteria of evaluation and assessment, there is a loss of commitment to the principles of reciprocity, obligation and community solidarity.[19]

In this process of becoming more "accountable," many women's NGOs have come to replicate the corporate model of organization.[20] This is a far cry from the small groups of women who came together in the 1960s and 1970s in many parts of the North and the South to raise consciousness, exchange views, and improve the situation of women. Joni Seager in *Earth Follies* and Mark Dowie in *Losing Ground* provide insightful critiques of the corporatization of mainstream environmental NGOs and its consequences. No such studies track the mainstreaming of women's groups where the same process is under way. However, glossy publications, high-powered seminars, and workshops conducted in lavish NGO quarters around the world have an increasingly common look whether they are environmental or women's NGOs.

Consumed with the responsibility of providing services and busy preparing project proposals, plans, and evaluations to donor specifications, many women's NGOs have become less willing or able to advocate for the political, social, and cultural change that was, in many cases, their original intention. Being burdened with providing services and depending on funding agencies to pay their rapidly increasing program, staff, rent, and other institutional costs means NGOs spend a lot of time in maintenance activities; they become more hesitant to take more politically risky positions in fear of losing their funds. In addition to setting forth criteria for funding, donors sometimes, by virtue of the funding they make available, appoint individuals to carry out a particular set of activities. When authority is conferred from the outside, the "appointed" individuals may or may not represent whom they claim.

This is not to say that all NGOs that are institutionalized necessarily become co-opted and incapable of effecting social change. However, there is a strong tow pulling NGOs to meet the directives of donors, to provide concrete services so that their effectiveness can be gauged and funds bestowed accordingly. Their funding is based on their records of "achievement," which are typically donor-defined.

Resisting "institutionalization," while a challenge, can be a source of great strength. Take the case of the Green Belt Movement (GBM) of Kenya that is spearheaded by Wangari Maathai. The GBM is acknowledged internationally as among the most effective environmental and women's NGOs. It consists of more than 50,000 members organized in more than 2,000 local community groups in 27 administrative districts of Kenya.[21] Since its inception in 1977, this grassroots, primarily women's network has planted more than ten million trees, reduced deforestation, and enabled communities to reap the benefits of balanced tree harvesting. The GBM has provided additional income and employment opportunities for rural women involved in the tree-planting campaign while fostering political consciousness and grassroots mobilization. The GBM has challenged the Kenyan government to protect the public interest. It has been able to do so while resisting institutionalization. In fact, its lack of institutionalization is underscored by a conspicuous absence of icons such as permanent headquarters or bureaucratic procedures (except for payment procedures). "The GBM has operated out of Mathai's three-bedroom bungalow.... Indeed, the only tangible icon of institutionalization is the routine of tree planting."[22]

I would argue that resisting institutionalization and "professionalization," as the GBM has deliberately done, has in no way lessened its effectiveness. In fact, I would go so far as to argue that it has allowed the GBM to act independent of political pressures, as the organization's survival does not rest on donor or government approval but on its members' tree-planting actions and the ability to galvanize them into political action. However, donor priorities and the new roles being assigned to NGOs are steering many in another direction, leading toward the mainstreaming of the NGO sector.

NGO–State Relationships

Numerous NGOs are controlled by governments and/or corporate interests and used to further their objectives. A striking example of government control over an NGO comes from Nigeria, though this type of relationship is found in many other settings as well. The National Council of Women's Societies (NCWS) is recognized by the Nigerian government as the only umbrella NGO representing women's interests.[23] All women's groups have to be affiliated with it in order to be officially recognized. A past president of the NCWS comments with unwavering loyalty on the organization's relationship to the state thus: "It's cordial; we owe absolute loyalty to the government irrespective of the government in power."[24] This unconditional loyalty is richly rewarded. NCWS members receive political patronage at local, state, and federal levels. This close and cozy relationship between the government and the "nongovernmental NCWS" has been interpreted by other Nigerian feminist activists as "direct government interference." They characterize the government's recent involvement and interest in women's issues as aimed at "neutralizing women's autonomous actions and promoting patriarchy and male domination within the female sphere."[25]

Other types of NGO-state relationships include NGOs acting as mediators, linking government agencies and services to local groups, and facilitating the efforts of various community groups to work together. In many countries NGOs must depend on governments for their funds and cooperate with government agencies in return for continued assistance. Increasingly, governments are contracting NGOs to implement policies and services where they are perceived to be more efficient and/or effective than government bureaucracies. However, there is a danger that, in promoting privatization, the government's role in guaranteeing the basic rights and needs of its citizens could be undermined.

Many NGOs seek to complement the public sector.[26] For example, many women's groups have a contract from their governments to provide women's health services. Through this process NGOs are drawn into a country's national development administration as the lowest rung of the service-delivery ladder.[27] Some have found this contractual relationship limiting, as the government retains its supervisory and regulatory role. In other instances, NGOs have abused government funds through fraud and corruption. In response, some governments are turning back to elected representatives to carry out the functions they had turned over to NGOs.[28] Many NGOs do not have cordial relationships with the state, and these are publicly harassed and censured. While there are fewer examples of governments harassing women's NGOs, there are numerous instances of human rights and environmental NGOs being viewed as enemies of their countries.

Some governments have been concerned about the evolving donor preference for NGOs as agents of development administration and services as opposed to governments. The increasing economic power that NGOs have been granted through outside agencies is viewed as a direct challenge "to the imperatives of statehood—territorial hegemony, security, autonomy, legitimacy, and revenue."[29] However, the sheer volume of economic assistance directly given to NGOs has made some governments see NGOs as a source of much-needed foreign exchange.[30] Current estimates of official aid to Kenyan NGOs accounts for about 18 percent of all aid received by Kenya annually. NGOs provide more than 40 percent of all health care services in Kenya and 40 to 45 percent of all family planning services.[31] The role that NGOs play as the major provider of services is an indictment of the failure of the Kenyan government in the area of social development. NGOs could pressure the government to maintain its commitment to provide basic needs or could step in to fill the vacuum while not letting governments off the hook.

Many African governments, recognizing the latent power of NGOs, view them as socioeconomic assets but handle them "more warily as political challengers whose benevolence needs to be directed and coordinated in order not to undermine the State."[32] Accordingly, many governments are formalizing their relationships with NGOs they regard as powerful economic entities. For example, the Kenyan government passed the NGO Coordination Act in 1990 to control the activities of NGOs. This need to control and constrain NGOs is echoed in Bangladesh, where the government has developed an NGO Affairs Bureau (NAB) to structure relationships between civil society and public authority, as well as those within civil society. In an assertion of statehood, the NAB has the authority to grant permission for NGO operations. The NAB's greater control over NGOs has already been seen where the state has felt its legitimacy challenged, using its legal and coercive power to hold NGOs in line.[33] It has accused many of the leading Bangladeshi NGOs of corruption, irregularities, and anti-state activities.

Most NGOs in Bangladesh have given up strategies to organize the poor, sanitized their activities (if not their rhetoric), and chosen the path of delivering economic assistance.... The decision by some NGOs to de-emphasize consciousness-raising signals that the government has already won the first round.[34]

Some NGOs have fought legislative control. They have mounted a challenge to governmental authority they believe to be authoritarian, stifling, and undermining of political participation. NGOs have challenged government authority and the state as the primary development agent, yet their motives and objectives for critiquing the state and its authority are fundamentally different from those made by the Bretton Woods Institutions. Many women's rights activists warn that the BWI are "destroy[ing] the state's capacity to put barriers in the path of free trade and capital flows."[35]

The BWI strip states of their ability to structure relationships between outside actors (in this case the standard bearers of "free trade") and those within its polity, whose interests it purports to represent. In the face of this onslaught of globalization, states are forced to beat a retreat from providing basic needs while the NGO sector is promoted as an alternative to government-provided services. In a nutshell:

The effect of the New Policy Agenda (grounded in neoliberal economic theory and liberal democratic theory) is to formalize, label, and use NGOs as service contractors, agents of democratization, or sources of innovation. NGOs become instruments for the delivery of services, democracy or innovation on the basis of clearly defined inputs, outputs and NGO interventions.[36]

Women's rights activists fear the undermining of sovereignty and the parallel process of supporting NGOs as more efficient providers of services.[37] They categorically warn:

Although NGOs can effectively influence the direction of public policies, and can implement exemplary programs, no amount of service provision by non-governmental organizations can substitute for the state in some of these critical areas referring to good health, education, clean water and fuel, child care and basic nutrition at reasonable cost for the majority of people.[38]

When women's NGOs have critiqued the state, the intent has been to reform state programs and policies, not to reduce the role of the state in providing/guaranteeing basic needs, as seems to be the goal of the BWI.

Development Alternatives with Women for a New Era (DAWN), an influential network of Southern women within the transnational women's movement, explains that members of social movements have challenged states to be more accountable to the needs of citizens and have worked to make the state and its processes more open, transparent, participatory, and accountable, and to strengthen countervailing institutions to executive power. This includes strengthening the hands of genuinely democratic legislative bodies, impartial judiciaries, and open communications and media, as well as the building of civil society to serve as watchdogs over the state. In sharp contrast, DAWN argues, the BWI, in the process of attaining their primary objective (free trade), have destroyed the legitimacy of states without working to attain serious institutional alternatives. In its searing critique, DAWN charges that "[the Bank's] support for transparency and NGO involvement in monitoring is confined to the social sector and to certain types of environmental effects, but is not part of the discussion around major economic policy loans in which the BWI is involved."[39]

Scaling Up

NGOs are made to conform to their new roles through the "scaling up" process. "Scaling up" is best understood as the flip side to the "scaling down" of government, as promoted by the neoliberal economic agenda.[40] The risks of scaling up are vividly projected in the attempt by the Microcredit Summit Organizing Committee to reach 100 million of the world's poorest families, especially the women of those families, with credit for self-employment by 2005. The Consultative Group to Assist the Poorest (CGAP) is a multidonor effort headed by the World Bank to address poverty through microfinance in developing countries. It builds upon the successes of the Grameen Bank (Bangladesh), Self-Employed Women's Association (SEWA, India), Women's World Banking (started in the United States), and other microenterprise lending projects that provide the poor with credit. Many of the microcredit NGOs are already quite large in terms of membership.[41] However, far greater bureaucratization and much heavier financial dependence on multilateral and corporate donors would be necessary to meet the new targeted goals. The CGAP is working closely with corporations and in fact is seeking to create a strong and committed corporate council.

Microenterprises are being touted by the World Bank and other donor and corporate entities as a panacea for alleviating poverty and as an instrument for women's empowerment. There is a great deal of laudatory literature regarding the way in which microcredit programs, primarily geared toward poor women, have provided women with the means for survival and a pathway to self-sufficiency and dignity. Yet, while the Grameen Bank in Bangladesh is promoted as one of the most successful small loan programs providing poor people with credit, it has also changed social and community norms and relationships in rural Bangladesh:

> Meanings of household and community no longer include expressions of collective responsibility but are recast in terms of the organization of social groups for the purpose of ensuring loan repayments.... The reorganization of the social collective to ensure loan repayment serves as a mechanism of social control rather than an arena for building social solidarity and creating relations of social obligation and reciprocal exchange.[42]

Thus, NGOs in Bangladesh, like the Grameen Bank, have been harbingers of the new international economic order. Their strength in rural areas, which lies in the training, employment opportunities, and credit they provide to the poor, has paved the way for resource extraction, and has provided access to a source of cheap labor and markets while privatizing social relations.

The Grameen Bank, a leader in the NGO sector, is charting ways to reduce government's role in providing welfare. Critics of the microcredit approach argue that the Grameen Bank model has sparked a movement to dismantle development initiatives and decentralize anti-poverty programs. Its ultimate objective seems to be geared toward the privatization of welfare with "shoeless women lifting themselves up by their bootstraps."[43] As part of this process, Muhammad Yunus, the founder of the Grameen Bank, has announced that the bank is working with the government to replace the nationalized health care system with a system for poor people on a "cost recovery basis."[44] If his proposals are adopted, it would create a two-tiered health care system.[45] Gina Neff argues that this dovetails with the World Bank's recommendation to create new markets and products for poor people.[46] A poor person's system of health care, paid for by poor people, would work to replace the nationalized health care system. The privatization of health care and dismantling of government programs that are part of the scaling-up process are in line with the political goals and orientation of neoliberal economic agendas. NGOs, whose power and influence dramatically increase due to support from outside agencies, have knowingly or unknowingly been seduced to comply with this agenda. In the scaling-up effort described above, government health services will most likely be eroded and the more political aspects of microenterprise lending, such as the emphasis on women's empowerment and challenging oppressive structures that is the goal of women's groups like SEWA, will most likely be sidelined.[47]

While the microenterprise program is a specific case depicting the political and economic ramifications associated with the scaling up of the microenterprise industry, Robert Chambers,[48] in a more general discussion, describes how pressures to disburse funds drive donor staff to dominate program and project agendas. He explains how large donors see the "absorptive capacity" of NGOs as "a restraint that hinders and delays expenditures." This makes donors push NGOs to spend more and faster to meet their project goals. In the rush for NGOs to spend, donor dominance is reinforced and the pattern of scaling up NGOs is affirmed. Thus, "logic forces the local to fit its imperious frame," reinforcing North-South hierarchies in this interaction. He notes:

> As bilateral and multilateral donors divert more of their funds to NGOs ... [NGOs] undertake more of the service functions previously performed by governments, they become more like hierarchical government organizations. This threatens the loss of some of the supposed comparative advantages of NGOs including sensitivity to local conditions, commitment to the poor, honest reporting.[49]

Other critiques discuss how the creativity of NGOs is stifled by donor imperatives that derive from a view of development as "essentially linear and predictable." These outside forces are transforming NGOs into routine service providers.[50].

The current large-scale USAID Population Assistance Program in Uttar Pradesh, India, underlines another set of problems associated with scaling up. Funds for this family planning initiative will be largely channeled through U.S. and Indian NGOs. Because of the scale of the project, the funds will be targeted toward more established groups that have the bureaucratic infrastructure and credibility to administer and manage larger grants. These NGOs will be more comfortable with the ideology, goals, and methods of USAID. Dependent on U.S. economic assistance, they will be more favorably inclined toward supporting U.S. foreign economic policy, particularly with respect to free trade and liberalization.

The significantly greater resources will increase the power and influence of these NGOs, compared with grassroots groups that may be more critical of such policies. Their greater funds and training, together with the clout they acquire through association with the U.S. and Indian governments, gives them a significant role in setting agendas and priorities. This further divides the NGO community into the "haves" and "have-nots." The net effect is that attention is deflected away from the causes of high fertility, poverty, and the low status of women, to technocratic and managerial innovations. The "haves" will answer and report to their granting agencies, while the "have-nots" will spend more of their effort in exposing these NGOs and mounting a critique of their practices, detracting from ongoing work. Thus, the influx of foreign funds and the concomitant ideology exacerbates differences, hierarchies, and tensions within the NGO community.

Another way in which NGOs are increasingly being molded by the international donor community to become more alike is witnessed in the drive to make NGOs accountable. Through the increased investment of multilateral agencies, and through technical assistance and training, NGOs are pressured to become more "efficient and accountable," to have greater "internal coherence," and to expand their scope of operations. Because of their outside financial and technical support, NGOs will most likely be more effective in providing family planning services than were government agencies without these inputs. Donor pressures on the Indian government will ensure that family planning programs continue to receive a greater share of already lopsided and diminishing health budgets, at the cost of other health needs. Bypassing the state as provider and guarantor of these services diminishes the government's sovereignty and legitimacy as well as whatever democratic controls exist over government agencies. Furthermore, issues of accountability and deeper foreign market penetration are serious consequences that need to be challenged. Concerned about the Indian government's handing over the social sector to NGOs and the escalation in NGO funds from donor agencies, a women's rights activist raises crucial issues of accountability. She observes:

> Money channeled through NGOs escapes a proper audit. Legally they are less bound than the government to be accountable to the public, and of course, they do not have to contest elections. Donor agencies have been pumping money into the NGO sector, because this sector is much more pliable than the government.... NGOs could be said to be running a parallel government in the country, with priorities determined abroad and with no accountability to the people.[51]

NGO Networks, Transnational Movements, and Alliances

There are many NGO networks that exist at local, national, and transnational levels that are dedicated to promoting women's interests. Formal networks usually provide their members with information, analysis, services, and other technical, training, and managerial assistance. Some serve as a forum for articulating a political platform or to push forward a campaign. Networks may be specialized or multisectoral and may facilitate contact among NGOs as well as with donors and governments. Some NGOs provide a venue for exchange and coordination of NGO activities. The strength of a network lies in its ability to bring many voices to bear on a particular issue and to mobilize a significant sector of the NGO community to take action. For example, WEDO, which represents a network of women's groups and activists around the world concerned with environmental issues, has led to women's voices and perspectives being heard in various important policy arenas. WEDO has been able to lobby for the inclusion of women's rights in major international documents in the series of international conferences that spanned the 1990s. It represents a broad range of women's issues in the policy formulation process. A host of other women's networks promote a women's agenda that has succeeded in bolstering feminists' leverage in global, regional, and national policy arenas. There is growing evidence that transnational issue networks have secured the expansion of women's rights.

The rapid growth of NGO networks can be partially explained by their popularity among donor agencies. Donors feel that, while they may not be willing or able to fund in every area, they can promote an issue by providing the means through which NGOs can communicate with one another, coordinate their efforts, and enhance their effectiveness. While networks have increased the effectiveness of groups, they have simultaneously centralized resources and decision making. Sonia Alvarez, in her discussion of women's networks focused on the series of U.N. conferences, discusses how they have failed to democratize information about national and international policy processes. Many within women's movements feel that networks have led to the centralizing of decision making and have monopolized resources and representation. She adds that

> feminist critics further complain that ... networks are often less inclusive, [and] internally democratic or fluid than the term "network" would appear to imply.... Though actively promoted by regional funders, many regional networks lack a real presence in our countries.[52]

While Alvarez is referring to the impact of U.N.-geared networks in Latin America, these very same issues are raised among women's NGOs in other parts of the world. Moreover, this critique has been made of networks that are not focused on changes at the United Nations. By virtue of having the ability to speak on behalf of a larger sector or determine access to resources or information among member groups, power is centralized in the hands of those who run the network. Some within the network get a more favored status, which inevitably leads to tensions.

Another critique of feminist NGOs and networks questions the appropriateness of national and international policy arenas as sites for feminist activism. The increased attention to these arenas as sites for organizing has sometimes distanced the priorities and organizing imperatives of women's NGOs and networks from the grassroots concerns of local women. This has exacerbated differences and led to splits within feminist movements. Questions remain regarding

> who such professionalized groups represent, who advocacy networks include and exclude, to whom they are ultimately accountable, and to what extent (transnational, national and local) civil society is itself ridden by unequal power relations grounded in class, race/ethnicity.[53]

As NGOs receive funds from an array of donors that often have divergent or competing agendas,[54] so do NGOs have competing agendas, and they vary greatly in their ability to gain access to power and resources. The difference in size and power among NGOs is often donor-driven, and gives some NGOs disproportionate advantages over others. Because of greater access to funds, the larger NGOs have paid professional staff and engage in strategic interventions to influence public policies or provide services. In sharp contrast, many NGOs or women's groups work through more informal organizational structures with significantly smaller budgets and no paid staff. The size, budget, and scope of the larger NGOs privilege their perspectives and politics. For the most part, the more professional and established NGOs tend to take fewer risks and costly political positions and are more amenable to conciliation and compromise. Less institutionalized NGOs find political spaces being usurped by NGOs with the financial means to conduct outreach and follow-up in local, national, and regional meetings.

The concern about bifurcation within women's movements reverberated through the 1990s series of U.N. conferences. Larger women's organizations with the resources and know-how to use the U.N. system to advance their position and agendas seized the momentum and often spoke ostensibly on behalf of others. For example, at the International Conference on Population and Development (ICPD, in Cairo, in 1994), the more mainstream women's health organizations helped engineer the so-called Cairo consensus. This overthrew the previous paradigm that focused on birth control and technological intervention, and made women's empowerment a central tenet of "just population policies." Many women's groups, especially those that have challenged population control policies over the past two decades, were skeptical about the consensus. They argued that there cannot be "feminist population policies," because the notion of population policies is inherently in conflict with the notion of women determining their own fertility. They saw the so-called consensus as the co-optation of women's powerful critiques of population policies.[55] They fear that participation in the U.N. conferences mainstreamed women's movements and straitjacketed women's activism. An analysis of Latin American feminist involvement in the international conference process noted:

> These more professionalized, policy-oriented sectors of the feminist field thus have become privileged interlocutors of public officials, the media, bilateral and multilateral aid and development agencies. Moreover, even when feminist NGOs deny that they represent the [whole] women's movement, they are too often conveniently viewed as such by elected officials and policymakers who can thereby claim to have "consulted" with "civil society" by virtue of involving a handful of NGOs in a particular policy discussion.[56]

Despite the pitfalls, women's rights NGOs have grown significantly in stature through transnational alliances. Work at the transnational level has not only produced international policy gains but in many instances has redirected energy and resources to local issues. For example, the very effective global campaign mounted by NGOs around violence against women put the issues of gender-based violence on policy tables around the world as well as on the U.N. agenda. The 16 Days of Activism campaign in 1991 against gender-based violence involved women's groups in dozens of countries. Hundreds of events, including petition drives, hearings, media campaigns, street theater, and cultural festivals, were organized to draw attention to this issue. Groups participating in the campaign determined their own objectives and activities, conscious of being part of a global effort. This coordinated global mobilization of women forced governments and international aid agencies to create mechanisms and structures and commit resources to address this issue. Capitalizing on the campaign, this network of women fueled the campaign at the U.N. Conference on Human Rights (Vienna, 1993) to integrate gender perspectives and women's human rights into the U.N. framework. They mounted a series of dramatic testimonies on the human rights abuses faced by women on the basis of their gender and demanded that women's rights abuses be seen as human rights abuses. The testimonies demonstrated the failure of existing human rights mechanisms to promote and protect the human rights of women.

While transnational NGO movements have proven very effective in using U.N. venues to promote their agendas and consolidate their power, some argue that this, too, has come at too high a price. For example, women's and environmental NGOs have been key players that have been seemingly strengthened by the U.N. conferences process. The series of U.N. conferences in the 1990s set goals and timelines for governments to deliver on a number of critical concerns. NGOs' participation in preparatory meetings enabled them to influence conference agendas and to have their concerns amplified at the local and international level. As a direct outcome of their organizing, more funds have been allocated to women's projects and women's key concerns. Despite these gains, the involvement in the U.N. conference process had a political cost. By choosing the U.N. conferences as a site for their organizing, NGOs had to operate within the framework set by the United Nations and government representatives. In many other instances these considerations were given precedence over local projects. In many instances NGOs found themselves working under too many constraints. Quite often they had to suggest changes within the confines of a preset framework that was inimical to their objectives.

Consider again the ICPD, generally considered to be a major step forward for women's empowerment, and the introduction of a new population paradigm. NGOs led by women succeeded in injecting feminist impulses into the Cairo Platform of Action. However, while women's rights and reproductive rights were promoted, they were embedded within the context of the dominant neoliberal agenda, which negatively affects women's health and aspirations for empowerment. Not only are the platform's references to financial and enforcement arrangements weak, they contradict the main principles and goals related to reproductive health, reproductive rights, and social development. While urging increased public expenditure, the platform also aims to increase private sector involvement, thereby promoting "the very privatization, commodification and deregulation of reproductive health services that, by its own admission, have led to diminished access and increasing mortality and morbidity of women who constitute the most vulnerable groups in both developing and developed countries," according to Rhonda Copelon and Rosalind Petchesky.[57]

In the context of shrinking health resources in general, the Cairo platform paid more attention to women's reproductive health. Copelon and Petchesky conclude that women's engagement in the Cairo conference process illustrates "the power of women's participation to change the dominant discourse of international politics and law." However, they also point out that:

> human rights and women's empowerment will be used as legitimizing
> rhetoric or as an instrument of male-dominated agendas to reduce or
> augment fertility, to promote religious or nationalist ideologies or to
> advance the hegemony of global market forces.[58]

Responding in the same vein, many within the women's movement
question the utility of investing time and effort to make changes in U.N. documents. Changes made at the international conference level are not structural.
While governments must abide by formal treaties, non-binding conference
statements do not effect changes on a domestic level, especially where there is
no sustained pressure by citizens to adhere to the spirit of these statements and
resolutions. While some NGOs have dedicated themselves to working to
"monitor" the promises made at U.N. conferences, tracking "accountability"
often deflects NGO energies and sucks them into the orbit of governments
and international lending agencies, where their impact is marginal and where
too often their politics are compromised.

Despite these pitfalls, non-involvement has its costs as well. Had
women's NGOs not used these U.N. conference opportunities to shape public
policy, other actors would have done so to the detriment of women's rights
and environmental objectives. DAWN argues that "such (global) action is
critical, because it is difficult if not impossible to challenge global actors, if we
are unwilling to act globally ourselves."[59] While DAWN argues that many
sections of the women's movement are not comfortable with such global action because it is too new and threatening to established modes of thinking,[60] I
believe that the radical factions of these movements oppose this engagement
for deeper reasons. They are concerned about using limited resources to respond to an agenda set by governments and U.N. agencies, rather than using
their resources to work for change outside of these international structures.
Lastly, the question of whether NGOs, through their participation, legitimize
governments and U.N. plans of action is an ongoing debate in the NGO community and is not limited to women's NGOs.

While the pros and cons of transnational networking are still being
thrashed out, the reality is that the women's movement is now thick with networks and loose coalitions. These networks connect up from the local to international level to link NGOs with governments, popular movements, and
funding agencies. This makes it sometimes impossible to extricate a local site
of activism from its transnational contexts. It requires that we understand
some NGOs as "fragmented sites that have multiple connections nationally

and transnationally."[61] For example, a women's group in India resisting population control is often in dialogue with and receives assistance from national and international coalitions of women's health advocates and organizations. While connected, the agendas and styles of these disparate players may not be wholly consistent. While there are certainly advantages to transnational connections, there are also some risks. A Southern NGO may increase its leverage through its transnational connections vis-à-vis national governments and funding agencies. However, in the process it may lose some of its autonomy or find its priorities reordered to fit the dictates of its transnational partners. Moreover, it may be exposed to greater attacks within the country where it is located because of its translocal connections. Thus, in many ways these transnational networks are double-edged swords that have to be wielded with great caution in order to be used to advantage.

Relationships Between NGOs and Transnational Corporations

Transnational corporations have become players in the "development industry." Some TNCs now boldly argue that they should be funded by multilateral agencies as "the most effective agents of development." Linda Powers, the vice president of global finance for the Enron Development Corporation, in testimony before the U.S. House of Representatives in January 1995, evaluated U.S. international aid policies. She argued that in pursuit of greater productivity, efficiency, and technological sophistication, official development aid should be diverted from the state to the private sector. Moreover, she stated that:

> Private parties, like our company and others, are now able to develop, construct, own and operate private infrastructure projects in these countries.... As an adjunct to these projects, to win local support, the private developers are installing substantial amounts of medical facilities, schools and the like to alleviate current problems in these countries.[62]

As TNCs assert themselves in the development arena, many NGOs and the development establishment are seeking TNCs as partners. Again, a striking example is the partnerships forged between NGOs providing microcredit and large corporate banks, as well as donor agencies, at the Microenterprise Summit that took place in Washington, DC, in February 1997. There, it was announced that large corporations will work with NGOs in reaching the poorest with credit. In this partnership, the world's poorest become the new market for TNCs. TNCs will be assisted in their efforts to penetrate these markets by

NGOs, governments, and multilateral agencies.

For some time now, corporations in the United States have been taking over some state welfare functions as the state pulls out of or contracts out these services. Welfare overhaul—that is, contraction of state funding and services and the outsourcing of these services—has "opened up opportunities in the business of poverty." There is now a "wave of business interest in the poor that has swept national corporations traded on Wall Street as they move deeper into sectors traditionally left to religious and philanthropic groups, public agencies, and mom-and-pop operations."[63] (This is not very different from the way that the "development industry" opened up opportunities in the business of poverty overseas and furthered Northern business interests.) Today, corporations as large as Lockheed Martin and Electronic Data Systems are bidding to privatize an array of state welfare and health care services. This is occurring even as critics and shareholders agree that, as "for-profit" organizations, they must place the interests of their shareholders ahead of what is in the best interest of their clients—in this case, the poor.

Distinctions Between NGOs and Social Movements

While NGOs are playing increasingly influential roles in the current political climate, because of the way in which they are easily manipulated and used by internal and external forces whom they must rely on for funds, other efforts and channels that seek to bring about social change need to be encouraged. NGOs should not be conflated with social movements, nor should they serve as substitutes for social movements. While an NGO is an organization, a social movement is an aggregation of people and organizations with a shared set of ideas that seeks to bring about social change consistent with a professed set of values. Therefore, NGOs may be a part of social movements, such as the women's, environmental, and fundamentalist movements, but by definition an NGO is narrower in scope, constituency, and impact.

Social movements and other forms of social dissent "cannot be controlled and are not likely sites for donor intervention."[64] New identities and new forms of politics and culture emerge from social movements, transforming social discourses and structures.[65] In many cases, broad social movements give direction to NGOs to generate a supply of activists for specific causes. In turn, NGOs can and have spurred the growth of social movements; for example, the coalescence of many environmental organizations birthed the environmental movement in the United States in the 1980s, which is far greater in scope than the NGOs that spawned it. NGO coalitions can constitute a significant segment of a social movement. In some instances, NGOs mediate the relations between social movements and states through their representation of the needs of particular groups. They translate the needs claimed by oppositional movements "into potential objects of state administration."[66] In some cases, NGOs have usurped the political space that was occupied by social movements and in this way contained grassroots mobilizations:

> No longer do citizens need to organize on their own behalf and engage in various forms of opposition, including social movements, rallies and other forms of dissent. Instead, the NGO sector, legitimized as a controlled, organized arena of public debate with institutional and financial support from the donor community, has come to speak on behalf of the citizenry, particularly those groups that have been targeted among the needy, women, and the poor.[67]

Though relationships between NGOs and social movements can be circular and mutually reinforcing, they can also be antagonistic. Some NGOs have been accused of exploiting and "selling people's movements at national and international forums." In Latin America in recent years, the relationship between NGOs and social movements has been tense as a consequence of growing "NGOization, formalized networking and transnationalization of the more policy-oriented sectors of the NGO movement."[68] Sharp lines have been drawn between NGOs and "the movement." NGOs have been characterized as engaging in:

> pragmatic strategic planning to develop "reports" and "projects" aimed at influencing public policies and/or providing advice or "asesoría" to the movimiento de mujeres (women's movement) and varied services to low-income women. Though sometimes engaging in similar asesoría and policy-oriented activities, the latter is understood to be made up of "militant" feminist groups or collectives that have largely volunteers, often sporadic, participants (rather than staff), more informal organizational structures, [and] significantly smaller operating budgets, and whose actions (rather than projects) are guided by loosely defined, conjectural goals or objectives.[69]

In Latin America, many activists in the women's movements have condemned NGOs for engagement in

> narrow, state-centric strategies that appeared to respond more to the logic of patriarchal domination than to an alternative feminist worldview. They worried that such strategies too often underplay the importance of continued feminist struggle in the realm of fomenting

gender consciousness and challenging patriarchal cultural norms.[70]

Thus, by designing their strategies to impact the state and respond to their programs and policies, women's discourses get sucked into the political structure rather than transforming the masculinist political structure of the state. This critique is by no means limited to Latin America but reverberates through feminist groups across the world.

Social movements are supported by local people who contribute their energy, ideas, and resources for a cause. They are not registered, they can participate in electoral politics, and do not have to meet either with governmental approval or funding priorities. Consequently, social movements can be less concerned than NGOs about governments taking action against them and can play profound roles in inducing social and political change. They have much greater public presence and resonance and incorporate the interests of a diverse body of actors. Social movements create alternative visions of politics, economy, and society.[71] To sum up the differences succinctly:

> Social movements have guiding principles, ideologies, and goals, whereas NGOs are a loose umbrella covering many different kinds of organizations, only some of which may view themselves as part of a social movement.[72]

The distinctions and differences between NGOs and social movements need to be clear so that they can work in synchrony where they have common goals and objectives.

Conclusion

In the new policy climate, many women's NGOs, like others in the NGO sector, may find themselves further overpowered and overwhelmed as they are given responsibility to deliver ever larger service programs. Critics argue that the new role being offered them is in the *administration of poverty* rather than its *alleviation*. They are increasingly to be service providers rather than those seeking to challenge the system, as they must depend on governments and international agencies as their sources of funds. However, even when they are given adequate resources to implement programs and services, their intervention could undermine the commitment of some governments to guarantee basic needs. NGOs may well be performing services and providing forms of welfare that are the responsibility of governments. Governments in turn will "look benignly and passively on while others carry out the tasks which are theirs, saving them money into the bargain."[73] Yet NGOs are usually poor substitutes for publicly funded services. Overwhelmed with meeting basic needs, many NGOs are no longer in a position to perform political advocacy and oppositional roles that gave NGOs their vibrancy and were in many cases their raison d'être. Donor dependency and escalating budgets render them less able to represent the concerns of the disenfranchised. Moreover, some of the smaller and less well-funded NGOs are outdone by NGOs that play the game as dictated by international donors and international capital, and by other nongovernmental players such as transnational corporations.

The difficult challenge is to balance the state's role as actor, arbitrator, and guarantor of the public good, while creating the enabling conditions for political participation as globalizing forces seek to reduce the roles and responsibilities of the state in the interests of global capital. A legitimate government must create such enabling conditions without stifling political activism, which includes but is not limited to NGO activism and vitality. NGOs in turn must be aware and alert to ways in which globalizing forces may manipulate their agendas and objectives. However, as this essay has argued, there is a real danger that many NGOs are increasingly becoming "an arm, not merely of government but of the new global economic order, however unwittingly, however involuntarily."[74]

DAWN suggests that social movements are best situated to take on the challenge of revitalizing and redirecting NGOs in keeping with their visions of social change. Yet I have shown how global processes and demands have, in some instances, created distance and tension among some NGOs and social movements. I have traced the way NGOs have lost touch or have had little interaction with social movements as they have been professionalized, "scaled up," and manipulated by the agendas of multilateral and bilateral donors. Where this has occurred there is a need for NGOs to realign themselves with social movements and examine ways in which they may have drifted away from their original intentions or popular bases. In this critical mode they can address some of their structural weaknesses and become more accountable "not only to their immediate constituencies but to companion actors in the movement for social transformation."[75] NGOs committed to expanding women's rights must also strategically renegotiate and reshape their interface with states. Where transnational corporations and emerging communal and fundamentalist formations are ascendant, they must strive to carve out independent spaces. It is only through such realignments that NGO efforts may contribute to greater social justice within and between countries.

Notes

I would like to acknowledge the critical readings and comments of several colleagues who helped me work through issues raised in this paper. They include University of Iowa graduate students Pratyusha Basu, Ned Bertz, Laretta Henderson, and Balamurli Natrajan; and my colleagues and friends Florence Babb, Anannya Bhattacharjee, Elsa Chaney, Michaeline Crichlow, Anne Donadey, Laura Donaldson, William Fisher, Paul Greenough, Betsy Hartmann, Ynestra King, Shira Saperstein, S. Shankar, Meredith Tax, Meredeth Turshen, and Eliza Willis, who were invaluable in providing insights, constructive criticism, and further references.

This article also appears in *Social Politics, International Studies in Gender, State, and Society,* Vol. 6, No. 1 (1998).

1. Jessica Mathews, "Power Shift," *Foreign Affairs,* Vol. 76, No. 1 (January/February 1997), 53.

2. Alan Fowler with Piers Campbell and Brian Pratt, "Institutional Development and NGOs in Africa," INTRAC NGO Management Series, No. 1 (1992), NOVIB, 7.

3. Michael Edwards and David Hulme, eds., *Beyond the Magic Bullet? NGO Performance and Accountability in the Post-Cold War World* (West Hartford, CT: Kumarian, 1996).

4. Ibid., 2.

5. Ibid., 2.

6. Barbara P. Thomas-Slayter,"Implementing Effective Local Management of Natural Resources: New Roles for NGOs in Africa," *Human Organization,* Vol. 51, No. 2 (1992), 136–43.

7. N. Uphoff, "Why NGOs Are Not a Third Sector: A Sectoral Analysis with Some Thoughts on Accountability, Sustainability and Evaluation," in Edwards and Hulme, eds., *Beyond the Magic Bullet?,* op. cit., 23–39.

8. Shelley Feldman, *NGOs and Civil Society: (Un)stated Contradictions.* ANNALS, AAPSS (1997), 51.

9. "Transnational Corporations at the UN: Using or Abusing their Access?" women, environment, and development primer (New York: WEDO, 1995), 3.

10. Cernea, in "Non-Governmental Organizations and Local Development," makes the case for grassroots economic associations of people, such as marketing co-ops, credit co-ops, etc., and other production-related economic services, to be considered NGOs. Michael M. Cernea, "Non-Governmental Organizations and Local Development," World Bank discussion paper No. 40 (Washington, DC: The World Bank, 1988), 15.

11. "Transnational Corporations at the UN: Using or Abusing their Access?" op. cit., 3.

12. Development Alternatives with Women for a New Era (DAWN), *Markers on the Way: The DAWN Debates on Alternative Development,* DAWN's Platform for the Fourth World Conference on Women, Beijing, China (Barbados: West Indies,

DAWN, 1995), 43–44.

13. Edwards and Hulme, *Beyond the Magic Bullet?*, op. cit.; L.M. Saloman, "The Global Associational Revolution: The Rise of the Third Sector on the World Scene," Occas Pap. 15, Baltimore Institute for Policy Studies, Johns Hopkins University, Baltimore, MD, 1993.

14. Mathews, "Power Shift," op. cit., 53.

15. Ibid., 54.

16. Myra Marx Ferree and Patricia Yancey Martin, eds., *Feminist Organizations: Harvest of the New Women's Movement* (Philadelphia: Temple University Press, 1995), 8.

17. Alan Fowler discusses how, in the early penetration of Africa, the colonial powers were accompanied by Christian welfare organizations, who together formed a model for formal "non-state service delivery allied to colonial interests." Later, in response to colonial oppression, many African countires established indigenous welfare organizations that provided services on an ethnic and voluntary basis. After independence, all sorts of foreign NGOs provided models for nonprofit service delivery that reflect Northern values and organizational structure. See Fowler, Campbell, and Pratt, "Institutional Development and NGOs in Africa," op. cit., 9.

18. "With respect to *origins,* many NGOs [in South Asia] have been founded by committed middle-class, educated people or professionals who want to do something about poverty alleviation…the great majority of NGOs ... state their major *purpose* as poverty alleviation." Marilyn Carr, Martha Chen, and Renana Jhabvala, *Speaking Out: Women's Economic Empowerment in South Asia* (London: Intermediate Technology Publications, 1996), 6.

19. Feldman, *NGOs and Civil Society*, op. cit., 50.

20. Joni Seager, *Earth Follies: Coming to Feminist Terms with the Global Environmental Crisis* (New York: Routledge, 1993); and Mark Dowie, *Losing Ground: American Environmentalism at the Close of the Twentieth Century* (Cambridge: Massachussetts Institute of Technology Press, 1995).

21. Stephen N. Ndegwa, *Two Faces of Civil Society: NGOs and Politics in Africa* (West Hartford, CT: Kumarian, 1996), 81.

22. Ibid., 86.

23. Hussaina Abdullah,"Wifeism and Activism: The Nigerian Women's Movement," in Amrita Basu, ed., *The Challenge of Local Feminisms: Women's Movements in Global Perspective* (Boulder, CO: Westview Press, 1995), 209–25.

24. Ibid., 218.

25. Ibid.

26. An example of this working relationship is the Bangladesh Rural Action Committee (BRAC), which, by the year 2000, will be active in nearly a quarter of Bangladesh's villages and an expanding proportion of urban slums. By the middle of 1992, BRAC's activities included 8,666 schools, 5,230 for 8-to-10-year-olds and 3,436 for 10-to-16-year-olds.

27. Fowler, Campbell, and Pratt, "Institutional Development and NGOs in Africa," op. cit., 12.

28. Stephen D. Biggs and Arthur D. Neame, "Negoitating Room to Maneuver: Reflections Concerning NGO Autonomy and Accountability within the New Policy Agenda," in Edwards and Hulme, eds., *Beyond the Magic Bullet?* op. cit.

29. Sumi Krishna, Environmental Politics: People's Lives and Development Choices (New Delhi: Sage Publications, 1996), 20.

30. Fowler, Campbell, and Pratt, "Institutional Development and NGOs in Africa," op. cit., 9–10.

31. Ndegwa, *Two Faces of Civil Society*, op. cit., 20.

32. Ibid.

33. Syed M. Hashemi, "NGO Accountability in Bangladesh: Beneficiaries, Donors and the State," in Edwards and Hulme, eds., *Beyond the Magic Bullet?*, op. cit., 124.

34. Ibid., 127.

35. Ibid., 39.

36. Biggs and Neame, "Negotiating Room to Maneuver," op. cit., 49.

37. DAWN, *Markers on the Way,* op. cit.

38. Ibid., 41.

39. Ibid., 39.

40. This was pointed out to me by my Grinnell College colleague Eliza Willis.

41. In 1995 SEWA already had more than one million clients in its credit programs. BRAC claims to be the largest NGO in the world. It serves 11 million households in 50,000 villages with a staff of more than 17,000 fieldworkers.

42. Shelley Feldman, *NGOs and Civil Society,* op. cit., 60. In the Grameen Bank model, small groups of recipients (mostly women) of small loans for microbusiness projects act as guarantors for one another. These groups of women who borrow money also exert peer pressure, making sure that loan repayment is carried out in accordance with the bank's terms.

43. Gina Neff, "Microcredit, Microresults," in Aspects of India's Economy, Vol. 21, October-December 1996, Research Unit For Political Economy, edited, printed, and published by Rajani X. Desai for R.U.P.E. Bombay, India, 68.

44. Ibid., 67.

45. Ibid., 73.

46. Ibid.

47. Programs like the Grameen Bank have long been criticized for reinforcing women's traditional roles. By working in their own small businesses, women are kept out of waged work, and most remain very poor. In addition, many of the loans given to women are directly invested by male relatives, and many women do not retain full or significant control of the businesses in their names.

48. Richard Chambers, "The Primacy of the Personal," in Edwards and Hulme, eds., *Beyond the Magic Bullet?,* op. cit.

49. Ibid., 246.

50. Vandana Desi and Mick Howes, "Accountability and Participation: A Case Study from Bombay," in Edwards and Hulme, eds., *Beyond the Magic Bullet?*, op. cit., 101.

51. Kalpana Mehta, "Population or Development: Search Conference Organized by UNFPA in India," in *Political Environments: A Publication of the Committee on Women, Population and the Environment*, No. 4 (Summer-Fall 1996), Hampshire College, Amherst, MA, 49.

52. Sonia E. Alvarez, "Knocking at the UN's Door: Contradictions in Policy-Centered Feminist Strategies of the 1990s" (paper presented at the XX International Congress of the Latin American Studies Association, Guadalajara, Mexico, April 17–19, 1997), 7–8.

53. Ibid., 8.

54. Between 1980 and 1993 the total spending of development NGOs rose from US$2.8 billion to US$5.7 billion. For further information, see Edwards and Hulme, eds., *Beyond the Magic Bullet?*, op. cit.

55. Jael Silliman, "The International Conference on Population and Development: A South Asian Point of View," *SAMAR*, Winter 1994, New York, 32–36.

56. Alvarez, "Knocking at the UN's Door," op. cit., 7.

57. Rhonda Copelon and Rosalind Petchesky, "Reproductive and Sexual Rights as Human Rights," in Margaret Schuler, ed., *From Basic Needs to Basic Rights* (Washington, DC: Women, Law and Development International, 1995), 355.

58. Ibid., 365.

59. DAWN, *Markers on the Way*, op. cit., 44.

60. Ibid., 45.

61. William Fisher, "Doing Good? The Politics and Anti-Politics of NGO Practices," *Annual Review of Anthropology*, Vol. 26 (1997), 450.

62. Subodh Wagle, "TN's as Aid Agencies? Enron and the Dabhol Power Plant," *The Ecologist*, Vol. 26, No. 4 (July/August 1996), 179.

63. "Deletion of Word in Welfare Bill Opens Foster Care to Big Business," *New York Times*, May 4, 1997.

64. Feldman, *NGOs and Civil Society*, op. cit., 60.

65. N. Frazer, *Unruly Practices: Power, Discourse and Gender in Contemporary Social Theory* (Minneapolis, MN: University of Minnesota Press, 1989), 11.

66. Ibid.

67. Feldman, *NGOs and Civil Society*, op. cit., 64.

68. Alvarez, "Knocking at the UN's Door," op. cit., 6.

69. Ibid., 5.

70. Ibid., 7.

71. Arturo Escobar, *Encountering Development: The Making and Unmaking of the Third World* (Princeton, NJ: Princeton University Press, 1995).

72. DAWN, *Markers on the Way*, op. cit., 44.

73. Jeremy Seabrook et. al, *NGOs and Social Change: A Collection of Es*says (New Delhi: Mulltiplexus, undated), 7.

74. Ibid., 7.

75. DAWN, *Markers on the Way,* op. cit., 44.

PATRIARCHAL VANDALISM
Militaries and the Environment

Joni Seager

Militaries are major environmental abusers. All militaries, everywhere, wreak environmental havoc—sometimes by accident, sometimes as "collateral damage," and often as predetermined strategy. If every military-blighted site around the world were marked on a map with red tacks, the earth would look as though it had a bad case of the measles.

Militaries are privileged environmental vandals. Their daily operations are typically beyond the reach of civil law, and they are protected from public and governmental scrutiny, even in "democracies." When military bureaucrats are challenged or asked to explain themselves, they hide behind the "national security" cloak of secrecy and silence—and it is military men themselves who get to define what "national security" is. In countries that are in the grip of martial law, militaries have an even more free and unhindered reign: with wide-ranging human rights abuses the norm under militarized regimes, environmental transgressions are often the least of the horrors for which critics try to hold militaries accountable, and thus even the fact that militaries *are* agents of major environmental degradation is often overlooked.

Militaries are powerful environmental ravagers. The reach of militarized environmental destruction is global. The most powerful military contrivances, nuclear and chemical "capability," push environmental capability to the limits—past the limits already for some of the radioactive, blighted wastelands created around the world by military testing, dumping, and adventurism.

Feminist analysis can shed new light on the intersections of patriarchy, power, militarism, and environmental destruction. If we want to understand the ways in which militarized environmental destruction reflects gendered processes and dynamics, we might start by focusing on four facets: the culture of militaries and the ways in which such culture shapes environmental agency, the role and construction of environmental policy and regulation, the role of environmental values and perceptions, and the differential nature of environmental impacts. All four of these are deeply "gendered"; all four are key to mapping the contours of militarized environmental relations.

But first, a brief review of the scope of the military environmental problem sets a context for subsequent analysis.

Toxic Tales

Militaries, with a reach from the local to the global, are among the biggest international environmental players. Anywhere in the world, a military presence is virtually the single most reliable predictor of environmental damage. Wherever there is a military presence (whether a base, a war zone, a storage facility, or a testing facility), one will almost inevitably find environmental damage. From Subic Bay to Goose Bay, from the mountains of Afghanistan to the deserts of Kuwait, from small-town Fernald, Ohio, to the South Pacific atoll of Kwajelein, the evidence of largely unfettered environmental "wilding" by the world's militaries is overwhelming and inescapable.

War

The most dramatic, obvious, and often the worst military environmental damage occurs in war. The globe is scarred by dead zones, "no-go" zones, and regions pushed over the brink of environmental sustainability by the actions of militarized combatants. A list of war-damaged regions (many of them still showing signs of environmental upheaval many years after the conflicts have ended) includes sizable portions of: the Falklands/Malvinas, El Salvador, Guatemala, Peru, Honduras, Nicaragua, Haiti, Guam, France, Belgium, Vietnam, Burma, East Timor, Sri Lanka, Angola, Somalia, the Persian Gulf, Iraq, Iran, Kashmir, the Solomon Islands, Papua New Guinea, Rwanda, Uganda, Sudan, Afghanistan, Cambodia, Laos, Mozambique, Kuwait, Lebanon, Yugoslavia, and Chechnya, among other places.[1]

The tools and tactics of war that produce the greatest environmental shock are too numerous and various to catalog in their entirety, but include the use of nuclear armaments and "regular" armaments made with depleted uranium (e.g., Persian Gulf); the hasty and unregulated disposal or abandonment of wastes and material of all types; saturation—a.k.a. "carpet"—bombing (e.g., Vietnam, Iraq, Laos); deliberate environmental sabotage (e.g., oil spills in the Persian Gulf War, Iraq); landscapes and marine environments littered with unexploded ordnance and mines (e.g., France, Belgium, Mozambique, Angola, Falklands/Malvinas); defoliation and the persistence of defoliant chemicals in the ecosystem (e.g., Vietnam, Peru, Guatemala, Nicaragua); "scorched earth" military tactics (e.g., Central America, Sri Lanka, Afghanistan, East Timor, Papua New Guinea); heavy equipment maneuvers through fragile ecosystems (e.g., Kuwait, Afghanistan, Iraq, Sri Lanka); entirely unregulated and hasty construction of war-support infrastructure such as airstrips, housing, and hospitals; and the wanton slaughter of wildlife and "harvesting" of timber, and other trafficking in ecological contraband, to finance combat activities (e.g., Nicaragua, Burma, Angola, Mozambique).

The burden of war is often heaviest in fragile environments—desert, alpine, and arctic—which are also often the environments with the most limited constituency of environmental concern. But environmental damage in a closed system is cumulative and feeds back on itself; whether we recognize it or not, military damage in one place—no matter how far away or seemingly unimportant—has global ripples.

Maintaining "Readiness"

Most militaries aren't at war most of the time. Instead, they are mostly maintaining a "state of readiness": keeping the military machine well oiled, testing weapons, conducting maneuvers. This apparently more passive side of military activity is, if anything, even more dangerous than war for the health of the environment and for the health of anyone who happens to live downwind, downstream, or adjacent to a military base, testing ground, or storage facility. Military sites top the list of the most toxic, most dangerous, and least regulated spots on earth.[2]

One of the reasons why a "normal" military presence is so deadly is that militaries consume, store, produce, and dispose of uniquely toxic materials: in addition to the more conventional materials such as propellants, oils, solvents, paints, and preservatives, military facilities often also house deadly chemical and radioactive substances (chemical weapons, bomb components, metal solvents), most of which are secret and almost none of which are subject to environmental oversight controls. The more dangerous, complex, and secret military activities are, the more grim and dangerous is the environmental fallout. Furthermore, militaries produce and use these materials—"routine" ones as well as the more exotic—in vast quantities. Militaries routinely generate waste end products—including cyanides, acids, heavy metals, PCBs, phenols, paints, and contaminated sludges—that may also include uniquely toxic components.

Bases and other military installations were the sleeping environmental hot spots of the late 1980s, and will be the source of some of the most persistent environmental catastrophes around the world throughout the 1990s. Ironically, sometimes the environmental damage at military facilities only comes into public view when the base is closed and conversion or "reuse" plans are considered. From the mid-1980s to the mid-1990s, most militaries in the industrialized world closed bases; significant numbers of closings occurred in Spain, Italy, Greece, Germany, the United States, Russia, Canada, the United Kingdom, Hungary, Estonia, Latvia, and the Philippines. In all of these places, environmental damage has been exposed during the closing process, and in many cases, plans to turn over the facilities to civilian uses have been canceled because the facilities are literally unusable. For example, estimates of the costs of closing former Soviet bases in Estonia alone reach well over US$4 billion; problems on these bases include fuel contamination of groundwater, radioactive waste, unexploded ordnance (much of which was dumped into the sea by the Soviet military), and leaking storage containers of unspecified hazardous wastes.[3]

The litany of military environmental damage could go on for pages and pages. The extent of militarized environmental damage in the former Soviet Union is particularly staggering: huge sections of the former Soviet Union are environmental hot spots as the result of military dumping, testing, and adventurism.[4] Several small islands off the Scottish coast remain "no-go" zones as a result of British military chemical testing during WWII. The Chinese military dumps nuclear waste in Tibet and tests nuclear weapons in the deserts of northwest China; the Kuwaiti military routinely conducts "live-fire" exercises in the desert; the Russian military continues to dump radioactive waste into Arctic waters; the militaries of Spain, Chile, and South Africa all have been accused of using wildlife sanctuaries for weapons testing.

Militaries, though, do not confine their environmental vandalism to domestic territory. Many of the world's largest military powers routinely export their most noxious activities to overseas territories, colonies, and allies. The South Pacific has been one of the favorite dumping and testing grounds for the world's militaries:[5] the British military tested its nuclear weapons in Australia and the South Pacific, the French in French Polynesia (and before that in Algeria), and the United States throughout the South Pacific. Around the world, from the Philippines to Germany, overseas bases and facilities—typically exempted from local environmental laws, and also beyond the reach of the environmental regulations of the nation of origin—are among the most notorious environmental hot spots.

The list of environmental costs of militaries must also include an assessment of the extent to which militaries disproportionately consume resources and produce pollutants. The U.S. Pentagon, for example, is the largest domestic consumer of oil. Worldwide, an estimated one-quarter of all jet fuel is used for military purposes; each year the world's militaries collectively use about the same quantity of petroleum products as does all of Japan, the world's second-largest economy.[6] Recent estimates suggest that emissions from the worldwide operations of armed forces alone account for 6 to 10 percent of global air pollution.[7] Militaries are the largest consumers of certain ozone-depleting substances. Military technicians kill thousands of animals annually in weapons, chemical, and materials tests; the U.S. military alone uses an estimated 540,000 dogs, cats, primates, and other animals yearly in torturous tests.[8] Modern armed forces are land-grabbers—they appropriate increasingly large expanses of land and airspace for their exclusive use. Modern militaries' appetite for land is growing: while a World War II U.S. Army battalion needed 4,000 acres to practice maneuvers, today's battalion needs more than 80,000 acres.[9] In the 1980s, it was estimated that militaries controlled approximately 1 percent of total territory in the top 13 industrial nations—this may sound small, but it represents an area roughly the size of Turkey.[10] In the Netherlands, the military directly controls about 1.1 percent, but indirect uses account for another 10.5 percent; at least one-third of the ecologically unique but fragile Waddensea is used militarily.[11] In the United States as a whole, the military controls about 2 percent of the land area. In Hawaii, one of the most militarized of U.S. states, estimates suggest that the military owns or controls from 10 to 25 percent of land on O'ahu, one of the main islands, and more than 10 percent statewide.[12]

And finally, an accounting of the high environmental costs of militaries must include recognition of indirect budgetary and policy effects. To the extent that the prerogatives of militaries are given high national priority, domestic programs, including environmental protection, will suffer. Since military and social programs have to compete for shares of limited national revenues (and attention), every increase in military budgets means a decrease in spending in sectors such as health, housing, and education. This is not a startlingly radical observation—in the 1950s, Dwight Eisenhower made the point directly: "Every gun that is made, every warship fired, signifies in the final sense a theft from those who hunger and are not fed, those who are cold and not clothed." Worldwide, expenditures on militaries continue to increase.

Ruth Sivard, a tireless researcher who monitors international military spending, estimates that in constant dollars, world military expenditures in 1994 were about 1.75 times the level of 1960.[13]

What's a Girl to Make of All This?

The distinctive approach of feminism is to look for the workings of gender—the omnipresent if sometimes "invisible hand" that shapes so much of the everyday world. The challenge for feminist environmental analysis is to assess whether environmental affairs may be "gendered," and if so, to what extent such a gender imprint "matters." In examining an environmental event, process, or condition, we should ask whether gendered presumptions, roles, or actions are at work; and if so, whether gender is merely incidental—unattended baggage, as it were, on the environmental journey—or whether it is an instrumental or causal factor in explaining (indeed, shaping) the state of the environment.[14]

I argue that gender is evident—and instrumental—in the militarized environmental arena in at least four main venues: in environmental "agency" (the role and conduct of agents, whether individual or organizational, that are key environmental players); in the construction of environmental policy; in the nature of environmental activism; and, finally, in the differential distribution of the impacts of environmental degradation.

Militaries, universally, share a distinctive gender profile. Everywhere in the world, militaries are deeply masculinized bureaucracies (a fact that is little changed by the introduction of small percentages of women into some of the world's militaries). A robust feminist scholarship on militaries and militarism provides the framework for understanding the links between militaries, militarism, and hypermasculinity; this point need not be elaborated here.[15] If we take as given the understanding that militaries are "distinctively gendered" organizations, then from an environmental interest the key question is, so what?

Does the masculinism that is deeply embedded within militaries and militarism have a bearing on the environmental agency of militaries? A feminist deconstruction of military-environment relations suggests that the answer is a resounding yes: the global devastation caused by militaries is directly a product of the militarized "cult of masculinity."

Natural environments are increasingly the direct target of military aggression; in militarizing the environment, militaries feed on and fuel the masculinist "prerogative" of men conquering nature. Even when the environment isn't a target of war, it is threatened by "normal" military activities in the pursuit of protecting "national security." All the people who are defining "national security" in every country of the world are men, and part of their agenda in defining national security is to protect their male and military privilege. Militaries cloak their environmentally dangerous activities by hiding behind the national-security defense, and they discourage environmentally responsible consciousness. In the military ethos, environmental consciousness is placed a distant second to more "serious" concerns about national security—and thus, men who would place environmental priorities above military ones are often cast as unpatriotic, even effeminate. This gender dynamic is hardened by the fact that, worldwide, most of the environmental grassroots activists are women, and most of the military bureaucrats they have to confront are men. The effects of militarized degradation of environments are not evenly distributed; men in the upper echelons of military hierarchies are the least likely to directly experience or even witness these impacts.

The disregard for the environment, and the complacency and disinterest with which militaries regard their environmental transgressions, hangs on a scaffolding of military privilege—a privilege that, in turn, is deeply rooted in a structure of militarized masculinity. Some of the structural components in military culture that produce an environmentally destructive ethos include a cultivation of hypermasculinity, secrecy, fraternity, and an inflated sense of self-importance.

Making a Culture of Destruction

The cultivation of hypermasculinity is structurally central to modern militaries. Militaries, especially at war, must construct a threatening enemy to bolster a macho drive in soldiers who might otherwise not be especially invested in their masculinity.[16] In recent warfare, the environment itself has been woven into the mix as a militarized target, and "ecocide" provides another arena for the play of militarized manhood. U.S. herbicide teams in the U.S.-Vietnam War rallied with the macho motto "Only We Can Prevent Forests," a play on the popular conservation slogan "Only You Can Prevent Forest Fires." In the Persian Gulf War, U.S. soldiers were widely portrayed—for the domestic audience—as taking on not only an evil enemy, but a forbidding environment, the "harsh desert wastelands" of the Middle East. The fact that nature is widely conceptualized as female adds the "allure" of a sexualized assault to military attacks against the environment; the military pendulum swings between protecting and assaulting feminized lands.[17] Men pitting themselves against the environment is not new; what military bureaucracies are doing is shaping this nature-conquering impulse into a war strategy.

Militaries use sanitized language to describe their activities as a means of distancing themselves from the consequences of their own actions. "Technostrategic" language, as Carol Cohn terms it,[18] plays an important role in warfare—it allows individual soldiers to perform sometimes horrible tasks with equanimity. Thus, human death is talked about as "collateral damage," plans to incinerate cities are described as "countervalue attacks," fusion bombs are called "clean weapons." Similarly, militaries use familiar and friendly terms to describe the environmental damage they inflict. The patterns that bombs make on the landscape are called "footprints"; saturation bombing is referred to as "carpet bombing"—as Helen Caldicott remarks, "Carpets are nice and soft and homely and domestic ... so carpet bombing must be okay."[19] Media commentators on military activities are often complicit in perpetuating deceptive descriptions of military damage. Helen Caldicott describes the commentary on the start of the Persian Gulf War:

> By God did they have a ball! You'd think it was a Superbowl match! Who were the commentators? White male Americans ... and were they excited! "Did you see that one? Look, Baghdad's lit up like a Christmas tree!" Christmas tree???[20]

More "ordinary" environmental transgressions by militaries also depend on a heady mix of masculinism, privilege, and power. After-the-fact investigations of military environmental neglect and damage, whether in the Soviet Union, Britain, or the United States, reveal that, in virtually every case, at least *some* base commanders, plant managers, or government officials had full knowledge of the ongoing environmental violations and did little to prevent or stop unsafe practices. While this fact may raise questions about the moral character of the individuals involved, more to the point, it raises serious questions about the institutional and structural contexts that shape military culture—a culture that appears to have a certain predictable universality: militaries from cultures and states that have little else in common share a distinctive environmental sensibility—namely, one of disregard.

Militarized secrecy is one key to understanding the social architecture of military culture. The veil of secrecy surrounding military programs protects militaries from public accountability, it imbues military actions with a sense of higher purpose, and it allows military men to feel invulnerable.

As cultural currency, the value of secrecy inflates with the power of the weaponry—as does the environmental cost. The U.S. military nuclear program—which has poisoned dozens of sites and thousands of square miles in the United States—illustrates the potent mix. The U.S. military jump-started the global nuclear bandwagon in the early 1940s in an urgent effort to develop—and use—the first nuclear weapons. A spokeswoman for the U.S. Department of Energy, commenting on the current state of environmental disaster at every one of the U.S. nuclear weapons facilities, explained: "We did inherit a lot of stuff. In 1943 the guys were doing the best the best they knew how, and the people who came after them didn't question what they'd done."[21] Robert Alvarez of the Environmental Policy Institute also identifies the early years of the nuclear program as crucial in setting the tone and direction for today's military nuclear programs: "From the beginning the program has been run with isolation, secrecy, self-management, and compartmentalization."[22]

Isolation and secrecy in the nuclear weapons program is not just a legacy of the 1950s. Managerial attitudes about environmental regulation of nuclear facilities appear to be almost as disdainful in the 1990s as in the midst of World War II; one Environmental Protection Agency official recently characterized the Department of Energy's approach toward U.S. environmental laws as "Look, Buster, don't bug me with your crap about permits. I'm building atomic weapons."[23] Surveillance and harassment of whistleblowers has been documented at several Department of Energy nuclear sites in the United States, including the Oak Ridge National Laboratory and Hanford.[24] In the early 1990s, an independent government task force found evidence that managers at Hanford and several other weapons facilities in the United States were using wiretaps and surveillance to intimidate and monitor workers within the plants who had voiced health and environmental concerns.[25] One of the targets of surveillance, a Hanford engineer who was dismissed because of his exposé about faulty monitoring equipment in the plant, reflected: "In a lot of respects the activities I have personally observed are similar to what we've heard about the KGB and the Gestapo. If you want to describe it as a police state, I think that's fair."[26] Another Hanford employee who voiced concerns about safety problems said she was threatened with dismissal, ordered to see a psychiatrist, harassed, and trailed by security agents.

The balance of power in the world of nuclear weapons and nuclear states pivots on a pyramid of secrecy, exclusivity, and fraternity.

Secrecy is the gatekeeper of power. All elites use secrecy to privatize access to knowledge. Men in power—male elites—have often used secrecy explicitly to exclude women from their preserve. Secrecy allows men to mystify the work that they do; it allows them to perpetuate the notion that what they are doing—whether that be mathematics or welding—is "too difficult" or "too complex" for women to understand.[27]

There are only five states in the world with declared nuclear weapons armaments, and another four or so that are essentially nuclear states; this is an exclusive group, often referred to as the "nuclear club." And a club it is, an exclusive knot of super-states. "Nuclear capability" is much coveted and jealously guarded, not only as a technics, but as a symbol of the full flowering of military might and state maturity—a signifier of a manhood of sorts.

This connection between masculinity and super-weaponry ("boys and their toys," as many feminists quip) was most recently revealed in the rhetoric surrounding the series of nuclear weapons tests set off by the governments of India and then Pakistan in May and June 1998. In mid-May 1998, the recently elected right-wing government of India set off a series of nuclear weapons tests. The proclamations of Indian government officials in the aftermath were full of bluster about the extent to which they would "now be taken seriously" and about pride in their new weapons "capacity." A leading nationalist and Bombay politician went straight to the point, saying, "We have to prove we are not eunuchs."[28]

In the wake of India's tests, considerable pressure was brought to bear on Pakistan's Prime Minister Sharif to retaliate in kind. The politically powerful army chief declared that "So far we have not disappointed our nation in respect of our security capability and we will never disappoint our people now"; he went on to say that the number of weapons Pakistan had was not important, "only the capability."[29] Pro-nuclear advocates in Pakistan played on themes of "competition" and the necessity of "measuring up" to India.[30] The *New York Times* reported that several of Prime Minister Sharif's critics called into question his manhood in order to goad him into a retaliatory nuclear test:

> Women in [Pakistan] traditionally wear stacks of thin gold bracelets. It is a symbol of femininity; conversely, the offering of a bracelet to a man is a symbol of his weakness. At a rally in Lahore, Mr. Sharif's hometown, Ms. Bhutto [the former Prime Minister and Sharif's chief political rival] ripped off her bracelets and cast them towards the crowd in a gesture that said: Give these to Mr. Sharif—he doesn't have the guts to stand up to India.[31]

Within nuclear states, the even more exclusive club is the fraternity of weaponeers—the men who dream up, design, and engineer the super-weapons of the nuclear age. Indeed, reports in the midst of the June 1998 nuclear weapons testing in South Asia suggest that it was nuclear scientists in Pakistan who were among the most eager to "prove themselves" by a Pakistan nuclear weapons test. In *Fathering the Unthinkable*,[32] Brian Easlea, a former nuclear physicist, argues persuasively that the context of the early atomic bomb projects in the United States and the United Kingdom was not only driven by masculinist paradigms, but was framed implicitly and explicitly by a "cult of masculinity." The development of nuclear weaponry brought together, for the first time, two of the most entrenched men's clubs—science and the military. (Science has long been an almost entirely male preserve, and male scientists have long used secrecy, mystery, and obfuscation to protect science as a male enterprise.)[33] This heady combination resulted in an impenetrable fusion of secretive masculine power. Physicists managed to harden the gender barriers of their discipline by allying themselves with the military; previously caricatured as woolly-headed, mild-mannered "sissies," physicists improved their public image (and their ability to garner government grants) inestimably by producing monster weapons in the 1940s and 1950s.[34] By combining forces, male scientists and military men forged an impenetrable alliance: military men got "the ultimate weapon," and physicists got to "prove their manhood." The hypermachismo and hypersecrecy that characterize nuclear weapons programs today—behind which egregious environmental violations are hidden—are a product of the fusing of masculinized science with militarized masculinity, both wrapped in the protective cloak of secrecy.

The world of the early nuclear weaponeers was a paramount men's club; historical and contemporary accounts of the communities of scientists and military men convened in Chicago, Berkeley, Los Alamos, Alamogordo, and Hanford in the 1940s and 1950s paint a "boy's world" picture.[35] Carol Cohn adds to Easlea's analysis in her study of the contemporary defense community—a community she describes as burdened by "the ubiquitous weight of [male] gender, both in social relations and language," that thrives on sexually explicit imagery and sanitized abstraction.[36] Cohn talks about the surprisingly transparent phallic imagery that pervades military discussions of military strength—a language of soft lay-downs, deep penetration, hard missiles. The history of the development of the atomic bomb is rife with "male birth" imagery: the Los Alamos bomb was referred to as "Oppenheimer's baby"; "Teller's baby" was born at the Lawrence Livermore labs. (Those who wanted to disparage Teller's contribution claimed that he was not the bomb's father, but the mother—i.e., that Teller merely "carried" someone else's idea.)[37] In the early tests, before they were certain that the bombs would work, the scientists expressed their concern by saying that they hoped the baby was a boy, not a girl—that is, a dud; when the bomb worked, the telegrams sent around the world crowed that the "baby is a boy." Cohn reports that mothering (denigrated) versus fathering imagery, female (negative) versus male (positive) sex-typing is still entrenched in the nuclear mentality.

New light is shed on the culture of nuclear destruction if it is understood as a private men's club, within which masculinity is both an explicit sexualized expression and an implicitly taken-for-granted context. The dominant representation of the early years of the atomic project is overwhelmingly one of nuclear scientists giving birth to male progeny with the ultimate power of violent domination over female Nature. The horror of work that consists of creating and "improving" tools of mass destruction is blunted by a culture that inculcates and values the male-socialized traits of separating morality and emotionalism from working and thinking. Disregard for the consequences, including the health and environmental costs, of the nuclear arms race is normalized within an insular, privileged fraternity. In thinking about the development of nuclear weaponry, we might reflect on the wry W. H. Auden poem about the militarized space program:

> It's natural the Boys should whoop it up for so huge a phallic triumph, an adventure it would not have occurred to women to think worthwhile.[38]

Making Policy

Most militaries are smugly certain of their importance in the national and global hierarchy. This distorted sense of self-importance has environmental effects. Representatives from one U.S. environmental organization that is currently suing the commander of an Air Force base comment that, "infected with the importance of their purpose, the military's fundamental mentality seems to be that they are simply not interested in mundane matters like environmental conservation."[39] Environmental safety is low on the list of military priorities. As one observer notes, "There is a bunker mentality.... Every penny that goes to safety programs is a penny taken from manufacturing nuclear warheads."[40] In another case, a commander of a military installation in Virginia, in a community confrontation over leaking PCBs from his base, explained his nonchalance about the environmental contamination by saying, "We're in the business of protecting your country, not protecting the environment."[41] This sense of a higher purpose, combined with male arrogance in the face of community pressure from activists who predominantly are women, allows the military to consider itself above the law.

But this deceit is not only of their own making. Militaries are protected by a structure of policies and priorities that insulate the military from environmental accountability. Key to this protective policy structure is something called "national security." It is in the name of "national security" that military facilities are exempted from environmental regulations and monitoring requirements, that militaries can shield themselves from outside interference, and that they are left as their own environmental watchdogs.

The "national security" knot is a perfect defense: it allows the military to deflect all questions, including questions about what they are doing in the first place that is supposedly in the interest of national security. "National security" is a vague and constantly shifting concept—it has no real or absolute meaning; it is whatever the military defines it to be. National security is defined and secured by a fraternity of men in government in concert with a fraternity of men in the military. While concepts of national security shift over time, one consistent hallmark of national security is that it is a realm of men. A recent survey of American government offices in which national security policies are formulated found that women occupy only 44 of some 1,015 policy-making positions (4.3 percent). Nor are women represented in the international arms-control bureaucracy: for example, of the 13 top-level positions at the newly created U.S. Institute of Peace, none is held by a woman.[42] Even at a time when women appear to be gaining access to conventional arenas of political power, the most jealously guarded of male inner sanctums remain defense, intelligence, and arms control.[43]

Meanwhile, the men in government who should be monitoring the military are typically in government positions of some significance; they have worked hard to arrive in positions of trust and to be privy to the most serious levels of government business. (Worldwide, women represent on average about 2 to 4 percent of government officials. In Scandinavian countries, where women represent approximately 25 percent of elected officials, there does seem to be a different consensus emerging about the nature of "national security," and one must wonder whether there is a relationship between these two facts.) For many men in government, one of the perquisites of power is being part of a privileged club, where men talk to one another about "serious" matters—like national security. Many of these men don't want to fall outside the national security "loop"; most of all, they don't ever want to be accused of not taking seriously national security or, worse, of being unpatriotic. Hedrick Smith, in his much-vaunted analysis of the workings of the U.S. government, *The Power Game*, describes the seductiveness, and significance, of being "inside the loop":

> Access in the power game is not merely physical; it is mental too. It is not only entry to the inner sanctum; it is being in the power loop—being chosen to receive the most sensitive information, as fresh grist for the policy struggle. Being "cut out" on information, or being "blindsided" as the power lingo has it, can be crippling…. In the national security power fraternity, the put-down comes in the form of one official asking another: "Are you in the loop?"[44]

In the United States, as elsewhere, the intangible bonds of fraternity between men in government and men in the military are hardened by more concrete partnerships among military services, defense contractors, and members of Congress from states where military spending is heavy and visible—a network of overlapping financial, industrial, and policy agendas that President Eisenhower loosely identified as the "military-industrial complex." Later in his book, Smith quotes a U.S. senator describing his initial introduction to the cozy relationships between the military and the government:

> It's slightly incestuous. I'm three months in office and I get invited to the Pentagon. An Army car picks me up. I arrive, and I'm taken to a nice office and order my breakfast. Well-dressed stewards, a four-star general on my right, the secretary of the Army to my left, one- and two-star generals around the table. I told General Wickham, the Army chief of staff, "If my battalion commander in Korea could see me now, he'd never believe it." Wickham laughed. He told me, "There is a kind of awe, and I hope you'll get over it. But there is a close relationship between Congress and the military."[45]

Revolving-door job connections and interlocking networks among defense contractors, military officials, and ex–government officials ensure a mutual self-interest in keeping military programs going, and in keeping external review or criticism to a minimum.[46]

There are very few governments in the world in which the military does not wield enormous influence.[47] Moreover, in an astonishingly high number of other countries, the military *is* the government. The environmental costs of this cozy convergence range from weak environmental oversight of the military to concerted repression of environmentalists to active participation by the state-military elite in environmental destruction (one of the most egregious examples of which is the wanton destruction of Thailand-Burmese forests by the combined commercial and military interests of three states).

Male bonding in the cause of national security is a powerful force, one that translates into specific policy initiatives—"gentlemen's agreements" for the environment, as it were. Militaries are routinely exempted from the restrictions of domestic environmental laws and international environmental treaties, usually on the rationale that environmental regulations might interfere with "military readiness"—although, in many cases, this rationale seems thin. For example, in 1988, a 29-nation treaty banning plastics dumping at sea specifically excluded military vessels, despite the fact that American Navy ships alone dump more than five tons of plastic waste overboard *daily*.[48] In 1986, the U.S. Congress passed a radical "Right to Know Act" that required industries and companies to report their toxic releases; the Department of Defense exempted itself from reporting its toxic chemical releases, and in fact it maintains that it does not know how much hazardous emissions it produces or what happens to the emissions.[49] In both national and international negotiations, militaries are routinely treated as "special case" agencies that need to be exempted from environmental controls. U.S. military bases in Japan, South Korea, and, formerly, the Philippines have virtually free environmental reign; during the Gulf War, no provision was made for the disposal of wastes left in the deserts of Saudi Arabia by the hundreds of thousands of coalition troops based there; "status of basing" and "status of force" agreements—the contractual arrangements that allow one country to operate military facilities in another—seldom include provisions for environmental protection.[50]

In the name of national security, militaries are largely left to be their own environmental watchdogs. The result of *this* particular gentlemen's agreement is a callous disregard for public health and safety impacts of military activities. The military record on environmental accountability is characterized in its entirety by suppression of health information, subterfuge, falsification of documents, duplicitous practices, cover-ups, flagrant disregard of public health, and harassment of activists.[51]

National security accords militaries a higher national purpose; this gives militaries privilege and priority in budget appropriations. Global expenditures on militaries are significant—and growing. Although military shares of domestic budgets vary widely, in most countries militaries consume a sizable proportion of national budgets. In more than a dozen countries in the mid-1990s, including Yemen, Mozambique, Saudi Arabia, and Oman, among others, military expenditures exceeded 10 percent of domestic GNP, and in some, notably Egypt and North Korea, they exceeded 25 percent. In much of the world, including states as diverse as China, Russia, Pakistan, and Greece, governments spend more on militaries than they do on health or education;

the Canadian government, usually considered to be a bit player in global militarism, spends 12 times as much on the military as it does on the environment.[52]

Best estimates put total worldwide military expenditures at about US$790 billion a year. Global military expenditures have been growing steadily over the past 20 years; however, while the overall trend is still upward, in the years between the mid-1980s and mid-1990s, there was some slowing of military expenditures in previous big-spender states, and military expenditures actually decreased in many countries. Between 1985 and 1994, of about 150 countries (for which data were available), 82 countries reduced military appropriations, but 59 increased military spending.[53] The "increasing military spending" countries include some of the poorer countries of the world, such as Myanmar, Sri Lanka, Sudan, and Sierra Leone; others on this list include Indonesia, Thailand, Malaysia, and South Korea. In South Asia, one of the poorer regions of the world, military expenditures grew by nearly 65 percent over the decade of the 1980s (and by 15 percent in Latin America and 10 percent in East Asia).[54] In 1998, the new nationalist Indian government, flush with its "successful" nuclear testing, increased military spending by 14 percent, bringing the total military outlays in India to about 19 percent of the total government budget (and the budget also included an increase of 68 percent for the India Atomic Energy Commission).[55]

There are environmental consequences when militaries appropriate national (and global) budgets. If military budgets increase, then spending on something else must shrink. Often the price of expanding military budgets is environmental neglect, increasing social inequality, and deterioration in the daily quality of life for hundreds of thousands of people. The effects of reductions in social welfare programs and deterioration in the environmental quality of life ripple through society unevenly: people on the economic margins, the poor, and the disenfranchised bear the brunt of social dislocation. Since, worldwide, women constitute the largest population living in poverty, when spending on social programs is reduced as a "trade-off" for military spending, it is women who suffer first and most deeply. Ironically, as militaries gain economic clout and their environmental record deteriorates, environmental monitoring programs themselves, usually chronically underfunded in the first place, are often early victims of budget cuts on the "social"-spending side of the national ledger. To the extent that military expenditures increase social inequalities and put downward pressure on the poorest segments of society, this can create a spiral of environmental destruction: for example, when landless or near-landless peasants become even poorer, they will move on to marginal lands; land degradation and deforestation in places such as Madagascar, Myanmar, Indonesia, and the Philippines are directly tied to these sorts of pressures.

There are more direct environmental trade-offs. Some recent comparisons, give a sense of the environmental cost of military spending:[56]

• For the price of one British Aerospace Hawk aircraft, 1.5 million people in the Third World could have clean water for life.

• The budget for the American "stealth bomber" program represents two-thirds of the costs of meeting U.S. clean water goals by the year 2000.

• The money spent on one nuclear weapons test could provide installation of 80,000 hand pumps to give Third World villages access to safe water.

• Ten days of European Economic Community military spending represents the annual cost to clean up hazardous waste sites in 10 EEC countries by the year 2000.

• The annual cost of a proposed anti-desertification program for Ethiopia was the equivalent of two months of Ethiopian military spending at 1989 levels.

• Four days of global military spending would fund the Tropical Forest Action Plan for more than five years.

• Two days of global military spending represents the annual cost of the U.N. Action Plan to halt Third World desertification.

• In ten days of the Persian Gulf War, the U.S. military spent the equivalent of the entire U.S. domestic annual budget for energy development and conservation.

The Worldwatch Institute (an environmental think tank) recently estimated that the global community would have to spend about US$774 billion during the final decade of this century if we wanted to reverse adverse trends in four priority areas: protecting topsoil on croplands from further erosion, reforesting the earth, raising energy efficiency, and developing renewable sources of energy.[57] This is a considerable and daunting sum—but less than the world spends on its militaries in a year.

In thinking about the relationships between masculinist prerogatives and military imperatives, there is a further, more complex, set of questions that might be broached: is it possible that the current global system of sovereign states (and the wars and national security mechanisms put into place to protect those private territories) is *itself* a product of *male* consciousness? Are sovereignty, nationalism, territoriality, and wars particularly *male* constructs? These are provocative questions, but ones increasingly salient for environmentalists as we are slowly coming, in the 1990s, to realize the costs and frustrations of trying to solve common global environmental problems through an international system that pivots exclusively around protection of sovereign "integrity."[58]

Given the gendered nature of the symbiotic relationship between state, military, and commercial power, it is important to note that when governments use the power of the state to repress environmentalists, or when they facilitate environmental abuses either by omission or commission, they are not only acting to protect their vested interests and private wealth—they are also acting to protect their *male* privilege and the sanctity of the *male* networks that sustain their power.

Making Trouble

Mainstream environmental groups commit only about 1 percent of their resources to weaponry and other military issues.[59] Thus, when environmentalists "take on" the military, it is most likely to be in the form of local activism by "amateur" troublemakers. This makes the gender dynamics of military-environment relations even more complex—because, worldwide, most community and grassroots environmental activists are women.[60] Women's grassroots environmental initiatives around the world range widely, from well-known groups such as the Chipko forest-protection movement in India and the Green Belt Movement in Kenya, to thousands of smaller groups that take on local environmental problems. Many of these issues bring women into direct conflict with militaries.

Because of their social location, often it is women who first notice degradation of a local environment. Women who spend more time in the home and local neighborhood, who spend more time tending to children, and who do most of the household chores are the first to notice unusual patterns of illness in the community, the first to notice persistent chemical odors or residues. Many of these women, reluctantly at first, become activists. They form neighborhood monitoring committees; they map out patterns of illness; they contact local and national media; and, often, in their campaign to find out what's going wrong in their neighborhood and to find someone responsible for cleaning it up, they come up against the military.

Confronting the military is something few people, especially women, are prepared for. Lois Gibbs, the whistleblower in the Love Canal (New York) toxic-waste site, reminds us that "many, if not most, women leaders in the [United States] hazardous waste movement are low- and moderate-income people, have formal educations that ended with a high school diploma, do not have any formal organizing training, have never before been involved in any other social justice issue, and come from and live in a very 'traditional' kind of lifestyle."[61]

Militaries seldom have to respond to questions about their actions. Militaries don't like to be challenged. Military men especially don't like to be challenged by women—worse, by "mere housewives," as they are typically cast. The hostility of powerful men colluding to protect secretive and intertwined vested interests from outsiders is heightened when the community activists who challenge them are women (or men) of a different class or race—perhaps Native American women in the American Midwest, or Filipina activists challenging American militaries in the Pacific.

When forced into a confrontation, sexism is usually the military's first resort: women community leaders repeatedly report that they have to endure arrogant, patronizing, and sarcastic military officials who try first and foremost to denigrate the authority and knowledge of the women challenging them. The fact that the community activists are women and therefore presumed to know little about "military matters" is the first challenge raised. If sexist intimidation doesn't quell community activism, militaries typically then threaten to close the facility that is under public scrutiny. In many communities, this poses a serious economic threat. Not coincidentally, this is also the tactic most likely to divide the men and women of the community, especially if the facility is a military base. Typically, more men than women are employed on military bases, or are employed at higher-paying jobs. Men are more likely than women to have emotional attachments to militaries or prior career attachments. Thus, the threat of closure often pits men and their jobs on one side versus women and public health on the other. Militaries consciously manipulate this threat to isolate women activists from family and community support.

Militaries construct a seductive dichotomy, with "men–military–national security" on one side, "housewives-environment-troublemaking" on the other. By setting up an opposition between "serious" national security concerns that are the province of men, and "trivial" environmental concerns that are the province of women, military officials not only manipulate ideologies of gender to protect their turf, but they widen the gap between environmental concern and militarized manhood, making it even less likely that environmental caring might be integrated into a military's mission.

Making People Sick

The social, health, economic, emotional, and logistical impacts of environmental degradation almost always vary with class, race, age, and sex—

sometimes because of biology, sometimes because of social location. The impacts of militarized environmental destruction are not borne evenly across a society. In many instances, a disproportionate burden falls on women and "minorities."

Women's social roles as family caretakers, and, in agrarian economies, as primary subsistence providers, situates them in the environmental front lines. In the aftermath of the Persian Gulf War, for example, women in both Kuwait and Iraq—even urban women unaccustomed to fashioning family provisions from raw materials—became the hewers of wood and carriers of water. A brief U.N. report from Iraq, several months after the war, observed that women and children were spending large parts of their day searching out food, fuel, and water, often carrying these supplies for miles. Indigenous peoples, too, paid a particular price of militarized environmental damage. The lands of the Bedouins were devastated: the desert ecosystem on which they rely was mined, bombed, and debased by the military presence in Saudi Arabia and the war in Kuwait and Iraq. Military activity, pollution, and oil spills dislocated the Marsh Arabs, a little-known population that lives in the wetlands and marshes of the Persian Gulf.

Since 1963, the United States has exploded 651 nuclear weapons or devices on the U.S. mainland; all the nuclear bomb testing sites in the continental United States are located on Native American lands, mostly on Western Shoshone territory in Nevada.[62] It is islanders in the South Pacific who have borne the greatest brunt of British, French, and American nuclear testing programs. Most of the nuclear weapons systems stationed in Europe and the United States have been tested on indigenous peoples' lands in the Pacific, without their consent and often without warning. Over the past four decades of nuclear testing, some Pacific islands have disappeared entirely ("vaporized," in military language), and many more have been rendered uninhabitable—and they will remain so for tens of thousands of years. Entire island populations have been dislocated, social disruption in the South Pacific as a result of military activities has been enormous, and the health consequences are incalculable. Women of the South Pacific living in the testing zones have experienced dramatic increases in reproductive failure and birth defects.

It is not unusual for the toxins used routinely by militaries to have particular health impacts on women. For example, the health of Vietnamese women has suffered, more so than men, from the poisoning of Vietnam. Dioxin, a primary contaminant in the millions of gallons of Agent Orange dumped by the U.S. military on Vietnam during the 1970s, persists in the food chain for decades. In human tissue, dioxin has a half-life of 12 years, which means that dangerous levels of dioxin are passed from generation to generation; lactating mothers are at greatest risk. Dioxin is highly carcinogenic, even in minute quantities, causing genetic mutations and any number of cancers. It also is a major teratrogenic (birth-deforming) chemical. In Vietnam today, women have the highest rate of spontaneous abortions in the world; birth defects occur at alarming rates; 70 to 80 percent of women suffer from vaginal infection; cervical cancer rates are among the highest in the world; and fetal death rates in pregnancy were 40 times higher in the early 1980s than they were in the 1950s.

Reproductive failures of all kinds are often the first indicators of severe environmental trauma. These health problems also have wider social consequences. In cultures where women are valued primarily for their reproductive capacities (and where is this not the case?), when those capacities are diminished, women who cannot or will not bear more children may face ostracization and a loss of their social stature; at a minimum, there is increased pressure on women to bear more children. In the aftermath of the Bhopal industrial disaster, for example, Indian feminists reported increasing rates of domestic violence, divorce, and abandonment—side effects of the mounting frustrations of increased poverty and ill health—suffered by poor women who were maimed by the chemical explosion.[63]

Conclusion

Militaries are among the biggest players in the global environmental arena. Environmental analysis that does not take into account the roles of militaries in local and global environments will be weak, and any prescription for environmental change that does not include reconfiguring military-environment relations will be partial and ineffectual.

If we want to understand the global environmental condition, we must understand the role of militaries. If we want to change it, we have to come to terms with gender.

Notes

1. The list of war-damaged regions and countries is extensive, and the literature on each is too large to quote here. As a starting point, I recommend Ruth Sivard *Annual Military and Social Expenditures* (Washington, DC: World Priorities); Daniel Faber, *Environment Under Fire: Imperialism and the Ecological Crisis in Central America* (New York: Monthly Review Press, 1993); Saul Bloom et al., eds., *Hidden Casualties: Environmental, Health and Political Consequences of the Persian Gulf War* (San Francisco: North Atlantic Books, 1994); Joni Seager, "Operation Desert

Disaster: Environmental Costs of the Gulf War," in Cynthia Peters, ed., *Collateral Damage* (Boston: South End Press, 1992); Donovan Webster, *Aftermath: The Remnants of War* (New York: Pantheon Books, 1996); and Joni Seager, *Earth Follies: Coming to Feminist Terms With the Global Environmental Crisis* (New York: Routledge, 1993).

2. For further information, see Joseph Gerson, ed., *The Deadly Connection* (Philadelphia: New Society Publishers, 1986); Seth Shulman, *The Threat at Home: Confronting the Toxic Legacy of the U.S. Military* (Boston: Beacon Press, 1992); Joni Seager, *The New State of the Earth Atlas* (New York: Simon & Schuster, 1995); Anne Ehrlich and John Birks, eds., *Hidden Dangers: Environmental Consequences of Preparing for War* (San Francisco: Sierra Club, 1990); Rosalie Bertell, *No Immediate Danger: Prognosis for a Radioactive Earth* (Summertown, TN: Book Publishing Company, 1985); *Deadly Defense: Military Radioactive Landfills* (New York: Radioactive Waste Campaign, 1988).

3. Bonn International Centre for Conversion, *Conversion Survey 1996* (London: Oxford University Press, 1996), 206.

4. Excellent overviews of Soviet military environmental damage are Murray Feshbach and Alfred Friendly Jr., *Ecocide in the USSR* (New York: Harper, 1992); and D.J. Peterson, *Troubled Lands: The Legacy of Soviet Environmental Destruction* (Boulder: Westview Press, 1993).

5. Good analyses of environmental damage in the South Pacific include Jane Dibblin, *The Day of Two Suns* (London: Virago, 1998); Robert Milliken, *No Conceivable Injury* (Victoria, Australia: Penguin Books, 1985); Peter Hayes et al., *American Lake* (New York: Penguin Books, 1986); and Bengt Danielsson and Marie-Therese Danielsson, *Poisoned Reign* (Victoria, Australia: Penguin Books, 1986).

6. Michael Renner, "Environmental Dimensions of Disarmament Conversion," in Kevin Cassidy and Gregory Bischak, eds., *Real Security* (New York: SUNY Press, 1993).

7. Michael Renner, "Assessing the Military's War on the Environment," in Worldwatch Institute, *The State of the World: 1991* (New York: W.W. Norton, 1991).

8. "Military Animal Abuse," *Animals' Agenda*, November 1990, 38.

9. Ted Olson, "Appetite for Land Growing," *Army Times*, April 9, 1990.

10. Michael Renner, "Assessing the Military's War on the Environment," op. cit.

11. Michael Renner,"Environmental Dimensions of Disarmament Conversion," op. cit., 98.

12. Kathy Ferguson, Phyllis Turnbull, and Mehmed Ali, *Rethinking the Military in Hawaii* (Honolulu: University of Hawaii, 1991), 8.

13. Ruth Sivard, *World Military and Social Expenditures, 1996* (Washington, DC: World Priorities Institute, 1996).

14. For a more complete elaboration of the conceptual framework for this femi-

nist analysis, see Joni Seager, *Earth Follies: Coming to Feminist Terms with the Global Environmental Crisis* (New York: Routledge, 1993).

15. The literature on gender and militaries is extensive. Key works include Cynthia Enloe, *Maneuvers: Militarizing Women's Lives* (Berkeley: University of California Press, 1999); Eva Isaksson, ed., *Women and the Military System* (New York: Harvester Wheatsheaf, 1988); Diana Russell, ed., *Exposing Nuclear Phallacies* (New York: Teacher's College Press, 1989); and Adrienne Harris and Ynestra King, eds., *Rocking the Ship of State* (Boulder, CO: Westview Press, 1989).

16. For an extended analysis of the militarized construction of masculinity, see Cynthia Enloe, *Does Khaki Become You?* (London and New York: Pandora Press and HarperCollins, 1988); Cynthia Enloe, *Maneuvers: Militarizing Women's Lives,* op. cit.; and Eva Isaksson, ed., *Women and the Military System* (New York: Harvester, 1988).

17. I am aware of only one study that attempts to trace direct links between the feminization of nature and the assault on nature by militaries: Mehmed Ali, Kathy Ferguson, and Phyllis Turnbull, "Gender, Land and Power: Reading the Military in Hawaii" (paper presented at the 15th World Congress of the International Political Science Association, Buenos Aires, 1991).

18. Carol Cohn, "A Feminist Spy in the House of Death," in Eva Isaksson, ed., *Women and the Military System,* op. cit.

19. Helen Caldicott, *Towards a Compassionate Society* (Westfield, NJ: Open Media, 1991).

20. Ibid., 4.

21. Gail Bradshaw is the spokeswoman, quoted in Matthew Wald, "U.S. Waste Dumping Blamed in Wide Pollution at A-Plants," *New York Times,* December 8, 1988.

22. Quoted in Stephen Kurkjian, "Dilemma of U.S. Nuclear Weapons Program," *Boston Globe,* November 13, 1988.

23. Quoted in Dan Reicher and S. Jacob Scherr, "The Bomb Factories: Out of Compliance and Out of Control," in Anne Ehrlich and John Birks, eds., *Hidden Dangers: Environmental Consequences of Preparing for War* (San Francisco: Sierra Club Books, 1992).

24. Matthew Wald, "Whistleblower at Nuclear Laboratory Was Disciplined, Labor Department Rules," *New York Times,* February 5, 1992; Keith Schneider, "Inquiry Finds Illegal Surveillance of Workers in Nuclear Plants," *New York Times,* August 1, 1991, A18.

25. Schneider, "Inquiry Finds Illegal Surveillance of Workers in Nuclear Plants," op. cit.

26. Ibid.

27. In the film *The Life and Times of Rosie the Riveter,* which chronicles the entry of American women into "men's professions" during the labor shortages caused by World War II, one of the women workers tells of her surprise when she found out

that welding was not a mystical and unattainable skill. "All these years," she exclaims, "men have been telling us how difficult welding is, how you have to study for years and years to get the skills.... They sold us a bill of goods!"

28. Quoted in John Burns, "India Glows With Pride," *New York Times*, May 13, 1998, A12.

29. Ibid.

30. Quoted in John Kifner, "Complex Pressures Dominated By Islam Led to Testing," *New York Times*, June 1, 1998, A6.

31. Ibid.

32. Brian Easlea, *Fathering the Unthinkable: Masculinity, Scientists and the Nuclear Arms Race* (London: Pluto Press, 1983).

33. For excellent analyses on the masculinist underpinnings of science, see Evelyn Fox Keller, *Reflections on Gender and Science* (New Haven, CT: Yale University Press, 1984); Sandra Harding, *The Science Question in Feminism* (Ithaca, NY: Cornell University Press, 1986).

34. A point suggested by Lisa Greber in "The Unholy Trinity: Physics, Gender and the Military" (unpublished B.A. honors thesis, Massachusetts Institute of Technology, 1987).

35. Probably the best study of the culture of the nuclear weapons project (though written with no particular gender awareness) is Richard Rhodes, *The Making of the Atomic Bomb* (New York: Simon & Schuster, 1986). For contemporary accounts of the world of weaponeers, see Robert Del Tredici, *At Work in the Fields of the Bomb* (New York: Harper and Row, 1987); Debra Rosenthal, *At the Heart of the Bomb: The Dangerous Allure of Weapons Work* (Reading, MA: Addison-Wesley, 1990); Hugh Gusterson, *Nuclear Rites: A Weapons Laboratory at the End of the Cold War* (Berkeley, CA: University of California Press, 1996).

36. Carol Cohn, "A Feminist Spy in the House of Death," in Eva Isaksson, ed., *Women and the Military System,* op. cit. See Cohn's bibliography in this article for a good list of feminist critiques of Western male rationality in the military system.

37. For more information on this mothering/fathering debate, see Easlea, *Fathering the Unthinkable*, chapter 4, op. cit.

38. W.H. Auden, "Moon Landing," in Charles Muscatine et al., eds., *The Borzoi College Reader* (New York: Knopf, 1971).

39. Cited in Stephanie Pollack and Seth Shulman, "Pollution and the Pentagon," *Science for the People*, May/June 1987.

40. William Vaughan, assistant secretary of energy during President Reagan's first term in office, quoted in *The Defense Monitor,* Vol. 18, No. 4 (1989).

41. Quoted in Will Collette, "Dealing with Military Toxics," Citizen's Clearinghouse for Hazardous Waste, 1987.

42. Barbara Ann Scott, "Help Wanted: Women Defense Experts and Decision-Makers," *Minerva: Quarterly Report on Women and the Military*, Vol. 6, No. 4 (winter 1988).

43. For example, see Hedrick Smith's description of the workings of U.S. government policy in chapter 6 of *The Power Game: How Washington Works* (New York: Random House, 1988).

44. Hedrick Smith, *The Power Game,* op. cit., 71–72, 78.

45. Ibid., 185.

46. For a fuller discussion, see Hedrick Smith, *The Power Game: How Washington Works,* op. cit., especially chapter 8l; Gordon Adams, *The Iron Triangle* (New York: Council on Economic Priorities, 1981); Helen Caldicott, *Missile Envy* (New York: Bantam, 1985), especially the chapter on the "Iron Triangle."

47. Generalizations about military influence in government admit the possible exception of a few countries with no standing military, such as Iceland and many of the Caribbean island nations, or the Scandinavian countries in which military influence appears to be somewhat contained. (The absence of a military sector can be documented for only a total of 19 sovereign nations; another 9 have a very limited military commitment, as indicated by reported military expenditures in Arthur Westing, ed., *Environmental Hazards of War* (London: Sage Publications, 1990), 70. It may not be coincidental that these "under-" or "un-militarized" countries are also prominent on the short list of those nations where women have gained the most access to formal political power.

48. The U.S. Navy has since volunteered to try to meet most of the provisions of this plastics pollution agreement, but it is not legally bound to do so.

49. National Toxics Campaign Fund, *The U.S. Military's Toxic Legacy* (Boston: National Toxic Campaign Fund, 1991).

50. Women's groups in Japan are fighting for environmental accountability on U.S. bases; for more information, see "Okinawa: Peace, Human Rights, Women, Environment," Okinawa Christian Center newsletter, Okinawa, Japan. For more information on environmental effects and agreements of the Gulf War, see Saul Bloom et al., eds., *Hidden Casualties,* op. cit.; and Joni Seager, "Operation Desert Disaster: Environmental Costs of the Gulf War," op. cit.

51. There are several good exposés of deliberate military and governmental malfeasance in obscuring and altering the environmental records of militaries. See, for example, Rosalie Bertell, *No Immediate Danger* (London: Women's Press, 1985); Nigel Hawkes et al., *The Worst Accident in the World* (London: Pan Books, 1986); Daniel Ford, *MeltDown: The Secret Papers of the Atomic Energy Commission* (New York: Touchstone, 1982); and Paul Loeb, *Nuclear Culture: Living and Working in the World's Largest Atomic Complex* (Philadelphia: New Society Publishers, 1986).

52. Figures from Ruth Leger Sivard, *World Military and Social Expenditures, 1996* (Washington, DC: World Priorities, 1996); K.S. Jayaraman, "Poor and buying weapons," *Panoscope,* No. 14 (September 1989); Jim Hollingworth, "Global Militarism and the Environment," *Probe Post,* fall 1990, Toronto, Canada, 42; "The Cost of the Persian Gulf War," Massachusetts SANE/FREEZE fact sheet, 1991.

53. Bonn International Centre for Conversion, *Conversion Survey 1996* (Lon-

don: Oxford University Press, 1996).

54. Nicole Ball, "Demilitarizing the Third World," in Michael Klare and Daniel Thomas, eds. *World Security: Challenges for the New Century* (New York: St. Martin's Press, 1994).

55. John Burns, "Military budget in India Is Increased by 14 Percent," *New York Times,* June 2, 1998.

56. Comparisons from Ruth Sivard, annual updates; Larry Tye, "Pulling Resources from the Military," *Boston Globe,* April 9, 1989, A1; World Commission on Environment and Development, *Our Common Future* (New York: Oxford University Press, 1987); Michael Renner, "Who Are the Enemies?" *Peace Review* (Spring 1989); National Commission for Economic Conversion and Disarmament, *The New Economy,* Vol. 1, No. 1, (August/September 1989), Washington, DC; and Center for Economic Conversion, *Plowshare,* Vol. 14, No. 2 (Spring 1989). An excellent compilation of information on the effect of military spending on women and women's programs in the United States is put out by the Women's International League for Peace and Freedom: *The Women's Budget,* Third Edition, 1988; Michael Renner, "National Security: The Economic and Environmental Dimensions" (Washington, DC: Worldwatch Paper No. 89, 1989).

57. Renner, "Environmental Dimensions of Disarmament Conversion," op. cit.

58. Feminist political scientists are increasingly interrogating the construction of the nation-state: Cynthia Enloe, *Bananas, Beaches and Bases: Making Feminist Sense of International Politics* (Berkeley, CA: University of California Press, 1989); Ann Tickner, *Gender in International Relations* (New York: Columbia University Press, 1992); Jan Jindy Pettman, *Worlding Women* (St. Leonard's, Australia: Allen & Unwin, 1996); V. Spike Peterson, *Gendered States* (Boulder, CO: Lynne Reinner Publishers, 1992).

59. Donald Snow, *Inside the Environmental Movement* (Washington, DC: Island Press, 1992), 53.

60. One of the few multinational studies of local environmental activism is Dianne Rocheleau, Esther Wangaari, and Barbara Thomas-Slayter, eds., *Feminist Political Ecology* (New York: Routledge, 1996).

61. Lois Gibbs, "Women and Burnout" (Arlington, VA: Citizens Clearinghouse for Hazardous Waste, 1988).

62. Bernard Nietschmann and William Le Bon, "Nuclear Weapons States and Fourth World Nations," *Cultural Survival Quarterly,* Vol. 11, No. 4 (1987), 5–7.

63. Padma Prakash, "Neglect of Women's Health Issues," *Economic and Political Weekly* (Delhi), December 14, 1985.

CONSUMPTION

North American Perspectives

H. Patricia Hynes

Sorting through a pile of books, pamphlets, and journal articles put aside for writing this piece on consumption, I came upon a report from a nongovernmental organization (NGO) promoting a simple, fairly low-cost solar cooker. The NGO, Solar Cookers International, recently undertook a pilot project with Somali women living in a refugee camp on Kenya's northeastern border with Somalia. A cadre of women was trained to teach some 2,000 other women in the camp how to use a solar cooker for cooking, baking, and boiling liquids.

When interviewed about the cookers' utility, refugee women described the hours they spent searching for sticks in the fragile desert environment (many left at 4 a.m. and returned at noon twice per week), the hazards of snakes and scorpions, the risk of being raped by bandits, and the need to trade food for fuel in the camp when fuel-gathering was inadequate. Solar cookers give them time, they said, for rest and for other tasks, including planting and nurturing trees in exchange for the cookers.[1] With the cookers, they are spared hours spent bending over open wood fires and inhaling wood smoke—the daily equivalent, in some cases, of many packs of cigarettes and the proximate cause of acute respiratory infections (the "most pervasive cause of chronic illness in developing nations").[2] Fire hazards to children are eliminated. And the food, cooked slowly in its own juices, is moister and tastier than fire-cooked meals.

The connections between solar cookers and environmental health extend farther still. Two of the highest risk factors for mortality and loss of healthy life among people in developing countries are malnutrition and contaminated water supply with concomitant poor hygiene.[3] The cooker can pasteurize water and milk; it retains more nutrients in the cooking process and can be

189

used to dry food for preserving. Moreover, the urban and rural poor—who pay upward of 20 percent of their disposable income for wood or charcoal— can buy fresh food in lieu of cooking fuel.[4]

Half of the world's people eat food cooked over wood and charcoal; more than three billion people depend on wood, biomass, and charcoal for the majority of their energy use.[5] Thus, the widespread dissemination of an easy-to-assemble and easy-to-use solar technology in sun-rich countries has enormous potential to save woodlands, to stem desertification and soil erosion, and to slow global climate change. (Who has more vested in saving local woodlands, pastures, and soil than the rural poor for whom these resources are the source of daily life?)

By chance, the solar cooker material lay near a pamphlet published by the Population Reference Bureau, Inc., which explicates the so-called population-environment nexus. A bar graph illustrates the consumption of primary materials (including fossil fuels, metal, and paper) and the production of hazardous waste by aggregate populations in the United States, other developed countries, and developing countries.

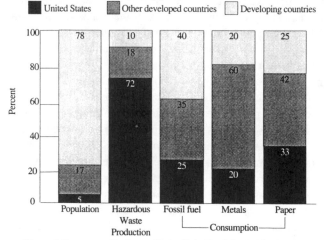

Figure 1. Share of Population, Hazardous Waste Production, and Natural Resource Consumption in the United States, Developing, and Developed Regions, 1990s.

Source: Natural Resources Defense Council, in Lori S. Ashford. *New Perspectives on Population: Lessons from Cairo. Population Bulletin* (Washington, DC: Population Reference Bureau, Inc.), Volume 50, No. 1 (March 1995), 30.

The accompanying analysis relies on the iconic population-consumption-technology formula, I=PAT, and a recent add-on variable called "carrying capacity": The impact of humans on the environment (I) is a function of their population size (P), their consumption of resources (A), the pollution impact of producing and consuming those resources (T), and the capacity of particular environments to support this human activity. (See H. Patricia Hynes, "Taking Population Out of the Equation," in this volume.) The populous poor (such as the refugee women in northeastern Kenya), the author argues, have increased incentives to exploit marginal forest and soil resources because of poverty and lack of economic opportunity; thereby, they can and do cause acute environmental degradation. Although the very poor of the developing world consume and pollute little in comparison to the developed world (as Figure 1 amply illustrates), they often live in critical, degraded habitats with minimal capacity to support humans. Thus, every stick taken by a woman for cooking the next meal, the argument implies, contributes to lowered water tables, soil erosion, desertification, and landslides. Slowing population growth among the very poor is the imminent solution to saving critical habitats from the survival consumption of the poor.

In the chance juxtaposition of the Solar Cookers International report and the Population Reference Bureau pamphlet, I found the crux of my argument for this essay on consumption: The consumption of resources by individuals, by governments and ruling elites, by semi-autonomous and secretive institutions such as the military, and by macroeconomic systems is embedded within the matrix of political economy and cultural values. Yet consumption—like demographics-driven theories of "population"—has been reduced to a mere empirical, per capita phenomenon, as if it were detached from those structural and ideological forces that result in wealth-building for some and impoverishment and poor health for others. The huge discrepancy in natural resource use between the wealthiest and the poorest peoples of the world (and its compelling injustice) withers and dissipates when the very poor are accused of having incommensurate impact on their local ecosystems by their minimal efforts to survive. Thus, the issue of consumption needs no less debate than feminists have given to population-control ideology.

What, then, is the content of recent North American critiques of consumption and consumerism? What are their strengths and weaknesses? What core elements of a woman-centered analysis can we bring to them?

Within this decade, a handful of analyses and practice-based responses have emerged to characterize, critique, and provide alternatives to consumption patterns and consumerist ideology in industrialized countries. Among the chief prototypes are three approaches: the "demographics of consumption," movements to simplify life and make consumer choices that are less environmentally damaging, and the computation of the ecological footprint.

Demographics of Consumption

Asking the question "How much is enough?" Worldwatch Institute researcher Alan Durning has amassed quite a stunning picture of the explosion in the consumption of consumer goods and services in the United States and worldwide.[6] He traces the origins of "consumer society" in the United States to the 1920s, with the emergence of name brands, the entrée of packaged and processed foods, the rise of the car as the popular symbol of American upward mobility, and the birth of mass marketing through advertising. Consumerism was stymied by the Depression and World War II, but it picked up enormous momentum in the United States after the war and was rapidly disseminated worldwide, under the gospel of development and the democratization of consumerism, to gain markets for expanding U.S. industries. To cite a few supporting statistics on the radical change in post–World War II consumption: People in the United States own, on the average, "twice as many automobiles, drive two and a half times as far, use 21 times as much plastic, and cover 25 times as much distance by air as their parents did in 1950."[7]

Durning's data on the growth in household appliance ownership over time embody the triumph of the central message of mass marketing: Greater

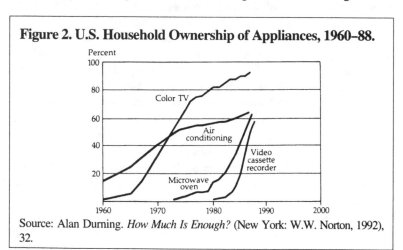

Figure 2. U.S. Household Ownership of Appliances, 1960–88.

Source: Alan Durning. *How Much Is Enough?* (New York: W.W. Norton, 1992), 32.

purchasing power and growing choice in the marketplace guarantee a better (and happier) life. Popular culture advertising underpins the macroeconomic maxim: An expanding economy—with rising per capita income and consumer spending—is a healthy economy.

Comparing global patterns of consumption leads Durning to a deeper inquiry into the qualitative differences in consumption among peoples in the world. He asks what kinds of resources people consume on a day-to-day basis and structures his answer around a comparison of consumption by diet, transport, and principal type of materials used. The result is three classes of consumption, the latter two being of much sounder environmental quality than the first, which has no sustainable characteristics.

Table 1. World Consumption Classes, 1992.

Category of Consumption	Consumers (1.1 billion)	Middle (3.3 billion)	Poor (1.1 billion)
Diet	meat, packaged food, soft drinks	grain, clean water	insufficient grain, unsafe water
Transport	private cars	bicycles, buses	walking
Materials	throwaways	durables	local biomass

Source: Durning, 27.

The primary focus of this tripartite view of consumption in the world—emerging from Worldwatch Institute and a number of liberal environmental, economic, and alternative-lifestyle circles in the United States—is the plight of the consumer class in the United States. Economist Juliet Schor points out that people in the United States work more hours today in their jobs than they did two decades ago, even though we are twice as productive in goods and services as we were in 1948. Why, instead of working more and having less leisure, do we not work less and enjoy more leisure, she queries. Describing the pitfalls of consumerism and the manufacture of discontent that keep middle-class people locked into a work-and-spend cycle, she calls for overcoming consumerism, revaluing leisure, and rethinking the necessity of full-time jobs.[8]

Both Schor and Durning hinge a key part of their prescription—that people rethink and modify their consumerist work- and lifestyles—on the question of happiness. National polls conducted since the 1950s show no increase in the percentage of people who report being "very happy," despite the fact that people now purchase almost twice the number of consumer goods and services they did in the 1950s. Time spent enjoying two of the classic sources of happiness—social relations and leisure—has diminished as people work more to purchase more nondurable, packaged, rapidly obsolete, nonvital goods and services.

Durning advocates that the consumer class be wary of the estimated 3,000 advertising messages that bombard us per day cultivating consumer taste and needs, and that we climb a few rungs down the consumption ladder by choosing durable goods, public transportation, and low-energy devices. In other words, he points to the consumption patterns of the 3.3 billion "middle consumer class" people in Table 1 as more sound and sustainable for the environment.

Voluntary Simplicity Movement

Arising from these same cultural observations, the voluntary simplicity, or new frugality, movement offers a new road map for those of the consumer class who wish to live better with less. Begun in Seattle and strong in the Northwest, this movement was given a high profile by the best-selling book *Your Money or Your Life*, a pragmatic self-help approach to living securely on less money in order to spend one's time in more meaningful social, personal, spiritual, and environmentally sustaining ways.[9]

In this movement, people learn to assess their real financial needs (with generous distinctions made between "needs" and "wants"), how to budget and invest to achieve financial independence on a substantially reduced income, and how to calculate the impacts of their lifestyle on the environment through household audits of energy, products, and waste. More than 300,000 people have developed "new road maps" for their future lives, based on core values they have identified in the process of rethinking what ultimately matters to them. Most reduce their cost of living by 20 percent immediately and, eventually, by even more; many "retire" from careers and full-time jobs to pursue personal and social interests.

If It's Good for the Environment and Good for the Person, What's the Problem?

How can we fault the appeal to happiness and to core values that these critiques of the consumerist culture make? They result in people living "more softly" on the Earth. They reach deeper into a person's self than the green consumer movement, which redirects, but does not necessarily reduce or challenge, consumerism. How many green products are designed for durability and marketed as such? The majority of green product manufacturers employ mass marketing techniques, including the cultivation of "need," and use shallow appeals to feel-good environmentalism to sell their products. Green consumers get locked into seesaw debates over plastic versus paper, for example, never learning that the debate is a foil that deters deeper questions of product durability and necessity. At its best, says Durning, green consumerism outpaces legislation and uses market tactics to reform the market; at its worst, it is "a palliative for the conscience of the consumer class, allowing us to continue business as usual while feeling like we are doing our part."[10]

The primary shortcoming of the "consumer treadmill" critique is that it is socially and politically underdeveloped. Focusing on average per capita consumption, Durning and others make little distinction among the highly disparate economic classes of people within the United States. While our society as a whole is locked into meat, packaged food, soft drinks, and throwaways—with a McDonald's on every corner—the gap between the poorest fifth and richest fifth of the United States begs for an environmental policy that is based on "a hunger and thirst for justice" as well as national concern about global climate change and the decline of personal happiness. The prescriptions to live on less, to get out of the rat race and enjoy more leisure, to examine one's personal values and organize one's life by those values, may not necessarily result in a more equitable or humanistic society. Those who choose voluntary simplicity, durables, and bicycles may live happily and stress-free across town from the angry (or depressed) involuntary poor, with no more empathy, solidarity, or insight into undoing social injustice. (Alternatively, of course, by choosing to live on less, people may end up in less expensive mixed-income neighborhoods, join their neighborhood associations, and, in so doing, meet and collaborate with the involuntary poor on neighborhood betterment.)

The focus on the cultivation of need by mass marketing and the lack of personal fulfillment, when divorced from an inquiry into the patterns and structures that reward the well-off and punish the poor, creates islands of better-living and more personally satisfied people without necessarily generating a sense of a new social movement or new society. "Twelve-step" programs to break the consumer habit offer good techniques borrowed from self-fulfillment and self-control support-group settings, but they are no substitute for social responses to persistent poverty, to misogyny that sells women as sex to be consumed, to child labor and sweatshops, to the consumption engine of militarism and military spending that siphons the life force out of societies, and to all oppressions of "the other."

Social consciousness within the environmental movement, on the other hand, speaks to people's civic and humanistic being, to their quest for a connectedness with others and the earth, to their desire to make the world more just and humane, as well as to the stressed, overworked, and seemingly optionless plight of individuals caught on the work-and-spend treadmill of late-20th-century industrial life. Taming consumption through a personal, spiritual quest is part of the answer, but not the whole one.

The Ecological Footprint

The intriguing epithet "ecological footprint" is shorthand for an analysis that more successfully integrates the calculation of consumer impact on the earth with the responsibilities of government, the right of every human to a fair and healthful share of the Earth's resources, and a deep concern for not overloading or degrading global ecosystems.[11] Here, too, the focus is primarily the North American consumer lifestyle and an accounting of its impacts on the environment. However, the goal is to calculate the size of the Canadian and U.S. ecological footprint compared with that of others in lesser-industrialized and non-industrialized countries and to determine how the oversized North American footprint can be reduced through better regional planning, more ecologically conscious consumption, and the restructuring of industrial technology and economics.

This ecological accounting tool, as geographer Ben Wisner points out so well, inverts "carrying capacity" to ask: Given nearly six billion people in the world, how should we live so as to enable all to live within the limits of the biosphere?[12] The premise of the ecological footprint is that although half the world lives in cities (and by 2020 an estimated two-thirds of people will), we live in a biosphere much larger than the physical boundaries of our cities and towns when we buy goods that are grown or made from resources outside our municipality or region and when we dispose of our wastes in the global atmosphere and marine environments. The ecological footprint is calculated by translating key categories of human consumption—food, housing, transport, consumer goods and services—into the amount of *productive land* needed to provide these goods and services and to assimilate their resultant waste.

Using assumptions about biomass substitutes for fossil fuels and so on, the authors of this method, Mathis Wackernagel and William Rees, calculate that the amount of land needed to support the average Canadian's present consumption, or ecological footprint, is 4.8 hectares.

Table 2. The Ecological Footprint of the Average Canadian, in Hectares per Capita.

	Energy	Built Environment	Agricultural Land	Forest	**TOTAL**
Food	0.4		0.9		**1.3**
Housing	0.5	0.1		0.4	**1.0**
Transport	1.0	0.1			**1.1**
Consumer Goods	0.6		0.2	0.2	**1.0**
Resources in Services	0.4				**0.4**
TOTAL	**2.9**	**0.2**	**1.1**	**0.6**	**4.8**

Source: Mathis Wackernagel, *How Big Is Our Ecological Footprint?* (Vancouver: University of British Columbia, 1993), 3.

In their calculations of ecologically productive land, Wackernagel and Rees estimate that an average of 1.6 hectares of land per capita is available worldwide for goods and services. In other words, the average Canadian uses three times as much of the earth's capacity as is available to every person; in other words, the average Canadian's ecological footprint is three times the size it ought to be, since everyone deserves a fair share of the global commons. Correspondingly, the average Indian ecological footprint is 0.4 hectares per person.

The average per capita consumption in Canada, as in every country, is a composite of the consumption of the rich, poor, and middle consumption classes. Thus, Figure 3 compares the ecological footprints of various Canadian households in order to show where the extremes of consumption lie and whose consumer lifestyle inordinately appropriates the carrying capacity of the Earth.

Three aspects of this analysis are particularly laudable. First, its starting

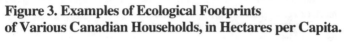

**Figure 3. Examples of Ecological Footprints
of Various Canadian Households, in Hectares per Capita.**

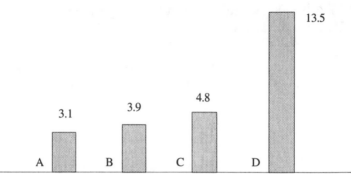

A. Single parent with child. Annual household expenditure: $16,000
B. Student living alone. Annual household expenditure: $10,000
C. Average Canadian family, 2.72 people. Annual household expenditure: $37,000
D. Professional couple, no children. Annual household expenditure: $79,000

Source: Wackernagel, 3.

point is the assumption that every human being has the same claim on nature's productivity and utility. Thus, it is inequitable and undesirable for North Americans to appropriate others' share of the global commons. Second, it promotes an urban and regional planning strategy that would reduce North Americans' footprint on the global environment by reversing sprawl through integrating living, working, and shopping; promoting bike paths and public transportation; and favoring the local economy. Third, it calls for a massive reform of industrial society to free up the ecological space needed by the poor to raise their standard of living, while enabling the well-off to maintain their high material standards.[13] Wackernagel and Rees's recommendations for restructuring industrialism to achieve a smaller ecological footprint on the world include reforms that are simultaneously being advocated by radical environmental economists:

• Shift taxes from income to consumption and include the full costs of resources and pollution in consumer products through environmental taxes and fees. Including true environmental costs in the full cost of products will motivate industry to make cleaner products and consumers to buy them; it will favor reuse, repair, and reconditioning of products.

• Invest in research into energy- and material-efficient technologies to achieve the "four- to ten-fold reduction in material and energy intensity per unit of economic output" needed in industrial countries to reduce the ecological footprint to a sustainable size.

• Invest the anticipated economic gains from the enhanced efficiency in remediating and restoring critical ecosystems.[14]

Even with a more structural approach to macroeconomic systems and the socially conscious goal of commonweal, certain footprints, in this analysis, remain invisible. Women have much less stake in the global economy than men—by virtue of having little political and economic power, as well as by holding different economic priorities, in many instances, from men. Thus, women have a smaller individual and structural footprint than men and male institutions. The economic and political institution of the military, for example (whose extreme impacts on economies, cultures, and ecosystems are analyzed elsewhere in this volume), arises from patriarchal concepts of power and methods of conflict resolution.

What insights and efforts can a woman-centered analysis bring to the issue of consumption in order to further the goals of redistributing and humanizing our use of natural resources, consumer goods, and services, and of mitigating and reversing our pollution impacts on ecosystems?

Conclusion

The commentary of Somali women refugees, when interviewed about the benefits of the solar cooker, provides a robust framework for the elements of a woman-centered analysis of the consumption-environment nexus.

Why are more than a billion women and girls consigned to spending hours daily collecting wood and biomass and ingesting smoke when the dissemination of technologies such as more efficient cook stoves and solar cookers would ease their lives; save their health; and conserve woodlands, soil, water, and biomass in critical ecosystems? Authors Kammen and Dove have identified a bias in science against "research on mundane topics" in energy, agriculture, public health, and resource economics akin to the initial prejudice against the "mundane economics" of the Grameen Bank.[15] Their analysis of the fallacies that underlie the inattention to labor-, time-, health- and environment-saving technologies is consonant with feminist critiques of science culture and science values.[16] According to the canon of science, the premier scientific work is basic research, uncontaminated by the needs of real people and characterized by objective and detached thought. The potential of "break-through discoveries" charges the rarefied atmosphere of science research and relegates revisiting old, unsolved, human-centered problems to second-tier science. In this first-order science, abstract theory, mathematical modeling, speed, distance, and scale are privileged over social benefits, qualitative methods, and the local and small-scale applications of "mundane" science. In other words, what might be seen as the subjectivizing, sociologizing, and feminizing of science popularizes and banalizes it.

Why, when a woman leaves a refugee camp to collect fuel for the next meal, must she fear being raped by men in the desert? And why, when she returns without enough sticks or does not have enough food for her family, must she be forced to have sex with male camp guards for food and fuel? The links between rape, food, fuel, and poverty in the Somali refugee camp exemplify the interconnectedness of women's unequal status in society, their sexual exploitation by men, and gender differences in the consumption of goods and services.

Worldwide, in every society and in every economic class, women are less financially secure than men. Insecurity and the need for survival goods and services create dependency; dependency causes women to sell or trade sex for food. Men who buy sex—and also spend money on gambling, alcohol, cigarettes, pornography, and sports—are spending income, in many cases, that is needed by their families for food, health, education, and home improvements. Studies of household economics demonstrate that women and men spend their incomes differently: men spend more on "luxury" items, and women, earning on the average less than men, spend more on the household needs of their families.[17]

Additionally, health data give insight into gender differences in consumer spending. For example, alcohol use is the leading cause of male disability in developed regions and the fourth leading cause for men in developing regions, while for women in developed regions, it is the tenth leading cause of disability. Depression is the leading cause of disease burden for women in developing and developed countries; poor reproductive health and suicide are the other leading causes of poor health for women in developing countries.[18]

Social goodness and community health, as the "ecological footprint" analysis affirms, are requisites and indices of a sustainable community. In our effort to reduce overconsumption through distinguishing genuine needs and consumerist wants, we must confront the consumption of so-called goods and services that are based on the sexual exploitation of women and girls and are often a consequence of war and environmental degradation, such as prostitution, pornography, and mail-order brides. The impeccable logic of environmental justice—that poor communities of color have been systematically exploited by polluters and industry by reason of race, and suffer disproportionately from poor health—holds for women as well. Like racial justice, a sexual justice that seeks to eliminate the sexual exploitation of women is fundamental to environmental justice, to community health, and to social goodness.

Notes

1. *Delivering on a Promise,* annual report (Sacramento, CA: Solar Cookers International, 1995).

2. Daniel M. Kammen and Michael R. Dove, "The Virtues of Mundane Science," *Environment,* Vol. 39, No. 6 (July/August 1997), 12–13.

3. Christopher J.L. Murray and Alan Lopez, *The Global Burden of Disease: Summary* (Boston: Harvard School of Public Health, 1996), 28.

4. Kammen and Dove, "The Virtues of Mundane Science," op. cit., 12.

5. Ibid., 11.

6. Alan Durning, *How Much Is Enough?* (New York: W.W. Norton, 1992).

7. Ibid., 30.

8. Juliet Schor, *The Overworked American: The Unexpected Decline of Leisure* (New York: Basic Books, 1991).

9. Joe Dominguez and Vicki Robin, *Your Money or Your Life* (New York: Viking, 1992).

10. Durning, *How Much Is Enough?*, op. cit., 125.

11. Mathis Wackernagel and William Rees, *Our Ecological Footprint: Reducing Human Impact on the Earth* (Gabriola Island, British Columbia and Philadelphia: New Society Publishers, 1996).

12. Ben Wisner, "The "Limitations of 'Carrying Capacity,'" *Political Environments* (Winter-Spring 1996), 1, 3–4.

13. Wackernagel and Rees, *Our Ecological Footprint,* op. cit, 144.

14. Ibid., 144–45.

15. Kammen and Dove, "The Virtues of Mundane Science," op. cit., 10–15, 38–41.

16. See Sue V. Rosser, *Female-Friendly Science* (New York: Teacher's College Press, 1990).

17. Sylvia Chant, *Gender, Urban Development and Housing* (New York: UNDP, 1996), 12–15.

18. Murray and Lopez, *The Global Burden of Disease,* op. cit., 21, 25–26.

NATIVE SOVEREIGNTY AND SOCIAL JUSTICE

Moving Toward an Inclusive Social Justice Framework

Justine Smith

While there is a growing awareness of the connections among various social justice issues, too many times activists continue to address those issues in a singular, focused, and isolationist manner. The current atmosphere in progressive circles pays much lip service to working collaboratively and inclusively. But in reality, the women's movement often has little to do with the environmental movement, the environmental movement has little to do with the economic justice movement, the economic justice movement has little to do with educational issues, and so on.

As an example, in 1997 I gave a presentation to a group of young activists and asked the participants how many of them thought protecting the environment was important. All raised their hands. I then asked how many of them thought supporting Native sovereignty was important, and only two raised their hands. I proceeded to explain how in the state of Wisconsin, one of the strongest defenses for the environment comes from tribal environmental protection programs and legal intervention from tribal governments. When asked how many of them were aware of this, nobody raised a hand.

This situation indicates that despite all the rhetoric, activists continue to prioritize "their" issue at the expense of the larger social justice struggle. Given this failure to see the broader picture, comprehensive, long-range social justice strategies are virtually nonexistent; effective collaborative efforts are few and far between; and divide-and-conquer tactics are often successfully employed so that groups that should be allies often become adversaries.

There is a general recognition in Native communities that although there are many distinct issues of importance impacting indigenous peoples today, all these issues are fundamentally connected and of equal value. To address one issue to the exclusion of others is to win the battle but lose the war. Consequently, Native rights activists reject a single-issue framework in favor of a framework of sovereignty. This sovereignty framework enables Native peoples to recognize and address various issues in a comprehensive manner. An example of the potential impact and application of Native sovereignty in a social justice struggle is the battle that has been taking place over the past several years against mining interests in northern Wisconsin. This struggle exemplifies how "Native sovereignty" elucidates the connections among seemingly disparate social justice issues. While mining development may ostensibly seem to be an environmental issue, its potential effects can be felt from the classroom to the doctor's office. Yet few non-Indian activists consider mining to be a pressing feminist or educational issue. Why? The example of mining in northern Wisconsin illustrates how would-be non-Indian allies of Native rights often unwittingly undermine not only the interests of Native people but their own interests when they operate from a paradigm of isolation rather than of sovereignty. Reframing contemporary struggles (such as the reproductive rights movement) using a sovereignty framework illustrates the potential impact Native sovereignty can have on the larger, global social justice movement.

Treaty Rights

Treaty rights are a primary component of the Native sovereignty movement. In 1983, Justice Barbara Crabb set a precedent with the *Voigt* decision by recognizing the treaty rights of the Lake Superior Band of Chippewas to hunt, fish, and gather in the ceded territories of northern Wisconsin.[1] This decision sparked a series of violent confrontations between non-Indians and the Chippewa who were attempting to exercise their treaty-protected rights to spearfish and gill-net. Many anti-Indian hate groups garnered local opposition to Chippewa spearfishing on the basis that Indians were gaining "special" rights to fish and were exhuasting the fish supply of Wisconsin lakes at the expense of non-Indians. (In fact, the Chippewa took only about 3 percent of the fish in northern Wisconsin; the majority of fishing was done by non-Indian sportsfishers, according to the Wisconsin Department of Natural Resources.)[2]

Buying into the rampant anti-Indian propaganda, some animal rights groups and environmental organizations joined these hate groups (e.g., Protect America's Rights and Resources and Stop Treaty Abuse) in opposing the Chippewa. At a 1990 Earth Day celebration in northern Wisconsin, an animal rights organization refused to let a Native American activist speak at the rally. They feared he would promote spearfishing, which they considered to be an act of brutality against fish. What both local non-Indians in northern Wisconsin and several animal rights and environmental organizations failed to understand was that this struggle was about much more than just fish. The larger picture of environmental degradation and increasing economic depression to which Natives active in the spearfishing struggle were trying to call attention was lost amid the rancorous fighting, largely orchestrated by multinational corporations that had a large financial stake in dividing the Indian and non-Indian communities in northern Wisconsin.

Mining

The presence of mining corporations in northern Wisconsin dates back to the earliest European settlements in the area. In fact, most of the early Indian treaties throughout the Lake Superior region were specifically written to cede mineral/mining rights.[3] The second wave of mining began in the 1970s and brought the interests of several multinational corporations to northern Wisconsin. In 1975, the Bureau of Mines, under contract with the Bureau of Indian Affairs (BIA), performed explorations on Indian lands throughout the country. In Wisconsin they found large deposits of copper and zinc. Gold and uranium were discovered to a lesser extent. This portion of the Great Lakes region was always known to be rich in mineral resources. It was not until the technological revolution in the 1970s and 1980s that mineral resource recovery became economically feasible.

One of the first mining companies to begin serious speculation in northern Wisconsin was Exxon. In 1975, Exxon Minerals Company, a subsidiary of the oil giant founded by John D. Rockefeller, located one of the largest zinc–copper sulfide deposits in the world (estimated at 55 million tons) near Crandon, Wisconsin. This land is adjacent to the Mole Lake Sokaogan Chippewa reservation. Situated in Forest County at the headwaters of the Wolf River, the deposit was estimated to contain enough mineral to produce ore for up to 25 years.[4] Exxon was not alone in its quest for financial profits (at one point Exxon estimated it stood to gain approximately $4.5 billion in profit from the mine). Other British and Canadian-based mining giants began staking claims on copper, zinc, and silver. All these discoveries were on ceded territory protected by treaty.[5] Tribes threatened by proposed mining development include the Chippewa, Oneida, Menominee, Potawatomie, and Stockbridge-Munsee.

Exxon's proposed mine at Mole Lake would have far-reaching environmental consequences. The Great Lakes bioregion is one of the most geologically and ecologically sensitive places in the hemisphere.[6] The mine itself would cover an area of more than 866 acres and produce 14,000 tons of ore a day. Over its lifetime it would generate an estimated 44 million tons of acidic waste, the weight of eight Great Pyramids in Egypt.[7] About half of this would be used to fill the mine shafts. The remainder would be dumped into tailings ponds 90 feet deep and spreading over 355 acres.[8]

More than 15,000 lakes, plus numerous rivers and streams, are part of the unique geology of Wisconsin. However, all these sources constitute only 3 percent of the water supply in the state because the vast majority of water is located in immense groundwater reservoirs. At Mole Lake, the proposed 2,500-foot mine shafts would drain groundwater "in much the same way that a hypodermic needle draws blood from a patient."[9] After use in the mining process, the water would then be discharged into the Wolf River, designated an "Outstanding Water Resource" by the state of Wisconsin and a "National Wild and Scenic River" by the United States. Operations would cause the water table to drop by as much as seven feet over a four-square-mile area.

The stakes at Mole Lake are greatly raised because the mine would be a sulfide mine. Sulfide wastes have a toxicity and persistence level similar to radioactive nuclear waste. When metals such as copper, zinc, silver, or gold are mined, metallic sulfide waste results. When this waste comes into contact with air or water, it oxidizes, forming sulfuric acid and highly poisonous heavy metals including mercury, lead, arsenic, and cadmium. In a wet area like Wisconsin, the potential for contamination is high. As one of Exxon's own engineers so aptly stated, "You couldn't think of a more difficult place to mine."[10]

In addition, no technology exists for reclaiming a sulfide mine, and the Bureau of Mines admits that contamination is a virtual certainty. The one difference between radioactive waste and sulfide waste is that over time, radioactive waste eventually degrades (albeit in about 10,000 years). Sulfide waste *never* degrades. Waste dumped into tailings ponds would eventually have to be treated. An area in California known as Iron Mountain is so contaminated from sulfide mining that streams flowing through the area are now classified as dead; those streams will never again be able to support aquatic or vegetative life of any kind. In England, there are sulfide mines nearly a thousand years old where toxic waste still persists.

Very few people realized the potential impact of the *Voigt* decision. Not only were the rights to hunt, fish, and gather in the ceded territories recognized, but the right to have things *to* hunt, fish, and gather in the ceded territories was also protected. In other words, if all the fish are contaminated with mercury and unfit for consumption, then the fish are for all practical purposes unavailable, and a recognized treaty right has been violated. Thus, anything that would harm a treaty-protected resource (such as fish, trees, or wildlife) violates the law. As Chippewa activist Walt Bressette states, "What is the point of having the right to spearfish if all the fish are contaminated with mercury?"[11] As a result, when a project potentially infringes upon a recognized treaty-held right, such as the potential environmental degradation caused by Exxon's mine in northern Wisconsin, Native nations have a legal right to challenge that project on the grounds of violation of treaty law.

While very few non-Indian activists recognized the importance of the *Voigt* decision at the time, multinational companies such as Exxon did. Mounting evidence suggests that these companies began funding anti-Indian hate groups (such as those mentioned previously) to divert attention away from the mining crisis and onto spearfishing. United opposition to mining from both Indians and non-Indians initially drove Exxon out of Wisconsin in 1986. But after sharp divisions were wedged between the two communities following the well-funded spearfishing protests, Exxon announced its return to the area in 1994 and is attempting to resume operations in Crandon.[12]

Animal rights and environmental organizations played right into these divide-and-conquer techniques of mining companies. Through their narrow definition of animal rights, they did not pick up on the fact that the treaties retaining the Chippewa's right to hunt, fish, and gather in the ceded territory in Wisconsin was (and is) one of the best protections against potential widespread environmental degradation throughout the northern part of the state. In fact, Native activists during the spearfishing struggle tried to focus attention on the devastation toxic contaminants brought to fish, wildlife, and the entire community, while attempting to organize Indian and non-Indian people alike to actively oppose any development that would further degrade the environment.

Repatriation

Even treaties have their limits. The paradigm of sovereignty allows for an even broader framework for social justice than do treaty rights. Repatriation is one example. A sovereign nation inherently possesses the right to identify and care for its members. When issues arise over burial sites, a tribe may exert jurisdiction and intervene on behalf of their deceased members. This very scenario occurred in northern Wisconsin surrounding the proposed Exxon mine. Evidence of a burial ground encircling the mine site gave the Mole Lake Chippewa more leverage to oppose Exxon's mining efforts.[13] They could not have done so by appealing to treaty rights alone; only by invoking their tribal sovereignty did this become possible.

Self-Governance

Another inherent aspect of sovereignty is the right to self-governance and regulation. Under the Environmental Protection Agency (EPA), regulatory laws may be drafted and enforced by individual states as long as they conform to federal guidelines. They can be *more* stringent than federal laws, but not less stringent. The EPA recognized the sovereignty of Native nations under "treatment as state" (TAS) status, which allows them to apply for regulatory authority just like a state. Several Native nations in Wisconsin have applied for TAS designation. The Forest County Potawatomie moved to have the air quality designation around their reservation upgraded to a Class I area pursuant to the Clean Air Act.[14] The Mole Lake Sokaogan and Menominee are seeking redesignation of their water quality under the Clean Water Act. While only the Potawatomie's actions would impact off-reservation activities, all these efforts would allow for closer monitoring of pollutants not currently covered by Wisconsin environmental laws.

Education

The battle over mining in Wisconsin is also fought on other fronts that often go completely unrecognized by activists. In Wisconsin, many mainstream environmental groups have been very visible when it comes to demonstrations, legislative lobbying, and, in some cases, grassroots organizing when opposing a major multinational corporation like Exxon from mining in the northern part of the state. But these same groups have been virtually non-existent when those same multinational corporations have added pro-mining propaganda to school textbooks and sent company representatives to do presentations in the local school systems to create a "pro-mining" environment. The educational system is so far outside the mainstream environmental movement's purview (with the exception of designing its own environmentally friendly curricula), such groups often are not even aware that a major battle is being fought in the classrooms by corporations, much less how to combat it. When a corporation like Exxon stands to gain close to $4.5 billion from mining, it can afford to invest in school education and to gain public support for its activities even if it means waiting a generation, especially when that generation has been spoon-fed pro-mining propaganda.

At the 1995 "Honor the Earth" gathering held in Mole Lake, local community residents spoke about this new battleground developing in the school classrooms. One man spoke about his daughter coming home from school one day and telling him about the guest speaker who visited her class. He was a representative of the Crandon Mining Company (which comprises two multinational mining corporations: Exxon and Rio Algom) who talked to the schoolchildren about all the benefits they would reap as a result of the proposed mine. The spokesperson told her class that lots of new jobs would be created and that maybe their parents would be some of those potential employees. Another parent reported that her child was told that he himself might be able to secure a high-salaried position with the Crandon Mining Company when he was older. Improvements would be coming to their town and a new era of economic prosperity could be expected. Even worse, the father discovered that new textbooks were being introduced to his daughter's class that discussed the positive new role of mining in Wisconsin. Consequently, Native activists are working with other embattled communities to counter the anti-environmental propaganda that goes unchallenged in local school curricula.

Gaming

Another front where the mining battle is being fought is in Indian gaming. Revenues generated by Indian gaming have in large part fueled tribal environmental and legal departments that have actively opposed mining. Attacks on gaming have been coming from both the federal and state levels. Up to this point, federal legislative actions against gaming (such as attempts to tax Indian gaming or to withhold federal aid to tribes who have gaming) have effectively been held at bay. On the state level, however, the attacks have been and continue to be relentless. Under the Indian Gaming Regulatory Act, Native nations must enter into compacts with the state in which they reside in order to operate gaming facilities. These compacts are subject to renewal every few years, as determined by the negotiating parties.

In Wisconsin, all gaming compacts must be renewed in 1998 and 1999. The governor has demanded that 20 points be satisfied by Native nations in order for them to receive their compact renewals.[15] Heading that list is nullification of treaty rights. Native nations must agree to relinquish their treaty rights in order to renew their compacts. One Native nation in Wisconsin has already withdrawn a lawsuit from federal court challenging the state's refusal to recognize their treaty rights. Another was forced to agree not to develop or attempt to enforce tribal environmental protection programs that might have off-reservation impacts. In addition, tribes were asked to agree to a "no-comment policy" on the compact renegotiations. While Native nations have honored the agreement in good faith, the governor has repeatedly violated the agreement by continually issuing inflammatory, anti-gaming rhetoric to the media. This has swayed public opinion against Indian gaming. To make matters worse, a recent Supreme Court decision has limited the ability of tribes to sue states that do not negotiate gaming compacts in good faith.

Many otherwise liberal religious organizations and denominations that otherwise support Indian rights have been fighting Indian gaming because they deem gaming an immoral activity. However, they do not offer tribes an alternative plan for economic development to replace gaming revenues. While they believe gaming causes social disintegration (which studies have shown not to be the case),[16] they have not addressed the mass social, environmental, and economic disintegration that will result if gaming revenues are suddenly cut from tribes that have not yet had the capital or time to create other means of economic development. They also do not recognize that, in many cases, tribal legal challenges (funded by gaming revenues) have posed the most effective challenges to mining and other devastating development proposals.

Victories

Fortunately, a broad-based coalition of citizens and organizations, through its extensive educational campaigns, has been successful in rebuilding the ties between Indian nations and non-Indians in northern Wisconsin in order to fight multinational mining conglomerates like Exxon. As a result of these collaborative efforts, in 1998 Exxon announced its withdrawal from mining operations in northern Wisconsin. Furthermore, through a series of broad-based, grassroots educational efforts, a mining moratorium bill was signed into law. The moratorium bill requires a mining company to prove that its operations would not result in environmental degradation. And environmental degradation that results from a corporation's past mining projects in other places (including other countries) can be used as evidence against that corporation during the permitting process. Groups that were fighting in the 1980s are beginning to see common cause. Similarly, environmental groups are increasingly appealing to treaty rights in their legal battles to stop environmental degradation.

Defining Sovereignty

While fighting for sovereignty is critical for Indian nations, it is important to clarify what sovereignty means. Simply uttering the term does not make a nation sovereign. A nation must have the economic, social, and political power to enforce its right to self-determination in order for sovereignty to have any true meaning. Furthermore, sovereignty must be exercised by the people of the community, not just a few members of the elite. Otherwise, sovereignty becomes simply another tool for neocolonial governments and multinational corporations to manipulate indigenous and Third World peoples.

In cases where it works to their economic benefit, corporations do not always oppose sovereignty. In fact, they come up in strong support of "Native sovereignty." For example, Northern States Power (NSP), an electric utility company in Minnesota, wanted to store radioactive nuclear waste near its power plant, which just so happens to border the Prairie Island Mdewakanton Sioux reservation. When the Prairie Island community invoked Native sovereignty to oppose the corporation's efforts, NSP did everything in its power to neutralize their efforts and eventually received permission to store the waste.[17] However, when NSP wanted to locate a monitored retrievable storage (MRS) facility for their radioactive waste, they approached the Mescalero Apache reservation in New Mexico as a potential site. When the state of New Mexico protested, NSP protested that the Mescalero were a sovereign nation and could do whatever they wanted with their land.

Native Sovereignty and Global Justice

Sovereignty is a useful paradigm for understanding not only Native struggles, but other struggles as well. One common response to Native issues is, "So how does any of that matter to non-Indian people?" One obvious response is that environmental degradation does not stop at political borders. Sulfide contamination from mining would contaminate not only the groundwater in the northeast portion of the state, but the Wisconsin and Wolf Rivers, which eventually empty into the Mississippi River and Lake Michigan watersheds, respectively. The potential health effects would impact massive populations in several states for generations. In addition, as Native activist Winona LaDuke has stated, "We are called First Nation people because whatever destructive plans are developed, they are always tried out on us first." What happens to Native peoples and Native nations will eventually happen to everyone. Defending and protecting Native rights and sovereignty is a first step toward preservation of the global community.

In addition, the framework of sovereignty is also helpful for informing other social justice movements. For instance, the reproductive rights movement frames the issues around individual "choice"—does the woman have the choice to have or not to have an abortion. This analysis obscures all the social conditions that prevent women from having and making real choices— lack of health care, poverty, lack of social services, etc. If a woman has an abortion because she cannot afford to have a child she would otherwise want, is that a real choice? In the Native context, where women often find that the only contraceptives available to them are dangerous, long-acting hormonal contraceptives (i.e., Depo-Provera and Norplant), where they are often subjected to medical experimentation without their knowledge and/or consent, where they live in communities in which unemployment rates can run as high as 80 percent, and where their life expectancy can be as low as 47 years, reproductive "choice" defined so narrowly is a meaningless concept. Instead, Native women and men must fight for community self-determination and sovereignty over their health care. Fighting for reproductive rights under the framework of sovereignty allows both Indian and non-Indian communities to address *all* the factors that prevent women from determining their reproductive lives.

Finally, adopting a sovereignty-like stance in other social justice movements allows for greater collaboration and cooperation with less danger of being co-opted. Imagine the potency of a coordinated, well-organized social justice movement that saw the connections among issues and backed each other whenever the situation arose. If every feminist, environmentalist, animal rights, anti-militarist, pro-labor, and racial justice activist had appeared on the boat landings in the early 1990s, the spearfishing protests would have turned into anti-mining rallies. And there is a certain accountability that occurs when movements work collaboratively rather than in isolation. It becomes much more difficult for an organization to issue ignorant (though politically popular) positions if it actively collaborates and works in consultation with other social justice organizations. This would have prevented the Sierra Club from issuing a position statement at the People of Color Environmental Leadership Summit in 1991 calling for increased development of national energy reserves in the lower 48 states, because they would have known that the vast majority of those energy reserves are located on Indian land and such legislation would translate into the wholesale violation of treaty rights, thereby destroying the very environment they sought to protect.

The potency of the sovereignty construct is just being realized in Native issues around the region, country, and hemisphere. However, it is important to realize that sovereignty is not a new construct. It has been a guiding, unifying, and empowering force for Native peoples for more than 500 years. It is also not unique to the United States or Canada. The struggle for self-determination, framed in terms of either sovereignty or independence, is present in virtually all liberation movements around the world. The potential potency of sovereignty for the entire social justice movement could be a powerful, though as yet untapped, political resource and a model for liberation.

Notes

1. David H. Getches, Charles F. Wilkinson, and Robert A. Williams, Jr., eds., *Cases and Materials in Federal Indian Laws*, 3rd ed. (St. Paul, MN: West Publishing Co., 1993), 22–23; Ronald N. Satz, *Chippewa Treaty Rights: The Reserved Rights of Wisconsin's Chippewa Indians in Historical Perspective*, transactions of the Wisconsin Academy of Sciences, Arts, and Letters Vol. 79, No. 1 (Madison, WI: Wisconsin Academy of Sciences, Arts, and Letters, 1991), 187–97.

2. Great Lakes Indian Fish and Wildlife Commission, *Seasons of the Chippewa* (Odanah, WI: 1995), 7.

3. Francis Paul Prucha, *American Indian Treaties: The History of a Political Anomaly* (Berkeley: University of California Press, 1994), 141.

4. Al Gedicks and Zoltan Grossman, "Exxon Returns to Wisconsin: The Threat of the Crandon/Mole Lake Mine," *The Circle* (April 1994), 8.

5. See generally Al Gedicks, *The New Resource Wars: Native and Environmental Struggles against Multinational Corporations* (Boston: South End Press, 1993).

6. "Call for Action on the Crandon Mine," *Milwaukee Area Greens*, Vol. 30 (Spring 1997), 1.

7. Wolf Watershed Education Project, *Save Our Clean Waters* (Madison, WI: 1996), 4.

8. Ibid.

9. Gedicks and Grossman, "Exxon Returns to Wisconsin," op. cit., 8.

10. Quoted in Larry Van Goethem, "Exxon Mine Will Feature Elaborate Waste Water Plan," *Milwaukee Journal*, March 28, 1982.

11. Walt Bressette, statement at Midwest Treaty Network Annual Conference, University of Wisconsin, Madison, May 1994.

12. Gedicks and Grossman, "Exxon Returns to Wisconsin," op. cit., 8.

13. U.S.C.A. Secs. 3001–13 (West. Supp. 1991); see Rennard Strickland, "Implementing the National Policy of Understanding, Preserving, and Safeguarding the Heritage of Indian Peoples and Native Hawaiians: Human Rights, Sacred Objects, and Cultural Patrimony," 24 Ariz.S.L.J. 175 (1992); Rennard Strickland, "Back to the Future: A Proposed Model Tribal Act to Protect Native Cultural Heritage," 46

Ark.L.Rev. 161 (1993); Walter R. Echohawk and Roger C. Echohawk, "Repatriation, Reburial, and Religious Rights," in Christopher Vecsey, ed., *Handbook of American Indian Religious Freedom* (New York: Crossroad, 1991), 63.

14. See *Nance v. EPA*, 645 F.2d 701 (9th Cir.), *cert. denied,* 454 U.S. 1081 (1981).

15. In a letter to Ms. Keller, Wisconsin governor Tommy Thompson stated, "Many citizens would like to see Wisconsin get something out of this [Indian gaming] process—no expansion of gaming, more revenue, elimination of spearfishing, a halt to applications to gain control over water and air standards." *Lac du Flambeau News*, October 1997.

16. Oneida Nation of Wisconsin, *Local Economic Impacts of Oneida Gaming* (November 1992).

17. North American Water Office, *Prairie Island Coalition Against Nuclear Storage* (Lake Elmo, MN: 1995).

THE STATE: FRIEND OR FOE?

Distributive Justice Issues and African American Women

Marsha J. Tyson Darling

This essay is about social constructions of African American women's sexuality; laws, policies, and actions of the state; the exercise of privacy rights; motherhood; and distributive justice. This essay is also about what happens when we consider the intersection of race, sex, and class—hence, what happens when we put African American women at the center of a discourse about distributive justice. Historically, most Black females have been deprived of the right to speak for themselves and rendered largely invisible. Others have insisted on representing Black females, most often out of a desire to control them by relying on popular beliefs about Black females and Black families. As the only population of women in America ever defined by law as chattel property, African American women are indeed very vulnerable to enduring beliefs, attitudes, and actions—often perpetuated by the state itself—that undermine their self-determination.

Whether through social policy rhetoric that fails to ensure substantive equality of opportunity or economic justice, or in paternalistic political jargon about the state's responsibility to better "control" poor African American females for their own good, through much of this century the state has undertaken to scrutinize, severely limit, and in some instances collapse the privacy rights of poor African American women and, by extension, their children. Indeed, through the decades of "Jane Crowism," and even since the civil rights movement, some agencies of the state, much of the press in the country, a substantial amount of the social science scholarship, and much of the popular culture have characterized poor Black women as promiscuous, lazy, and lacking motivation or merit (a time-honored measure of moral deservability). The marginalization of Black women has very often been presented as evidence of African American female inertia and unworthiness.

The ideological legacy that has derived from the intersection of racism and sexism is that poor and working-class African American women have most often been represented as lacking the moral right, political authority, economic power, or cultural know-how to represent themselves as authorities of their own lives. This ideological legacy can aptly be called paternalism in its most benign manifestation, and oppression in its most disempowering manifestation. Either way, African American women have seldom experienced in their lives the state's active interest in their empowerment. Instead, generations of African American women and their allies have repeatedly attempted to construct a liberating and legitimizing basis for interactions with the state.

The state's role in including or marginalizing any group in society is particularly revealing for what it tells us about the social construction of the state's interests. When the state represents its compelling interests as inclusive of the civil and human rights of African American females, then there is a basis in law, jurisprudence, ethics, and social policy, taken together, by which even poor African American women are accorded the constitutional provisions of freedom, privacy, equal protection, and due process under the law. The refusal to recognize such rights for poor African American women, given the historical legacy of the constructed rationales explored in this essay and in other scholarship on the issue, is the driving force behind state intrusion into the privacy rights of African American women in contemporary society.

In contemporary society, the ideological rationale for the state's control and repression of many Black females derives from beliefs that have persistently popularized and institutionalized representations of Black female irrationality, promiscuity, laziness, and emasculating temperament. The consequence of state abandonment of Black female civil rights has been to intensify the marginalization and invisibility of poor Black females and the intensification of poverty for poor Black children.

Essentially, this essay considers the question of what happens when we place African American females at the center of discourses about: (*a*) the exercise of constitutional rights regarding privacy, equal protection under the law, and due process; and (*b*) innovations in genetic biomedical technology that raise troubling questions about the potential for the abuse of poor African American women. This essay's chief contribution is its examination of the historical factors that have contributed to the social construction of African American women as "other," as undeserving of state protection. Ranging from the letter of the law and social custom in the American colonies to eugenics-driven public policies in the 20th century, racist and misogynist ideologies and theories in law, medical science, public health, much of social science scholarship, and the provision of social services have served as reflections of the social constructions of Black women as "other." No contemporary discourse of this issue should proceed without a candid evaluation of the impact of this legacy of exclusion. And no discussion of at-risk populations in an age of genetic experimentation should naively suppose that poor African American women's constitutional rights are safeguarded.

It is important to say at the outset that the social consequences of pejorative beliefs about poor African American females have derived from theories of biological determinism. In their many guises, theories of biological determinism have generally served to construct and legitimize racist, sexist, and classist beliefs and actions against the poor, women, and people of color. As it has been constructed and used, biological determinism is at the root of the idea that those who have been most marginalized from the sources, structures, and institutions of authority and privilege are least deserving of rights, because they are believed to be genetically inferior and hence less valuable to society. Throughout this century the marginalized have been the most vulnerable, as the agencies of the state often undertook to define "compelling interests" and to construct social policies predicated on racially and sexually prescribed normative and ethical considerations of "worthiness" and "deservability." In this regard, theories of biological determinism have been complicit in constructing all women, but especially poor African American women, as the "undeserving other."

It is important to examine the consequences of how the state has increasingly defined society's good as inimical to the rights of privacy in motherhood, medical confidentiality for at-risk women, and civil rights protections from coercion in the context of informed consent and choice for poor and marginalized females.[1] In this vein, historical representations of African American female sexuality are central to any assessment of 20th-century social policies directed at Black women, for at the root of much contemporary decision-making that affects social policy are beliefs about Black women that remain mired in decades-old, but firmly entrenched, attitudes and forms of misogyny directed toward African American females.

A word about the social construction of the "state" is in order here, for this essay challenges a narrow and limited theoretical definition of the "state." To begin with, the state is often referenced as an impersonal structure charged with overseeing the administration of government. As feminist scholars have pointed out, such a theory of the state focuses on the state as a "thing" rather than as a "process."[2] The "state" is a governing entity made up of values; beliefs; traditions of male ownership and control; and the expropriation, domination, and selective representation of citizenship rights, thereby establishing selective participatory democracy. In the context of this essay, the social services system represents an example of an institution of the state that operates to prioritize beliefs constructed and legitimized according to racial, sexual, and class values and mores.

Pejorative references to many poor African American females as "welfare queens," even when the majority of women receiving social service assistance are white, represent the ways in which perceptions of welfare recipients who are the very poor are sexual and racial. As the discourse about welfare is racialized, poor women receiving state assistance have been represented as undeserving, and even as doing too well to be assisted by the dollars of others. Such a pejorative emphasis on poverty-caused entitlement derives from culturally reinforced ideas about the "undeserving poor" and "bad mothers." (Meanwhile, entitlements for the middle class—like the upward redistribution of income from income-tax deductions for real estate taxes and home mortgages—and corporations flourish.) Hence, for the most part popular perceptions of poor African American females on welfare are responsible for much of the belittling and austere treatment many poor Black females often receive from social service agencies, law enforcement institutions, and many scholars and policy analysts in the business of constructing public policy.

From the colonial era to the decades of suffrage reform and then civil rights protest in this century, most state and federal laws were created as entitlement vehicles for actualizing self-determination for white males of European ancestry. Throughout those many decades, the state has operated to establish institutional structures and operations that legitimize white-skin privilege and, through the institution of the family, male sexual ownership of women. Since skin-color privilege defined "freedom" and "humanity" in the colonial era, white women were among the "free" and "human" in a social setting where African women were without human rights, being defined as "chattel." And, until this century, Native American women were defined and treated as the enemy.

The absence of any human rights for enslaved women abrogated their fundamental humanity and reduced them to "movable property" and units of production and reproduction. While there is little dispute that enslaved women often did the same work as enslaved men, the expropriation of enslaved African women's reproductive sexuality for the financial gain of white males is important to note because of the ways in which social custom and law opened the way for white males to financially profit from the pregnancies that were often the consequence of interracial reproductive sex with enslaved women.

In this vein, white settler males established social customs in the colonial era around which they fashioned laws that prescribed social relations based on the desire to physically exploit captive African men and women. Responding to the presence of increasing numbers of mulatto children born from interracial sexual relations between white men and enslaved African females, the Virginia House of Burgess in 1662 led the colonies with a statute that rendered the paternity of children born to enslaved African females inconsequential, at the same time extending enslavement beyond the generation of enslaved women bearing interracial children. Both intentions were responsible for beginning the process of institutionalizing the expropriation of Black female reproductive sexuality for the purpose of breeding a slave population born in the colonies with both European and African fathers. Statutory law clearly reflected the relatively early decision to expropriate the reproductive sexuality of enslaved African women:

> 1662 Act XII. Children got by an Englishman upon a Negro woman shall be bond or free according to the condition of the mother.[3]

Hence, from the colonial era until well into the 19th century, the vast majority of enslaved African or mixed-race women exercised no human rights based on skin color, sex, religious affiliation, or national origin.

The fact that many poor white Englishwomen were indentured should not be misconstrued to mean that the social reality of indentured servant status for white women approximated the social meaning of the entire absence of human rights. And while we can certainly find some examples of the deplorable treatment of some poor white female servants, no one in either the colonies or in the creation of the Republic legislated the expropriation of the sexual and reproductive organs of white women, no matter how poor, for the personal and economic use of a different race of men. References to Black females as "wenches" remind us that enslaved African women were referenced, legislated, and treated as non-sentient "things," non-humans in a property system. The legacy of this legally sustained social custom, which spanned 200 years into the 19th century, is still with us in this century, as persistent racism and sexism often continue to influence white male and female perceptions of Black female sexuality even today.

In the 19th century, the social construction of enslaved women as "other" was handed its most potent weapon by white male medical and scientific professionals. Reflecting on the representations of Black females as akin to the "Hottentot Venus," leading white male medical professionals were among the professionals who positioned themselves to speak in ways many whites regarded as definitive.[4] The Southern white male doctors who laid the intellectual groundwork for still later beliefs about Black females were often men convinced that living in a system in which they and other white men controlled and possessed property rights over Black female sexuality qualified them as experts on Black female sexuality. Discussing Black female genitalia, a leading medical publication proclaimed Black female sex as reflecting the "atrophic condition of the external genital organs in which the labia are much flattened and thinned, approaching in type that offered by the female anthropoid ape."[5]

Reflecting on Black female and male sexuality and mental capacity, three medical views surfaced that are revealing of how white constructed beliefs about Black females influenced the range of concerns white doctors and scientists pondered in the 19th century. Commenting on Samuel George Morton, "empiricist of polygeny," biologist Stephen Jay Gould implicates the prejudices and biases of Morton's largest, most copious, and most influential work, *Crania Americana,* published in 1839. Morton is quoted as representing a female Hottentot prototype as "the women are represented as even more repulsive in appearance than the men."[6] Indicating the preeminent authority that physicians exerted on topics related to race and sex relations, John S. Haller Jr.'s now-classic study of scientific attitudes in the second half of the 19th century represents a scientific view of interracial sex:

> One of the characters of the Ethiopian race consists in the length of the penis compared to that of the Caucasian race. This dimension coincides with the length of the uterine canal in the Ethiopian female, and both have their cause in the form of the pelvis in the Negro race. There results from this physical disposition, that the union of the Caucasian man with an Ethiopian woman is easy and without any inconvenience for the latter. The case is different in the union of the Ethiopian [man] with a Caucasian woman, who suffers in the act.[7]

In the 20th century, many of the nation's health care practitioners and providers, scientists, and scientific researchers have been trained or influenced by racist and misogynist beliefs about Black female sexuality, even as they set about to further disparate treatment for Black females, particularly in the area of reproductive rights. So widespread and pervasive was the vilification of Black female sexuality that many professionals in the public health movement, the birth control movement, and, still later, the social welfare movement internalized many of the pejorative racist and sexist beliefs constructed into humanities, science, and social science scholarship and popular culture in earlier decades.

In the late 19th and early 20th centuries, eugenics provided an ideological defense of the control of Black female reproductive sexuality.

> The word *eugenic* comes from the Greek word *eugenes* (eu [well] and genos [born]). The term refers to improving the race through the bearing of healthy offspring. Eugenics is the science that deals with all influences that improve the inborn quality of the human race, particularly through the control of hereditary factors. A eugenic program is a public policy structure designed to have its effect on gene frequencies in whole populations. Negative eugenics is a systematic effort, whether decisional or programmatic, to minimize the transmission of genes that are considered deleterious.... Another term that is relative is *genocide,* which is the deliberate extermination of an entire human ethnic, political, or cultural group.[8]

For example, just when white public officials raised alarms about the emerging birth control movement for giving rise to white race suicide and declining white fertility rates, many of these very same public health officials often viewed Black female sexuality as something aberrant, and in need of containment and repression. Indeed, white racism constructed and sustained the harrowing movement for "nativism" that produced the Johnson Restrictive Immigration Act of 1924. It was the eugenics movement's emphasis on eclipsing the right of reproductive freedom and choice from those deemed "unfit" that signaled its danger to African Americans. Forcible sterilization was the principal medical procedure used by eugenicists. Thirty states had involuntary sterilization laws on the books by 1931. Most of the these laws required sterilization of persons who were deemed "unfit." According to research on the legacy of eugenics:

> A review of the history of eugenic sterilizations in the United States makes it evident that many abuses have occurred since thousands of

persons who were not mentally retarded were forcibly sterilized. Many individuals were also involuntarily sterilized mainly because of their race (black) or because of poverty and inability to pay for the care of themselves and their children (*Buck vs. Bell Superintendent*, 1927).[9]

We may never know exactly how many times sterilization instead of contraception was provided to or forced onto Black women and other women of color.

Just as the ideology of white supremacy spurred the eugenics movement and shaped the construction and emergence of theories driven by eugenics formulations in most science and social science disciplines throughout the early decades of the 20th century, the eugenics movement directly influenced the emerging birth control movement.[10] For instance, African American women's issues were marginalized in the birth control movement because most white men and white women struggled along under the highly destructive illusions and mythologies created by the convergence of racism and sexism. By the time the American Birth Control League merged with the Clinical Research Bureau to form the Birth Control Federation of America in 1939, racism and sexism were institutionalized as "science" and human-uplift social policy by the eugenics-influenced medical and science professionals, who built their reputations by accepting most of the ideas about people of color that derived from the nativist and eugenics movements. Few whites could see that many African American women were as interested in limiting birth rates, so as to improve the quality of life for live births, as white women.[11]

Many whites believed that African American female sexuality and reproductive behavior had to be controlled from outside the Black family by white officials and white agencies. Unfortunately, so convinced were many health professionals and reproductive rights advocates like Margaret Sanger and others—some of whom counted themselves as feminists—of the runaway sexuality and "breeding" capacity of especially poor African American women that Black women's needs were marginalized in the emerging birth control movement.[12] Long accustomed to viewing Black women as little more than baby-breeding machines, many were unable or unwilling to perceive Black female sexuality as anything but out of control.

So powerful were those who advocated a racially and sexually prescriptive delineation of the human species into separate and distinct racially defined "species" that the emerging public health movement, like the later social welfare movement, bore the impress of eugenics racism and misogyny. Essentially, the eugenics-driven, racist beliefs of the day presented Black males and females as a separate race, a subspecies. Scholars have focused on the medical travesty that the infamous Tuskegee syphilis experiment indicates, wherein several hundred Black men from the rural South repeatedly visited and left public health clinics untreated for advanced stages of syphilis. Importantly, not only were 431 African American men with syphilis released untreated by the U.S. Public Health Service back into rural communities of women and children, thereby spreading syphilis still further, but they were kept away from treatment intervention even when penicillin was available. Essentially, the Black men used in the 40-year human experimentation project were betrayed by the doctors representing the U.S. government.[13]

Many of the Black men with "bad blood" had sex with Black females without knowing that they were spreading untreated syphilis through populations of uninfected women. Obviously, the medical health of the many women and children who contracted syphilis were of no concern to U.S. public health care providers, nor was the fact that the trust given to doctors representing the government was betrayed by their complicity in ensuring that so many Black men with syphilis passed syphilis to women and the unborn. Since we know that syphilis as a venereal disease is far more difficult to discern in women, the intensity of what the omission suggests is immense, for while Black men routinely made trips to be examined, and at least might have thought that something was wrong with them, scores of already poorly nourished Black women, who received very little if any health care or prenatal care, were knowingly betrayed by the U.S. Public Health Service.

What has not been said is that by allowing 431 Black men with advancing stages of syphilis to travel to and from their homes, intermingling with single and married Black women, the U.S. Public Health Service subjected multiple communities of Black families to untreated syphilis. It is important to consider that the doctors in charge of the experiments went to great lengths to ensure that the syphilis went untreated, including, when possible, foreclosing the option that the afflicted Black men could go elsewhere and receive treatment. The conclusion that emerges from the historical evidence is that in the minds of the nation's leading doctors, African American male and female sexuality was a "mechanism" or a "thing" different from white sexuality, and warranting of study without remorse. The medical code of Hippocrates and constitutional guarantees of equal treatment were swept away, as were any considerations of consent, impact on larger communities of previously uninfected females and children, or the ethical questions raised by interfacing with patients in dishonest, deceitful ways that promote their contagion and suffering.

Poor Black women bore the brunt of racist and misogynist beliefs, for they were not among the groups of educated or professional Black women most able to avoid dependency on state-organized and -funded interventions on behalf of public health, birth control, and subsidized social welfare benefits. Increasingly, eugenics thinking and racial medicine were responsible for the tendency of many health and science professionals to perceive and represent poor Black females as the undeserving poor. It is clear that the processes of the state encroaching on the rights of Black women in the name of "good medicine," "good science," and "good family planning" descend from beliefs and actions that reach all the way back to the convergence of the social construction of Black female sexuality under the institution of slavery and racial medicine. So prevalent were the pejorative beliefs about poor and working-class Black women, most often believed to be uninterested in aspiring to be like middle-class white women, that some educated middle-class Black men and women internalized negative beliefs about poor Black women, especially those beliefs that were alleged to be predicated on theories arising from social science scholarship. Hence, poor Black females were rendered invisible, their real lives seldom, if ever, represented through their own words.

Often, the underlying stereotypical beliefs that have dominated much social policy thinking betray African American female attempts to build empowering interactions with the health care community. In the medical and social science community, concepts like "pathology" have been used to legitimize distancing resources from Black women. Indeed, the background to popularized beliefs that Black female sexuality poses a danger to society is linked with the grafting of "pathology" onto prevailing representations of Black females as Jezebel, Sapphire, and Mammy.

In the 1960s the word "pathological" entered the white mainstream as the social science assessment of the Black family.[14] True to the tenacity of racist and sexist representations of Black female sexuality as a "thing," and hence Black women as things, apart, unintelligible, and backward, Black women emerged in the widely circulated social science scholarship as emasculators of male authority, domineering wives, and unfit mothers—basically dysfunctional.

In other words, the denigrating stereotypes of Sapphire and Jezebel, and the additional representation of Black females as "deviant," implying sickness and craziness as personality disorders, were constructed into social science theory, thereby renewing the representations that had worked to effectively marginalize Black females. In addition, "pathology" as a personality disorder was grafted onto the older forms of representational oppression, and a still newer and more deadly representation of Black females and the families they nurtured emerged. In many ways, the fate of poor Black females in still another age of social policy formulation was sealed in marginalization, subordination, and inferences of personality disorder and craziness.

As in so many other decades, in the 1960s the full force of racial, sexual, and socioeconomic oppression was laid fully and squarely on the backs of those already victimized. Professor William Ryan named the syndrome clearly in his classic work *Blaming the Victim*.[15] Essentially, the needs and developmental issues confronting poor and working-class Black women slipped largely into further obscurity, as influential spokespeople on behalf of Black women's self-empowerment needs were few. Even the emerging women's movement largely ignored the needs of poor Black women by eclipsing the consequences of race and instead focusing on a presumed similarity of gender experience across ethnicity.

Most African American communities, eager to support Black manhood and promote Black male leadership and the patriarchal middle-class family, sent Black females mixed messages. In those messages, Black women were to know their place, work hard, support the empowerment of "their" men, bear more children and devote their lives to them, and take care of the elders, the sick, and the infirm. Nowhere in the messages about what constituted a "good woman" was there the acknowledgment that Black women also needed support, leadership opportunities, especially at the grassroots level, and serious time set aside for self-development, nurturance, and mentorship of one another. Black females were called upon to have no centerplace of their own, to serve everyone else in relative obscurity, to be long enduring and slow to complain. Long accustomed to being treated as the mules of the world by most whites, poor Black females slipped even farther down the personhood ladder, as increasingly explicit expressions of misogyny were acted out and often denied, tolerated, or represented as the victim's fault in Black communities. Too often, Black female attempts at self-help were met with suspicion as only Black women seemed to be speaking and writing about the permeation of misogynistic beliefs and actions into Black communities, where there had previously often been far more egalitarianism than in white America.

With each passing decade, the misogynist messages in much of social science scholarship, the media, and popular culture spread ever more extensively through American culture. Quite frankly, most whites and even many African Americans too often sent Black women the message that sexual violence, rape, incest against women and children, and domestic battering were somehow just personal dilemmas, for seldom did even African American male leadership speak to issues of incest, domestic violence, rape, and the ethos of male sexual conquest and its relationship to abandoned pregnant females. Out of the malaise of everybody's wanting to be more important, worthy, and deserving than African American females came invisibility for those issues most oppressive to poor Black females.

Poor African American females are of particular concern in this essay because, along with women of color on reservations, in barrios, and in impoverished rural and urban areas across the country, they exercise the fewest constitutional and civil rights of any women in the United States. Poor African American females have been subjugated by pernicious and enduring negative beliefs initially constructed to defend slavery and used in this century to blame, shame, and abandon Black females. Our attention should be focused on protecting the constitutional, civil, and human rights of poor marginalized women, because poverty among women is increasingly producing impoverished children. Traditional tools for building positive female self-image, self-esteem, and self-respect are under siege from the state and sometimes from within the Black community.[16] Increasingly, desperately poor African American households and even families are distanced from a small, educated, and prosperous Black middle class. Consequently, poor women are often rendered invisible in their oppression and, as such, are all too often victimized as the state structures and mechanisms of domestic and international development increasingly abridge and/or deny their rights.

In the United States, where entitlement is socially constructed, the perception of one's moral status affects one's access to the exercise of entitlement. By constructing and validating a moral basis for individual worthiness and then establishing that poor Black females are undeserving of entitlement based on moral status, the state has often constructed a definition of female behavior that is morally repulsive, ethically indefensible, and in many cases criminally prosecutable. Increasingly, agencies, legislatures, and some courts across the country are acting to define state interest in a manner that justifies the disparate and unequal treatment of poor Black females in the criminal justice system. Not surprisingly, the issue centers around Black female reproductive sexuality.[17]

In a century where "racial medicine" has become a tremendously controversial health policy because it has been so influenced by eugenics thinking, discussions about African American female sexuality and reproductive behavior cannot but concern audiences of professionals and scholars interested in the intersection of health policy, socioeconomic status, medical jurisprudence, and ethics. Likewise, if "racial medicine" has influenced some number of medical practitioners, public health officials, scholars, social service workers, and administrators to perceive African American females as sexually promiscuous, out of control, incapable, and perhaps even undeserving of self-directed development, then increasingly the criminal justice system has intensified its efforts to identify, entrap, and criminalize African American female drug use, particularly during pregnancy.[18]

At exactly the same time that public health structures and operations have intensified efforts to more directly interface with rising health problems, the courts and the criminal justice system are evolving case law precedents that establish, define, and redefine socially acceptable boundaries for drug-impaired felony prosecution. In terms of African American women, it is the combination of pregnancy and drug use that has propelled a social, law enforcement, criminal justice, legal, and political movement in at least 25 states to criminalize and disproportionately prosecute poor pregnant Black females, who for the most part depend on state assistance. While the combination of drug use and pregnancy is in no way racially prescribed, the criminalization of drug use during pregnancy is a precedent being erected on the backs of mostly young, poor, sexually abused, pregnant Black females.[19]

Importantly, judgments against drug-impaired pregnant females are arising out of a moral force that is fueled by racist beliefs long embedded in popular notions about Black female sexuality and personality. This is clearly borne out by the fact that despite research findings that pregnant drug use cannot be predicted by either race or socioeconomic factors, it is the most vulnerable, young, poor, Black females who are being singled out for prosecution. Of further importance, the moral judgments against poor women have encouraged the courts to allow officers of the state's judicial apparatus to "hold harmless" and grant immunity to medical providers who report drug-using pregnant women to local law enforcement officials.[20]

Researchers have reported that the consequences of utilizing the prenatal treatment clinic as a drug detection point has been to reduce the numbers of poor pregnant Black females who use medical facilities, where, because of their skin color, their urine is the first tested.[21] Obviously, this compounds the already immense challenge of facilitating the greater access, affordability, and utilization of prenatal care among poor Black females. The question arises whether the state's intention to increase prenatal care among poor women, thereby increasing the quality of care given to infants at the crucial fetal stage, is consistent with the policy of making prenatal clinics for poor women places where trust and confidentiality do not prevail.

The issue here is not whether drug-impaired pregnant women are at risk and place their unborn fetuses at risk, for clearly they are at risk and sustain risk conditions for unborn fetuses. However, the most fundamental issue here is, what are the rights of privacy, equal protection under the law, due process, and access to drug addiction treatment for impoverished Black females who have no recourse but to seek medical, legal, and social service assistance from the state? How can the state seek to compromise privacy, due process, and equal protection under the law in circumstances where poor Black females are being prosecuted disproportionately for the same offenses that others also commit? How can the state commit itself to this tactic and at the same time protect constitutional rights for poor women?

Without question this is a compelling ethical as well as legal issue in which the state and the courts are constructing interests that are often adverse to young, poor, African American females. How is it consistent with constitutional interpretations in support of civil rights to make the condition of pregnancy the basis for disparate and unequal treatment? How can the state intervene to support fetal rights, criminalizing pregnancy under a conditional set of circumstances presented as protective of fetuses, while not moving to intervene where legal drug use, like alcohol abuse during pregnancy, renders harm, such as fetal alcohol syndrome?

The issue that undergirds much of the criminalization of drug use during pregnancy is the creation of a category of civil rights for fetuses, specifically constructed as "adverse." The premise behind establishing fetal rights that must be protected by the state in opposition to the rights of pregnant women or mothers is that women are acting against the civil rights of fetuses.[22] The implication in such a narrowly tailored construction of causality is that only individual women are to blame for abrogating rational choices and decisions in support of full-term, healthy pregnancies. Certainly, while it is important to encourage females to keep wanted pregnancies, it should also be important to encourage young African American women to care about themselves. From a constitutional point of view, the issue is privacy, self-determination, and choice. From an ethical point of view, the challenge is to facilitate building self-esteem and empowerment as the bases of self-loving choices. Importantly, there are signs that some courts are ruling that states cannot punish drug-using pregnant females for the negative consequences of their drug use on unborn fetuses. Hopefully, this progressive direction of the courts will be accompanied by a reassessment of public policies that direct dollars toward much-needed treatment, education, and self-esteem enhancement, or "recovery work."[23] Such measures would go a long way toward grappling with the intersection of race, sex, and class in terms of distributive justice.

Arguably, choice should proceed from education and opportunities for self-empowerment, not from austere and punitive state-legislated interventions in women's reproductive sexuality and behavior. While we cannot and should not be indifferent to the destructive impact of illegal drug use during pregnancy, neither should we confuse helping females become healthy mothers with usurping and controlling pregnant female sexuality.[24] While much good scholarship has been offered that elucidates much of this controversy, it is important to say that in the context of poor Black women, who themselves have seldom exercised their own civil rights, the state is forcing many to undertake social reproduction with few if any social or systemic supports, except for those constructed and maintained by African American folks themselves.[25]

In raising the issue of reproductive rights for Black females, more is at stake than the codification of enduring beliefs about Black female sexuality into contemporary thinking. Frankly, white male patriarchy has established a legacy of property interests in Black females that, unlike the control white males have exerted over white females and children, in no way builds or furthers self-determination or familial survival for Black females. In other words, racism and misogyny operate at this level to judge and condemn Black female sexuality, offer little if any vehicle for empowerment, and deprive many poor Black communities of the support to existing familial structures that would likely enhance the quality of life for the next generation of Black children. The spiraling numbers of Black children growing up in state institutions and orphanages testify not only to a crisis of impoverishment in many Black communities and households, but also to a systemic problem of economic abandonment and political marginalization of the poor, especially women and children.

Without some serious attention to the ways in which white, patriarchal agencies and institutions dominate poor Black families without ensuring the empowerment and survival of Black women and their children, many African American communities will experience a level of trauma and loss of control of the most basic institution in Black communities. In an age where even the white, middle-class nuclear family is giving way to single-parent families and escalating divorce rates, Black people can ill afford to pretend that the solution is to relinquish control over poor families to the state, for to do so is to allow the machinations of the state to shame and dismember Black households, criminalizing Black female reproductive sexuality.

Realistically, if Black females have no rights, what rights will Black children have, and who within the state will protect those rights? For as long as advocacy groups have worked to raise consciousness and a call to action on behalf of at-risk children, it has been extremely difficult to move an agenda forward that deals with empowering the women who are principally responsible for living with and caring for their children.[26] Clearly at issue are longstanding negative beliefs about poor women, many of whom are African American.

States are being forced to provide for unprecedented numbers of infants impaired and suffering fetal toxicity from the disabling effects of crack addiction. Infants are being born with debilitating physical impairments—specifically, low birth weight, hyper-irritability, abruptio placenta, and infant neurobehavioral deficits. Many infants are taken from their mothers, and some are abandoned by women who cannot take care of themselves or their infants. However, sometimes there is a policy in place that disallows guardianship by other non-drug-using family members, thereby severing the infant from a kinship system that is an alternative to foster care. And, despite the extent of the crisis, there are still states where interracial adoption is outlawed, and adoption of abandoned infants by single or alternative-lifestyle parents is forbidden.[27]

While the issues are complex, scholars, legal experts, and activists doing "recovery work" for women are concerned that states are responding by selectively "blaming" and "punishing" poor urban and rural women, who are disproportionately African American. Essentially, in the context of normative considerations of equity, civil rights, privacy, and access to the range of resources necessary to pursue economic empowerment, most of the women being prosecuted through the criminal justice system are being abandoned, instead of being treated and helped to become financially independent. This is an acute human development and social policy issue, as very often pregnant drug-using women experience tremendous difficulty accessing drug treatment facilities that will provide services to pregnant women or women with children. Essentially caught between a rock and a hard place, many pregnant women who have sought treatment have confronted significant challenges. In 1989, of the 78 drug treatment facilities located in New York City, 54 percent excluded all pregnant women, 67 percent would not accept pregnant women on Medicaid, and 87 percent would not accept pregnant women on Medicaid who were addicted to crack-cocaine. In California, of 366 publicly funded drug treatment programs, only 67 treated women, and only 16 were able to accommodate children. In Ohio, where there were 16 women's recovery programs, only 2 accommodated children.

Clearly, this presents legal, economic, and political consequences for drug-impaired pregnant women, drug-addicted infants, and states. The legal consequences are acute: the punishment for simple possession and use of crack-cocaine amounts to a misdemeanor—unless the accused is a pregnant woman. This issue raises crucial questions about the state's narrow construction of legal precedent on the premise that "harm" is conveyed to fetuses by delivery of crack-cocaine or heroin through the umbilical cord. What are the consequences of focusing on damage done to unborn fetuses by only drug-impaired pregnant females, to the exclusion of assessing the impact of male drug impairment and its possible role in damaging fetal DNA?

In most of the states presently prosecuting pregnant women who are users of crack-cocaine, it is the condition of pregnancy for women that brings a felony criminal charge, primarily because it is the condition of pregnancy that requires that females interface with the medical establishment. Several questions arise, the most important one being, on what normative and constitutional grounds is it permissible and tolerable to deny pregnant women the same legal rights as everyone else? Also, a question arises as to the constitutionality of attributing moral weakness to the condition of drug use during pregnancy, and requiring court-ordered medical and surgical intervention, particularly in light of precedent-setting Supreme Court decisions in which the Court represents drug addiction as a disease and not a moral weakness (*Linder v. United States,* 1925), and in which the Court challenges the exercise of state power in its ruling regarding forced tubal ligation sterilization (*Skinner v. Oklahoma,* 1942).[28]

In addition, how do the historical legacy of abusing the human and civil rights of Black women through 200 years of enslavement, the social construction of pejorative beliefs about Black women's sexuality, and the personality disorders projected onto Black females by social science theories factor into the apparent greater readiness of police and prosecutors to arrest and prosecute young, poor Black women? This concern extends to "reporting" and "screening" procedures and mechanisms, since, according to the American Civil Liberties Union (ACLU), the disproportionate arrest and prosecution of Black American women contributes to an image of the crisis of drug-impaired mothers as a Black problem.[29]

In the early 1960s, of 167 prosecutions on drug-related felony charges in 25 states, approximately 130 were of Black women, 87 were in South Carolina, and 50 in Florida. It is poor women, Black females dependent on state-provided assistance, who are being singled out for specific disparate and unequal treatment. The very women who have access to the least resources with which to protect their legal and civil rights, their rights to privacy and due process, are the women targeted by the state. It is simply not true that more pregnant Black females abuse illegal drugs. Indeed, according to the ACLU and other reporting agencies, there is a drug crisis affecting women across racial and ethnic lines, but the criminal justice system is targeting Black women for prosecution.[30]

Legal researchers have questioned the consequences of states' requiring pregnant women who take drugs to forfeit, not waive, their rights. In an impressive volume, *The Criminalization of a Woman's Body,* legal professionals and scholars note the deliberateness with which states have charged pregnant women with felonies. Notably, felons relinquish their right not to be interfered with by the agencies, mechanisms, and instrumentalities of the state. Impoverished Black women convicted of felonies are often at the mercy of punitive efforts in the social services system, criminal justice system, medical system, and legislative system.[31]

There is also a substantial body of scholarship that traces increases in court-ordered medical interventions. The state has been allowed to force medical and surgical procedures on women, and to impose prison sentences or conditional "supervised" paroles (during which women are compelled to report on the most intimate details of their sexual and personal lives or face immediate imprisonment). This is a particularly troubling practice for women with children, who may have used drugs during a later pregnancy, but who often are forced to forfeit custody of their older children. To many observing this disturbing trend, it appears that the state has unleashed a war on poor, pregnant Black females. A number of cases signal the state's questionable actions regarding Black female civil rights and illustrate how the instrumentalities of the state take over in the context of the criminalization of female drug use during pregnancy.[32] While scholars and legal experts have been clear to point out that female sexuality and reproductive behavior are being criminalized, the fact that most of the females being identified and prosecuted through the criminal justice system are poor and Black should qualify our remarks about the criminalization of female sexuality in the context of drug use during pregnancy.

Black women are marginalized and often treated as non-persons in the legal and public policy decisions that abridge or deny their right to privacy.

Reproductive sexuality and individual civil rights for Black females are at the center of the controversy. On the surface, the use of the contraceptive Norplant appears uncomplicated by issues of "choice" versus "coercion." Often drawing on pejorative beliefs that have consistently been used to stigmatize Black female reproductive sexuality, however, the state has recently targeted poor Black females in inner-city areas for implementation of this invasive contraceptive technology.[33] There are those who argue that the courts should order poor women receiving state assistance to use long-acting contraceptives:

> Because it does not require constant monitoring and is nearly fool-proof, Norplant is an appealing candidate for use as a method for controlling the reproduction of women who courts or others deem unfit to be mothers, either because they have been convicted of child abuse or because they are drug users. The use of Norplant could be required as a condition of probation. In addition, Norplant may be used as an incentive to women on welfare or as a condition of receiving further benefits to induce them to have fewer children and thus to lower welfare costs.[34]

Such a requirement establishes still another social policy that requires poor Black females to agree to undertake limited social reproduction without the forms of legal and social support available to middle-class women. This is a crucial issue that contributes to the feminization of poverty, as the impoverishment of and the denial of civil rights protections to many poor Black females place them and their children at risk of being treated in an arbitrary, whimsical, or inhumane manner.

Significantly, in this century the state has implemented reproductive technology that has negatively impacted women of color. Often swept aside in conversations about women's problems in the context of economic development, "Operation Bootstrap," a U.S.-funded sterilization program in Puerto Rico, showed the extent to which population planning programs often utilize women of color for experimentation of new reproductive technologies or drugs. The role of racism and sexism in the state's implementation of controversial contraceptives like Depo-Provera among populations of poor women, who exercise far less "choice" than more economically and racially privileged women, is well documented. Norplant is only the newest drug to be used to affect reproductive sexuality among poor women. Significantly, Norplant, which is composed of silicone tubes that release a synthetic version of progestin, has to be inserted beneath a female's skin, and as such, becomes a part of her body—she relinquishes control. While conceivably a female should be able to have the contraceptive implant removed by a doctor at any time, social service benefits have sometimes been made contingent upon leaving the rods in poor women's bodies, even though they might experience negative consequences. This is often an invisible issue because the women affected are largely invisible.

Poor women were the first to receive Norplant in Maryland, and many questioned whether the state was engaging in coercion when choice should have been operative. There have been disturbing reports from poor women in Baltimore that they are being coerced into using Norplant. Equally disturbing are reports that poor Black females with teenage daughters are being coerced into pressuring them into using Norplant. Importantly, while Norplant is largely effective in preventing pregnancy, it is ineffective in preventing the spread of sexually transmitted diseases. Given the poor HIV/AIDS-prevention-information outreach to Black communities, contraceptive devices like Norplant can easily be misunderstood to provide more protection than in fact they do. If Norplant becomes a quick fix, then the state will have abandoned poor Black females to its own agenda of limiting the financial costs of supporting and caring for increasing numbers of teen births, while devising largely ineffective educational efforts to promote HIV/AIDS and sexually-transmitted-disease prevention.

A progression of events is setting a historical precedent even as we speak. As with all precedents, the past becomes significant and consequential for the present. Importantly, choices and decisions made by privileged men and women in the latter 20th century are giving rise to an age in which biomedical technology will redefine the family by implementing laws, social policies, ethical standards, and medical procedures that increasingly re-situate and renegotiate the role of the state in the lives of all women.[35]

At exactly the same time as poor Black female sexuality and reproductive behavior are being criminalized, there is an effort to commercialize and colonize the female body, its reproductive organs, and fetal tissue. Viewed in this manner, it is possible to see that both the criminalization of poor Black female sexuality and the increasingly popular perception that Black women's wombs should be for hire (i.e., through contract motherhood, or what some have called "surrogate motherhood") has derived from long-standing perceptions and beliefs about Black females as unfit mothers of their own children, but apt vehicles and containers for other people's property in the form of unborn children.

With the introduction and use of invasive contraceptive drugs that have been promoted among poor Black females of childbearing age, the state has developed policies and practices that, like earlier infringements on African American women's rights, continue to blur the line between coercion and choice.

If the state does differentially criminalize crack-cocaine use in pregnancy in ways that reflect the construction of racist and misogynist beliefs about Black female sexuality, and ties social benefits to the use of invasive birth control methods, what is to prevent the state from arguing for other "conditions" that warrant the disparate treatment of Black females because of some perceived "fault" of pregnant Black females? Given how the state has constructed its interest in fetal protection against real or imagined abuse, and given how the state has furthered its intrusion into the privacy rights of poor women through legal precedents that have made Norplant a necessary and efficient means for controlling poor Black female reproductive sexuality, at this point there is little to prevent the state from pressuring or requiring poor Black females to undergo prenatal gene therapy to correct chronic, debilitating, and expensive genetic mutations that afflict fetuses.

The line between female rights in pregnancy has already blurred to the point that race and class largely determine the extent to which the state and its representatives seek to identify, morally condemn, prosecute, and criminalize drug use during pregnancy. Given the moral climate in many places in the country, requiring poor Black females to undergo corrective gene-therapy surgery would be an extension of the mind-set that characterizes most poor Black women as morally unworthy of caring for the interests of unborn fetuses.

Since adverse fetal rights is a position that rests on the belief that women are engaging in harmful conduct toward fetuses, the state could construct its interests on behalf of fetuses around the cost-efficiency of having poor women undertake pre-birth gene therapy to correct genetic mutations, like sickle-cell anemia. Sickle-cell anemia is characterized as "chronic inherited anemia, primarily affecting Blacks, in which red blood cells sickle, or form crescents, plugging arterioles and capillaries. Like a number of other genetic mutations (i.e., hemophilia, cystic fibrosis, muscular dystrophy and ADA deficiency) sickle cell anemia derives from the genetic information coded into the nucleus of human chromosomes."[36]

In recent years medical researchers have identified the genes that are responsible for transmitting sickle-cell anemia through procedures associated with gene mapping. Gene mapping results from genetic testing to identify, isolate, and diagnose specific genes that may be associated with diseases. In sickle-cell anemia, one or both genetic parents contribute a gene for the disease. Researchers at the Human Genome Project have identified the 11th chromosomal pair as the location of the genes responsible for sickle-cell anemia. Currently, medical researchers are able to provide a DNA test to ascertain the presence of sickle-cell anemia.[37]

But a disquieting recent case involving genetic screening for sickle-cell anemia bears remembering. While the testing for sickle-cell anemia was not prenatal, the discrimination that occurred against African Americans is instructive for the considerations raised in this essay. In the early 1970s the government undertook a large-scale sickle-cell-anemia-testing project. By the middle of that decade the U.S. Air Force Academy was excluding sickle-cell carriers, a number of commercial airlines and many employers fired Black personnel with sickle-cell, and a number of insurance companies raised the premiums of sickle-cell carriers. Often, there was little if any distinction made between those persons whose blood showed evidence of the trait, and those who had the disease itself.[38]

Consistent with how adverse fetal rights have evolved alongside the social construction of "good" motherhood, it might not take much for the state to represent morally deserving mothers as mothers willing to undergo a corrective procedure to change an otherwise debilitating condition like sickle-cell anemia, hemophilia, or ADA deficiency, which might not afflict either genetic parent but would prove chronic or fatal to the child born with the disease.[39] Theoretically, a woman's or couple's right to choose would guard their constitutional right to privacy. Realistically, one's race and class actually shape the degree to which one exercises "rights." Therefore, in the context of reproductive sexuality, poor Black females exercise few if any protected rights, and could arguably be coerced into undergoing gene therapy, especially if the state argued that, from a cost-efficiency perspective, it costs less to subsidize gene therapy than to care for a lengthy, perhaps lifelong, chronic health condition such as sickle-cell anemia.

The genetics revolution is profoundly redefining social relations, because the state is in the process of redefining what life and individual rights will mean in the age of emerging biomedical technology. One thing is certain, namely, that the promise of unlimited good in the genetics age will operate against a historical backdrop replete with examples of the social construction of African American women as "other" that have created a social environment of disparate and unequal access to constitutional protections. As in previous centuries, the question will be, is the state friend or foe?

Notes

A version of this essay was presented at the Black Women and the Academy Conference at the Massachusetts Institute of Technology in Cambridge, Massachusetts, in 1994. I would like to thank Ms. Lea Scarpulla-Nolan for her research assistance, and Dr. Leona Fisher for her editorial suggestions and scholarly insights.

1. See the really fine collection of essays that deal with a broad range of reproductive issues, public policies, and laws edited by Sherrill Cohen and Nadine Tabb, *Reproductive Laws for the 1990s* (Clifton, NJ: Humana Press, 1989); and Rima D. Apple, ed., *Women, Health, and Medicine in America* (New Brunswick, NJ: Rutgers University Press, 1992).

2. See R.W. Connell's discussion of gender politics in "The State, Gender, and Sexual Politics: Theory and Appraisal," *Theory and Society,* Vol. 19 (1990), 508–10; also, Ellen M. Charlton, Jana Everett, and Kathleen Staudt, "Women, the State, and Development," in *Women, the State and Development* (Albany, NY: State University of New York Press, 1989), 5.

3. A. Leon Higginbotham Jr., *In the Matter of Color, Race and the American Legal Process: The Colonial Period* (New York: Oxford University Press, 1978), 43.

4. See especially scientist George Cuvier's reflection on the "Hottentot Venus" after she died in Paris:

> She had a way of pouting her lips exactly like we have observed in the orang-utan. Her movements had something abrupt and fantastical about them, reminding one of those of the ape. Her lips were monstrously large. Her ear was like that of many apes, being small.... I have never seen a human head more like an ape than that of this woman.

P. Topinard, *Anthropology* (London: Chapman and Hall, 1878), 493–94.

5. See E.B. Turnipseed, "Hymen of the Negro Women," *Richmond and Louisville Medical Journal,* Vol. VI (1868), 194–95; Turnipseed, "Some Facts in Regard to the Anatomical Difference between the Negro and White Races," *American Journal of Obstetrics and Diseases of Women and Children,* Vol. X (1877), 33; C.H. Fort, "Some Corroborative Facts in Regard to the Anatomical Difference Between the Negro and White Races," *American Journal of Obstetrics and Diseases of Women and Children,* Vol. X (1877), 258–59.

6. See Stephen Jay Gould, *The Mismeasure of Man* (New York: W.W. Norton, 1981), 56.

7. John S. Haller, Jr., *Outcasts from Evolution: Scientific Attitudes of Racial Inferiority, 1859–1900* (Urbana, IL: University of Illinois Press, 1971), 56.

8. Kenneth, L. Garver and Bettylee Garver, "Eugenics: Past, Present, and the Future," *American Journal of Human Genetics,* Vol. 49 (1991), 1109.

9. Ibid., 1111–12; also, P. Reilly, "The Surgical Solution: the Writings of Activ-

ist Physicians in the Early Days of Eugenical Sterilization," *Perspectives on Biology and Medicine,* Vol. 26 (1983), 637–56; Reilly, "Involuntary Sterilization in the United States: A Surgical Solution," *Quarterly Review of Biology,* Vol. 62 (1987), 153–62.

10. See especially Ruth Hubbard, *The Politics of Women's Biology* (New Brunswick, NJ: Rutgers University Press, 1990), 143; and generally, Linda Gordon, *Woman's Body, Woman's Right* (New York: Grossman Press, 1976).

11. Jessie M. Rodrique, "The Black Community and the Birth-Control Movement," in Ellen Carol DuBois and Vicki L. Ruiz, eds., *Unequal Sisters: A Multicultural Reader in U.S. Women's History* (New York: Routledge, 1990), 333–44.

12. Angela Y. Davis, *Women, Race & Class* (New York: Random House, 1981), 202–20.

13. James H. Jones, *Bad Blood: The Tuskegee Syphilis Experiment* (New York: The Free Press, 1981).

14. Daniel Patrick Moynihan, *The Negro Family: The Case for National Action* (Washington, DC: Department of Labor, Office of Policy Planning and Research, 1966).

15. William Ryan, *Blaming the Victim* (New York: Vintage, 1972).

16. Martha E. Gimenez, "The Feminization of Poverty: Myth or Reality?" *Social Justice,* Vol. 17, No. 3, 43–69; Regina A. Arnold, "Processes of Victimization and Criminalization of Black Women" *Social Justice,* Vol. 17, No. 3, 153–66; Linda Burnham, "Has Poverty Been Feminized in Black America?" in Rochelle Lefkowitz and Ann Withorn, eds., *For Crying Out Loud: Women and Poverty in the United States* (New York: Pilgrim Press, 1986), 69–83.

17. Michael Burke, "Cocaine Moms Are Not Coddled in Pensacola," *Pensacola News Journal,* March 4, 1990, 1A; Victoria Churchville, "D.C. Judge Jails Woman as Protection for Fetus," *Washington Post,* July 23, 1988, 1; Selwyn Crawford, "Legal System Grapples with Newborn Addicts," *Dallas Morning News,* July 19, 1989, 1A; James Epes, "Infant Taken Away from Mother Charged with Criminal Neglect," *Peidmont News,* August 23, 1989; B. Henderson, "Mothers of Infant Addicts: Does Prosecution Help?" *Charlotte Observer,* August 26, 1989; John Kennedy, "Cloudy Future After Infant-Cocaine Case," *Boston Globe,* August 23, 1989, 1; J. Kirby, "Judge Orders Cesarean Birth Despite Family Refusal," *Marietta (GA) Daily Journal,* May 2, 1989, 1; Dan Keating, "Woman Faces Charges of Abuse of Unborn Child," *Miami Herald,* January 13, 1990, B1; Patrick Young, "Woman Charged After Giving Birth to Addict," *Indianapolis Star,* October 7, 1989.

18. Loren Siegel, "The Criminalization of Pregnant and Child-Rearing Drug Users," *Drug Law Report,* Vol. 2, No. 15 (1990), 169–76; Paula J. Caplan and Ian Hall-McCorquodale, "Mother-Blaming in Major Clinical Journals," *American Journal of Orthopsychiatric Association,* Vol. 55, No. 3 (1985), 345–53; George J. Annas, "Forced Cesareans: The Most Unkindest Cut of All" *Hastings Center Report,* Vol. 12 (1982), 16–17, 45; Molly McNulty, "Pregnancy Police: The Health Policy and Legal

Implications of Punishing Pregnant Women for Harm to Their Fetuses," *New York University Review of Law and Social Change*, Vol. 16 (1987–88), 277–319; Kary L. Moss, "Legal Issues: Drug Testing of Postpartum Women and Newborns as the Basis for Civil and Criminal Proceedings," *Clearinghouse Review* (March 1990), 1406–14; National Criminal Justice Association, "State Courts Debate Prosecution of Pregnant Drug Users," in *Justice Research* (March/April 1992); L.J. Nelson and N.M. Milliken, "Compelled Medical Treatment of Pregnant Women," *Journal of the American Medical Association*, Vol. 259 (1988), 1060–66; Dorothy E. Roberts, "Drug-Addicted Women Who Have Babies," *Trial* (April 1990), 56–61.

19. Lynn M. Paltrow, compiler, *Criminal Prosecutions Against Pregnant Women: National Update and Overview* (New York: American Civil Liberties Union Reproductive Freedom Project, April 1992); Jacqueline Berrien, "Pregnancy and Drug Use: The Dangerous and Unequal Use of Punitive Measures," *Yale Journal of Law and Feminism,* Vol. 2, No. 2 (1990), 239–50; Judy Scales-Trent, "Black Women and the Constitution: Finding Our Place, Asserting Our Rights," *Harvard Civil Rights Civil Liberties Law Review,* Vol. 24, No. 1 (1989), 9–44; Kary L. Moss, "Substance Abuse During Pregnancy," *Harvard Women's Law Journal,* Vol. 13 (1990), 278–99.

20. Janet Gallagher, "Fetus as Patient," in Sherrill Cohen and Nadine Taub, eds., *Reproductive Laws for the 1990s* (Clifton, NJ: Humana Press, 1989).

21. Molly McNulty, "Pregnancy Police," op. cit.

22. Dawn E. Johnsen, "The Creation of Fetal Rights: Conflicts with Women's Constitutional Rights to Liberty, Privacy, and Equal Protection," *Yale Law Journal,* Vol. 95 (1986), 599–625; Patricia King, "Should Mom Be Constrained in the Best Interests of the Fetus?" *Nova Law Review,* Vol. 13 (1989), 393–404; Watson A. Bowes Jr. and Brad Selgestad, "Fetal Versus Maternal Rights: Medical and Legal Perspectives," *Obstetrics and Gynecology,* Vol. 58, No. 2 (1981), 209–14; Jeffrey L. Lenow, "The Fetus as a Patient: Emerging Rights as a Person?" *American Journal of Law and Medicine,* Vol. 9 (1983–84), 1–29; Janet Gallagher, "Prenatal Invasions and Interventions: What's Wrong with Fetal Rights," *Harvard Women's Law Journal,* Vol. 10 (1987), 9–58; George J. Annas, "Predicting the Future of Privacy in Pregnancy: How Medical Technology Affects the Legal Rights of Pregnant Women," *Nova Law Review,* Vol. 13 (1989), 329–53.

23. Although appellate court rulings in no way preclude state legislatures from enacting punitive laws that would thereby obligate the court to rule differently, for the time being several appellate courts have refused to allow state-level child-endangerment laws to furnish the statutory basis for punitive action against drug-using pregnant women; see "States Cannot Punish Pregnant Women for 'Fetal Abuse,' Courts Say," *Trial* (May 1992), 11–12, 14; Deborah Mathieu, "Respecting Liberty and Preventing Harm: Limits of State Intervention in Prenatal Choice," *Harvard Journal of Law and Public Policy,* Vol. 8, No. 1, 19–55.

24. Wendy Chavkin, Machelle Harris Allen, and Michelle Oberman, "Drug Abuse and Pregnancy: Some Questions on Public Policy, Clinical Management, and

Maternal and Fetal Rights," *Birth,* Vol. 18, No. 2 (1991), 107–12; Patricia A. King, "Helping Women Helping Children: Drug Policy and Future Generations," *Milbank Quarterly,* Vol. 69, No. 4 (1991), 595–621; Walter B. Connolly Jr. and Alison B. Marshall, "Drug Addiction, Pregnancy, and Childbirth: Legal Issues for the Medical and Social Services Communities," *Clinics in Perinatology,* Vol. 18, No. 1 (1991), 147–86; Mary Haskett et al., "Intervention with Cocaine-Abusing Mothers," *Families in Society: The Journal of Contemporary Human Services,* Vol. 25 (October 1992).

25. Mimi Abramovitz, "Poor Women in a Bind: Social Reproduction Without Social Supports," *Affilia,* Vol. 7, No. 2 (1992), 23–43.

26. See staff report, *A Children's Defense Budget: An Analysis of Our Nation's Investment in Children* (Washington, DC: Children's Defense Fund, 1993); staff report, *The Economic Status of Black Women: An Exploratory Investigation* (Washington, DC: U.S. Commission on Civil Rights, October 1990); staff report, *Women and Poverty* (Washington, DC: U.S. Commission on Civil Rights, June 1974); U.S. House of Representatives Select Committee on Children, Youth and Families, *No Place to Call Home: Discarded Children in America* (Washington, DC: U.S. Government Printing Office [USGPO], 1990); U.S. House of Representatives Select Committee on Children, Youth and Families, *Keeping Kids Safe: Exploring Public/Private Partnerships to Prevent Abuse and Strengthen Families* (Washington, DC: USGPO, 1992).

27. U.S. House of Representatives Select Committee on Children, Youth and Families, *Getting Straight: Overcoming Treatment Barriers for Addicted Women and Children* (Washington, DC: USGPO, 1990); U.S. House of Representatives Select Committee on Children, Youth and Families, *Beyond the Stereotype: Women, Addiction, and Perinatal Substance Abuse* (Washington, DC: USGPO, 1990); U.S. House of Representatives Select Committee on Children Family, Drugs and Alcoholism, *Drug-Addicted Babies: What Can Be Done?* (Washington, DC: USGPO, 1990); U.S. House of Representatives Select Committee on Children, Youth and Families, *Born Hooked: Confronting the Impact of Perinatal Substance Abuse* (Washington, DC: USGPO, 1989); U.S. House of Representatives Select Committee on Children, Youth and Families, *Placing Infants at Risk: Parental Addiction and Disease* (Washington, DC: USGPO, 1986); U.S. House of Representatives Select Committee on Children, Youth and Families, *Law and Policy Affecting Addicted Women and their Children* (Washington, DC: USGPO, 1990); U.S. House of Representatives Select Committee on Children, Youth and Families, *Child Abuse Prevention and Treatment in the 1990s: Keeping Old Promises, Meeting New Demands* (Washington, DC: USGPO, 1992); U.S. House of Representatives Select Committee on Narcotics Abuse and Control, *Cocaine Babies* (Washington, DC: USGPO, 1987); U.S. House of Representatives Select Committee on Narcotics Abuse and Control, *On the Edge of the American Dream: A Social and Economic Profile in 1992* (Washington, DC: USGPO, 1992); U.S. House of Representatives Select Committee on Narcotics Abuse and Control, *Drug Abuse Treatment: A Review of Current Federal Programs and*

Policies (Washington, DC: USGPO, 1992); U.S. House of Representatives Select Committee on Children, Youth and Families, *Abused Children in America* (Washington, DC: USGPO, March 1987).

28. Jacqueline Berrien, "Pregnancy and Drug Use: The Dangerous and Unequal Use of Punitive Measures," *Yale Journal of Law and Feminism*, Vol. 2, No. 2 (1990), 239–50; Berrien, "Pregnancy and Drug Use: Incarceration Is Not the Answer," in Marlene Gerber Fried, ed., *From Abortion to Reproductive Freedom: Transforming a Movement* (Boston: South End Press, 1990).

29. See especially Loren Siegel, "The Criminalization of Pregnant and Child-Rearing Drug Users," *Drug Law Report*, Vol. 2, No. 15 (1990), 169–76.

30. See especially "State by State Case Summary of Criminal Prosecutions Against Pregnant Women and Appendix of Public Health and Public Interest Groups Opposed to these Prosecutions" (American Civil Liberties Union memorandum, New York, September 26, 1990, July 26, 1990); "Update of State Presentation Regarding Drug Use During Pregnancy" (American Civil Liberties Union memorandum, New York, May 22, 1990).

31. The entire volume is excellent. See Clarice Feinman, ed., *The Criminalization of a Woman's Body* (New York: Haworth Press, 1992).

32. Lynn Paltrow, "Criminal Prosecutions Against Pregnant Women," op. cit.

33. Barbara Kantrowitz, Pat Wingert, and Elizabeth Ann Leonard, "A 'Silver Bullet' Against Teen Pregnancies?" *Newsweek*, December 14, 1992.

34. Jim Persels, "The Norplant Condition: Protecting the Unborn or Violating Fundamental Rights," *Journal of Legal Medicine*, Vol. 13 (1992).

35. U.S. House of Representatives Select Committee on Children, Youth and Families, *Alternative Reproductive Technologies: Implications for Children and Families* (Washington, DC: USGPO, 1987); Warren Freedman, *Legal Issues in Biotechnology and Human Reproduction: Artificial Conception and Modern Genetics* (New York: Quorum Books, 1991); Virginia Walther and Alma T. Young, "Costs and Benefits of Reproductive Technologies," *Affilia*, Vol. 7, No. 2 (1992), 111–22; Ellen Holmes and Laura M. Purdy, eds. *Feminist Perspectives in Medical Ethics* (Bloomington, IN: Indiana University Press, 1992).

36. Within each of the 100 trillion cells in the human body (except red blood cells) is a nucleus with 46 chromosomes, arranged in 23 pairs. Coiled, spiral-shaped strands of deoxyribonucleic acid (DNA) molecules fill the chromosomes and impart instructions to the cell.

37. Philip Elmer-Dewitt, "The Genetic Revolution," *Time: Special Report on Genetics, the Future Is Now*, Vol. 143, No. 3 (1994), 46–53; Rick Weiss, "Human Gene Therapy Achieves a Milestone," *Washington Post*, April 1, 1994, A1; George J. Annas and Sherman Elias, eds., *Gene Mapping: Using Law and Ethics as Guides* (New York: Oxford University Press, 1992); Sharon J. Durfy, "Ethics and the Human Genome Project," *Arch Pathology Lab Medicine*, Vol. 117 (May 1993), 466–69; Earl Ubell, "Is Mending Sick Genes a Miracle Cure?" *Parade Magazine*, January 16,

1994, 8–9; Steve Jones, "A Brave New, Healthy World?" *Natural History,* Vol. 103, No. 6 (1994), 72–74; Beverly Merz, "Designer Genes: Gene Therapy Takes Aim at Growing List of Serious Diseases," *American Health,* Vol. 12, No. 2 (1993), 46–54.

38. See "Reproductive Ethics," *Congressional Quarterly Researcher,* Vol. 4, No. 13 (April 6, 1994), 289–312.

39. Benno Muller-Hill, "The Shadow of Genetic Injustice," *Nature,* Vol. 362 (April 8, 1993), 491–92; Sharon J. Durfy, "Ethics and the Human Genome Project," *Arch Pathol Lab Medicine,* Vol. 117 (May 1993), 466–69.

HIGH-TECH, POP-A-PILL CULTURE

"New" Forms of Social Control for Black Women

April J. Taylor

As Black women in the United States enter the new millennium, the threat of packaged forms of better health offered by pharmaceutical and biotech companies looms large. These companies promote and push products for health problems we face, and some we don't. Their ambitious marketing schemes hyper-medicalize women's bodies, making the corporatization of health care inevitable and reducing our access to indigenous or alternative healing practices. This paper explores how these methods are particularly used to control and disempower Black women.

Within the past few months, the U.S. public has been inundated with drug crazes. Once touted as the miracle drug for weight loss, fenfluramine has now been pulled from the market for many reasons, but mainly for cardiovascular dysfunction. Social and mental stresses, a product of economic uncertainty and intense social unrest, are often misdiagnosed as depression. Prozac, the omnipotent wonder drug, is offered as the cure-all. Similarly, prescription pills and birth control methods are manufactured and proffered as panaceas for practically any ailment, and are marketed and made available to wide segments of the population. High-tech, intrusive contraceptive methods are advertised in slogans promoting "choice," "responsibility," and "freedom." I argue that this campaign is aimed at the women most feared for their reproductive abilities—Black women.

242

In the United States, Black women have always faced political, economic, and social conditions that have compromised our economic livelihoods, health, and well-being. In a country that professes wealth, democracy, and the world's best health care system, the current status of Black women's health tells another story. A cursory look at the following statistics indicates that something is dangerously awry. There are roughly 17 million Black women in the United States, and we live mostly in urban areas. Poverty affected 32 percent of all Black women in 1995, and two-fifths of Black women both under the age of 18 (42 percent) and 75 years of age and older (38 percent) reported incomes below the poverty level.[1] Forty-five percent of all Black households were headed by Black women—and had a median income of about $15,600.[2] Black women experience a higher rate of depression than any racial and ethnic group, and Black women report the shortest life expectancy.[3] Black women suffer from a cervical cancer rate that is more than double that of white women,[4] and while Black women are being diagnosed later in life with excessive rates of breast cancer, they are twice as likely as white women to die as a result.[5]

Studies find that three of the four hazardous waste landfills in the Southeast were located in predominately poor or Black areas.[6] Additionally, Black women, who are disproportionately affected by diabetes, have a greater tendency to be overweight, which is a precursor for high blood pressure and many other health problems. And finally, perhaps one of the most urgent public health issues facing Black women today is HIV/AIDS infection. Black women are disproportionately affected and "account for nearly three-fifths of all cases amongst women."[7] It is estimated that by the year 2000, more than 60 percent of all HIV/AIDS cases will be Black women. HIV/AIDS is further compounded by the racial, sexual, political, economic, and social factors that make it one of the most complex epidemics in our history.[8] The violent, systemic nature of racism, white supremacy, and global capitalism devastates the sociopolitical health status of Black women. When we also factor in eugenic thinking, which often determines public policy, this creates fertile ground for right-wing policies that determine how the medical-industrial complex renders "service" to Black women.

U.S. history reveals that Black women have faced political and governmental policies that have encouraged our treatment as victims of medical mistreatment and experimentation. Couple this with notions of hypersexuality, stereotypes of making too many babies, and views that Black women are problematic entities—notions commonplace in this culture—and you have

Black women who are demonized and essentially relegated to non-woman status.[9] We have learned of the sterilization of young Black women, such as in the infamous case of the Relf sisters of Mississippi;[10] the Tuskegee syphilis experiment, in which Black men were not treated as the course of syphilis played out; and the outright denial of medical attention to Black women in hospital emergency rooms.[11] These are some of the more noted historical cases of medical mistreatment. Today, Black women still receive compromised health care and face some of the same dehumanizing conditions, as they did in the past. Black women bear the brunt of "deciding" between injectable contraceptives and prison,[12] and are still dubbed parasitic "welfare queens" by Republican and Democratic administrations. We have been defined as hypersexualized vessels to be conquered and marketed for misogynist purposes. Black women also are projected to have genetically deficient and violent children.[13]

Viewing the medicalization of Black women's bodies in this context, we see how these "new" methods still control women's fertility and sexuality. Companies amass incredible amounts of profit capitalizing on inequality, racism, and gender bias. For all women—but especially women who are economically and politically exploited, who are women of color, who are Black—these are not "new" social controls. The fundamental philosophies and objectives of these "new" methods are still the same, but they are packaged differently. High-tech contraceptive methods, such as Norplant and Depo-Provera, which are marketed to young and poor women, the experimental use of the chemical sterilizing agent Quinacrine, and the use of immunological contraceptives are all components of eugenic policies to control certain populations. The "genetic revolution," aimed at gene mapping and manipulation, is cause for all people to be alert about the future and their health care (or lack thereof). We must be very careful of promises of new and improved health care. These attempts to control fertility are consistent with the insidious quest to blame women, especially women of color, for the problems of the world. Meanwhile, the corrosive advancement of capitalism persists, racist attacks continue to occur, and women, especially Black women, find themselves sicker and sicker in this high-tech, pop-a-pill culture.

For this paper, I shall limit discussion to contraceptive abuse, the use of Norplant and Depo-Provera, and the efforts of Black women to assert reproductive autonomy. Additionally, I illuminate the use, misuse, and potentially abusive road down which genetics, "the new science" for health, may lead us.

Contraceptives

In discussing contraceptives in the United States, high-tech, invasive, and provider-dependent methods such as Norplant and Depo-Provera are often pushed upon women as though they were methods with curative powers. If one were to peruse any of the magazines targeted at Black and young women, one would see ads for Depo-Provera and Norplant appealing to youth, independence, and beauty. Given the highly aggravating side-effects that a vast number of women indicate with usage, we must ask ourselves, why is it that these ads constantly appear in Black women's magazines such as *Essence* and *Heart & Soul?*

Why are they marketed to women without emphasizing that hormonal methods do not protect one from sexually transmitted diseases? Contraceptive access in this country is such a strange paradox. On the one hand, access and availability for many methods are deemphasized and appear to be limited. Yet there seems to be widespread marketing of hormonal methods as the cure-all to unwanted pregnancy, disregarding the threat of HIV/AIDS. In the course of researching birth control methods, many researchers, women, and even "feminists" take issue with women who critique intrusive hormonal methods. One such controversy rages over Norplant.

Norplant

Norplant (levonorgrestral), a problematic and highly controversial contraceptive, was developed by the Population Council, a New York–based agency with affiliates around the world that promotes and develops contraceptive methods. Norplant was approved by the Food and Drug Administration (FDA) in 1990. It primarily works by suppressing ovulation. In her book *Women as Wombs,* Janice Raymond contends that "the development of Norplant is viewed as a technical solution to women's fertility that is supposedly out of control."[14] Immediately, the contraceptive "magic bullet" had arrived: a method that was lauded as safe, effective, invisible, and worry-free, that offered "freedom" and increased women's "choices." Many women were perhaps eager for the arrival of such a method, but others were cautious about this device, which requires the implantation of six silicone rods into the upper arm, to be left in place for up to five years. Two days after FDA approval, the *Philadelphia Inquirer* ran an editorial stating that Norplant should be used as a solution to contain Black poverty.[15] Shortly thereafter, Darlene Johnson, a Black mother accused of child abuse, was ordered to have Norplant inserted in her arm. This marked the first known case of coercive, legal sanction of

Norplant.

As news of Norplant spread, many legislative houses discussed its efficacy for curtailing the sexual activities of the poor and the ubiquitous "welfare queens." According to legal scholar Dorothy Roberts, "welfare became a code word for race," and "people can avoid the charge of racism by directing their vitriol at the welfare system instead of explicitly assailing Black people."[16] Legislatures in 13 states proposed nearly two dozen bills designed to use Norplant as an instrument of social engineering—tying welfare payments to Norplant use and enticing women to accept the method through financial incentives.[17]

Some of the known side effects of Norplant use are:

> headaches, weight gain, loss of libido, nausea, dizziness, acne, breast tenderness, hair loss, swelling of the ovaries, ovarian cysts, menstrual disruption and irregularities, excessive bleeding, anemia, depression, nervousness and change in appetite.[18]

Furthermore, Norplant's effectiveness diminishes if a woman weighs more than 154 pounds. A major question still remains, especially for younger women: what are the long-term effects of usage? Given that Black women suffer disproportionately from many health ailments such as hypertension, diabetes, depression, and weight problems, Norplant's effectiveness may diminish as dangers to our health are elevated.

Norplant is currently being challenged in the United States by many women suffering side effects and experiencing problems with removal. There are about one million Norplant users in the United States, and thousands of women have joined class-action lawsuits against Wyeth-Ayerst, the U.S. manufacturer. Women have alleged that the dangers of the device were not adequately disclosed by its manufacturer. Furthermore, the insufficient number of personnel trained to remove the implants showed negligence on the part of the manufacturer. More than 400 lawsuits have been filed, including class-action suits representing 50,000 women in well over five states.[19]

Women involved in the suits are young women, women of color, and poor women who've found it difficult to get the device removed.[20] Unfortunately, in some cases, young women have resorted to traveling to different states at their own expense or using drastic measures such as digging instruments into their arms to remove the rods.[21] For the many women who cannot afford to have the implants removed, Wyeth-Ayerst has created a fund called the Norplant Assistance Removal Fund. However, for poor women who cannot contribute anything to the costs of removal, Wyeth-Ayerst requires that they sign a waiver form absolving the corporation from all legal action that could be taken against them.[22]

As a result of these suits, we now have information that indicates how many women have had great difficulty with this contraceptive method. Since these disclosures, Norplant's popularity has rapidly declined. A "study of 900 poor women in New York, Pittsburgh and Dallas, with concerns about Norplant, indicated a significant decline in the number of women requesting Norplant ... from about 100 a month in the last six months of 1993 to fewer than 10 a month in January of 1995."[23] Women are engaged in a battle to hold pharmaceutical companies and their health care providers accountable for this negligence. Unfortunately, the historical reality is that the courts have been unkind to Black women in cases involving bodily integrity. In one class-action case in Texas, "a federal judge ruled against the plaintiffs [the women], finding that Wyeth-Ayerst had adequately notified the doctors about Norplant's potential," and consequently, the "fate of the other lawsuits, and Norplant's widescale distribution, remains uncertain."[24] This uncertainty, however, leaves room for a contraceptive competitor, whose history of use and abuse has been even more problematic—Depo-Provera. Given all the public exposure surrounding Norplant and its association with controversy, Depo-Provera is very appealing to many women, but there are many teens and other women who may be unaware of the history and struggles against the drug.

Depo-Provera

Depo-Provera (depo medroxyprogesterone acetate), often called "the shot" or Depo, is manufactured by the UpJohn Corporation. Depo is a synthetic hormone that is injected into the arm every three months and works, like Norplant, by suppressing ovulation. Also like Norplant, Depo is not a barrier method and does not protect a woman from sexually transmitted diseases. The FDA withheld approval of Depo in 1967, 1978, and 1983.[25] Depo was finally approved in 1992 in the United States, despite the fact that groups such as the National Women's Health Network and the National Black Women's Health Project lobbied against its approval. Even before it was approved, it was offered to women as an unapproved yet "safe and effective" contraceptive method.

One main issue of the campaign against Depo had to do with safety. Contraceptive developers seemed more concerned about efficacy of the drug than with the safety and well-being of its users. Safety and efficacy are treated separately when it comes to women's health and well-being. The standard for acceptance of a drug should be based on a woman's comfort, safety, and satisfaction, as well as on minimal side effects, all fitting into the context of her life. When it comes to what we put in our bodies, safety and the long-term effects on the body should be paramount conditions for usage.

In the case of Depo, initial experimental trials of the drug failed. Depo was originally designed as a drug to prevent miscarriage and to stop premature labor—it didn't work, but it was observed that it did make women infertile for a period of time.[26] UpJohn decided to manufacture the drug in 1963 as a contraceptive. From the early trials, there were questions about its carcinogenicity. Animal studies in the early years indicated that beagles injected with Depo developed cancer. Proponents of Depo tried to dismiss those claims by saying that beagles were prone to getting cancer. If this was the case, then why were the dogs used in the study in the first place? Studies indicate that the use of Depo may increase the risk of breast cancer in women under the age of 35. Then why is it offered as an alternative to Norplant, when Black women suffer from a higher morbidity rate from breast cancer?[27] Although it may be debatable whether or not Depo causes breast or cervical cancer, the long-term effects, especially among young women, are still unclear.

Early on, Black women were used as subjects in clinical experiments involving Depo. From 1967 to 1978, the largest U.S. Depo study was conducted at Grady Memorial Hospital in Atlanta, Georgia. Fourteen thousand women were injected with Depo-Provera.[28] More than 50 percent were Black, low-income, and rural women. The trials were conducted on many of these women without their knowledge or consent, flagrantly violating FDA regulations. It was not disclosed that these women were in the middle of a vast human experiment, nor were mechanisms in place for their follow-up care. Depo-Provera is now on the market despite the fact that no long-term studies have been done.

Today, many grassroots women's groups have called for a moratorium on Depo. Groups like the National Latina Health Organization, based in California, contend that, after long years of fighting against Depo, "the FDA invited UpJohn to re-apply for approval ... and even during the hearings, women's groups and activists were given a lesser amount of time for their case compared to that of UpJohn; the histories of Latina, Native American, and Black women were not included."[29]

In a recent study of Depo users, 33 percent were under the age of 19, 84 percent were Black women, and 74 percent were low income.[30] Many ads are directed at the MTV generation, with images of street-smart young women avoiding pregnancy and looking good. Given this, there's a strong probability that these women will face the prospect of serious health issues as a result of prolonged use of Depo. With the rise of Depo use, as with all forms of non-barrier control methods, women could face higher incidence of HIV/AIDS infection. Could this be the major factor in the high HIV/AIDS rate among Black women?

The issues surrounding contraceptives reflect but a segment of the systemic ways in which control is exercised over women's lives. With the spread of a "genetic revolution," many people stand to be exploited, discriminated against, and rendered medically deficient if we do not remain aware of the intersection of genetics, corporate control, and our health care.

Genetics

Genetic research is on the rise, and biotech companies are emerging all over the world with the goal of patenting, discovering, and creating life forms. The development of Dolly, the cloned sheep in Scotland, is just one recent example. Just as contraceptives are being marketed to a new generation of women, gene therapies and research are also being offered to women as a new form of medicine. Women's health activists have cause for concern when we hear of genetic research to collect and map out DNA samples of hair tissues, cheek cells, and plant materials, all supposedly for the benefit of our health. As with high-tech contraceptive use, there is a great potential for abuse and misuse of genetic therapies.

The information that scientists and biotech people are collecting will be stored at the Human Genome Project and the Human Genome Diversity Project. Samples are analyzed and reproduced, especially samples of indigenous peoples. Scientists say that they will be able to find the genetic material that could offer cures to those suffering from many diseases. In the quest for genetic panaceas, alliances have been forged between biotech corporations and neo-Malthusians. A recent article in *Forbes* magazine titled "Monsanto v. Malthus" featured biotech firms, genetic scientists, and transnational corporations who are lauded for saving the world against "growing population" and food shortages through the development of genetically altered food products. An example of this is the "New Leaf Potato Plus (NLPP)" created by the Monsanto Corporation. The NLPP will enable the potato to have super-protection against viruses and "menacing" insects. Robert Shapiro, CEO of the Monsanto Corporation, exclaimed that all they want to do is to make people healthy and improve their health. How does Monsanto hope to improve our health? He states:

> Scientists in the St. Louis–based company have genetically re-arranged the genetic sequence of a potato to make it higher in starches and lower in water. So that when it's cut into french fries, the genetically engineered potato absorbs less oil in the deep fryer ... so when you visit McDonald's, you won't get anymore of those limp french fries.[31]

In a nutshell, the concern isn't really about our health or well-being but about consumption, profits, and the control of food production. The corporate entities search for "the" gene that makes us fat or "the" gene that "causes" heart disease so that we may continue to consume corporate products and buy health solutions from them. The bottom line is corporate technology's morbid fascination with the manipulation of life and profit. Monsanto has a six-billion-dollar collection of companies in the areas of drugs, agriculture, and food in order to cash in on "the genetic revolution." As for the direct connection between our bodies and genetics, there has been growing concern and controversy in the United States surrounding breast cancer and genes.

Breast Cancer

Breast cancer is at epidemic proportions in the United States, and one in nine women will be directly affected. Black women are disproportionately affected by breast cancer and are twice as likely as white women to die from it. Everywhere there are stories of women who have had or who are fearful of getting breast cancer. And what do we hear is occurring in the scientific world? Scientists have located the gene that "causes" breast cancer. Consequently, they are now marketing a test to women to determine if they have a predisposition for developing breast cancer by looking for the genes BrCa 1 or BrCa 2, which have more than 125 variations. The breast cancer test, which is being offered by a Utah biotech company called Myriad Genetics, offers the test to a woman for the price of $2,400. Even if one were tested, the result would not definitively indicate one's chances of getting cancer. Let's look at a few possible scenarios:

- Woman A wants to get tested, and she sends off her sample to be analyzed by Myriad. Her test is returned as positive. This may cause her to worry and to bemoan the fact that she will get breast cancer. But information provided to her does not definitively tell her that she *will* get breast cancer, only that her possibilities are increased, and she may be at a greater risk.

- Woman B gets tested, and her test comes back negative for BrCa 1 or 2;

she feels quite relieved and thinks that she will not get breast cancer. Yet this does not necessarily mean that she will not get breast cancer in her lifetime. There are numerous other possibilities, but in each scenario, what is the value in being tested? What is the woman really gaining? The breast cancer gene accounts for only 5 to 10 percent of all cases of breast cancer, but the majority of women who contract the disease will more than likely get it via environmental toxins in their food, water, or neighborhoods. In making a decision to get tested, a woman must pay close to $2,400 to a biotech firm to supply her with information that may not be of any use to her. If her test comes back positive and she is advised, as many women are, to get a prophylactic mastectomy, she must pay more money for the procedure, hospitalization, and care. Importantly, there is no guarantee that she still won't get breast cancer. Meanwhile the woman is spending money to ease and assure herself, but there is no guarantee that she will remain healthy. But one thing is guaranteed: Myriad Genetics boasts an estimated $400 million to $500 million market for the breast cancer test and will possibly earn much more in the future.

What is painfully certain is the fact that if you are a poor woman or a Black woman, your chances of contracting and dying of either breast or cervical cancer are significantly higher than for other women. Many Black families live near toxic waste sites, have access only to poor quality food and poor health care, and are living in immuno-suppressing conditions that can cause gene mutations. Instead of looking for genes, it would be more appropriate to investigate the toxicity of food or dump sites in neighborhoods. Given the history of medical abuse in this country, there's a strong possibility that biotech companies will target Black people either to present them with costly cures or to extract their own genetic information to use against them. In a recent case at a lab at the University of California, Black and Latino women employees who thought they were being checked for their cholesterol levels were checked for "syphilis, sickle cell traits, and pregnancy."[32] One Black woman pointed out that she felt violated and thought, "do they think all Black women are nasty and sleep around?"[33] The secret testing made many workers feel as though they were a part of some larger secret study to track people of color. The potential for abuse is all around us, and, given the discrimination that Black people face, Black women will continue to be medically victimized and used as experimental tools for the expansion of the white corporate model of health care.

What We Can Do

In an age where profit reigns, where solutions are "discovered" and then sold to us, what can we do for ourselves? Black women have always fought for their dignity and rights. Black women have often held in their hands curatives, herbs, powders, and plants that would comfort, console, and heal them. With economic woes and cultural divisions among us, and problems of violence and despair eating away at our solidarity, how can we combat ominous threats to our well-being? I think there's no other way but to organize (locally, nationally, and internationally), communicate, read, critique, and disseminate information, to take a stand and work to make real changes. We need to stay informed and keep political pressure on the very forces that are trying to divide us.

One major endeavor that has been most successful and fulfilling for me has been my experience of participating in the International Black Women's Cross-Cultural Studies Institute, led by Dr. Andree Nicola McLaughlin of Medgar Evers University in New York. McLaughlin is a master organizer when it comes to joining Black women of the African Diaspora and fellow sisters from the South. The institute is held every two years and is hosted by different grassroots women's groups in a chosen country. An important aspect of the institute is that it has branches that focus on different sets of issues such as health, communications, human rights, and legislation. Although the institute does not have solid funding, the group manages to come together and to support women who attend. The importance of this effort is in its success in demonstrating and supporting the needs of Black women. Critical discussions are held on race and racism, solidarity is forged among sister partners from various parts of the world, and lasting friendships and bonds are made.

This is so important for all Black women throughout the world, who face daily political disenfranchisement, economic displacement, racial discrimination, and misogyny. It is so important that, during this time of technological "advances," Black women come together, organize, and create their own solutions to the problems we face. We must not rely on or even trust the medical-industrial complex, which manufactures a corporate vision of health. Although the onslaught may be overwhelming, by organizing and staying connected, we can take control of our health and destinies.

Notes

1. Wilhelmina Leigh et al., in *Women of Color Health Data Book,* draft copy (Washington, DC: Office of Research on Women's Health, NIH, June 1997), 13.

2. Ibid., 13.

3. Ibid., 14.

4. Ibid., vii.

5. Lorna Scott McBarnettee, "African American Women," in Marcia Bayne-Smith, ed., *Race, Gender and, Health* (Thousand Oaks, CA: Sage Publishing, 1996), 51.

6. Leigh, *Women of Color Health Data Book,* op. cit., 14.

7. Wilhelmina Leigh, *The Health Care Status of Women of Color* (Washington, DC: Women's Research and Education Institute, 1994), 26.

8. Conversation with HIV/AIDS educator Rosie Muñoz-Lopez, September 25, 1997.

9. Jill Nelson, *Straight, No Chaser: How I Became a Grown-up Black Woman* (New York: J.P. Putnam & Sons, 1997), 19. Throughout her book, Nelson highlights how Black women have been rendered voiceless on the one hand and demonized on the other.

10. Martha C. Ward, *Poor Women, Powerful Men* (Boulder: Westview Press, 1986), 95.

11. Angela Davis, "Sick and Tired of Being Sick and Tired: The Politics of Black Women's Health," in Evelyn White, ed., *The Black Women's Health Book: Speaking for Ourselves* (Seattle: Seal Press, 1991), 20.

12. Michael Lev, "Judge Is Firm on Forced Contraception but Welcomes an Appeal," *New York Times*, January 11, 1991, Section A. Discusses the case of Darlene Johnson.

13. Dorothy Roberts, *Killing the Black Body: Race Reproduction and the Meaning of Liberty* (New York: Pantheon Books, 1997), 8. This is probably one of the best books written on Black women's health. The author has done a thorough and comprehensive job.

14. Janice Raymond, *Women as Wombs* (San Francisco: HarperCollins, 1993), 19.

15. "Can Contraception Reduce the Underclass?" (editorial), *Philadelphia Inquirer*, December 12, 1990, sec. A, p. 18.

16. Roberts, *Killing the Black Body*, op. cit., 112.

17. "Topics for Our Times: Norplant Coercion—An Overstated Threat," *American Journal of Public Health*, Vol. 87, No. 4 (April 1997), 550.

18. Eve Ollila et al., "Experience of Norplant by Finnish Family Planning Practitioners," in Women and Pharmaceuticals Project, *Norplant Under Her Skin* (Netherlands: Eburon, 1993), 64.

19. Jennifer Washburn, "The Misuses of Norplant: Who Gets Stuck," *Ms. Magazine*, Vol. 7, No. 3 (November/December 1996), 33.

20. Ibid., 34.

21. Roberts, *Killing the Black Body*, op. cit., 131.

22. Washburn, "The Misuses of Norplant," op. cit., 34.

23. "New Data Show Norplant Safe and Effective," Damers Christenson. *Medi-*

cal Tribune for the OG/GYN, May 1, 1997. (Article faxed to the author. A copy will be sent upon request.)

24. Roberts, *Killing the Black Body,* op. cit., 128.

25. Lynette Dumble, "In the Name of Freedom: Hazardous Contraception for Marginalized Women" (paper presented at the fifth Women and Labour Conference, MacQuarie University, South Wales, 1995).

26. Women's Health Information Resource Collective, "Depo Provera: How Does It Work?" (North Carlton, Australia), 2.

27. "Depo-Provera and Implants Prove No Competition for No. 1 Choice Ocs.," *Contraceptive Technology Update,* Vol. 14, No. 12 (December 1994). This article gives an account of a practitioner who urges women who leave Norplant to use Depo instead.

28. Amy Goodman and Kyrstyna von Henneberg, "The Case Against Depo," *Multinational Monitor,* Vol. 6, Nos. 2 and 3 (February and March 1985), 7. This is probably the best historical account of the slow early trials and struggles against Depo's approval.

29. *Depo Provera Factsheet* (Oakland, CA: National Latina Health Organization, June 1993).

30. *Contraceptive Technology Update,* Vol. 14, No. 12 (December 1994), 162.

31. Robert Lenzner and Bruce Upbin, "Monsanto v. Malthus," *Forbes Magazine,* Vol. 159, No. 5 (March 1997), 58. This article gives a good view of how genetic agribusiness intends to make consumption so much easier by consuming fast food.

32. Dana Hawkins, "A Bloody Mess at One Federal Lab," *Newsweek,* Vol. 122, No. 24 (June 23, 1997), 26.

33. Ibid., 26.

LEGAL, BUT...

Abortion Access
in the United States

Marlene Gerber Fried

Reproductive freedom, the right of a woman to control her own childbearing, implies the right to have children and the right not to. Safe, legal, and accessible abortion, a necessary component of a full reproductive rights and health agenda, remains out of reach for millions of women. This has devastating consequences. Worldwide mortality from illegal abortion remains a major threat to women's health and well-being. Thirty-nine percent of the world's women live in countries where abortion is illegal. Eighty thousand women die annually from unsafe abortions, and there are 20 million unsafe abortions each year.

Despite these grim statistics, efforts to change this situation face formidable opposition from the Vatican, conservative Islamic movements, the Christian Right, and the anti-abortion movement, who together have succeeded in limiting abortion access through legal and extra-legal activities.

Women worldwide have organized against these forces, showing that the anti-abortion political agenda is essentially a way of enforcing patriarchal domination. The global women's movement has affirmed abortion, contraception, and other reproductive needs as part of its agenda. Unfortunately, threats to women's reproductive self-determination have also come from those who have been seen as allies. In trying to control their sexual and reproductive lives, women worldwide face a double challenge: from fundamentalism on the one side and, on the other, population-control programs that aggressively seek to limit women's fertility through unsafe and unethical means.

Because of the tendency to separate the abortion issue from other aspects of reproductive rights, the threat to reproductive choice posed by population-control policies has been obscured. In fact, all the major population organizations are seen as part of the pro-choice movement because of their staunch support for the legalization of abortion and their opposition to legal restrictions and other obstacles to access. For the most part, pro-choice organizations have been unaware and/or uncritical of the population-control politics of these groups. Population groups have even solicited the support of pro-choice organizations in attempts to create a consensus around overpopulation as an environmental threat.

It is important to bring these issues to the forefront of the pro-choice movement, especially now, when the ideology that blames low-income women's fertility for their poverty is being used to justify punitive welfare policies aimed at deterring poor women from having children. Currently in the United States we have an opportunity to expose the links between coercive population control in the developing world and coercive policies in the United States. Navigating the double challenge is difficult. We must tread carefully here and distinguish our feminist critique of population-control policies from the anti-abortion movement's opposition to abortion and all forms of birth control. One way to make our position clear is to continue strong advocacy for safe and accessible abortion.

Despite 25 years of legal abortion, the battle over abortion rights continues to be in the forefront of U.S. politics. The lack of access to abortion for millions of women is a function of persistent legal and illegal activity on the part of the anti-abortion movement, which has pursued a dual strategy to recriminalize abortion in the long run and to decrease access to abortion in the short run. They have achieved major legal restrictions, including the denial of public funding for abortion and the requirement that young women obtain parental consent for an abortion.

As the following case illustrates, the obstacles to abortion access in the United States persist. Mary calls me from South Dakota, asking if we can help. "Susan," her 17-year-old daughter, is pregnant. The man involved is the father of Susan's two-year-old child, but she has a restraining order against him. She is in her second trimester, and the only clinic in her state does not do abortions past 14 weeks, so she will have to travel 1,000 miles to have the abortion. Mary and Susan have tried, but they cannot raise all the money needed for the trip and the procedure. The man's mother could contribute, but she is pressuring Susan to have the baby and give it to her to raise. Mary is worried and scared. She is also angry, having called all the pro-choice groups she has ever heard about and having found no resources for women and girls in her daughter's situation.

At the National Network of Abortion Funds, we get many calls like this one from women all over the United States, women in prison, young women, women who have been raped, "undocumented women" (women without legal residency papers), women without resources. We repeatedly hear the desperation of girls and women, like the 17-year-old with one child who drank a bottle of rubbing alcohol to cause a miscarriage, and the 14-year-old who asked her boyfriend to kick her in the stomach and push her down the stairs—as if abortion had never been legalized.

Although legal abortion is one of the safest surgical procedures in the United States today—comparable to a tonsillectomy—and although it is relatively inexpensive compared with other surgical procedures, it remains out of reach for thousands of women who, like Mary's daughter, find that the expense, location and shortage of services, burdensome legal restrictions, and threats and violence from anti-abortion activists create daunting barriers. Her case also raises questions about the role pro-choice organizations should play in helping women obtain abortions.

Strategies of harassment and terrorism aimed at women seeking abortions and at abortion providers have led to a serious decrease in abortion services, a shortage of providers, and a lack of training opportunities. Battles over particular restrictions are ostensibly about the conditions under which legal abortions are available, but they are also symbolic fights about who will control women's lives. Abortion is a profoundly radical act, an assertion, however constraining the circumstances, of women's power. The mainstream pro-choice movement in the United States has avoided casting the issue in these terms.

Abortion has been marginalized and stigmatized in the United States, and pro-choice forces have been intimidated. Restricting access for young women and denying public funding for abortions are strategic ways to isolate and stigmatize the doctors who perform abortions, the hospitals and clinics where abortions are provided, abortion itself, and, ultimately, the women who have abortions. Indeed, women bear the brunt of social disapproval. Today, even the many supporters of abortion rights define abortion as a necessary evil. President Clinton, who is pro-choice, describes his position in terms of a commitment to keeping abortion safe and legal, but to making it rare. In current efforts by the anti-abortion movement to ban a specific late abortion procedure called intact dilation and extraction (D&E), voices on all sides portray second- and third-trimester abortions negatively. Since 1995, the anti-abortion movement has worked to ban this method of abortion in the United States and the United Kingdom, and has successfully sensationalized this issue.[1]

This paper gives a picture of the status of legal abortion from the vantage point of those women who bear the brunt of restricted access—low-income women, women of color (who comprise a disproportionate number of the poor), and young women. As such, it emphasizes the losses rather than the gains that have accompanied the legalization of abortion and the inadequacy of the pro-choice political responses. I argue for placing the abortion issue in the broader context of women's rights, social justice, and opposition to population control.

Eroding Abortion Access Funding

Within the system of privatized health care in the United States, a large majority of abortions are paid for by the patients themselves. About one-third of women do not have employment-linked health insurance. One-third of private plans do not cover abortion services, or only cover them for certain medical indications. At least 37 million Americans have no health care coverage at all, including nine million women of childbearing age.[2]

Abortion is the only reproductive health care service for which Medicaid does not pay. Medicaid is a publicly funded program that covers "necessary medical services" for people whose combined income and resources are considered insufficient to meet the costs of medical care. However, because the eligibility ceilings are set so low, Medicaid covers fewer than half of those who live in poverty.[3] Federal Medicaid coverage was available for abortion from the time state-level abortion laws began to be liberalized in the late 1960s until 1977, four years after *Roe v. Wade* made abortion legal nationwide. Since then, each year the U.S. Congress has passed different versions of the Hyde Amendment, which prohibits federal funding of abortion. Initially, the only exception to the Hyde Amendment was in cases of life endangerment of the pregnant woman. Most states, which can make their own regulations as long as these do not contradict federal rulings, have followed the federal precedent. In 1993, federal exceptions for rape and incest were added, but only after a long battle. Even this minimal "liberalization" had to be fought out in court when several states refused to comply.

The impact of the Hyde Amendment has been devastating. Between 1973 and 1977, the federal government paid for about one-third of all abortions. Now it pays for virtually none.[4] Since the average cost of a first-trimester abortion is US$296 (nearly two-thirds the amount of the average maximum monthly welfare payment for a family of three), some welfare recipients cannot afford abortions at all. It is estimated that 20 to 35 percent of women eligible for Medicaid who would have had abortions if funding had been available have instead carried their pregnancies to term.[5] Others are forced to divert money from other essentials such as food, rent, and utilities. Even when women have been able to raise the money, the time it takes to search for funding makes it more likely that they will need a more costly and difficult second-trimester procedure. It is estimated that one in five Medicaid-eligible women who have had second-trimester abortions would have had first-trimester abortions if the lack of public funds had not resulted in delays occurring while they tried to raise funds.[6]

Decreasing Services

The provider shortage has come to public attention only in the past few years, although it represents a major threat to abortion rights. The number of abortion providers (hospitals, clinics, and physicians' offices) has declined since the 1980s,[7] and services are very unevenly distributed. Nine in ten abortion providers are now located in metropolitan areas; about one-third fewer counties have an abortion provider now than in the late 1970s. Ninety-four percent of non-metropolitan counties have no services (85 percent of rural women live in these underserved counties). One quarter of women having abortions travel more than 50 miles from home to obtain them.[8] These are all particularly severe aspects of an overall rural health care problem in the United States. A car, necessary to reach most health care facilities (especially reproductive health care facilities), is beyond the means of many of the rural poor.

Abortion is considered a form of semi-urgent medical care for several reasons, including the fact that the risk of complications increases as a pregnancy advances, and because abortion becomes impossible if it is delayed too long. Yet women seeking abortions must cope with a number of barriers that do not obstruct other kinds of semi-urgent medical and surgical care.[9]

As older physicians retire, there are fewer medical students being trained in abortion techniques to take their place. Despite the fact that abortion is the most common surgical procedure women undergo, almost half of graduating residents in obstetrics-gynecology have never performed a first-trimester abortion. Many hospitals do so few abortions that they cannot even qualify as appropriate training sites.[10]

Anti-abortion violence and harassment aimed at doctors and medical students contribute to this situation.[11] Clinics and providers have been targets of violence since the early 1980s. Thus far, 1993 was the peak year for anti-choice violence, but levels remain unacceptably high. These acts included death threats, stalking, acid attacks, arson, bomb threats, invasions, and blockades. In three separate incidents, five clinic workers (two doctors, a volunteer escort, and two receptionists) have been murdered at abortion clinics.[12]

Restricting Young Women's Abortion Rights

Another area in which the anti-abortion movement has had considerable legislative and ideological success is in restricting abortion for young women. About 40 percent of the one million teens who become pregnant annually choose abortion. Laws requiring that minors seeking abortions have either parental consent or notification are enforced in 27 states.[13] Health care providers face loss of license and sometimes criminal penalties for failure to comply.

Although the supporters of such laws claim that they are meant to protect the health and promote the best interests of young women, in fact they are a threat to young women's health and well-being. Parental notification or consent laws, which include provisions for judicial bypass for young women who cannot or are unwilling to involve their parents, often require travel, extra time, and money. Although most teens who request a judicial bypass are ultimately given permission by the court to have an abortion, the process may be humiliating and traumatizing. Judicial bypass requires a young woman to discuss her pregnancy and personal details about her life in front of strangers in a courtroom. Although these procedures are supposed to be confidential, in rural areas and small towns, a young woman may find that confidentiality is threatened or impossible to maintain.[14]

In addition to the aim of limiting abortion rights, the battles over restricting abortion in the United States are also used by conservatives as a vehicle for advancing a far-reaching economic and political agenda, which includes dismantling and privatizing the public health and social welfare system. These conservative forces also aim to restore "traditional" patriarchal families and values—for example, through punitive deterrents to out-of-wedlock pregnancy. Low-income women, especially women of color, young women, immigrants, and gays have been convenient scapegoats for these forces, and have been blamed for everything that is currently wrong in the United States—from increasing violence and drug use to rising levels of poverty. Failure to address this broader picture, even at the level of rhetoric, has been a real weakness of the pro-choice movement in terms of framing adequate responses and forming effective political alliances.

Instead, abortion rights forces in the United States have focused primarily, and successfully, on preserving the basic legality of abortion. They have not, however, succeeded in preserving or expanding accessibility to abortion, or in gaining legitimacy for abortion. Pro-choice strategies have not stopped opponents of abortion from curtailing the abortion rights of millions of U.S. women.

The anti-abortion movement has also used access issues to further its long-term political objective of re-criminalizing abortion. Battles over legal restrictions have weakened and fragmented the pro-choice movement. For example, the failure of the mainstream pro-choice organizations to mobilize in opposition to public funding prohibitions angered low-income women and women-of-color organizations. At the same time, the anti-abortion movement has been able to use such battles as an opportunity to consolidate their movement, draw in new supporters, and build support for other restrictions on abortion. They have also won significant ideological and symbolic victories.

Narrowing the Vision: Fighting for Choice

Earlier battles for abortion rights are a reminder of how much ground has been lost since 1973—in the concrete losses discussed above and at the ideological level. In the fight to legalize abortion, the women's liberation movement of the 1960s and 1970s located its demands for abortion rights in the context of sexual freedom and a broad program of women's rights. Its call for abortion on demand was a bold assertion that women need to make, and should have the right to make, their own decisions about sex and fertility. This position was in contrast both to those supporters of legal abortion who took a public health perspective and to those who saw women primarily as the victims of illegal abortion. For the women's liberation movement, the legalization of abortion was considered to be a significant step, but only a step, in expanding women's autonomy and freedom.

Although this perspective did not prevail in the U.S. Supreme Court's judgment in the case of *Roe v. Wade*, it was a significant political statement and rallying point.[15] In the post-legalization battles to defend and maintain the legal right to have an abortion, that voice has been marginalized and replaced by a politics of defensiveness that has shaped the strategies and goals of the most visible, mainstream pro-choice organizations. The pro-choice movement that emerged in the 1980s was formed in reaction to an all-out anti-choice offensive that included initiatives in federal, state, and local legislatures; courts; abortion clinics; and the media. In the effort to hold onto past gains and to avoid alienating possible supporters, this movement avoided talking about women's rights and in some cases even talking about abortion. The focus was on the intolerance and extremism of the other side.[16]

During the Reagan-Bush era in the 1980s, in the face of the fierce attack by an aggressive anti-abortion movement, efforts were made to make pro-choice demands more palatable by sanitizing them. Even using the word "abortion" was considered too controversial. The movement favored the more euphemistic notions of "choice," "personal freedom," and "privacy," in hopes that this was a discourse that even conservatives couldn't find objectionable.

The movement's agenda was narrowed to safe, legal abortion. In the conservative climate of the 1980s, pro-choice forces were pressured to settle for less and to make compromises. In addition to the problematic effects on the movement itself, this was not a successful strategy for defending abortion rights. Doing so against ongoing and systematic attacks requires a movement that presents itself openly as committed to a broader and deeper understanding of the significance of abortion to women's lives.

The shift in approach has also had other consequences for the development of the pro-choice movement. "Fighting for choice" is an appeal to those who already have choices, not to those who do not—low-income women, women of color, young women. While these are the women who have borne the brunt of the attacks on abortion access, they are not well represented within the pro-choice movement. Until very recently, however, fighting for access has been the weakest part of the pro-choice strategy. It has taken very dire circumstances to change this.

For example, the movement has been wary of directly challenging parental involvement laws. Even among supporters of abortion rights, young women's rights remain an "unpopular" cause. The conservative view, that parents have a right to control their daughters' behavior, clearly resonates. Because of this, pro-choice activists have preferred to create mechanisms that enable young women to have access in spite of the laws, such as free lawyers, rather than attempting to repeal parental consent laws. The issue became a visible part of the pro-choice agenda only after the death of Becky Bell in 1989, a white, middle-class teenager who had an illegal abortion because she did not want to let her parents know that she was pregnant.

Although these erosions in women's right to an abortion in the United States have shaped women's abortion experiences, the voices of the women who are denied access to abortion have remained virtually unheard in the abortion debate. Hence, many people, even those who favor abortion rights, are unaware of the realities of diminishing access and feel no urgency to do something about the erosions. In fact, the mainstream, predominantly white pro-choice movement has always responded weakly, if at all, to restrictions on low-income women's abortion rights. It was only in the 1980s, when all women's rights were threatened, that hundreds of thousands of women flocked to defend abortion clinics and the *Roe v. Wade* decision. There have been no comparable large-scale mobilizations to protect or reinstate the rights of low-income women. Fighting for the rights of low-income women has been left to smaller, more "radical" groups, marginalized by the mainstream of the movement, and to women-of-color organizations that see clearly the importance of such battles. They have had to push hard to bring the mainstream movement to this perspective.[17]

These failures of strategy have contributed, however inadvertently, to the ability of the anti-abortion movement to control the terms of the public debate. They have been the ones taking bold initiatives, not shying away from unpopular political stands, and all-too-eagerly seizing the moral terrain.

Stigmatizing Abortion—Demonizing Women

Generating moral disapproval of abortion has been high on the anti-abortion movement's agenda. Their adherents have made moral disapproval a key strategy in their efforts to restrict and recriminalize abortion and have successfully used it as a vehicle for shaping public opinion. For example, in the area of public funding, they have made appeals such as "Abortion may be legal, but why should we be forced to pay for something that is morally repugnant (to us)." They have been increasingly successful in suppressing the parentheses and in portraying the matter as if there were a universal consensus that abortion is morally illegitimate.

Anti-abortion extremists have taken up this moral mandate in their campaigns against abortion providers. They use the assertion of the moral "illegitimacy" of abortion to justify the claim that anyone participating in abortion-service delivery is morally tainted and must be stopped. It has not been difficult for such extremists to then seize this as justification for their acts of violence.

Thus, women who have abortions are portrayed as selfish, sexually irresponsible, unfeeling, and morally blind individuals who kill their own children for "convenience." Only the women whom they see as true victims—those seeking abortions for pregnancies resulting from rape or incest—are above contempt. But even in those cases (while deserving of sympathy), they argue, the women should have the babies, not abortions. In short, they believe women simply cannot be trusted to make the right decisions, but must be controlled.

The same contempt for women, especially those who have the fewest resources, pervades other aspects of the conservative political agenda, which calls for the restoration of the stigma of illegitimacy and a renewed emphasis on the connection between illegitimacy, poverty, and social decay.[18] As solutions to the social ills they identify, conservatives have proposed a series of callous, punitive, and coercive measures designed to control the lives and reproductive capacity of poor women. These include proposals that would reduce a parent's welfare benefits if their child skips school, requiring that minors get married as a condition of receiving benefits, and requiring women receiving welfare benefits to accept long-term contraceptive implants so that they do not have more children who need social support.

These proposals are derived from an analysis that considers poverty to be caused by poor women having too many children, not by racism, sexism, or the lack of jobs that pay a living wage, and certainly not by the lack of government support for low-income families. These so-called welfare reforms have been designed with the overt intention of making it more difficult for single and adolescent mothers and their children to survive economically. Thus, social welfare support has been made conditional on "good" behavior and on the grounds of social disapproval; punishment has been substituted for meaningful social policy. Little attention and less money is being given to support young mothers or to enhance educational and job opportunities for young women with low incomes.

As in many developing countries, blaming social problems on women's sexuality and reproduction has been used in the United States as a justification for different forms of population control—coercive sterilization, the imposition of long-term contraceptives on low-income women of color, making welfare benefits contingent on having abortions, and, at the same time, making abortion unobtainable. It is not insignificant that while refusing to pay for abortions for this population of poor women, Medicaid continues to cover sterilization.

Most recently, contraceptive implants have been used as an instrument of coercion. For example, low-income teenagers have been the focus of aggressive campaigns in favor of implants, and legislation has been proposed tying welfare benefits to the acceptance of this method. One woman, convicted of child abuse, was offered a "choice" between jail or implants, which raised fears about potential abuse of this method.

Behind these efforts to control women's reproduction is a misogynist contempt for women's sexuality, intertwined with racism. There is a thread linking these policies, which affect low-income women the most, to policies aimed at controlling all women. Welfare restrictions limiting the possibilities for low-income women to have children are the other side of the coin of abortion restriction. Both deny a woman the right to control her own childbearing.

While conservatives may be spearheading these efforts, they have been joined by many liberals, and the effort to stop young, low-income women from having children has appeal even in pro-choice circles. Historically, the pro-choice movement in the United States has focused only on women's efforts not to have children. At best, its definitions of reproductive choice have not adequately encompassed or supported women's rights in relation to having or caring for children. At worst, abortion rights proponents have embraced population-control arguments directed against the fertility of low-income women and women of color. Strategies are needed that actively resist both population control and opposition to abortion.

Expanding the Vision of the Pro-Choice Movement and Increasing Access

A bolder, non-defensive posture is required for both short- and long-range strategies. In order to increase all women's access to abortion, larger battles must ultimately be fought for economic, sexual, and racial justice. The abortion rights movement has to advocate the morality of women's autonomy and the rights of all women, including the young, to make their own reproductive decisions, including decisions to have children.

Fighting for women's rights in terms of access is an important step, both because women who are denied them are in dire need of abortion services, and in order to strengthen political support for abortion rights overall. Restoring Medicaid funding for abortion would be an important step toward increasing access for all women.

Some analysts believe that the newer methods of early abortion (both drug-induced and surgical) have the potential to increase access to abortion. However, the most important factors causing later abortions are not related to the technique involved but to barriers to access. These disproportionately occur among low-income women, women of color, and young women. There may well be less public sympathy for these women, at the present time, than there is for fetuses. If so, then the challenge to the pro-choice movement is to change this.

Clinic violence has received heightened official attention since Bill Clinton became president and in the wake of the murders of abortion providers. The Freedom of Access to Clinic Entrances Law was passed in 1994, making it a federal crime to impede access to abortion clinics. Local ordinances with similar effect have also been passed. Abortion clinics have increased their own security precautions. While clinics are, for the most part, no longer sites for large-scale demonstrations and counter-demonstrations, anti-abortion picketing continues on a smaller scale. Incidents of violence have decreased, but those that do occur are serious and have a chilling effect on the entire domain of abortion-service delivery.

It has been difficult to mobilize pro-choice activism in this period, when demands for privatization are drowning out calls for public services and there has been a steady decrease in access to all forms of health care for the poor. However, it is important to recognize current efforts within the pro-choice movement to focus on the needs of low-income women and on access issues. A number of activist groups and all the major pro-choice litigation centers are working at the state level to oppose new efforts to prohibit public funding, find loopholes in existing legislation, and repeal restrictive laws. Efforts are also being made to increase the number of abortion providers by changing regulations that prevent midlevel practitioners from performing them and by increasing the numbers of training sites where providers can learn to do abortions.

Grassroots strategies include providing direct economic assistance to women for abortions, creating self-help groups that teach women how to maintain their health, and mobilizing campaigns to increase the number of abortion providers and the availability of abortion services. In the past few years, the large mainstream organizations have included opposition to welfare reform in their agendas as well.

The leadership for broadening the vision and strategies of the pro-choice movement in the 1980s and 1990s has come from several women-of-color reproductive rights groups, which have a more inclusive vision and agenda based on the needs of women in their own communities. For example, a 1993 battle to restore Medicaid funding for abortion was spearheaded by the National Black Women's Health Project, which has also taken the lead in monitoring and publicizing the coercive abuse of contraception. Groups like this locate abortion within a broader agenda of women's health and reproductive choices. They also advocate the building of a more inclusive movement, bringing in the voices of women who have been excluded, and championing those voices.

Successful strategies that address the funding issue are not easy to find at a time when public funding is so politically unpopular. At the level of national policy, there has not been a campaign to restore federal Medicaid funding for abortion since the failure of these efforts in 1993.

Ultimately, securing abortion access requires that abortion services be part of comprehensive health care available to all women. In spite of the fact that the United States is very far from this, even as an ideal, pro-choice groups must take up this challenge. This means directly opposing the scapegoating of low-income women and building support for their rights.

In sum, the abortion debate needs to expand to include the voices of those who have been hit hardest by the gradual disappearance of access to abortion. Further, it needs to reshape public opinion so that the needs and rights of all women are respected. This requires placing abortion rights in the context of a larger human rights and social justice agenda. Concretizing this sweeping prescription into workable strategies and messages is the most challenging task facing the pro-choice movement in the United States today.

Notes

A longer version of this paper appears in Rickie Solinger, ed., *Abortion Wars: A Half Century of Struggle, 1950–2000* (Berkeley: University of California Press, 1998). It is printed here with their kind permission. A version also appears in *Reproductive Health Matters,* May 1997. Correspondence may be addressed to: Marlene Gerber Fried, Civil Liberties and Public Policy Program, Hampshire College, Amherst, MA 01002, USA (mfried@hamp.hampshire.edu).

1. This is a method in which the fetus is given an injection so that it dies in the womb. Fluid is then removed from the cranium, as this is the only way to bring the head out without causing tears or bleeding in the woman's cervix, and the fetus is removed intact. This method is used in the third trimester of pregnancy when the life of the pregnant women is at risk, or in cases of serious fetal anomaly. It is rare to the extent that the overwhelming majority of abortions are performed in the first trimester. It may also be used from 20 to 24 weeks of pregnancy if a doctor determines that it is the best procedure to use in the circumstances. This procedure is also referred to as "D and X." The anti-abortion movement calls the procedure "partial birth" abortion and has portrayed it as infanticide. Although the U.S. Congress may vote to ban this method, courts in the United States have said that the following determinations may not be made by legislatures but must be left to the physician attending a woman: when a particular fetus is viable, which abortion method is appropriate to use in specific circumstances, and what constitutes a threat to a particular woman's life

or health. See *Late Term Abortions: Legal Considerations* (New York: Alan Guttmacher Institute, 1997).

2. S. Lerner and J. Freedman, "Abortion and Health Care Reform," *Journal of American Medical Women's Association (JAMWA),* Vol. 49, No. 5 (1994), 44.

3. P. Donovan, *The Politics of Blame: Family Planning, Abortion and the Poor* (New York: Alan Guttmacher Institute, 1995).

4. Ibid., 131. Donovan points out that even before the Hyde Amendment, not all women in need of subsidized abortion services were able to obtain them, either because the services were not available or accessible to them or because the states had policies prohibiting coverage.

5. S. Henshaw, "Factors Hindering Access to Abortion Services," *Family Planning Perspectives,* Vol. 27, No. 2 (1995), 54–59, 87.

6. *Abortion Delivery in the United States: What Do Current Trends and Nonsurgical Alternatives Mean for the Future?* (New York: Alan Guttmacher Institute, 1995).

7. A. Frye et al., "Induced Abortion in the United States: A 1994 Update," *JAMWA,* Vol. 49, No. 5 (1994), 131–36.

8. Fact sheet prepared by the Alan Guttmacher Institute for a Septermber 1995 press briefing.

9. Henshaw, "Factors Hindering Access to Abortion Services," op. cit.

10. Training for first-trimester abortion is required in only 12 percent of Ob-Gyn residency programs, and for second-trimester abortion, in only 7 percent. It is not offered at all in 30 percent of programs. Carolyn Westhoff, "Abortion Training in Residency Programs," *JAMWA,* Vol. 49, No. 5 (1994), 159–62, 164.

11. More recently, anti-abortion activists have also targeted medical students. A group called Life Dynamics promoted their agenda with *Bottom Feeder,* a so-called joke book that was sent to 35,000 medical students. One of the jokes in it says: "What do you do if you find yourself in a room with Hitler, Mussolini, and an abortionist, and you have only two bullets? Answer: Shoot the abortionist twice." This mailing was meant to intimidate medical students, both by stigmatizing abortion and by telling all those who received it that the anti-abortion movement knew where they were living.

12. In 1993, Dr. David Gunn was murdered in Pensacola, Florida, by Michael Griffen. In 1994, at the same clinic, Dr. Bayard Britton and clinic escort James Barrett were murdered by Paul Hill. In 1994, in Brookline, Massachusetts, John Salvi murdered Shannon Lowney at the Planned Parenthood Clinic of Greater Boston and LeeAnn Nichols at the nearby Preterm Health Services. In 1998, Robert Sanderson, an off-duty police officer, was killed by a bomb at a clinic in Birmingham, Alabama.

13. Thirty-eight states have adopted parental involvement laws. See *Restrictions on Young Women's Access to Abortion Services* (New York: Center for Reproductive Law and Policy, November 1996).

14. *Mandatory Parental Consent and Notification Laws* (New York: Center for

Reproductive Law and Policy, November 1995).

15. *Roe v. Wade,* the 1973 U.S. Supreme Court decision that legalized abortion, was a compromise among various positions. The court decided to place abortion within the scope of the right to privacy and state intrusion into the doctor-patient relationship, rather than under a right of bodily autonomy. The decision asserts that any restriction on abortion during the first trimester of pregnancy is unconstitutional, and that during that period, the decision to have an abortion is left to the pregnant woman and her physician. In the second trimester, the state may protect its interest in the pregnant woman's health by regulating the abortion procedure in ways reasonably related to her health. In the third trimester, the state may restrict and even prohibit abortion because the state has an interest in protecting the fetus after it has become viable.

16. Janet Hadley makes similar observations in "The 'Awfulisation' of Abortion" (paper presented at the conference Abortion Matters, Amsterdam, March 1996, and excerpted in *Women's Global Network for Reproductive Rights Newsletter,* Vol. 54, No. 5 [1996], 6).

17. In 1993 the National Black Women's Health Project spearheaded a campaign to repeal the Hyde Amendment. This was the first concerted effort by the pro-choice movement to take on the funding issue since this amendment was initially passed in 1977.

18. Charles Murray, one of the most influential ideologues of "welfare reform," described illegitimacy as "the single most important social problem of our time, more important than crime, drugs, poverty, illiteracy, welfare, or homelessness because it drives everything else." Charles Murray, "The Coming White Underclass," *Wall Street Journal,* October 29, 1993.

ABOUT THE CONTRIBUTORS

Asoka Bandarage is Associate Professor of Women's Studies at Mount Holyoke College. Her article first appeared in *Hunger Notes* (vol. 19, no. 4, Spring 1994), and the issues here are discussed at length in her book *Women, Population and Global Crisis: A Political-Economic Analysis* (London: Zed Books, 1997). She is also the author of *Colonialism in Sri Lanka: The Political Economy of the Kandyan Highlands, 1833–1886* (Berlin: Mouton, 1983) and many articles on international political economy, culture, gender, and the environment. She serves on the steering committee of the Committee on Women, Population, and the Environment and the editorial boards of *Hypatia* and the *Bulletin of Concerned Asian Scholars.* She works as a consultant to grassroots organizations in the area of women and international development.

Marsha J. Tyson Darling is Associate Professor of Women's Studies and History at Georgetown University. She is a Rockefeller Foundation Visiting Scholar at the Oral History Research Office at Columbia University, where she is doing research on the impact of microcredit opportunities on working-class women in New York City's ethnic communities. She has worked as a testing director of a sickle-cell anemia project in upstate New York and has served as board member for the National Black Women's Health Project. She is the editor of a book of essays titled *African American Studies: Significant Issues* and a two-volume collection of court cases, legal documents, and essays titled *Race, Redistricting and the Constitution: Sources and Explorations of the Fifteenth Amendment.* She is preparing a manuscript for a book titled *Emerging Biomedical Technologies and Social and Legal Rights for Women,* and she is a member of the Committee on Women, Population, and the Environment.

Marlene Gerber Fried is the director of the Civil Liberties and Public Policy Program at Hampshire College, where she is also Professor of Philosophy. She is a Visiting Scholar at the Bagnoud Center for Health and Human Rights at the Harvard School of Public Health. She is a longtime reproductive rights activist and is founding president of both the National Network of Abortion Funds and the Abortion Rights Fund of Western Massachusetts. She is also on the steering committees of the Abortion Access Project and the Committee on Women, Population, and the Environment.

Betsy Hartmann is the Director of the Population and Development Program at Hampshire College and a founding member and co-coordinator of the Committee on Women, Population, and the Environment. She is the author of *Reproductive Rights and Wrongs: The Global Politics of Population Control* (South End Press, 1995) and coauthor of *A Quiet Violence: View from a Bangladesh Village* (Food First and Zed Books, 1983). She is a longstanding activist in the international women's health movement and is currently working on a longer project on environment and security.

H. Patricia Hynes is Director of the Urban Environmental Health Initiative and Professor of Public Health at Boston University School of Public Health, where she works on issues of urban environment, feminism, and environmental justice. An environmental engineer, Hynes won the Environmental Service Award of the Massachusetts Association of Conservation Commissions. In 1987 she won a German Marshall Fund Environmental Fellowship to do a comparative study of lead contamination and environmental policy in Western Europe and the United States. She is author of *The Recurring Silent Spring* (Pergamon, 1989) and *EarthRight* (Prima, 1990). Her current work, *A Patch of Eden* (Chelsea Green, 1996), a book on community gardens in inner cities and their potential for social justice and urban ecology, won the 1996 National Arbor Day Foundation Book Award.

Ynestra King is a founding member of the Committee on Women, Population, and the Environment. Her germinal writings on the relationships between feminism, ecology, and militarism have contributed to the collective thinking of CWPE. She taught for many years at the New School for Social Research and has been a Visiting Scholar at Rutgers University and Columbia University. Recently she has begun writing about disability, and she is at work on a memoir and a collection of her essays. She lives in New York City with her seven-year-old son, Micah.

Joni Seager is a feminist geographer and a professor and Chair of the Geography Department at the University of Vermont. Her most recent books include *Earth Follies: Coming to Feminist Terms with the Global Environmental Crisis* (Routledge, 1993) and *The State of Women in the World Atlas* (Penguin, 1997).

Jael Silliman is Assistant Professor in Women's Studies at the University of Iowa. She has worked on health and reproductive rights, environment, and alternative development issues for the past two decades as an activist, practitioner, and foundation officer. She is currently the Board Chair of the National Asian Women's Health Organization, a member of the Committee on Women, Population, and the Environment, Secretary of the International Projects Assistance Services (IPAS), and a board member of the Reproductive Health Technologies Project. She has written several articles on women's health, population, development, and environmental justice issues.

Andy Smith (Cherokee) is a co-coordinator of CWPE and is a member of Women of All Red Nations. She holds an M.Div from the Union Theological Seminary in New York City.

Justine Smith was co-organizer of Women of All Red Nations in Chicago and has served on the boards of American Indian Health Services and the Midwest Treaty Network. In addition, she has worked as a social studies and Indian culture instructor for a Native American alternative high school and served as an Assistant State Director for a regional environmental organization. Currently she serves as the Youth Coordinator for the Native American Ministry in Milwaukee.

Meredith Tax is President of Women's WORLD (Women's World Organization for Rights, Literature & Development), an organization of politically committed women writers from around the world concerned with the importance of cultural struggle and the role of women writers in it, and gender-based censorship—the historic, worldwide silencing of women's voices—as a major obstacle to women's achievement of equality, sustainable livelihoods, and peace. This essay was discussed at international meetings by a working group consisting of Marjorie Agosin (Chile/United States), Ama Ata Aidoo (Ghana), Ritu Menon (India), Ninotchka Rosca (Philippines), and Mariella Sala (Peru).

April J. Taylor has been working on health issues related to Black women for a number of years. She is currently mapping together an International Black Women's Health Network and is working on a master's degree in Public Health. She is a coauthor of the chapter on holistic health and healing in *The New Our Bodies Ourselves* and has traveled extensively in the United States and overseas to address issues of women's health.

Meredeth Turshen teaches gender and development and Third World social policy at the Edward J. Bloustein School of Planning and Public Policy, Rutgers University. She has written three books: *The Political Ecology of Disease in Tanzania* (1984), *The Politics of Public Health* (1989), and *Privatizing Health Services in Africa* (1999), all published by Rutgers University Press, and has edited three others: *Women and Health in Africa* (Africa World Press, 1991), *Women's Lives and Public Policy: The International Experience* (Greenwood, 1993), and *What Women Do in Wartime: Gender and Conflict in Africa* (Zed Books, 1998). She serves as Political Co-Chair of the Association of Concerned Africa Scholars and as contributing editor of the *Review of African Political Economy.*

INDEX

About South End Press

South End Press is a nonprofit, collectively run book publisher with more than 200 titles in print. Since our founding in 1977, we have tried to meet the needs of readers who are exploring, or are already committed to, the politics of radical social change. Our goal is to publish books that encourage critical thinking and constructive action on the key political, cultural, social, economic, and ecological issues shaping life in the United States and in the world. In this way, we hope to give expression to a wide diversity of democratic social movements and to provide an alternative to the products of corporate publishing.

Through the Institute for Social and Cultural Change, South End Press works with other political media projects—*Z Magazine*; Speakout, a speakers' bureau; and Alternative Radio—to expand access to information and critical analysis. If you would like a free catalog of South End Press books, please write to us at: South End Press, 7 Brookline St., #1, Cambridge, MA 02139-4146. Visit our website at http://www.lbbs.org/sep/sep.htm.

Related Titles

Reproductive Rights and Wrongs:
The Global Politics of Population Control
by Betsy Hartmann $18

From Abortion to Reproductive Freedom:
Transforming a Movement
Edited by Marlene Gerber Fried $14

Dragon Ladies:
Asian American Feminists Breathe Fire
Edited by Sonia Shah $17

50 Years Is Enough: The Case Against the World Bank
and the International Monetary Fund
A Project of Global Exchange, edited by Kevin Danaher $16

When ordering, please include $3.50 for postage and handling for the first book and 50 cents for each additional book. To order by credit card, call 1-800-533-8478.